COLLECTED WRITINGS OF
Edgar Allan Poe

VOLUME 4

WRITINGS IN *THE BROADWAY JOURNAL*

NONFICTIONAL PROSE

Part 2, The Annotations

Edgar Allan Poe

From a quarter plate daguerreotype made at William Abbott Pratt's Daguerreotype Gallery, Richmond, Virginia. September 1849

Edgar Allan Poe

WRITINGS IN *THE BROADWAY JOURNAL*

NONFICTIONAL PROSE

Part 2, The Annotations

Edited with Introduction
by
BURTON R. POLLIN

GORDIAN PRESS
NEW YORK
1986

Collected Writings of Edgar Allan Poe
Volume 4

Published by Gordian Press
85 Tompkins Street
Staten Island, NY 10304
First Printing

Library of Congress Cataloging-in-Publication Data

Poe, Edgar Allan. 1809-1849.
   Writings in the Broadway journal.

   (Collected writings of Edgar Allan Poe ; v. 3–4)
   Includes index.
   Contents: pt. 1. The Text — pt. 2. The annotations.
   I.   Pollin, Burton Ralph.   II.   Broadway journal.
III.   Title.   IV.   Series: Poe, Edgar Allan, 1809-1849.
Works. 1981 ; v. 3-4.
PS2619.P64   1986   818'.309   86–18426
ISBN 0-87752-233-2 (pt. 1)
ISBN 0-87752-234-0 (pt. 2)

FOREWORD

Some word of explanation must be given to the wide circle of students of Poe for my issuing Poe's works in the *Broadway Journal* as the next two volumes of his *Collected Writings*. The first volume, consisting of his three longest narratives, (the *Imaginary Voyages*), methodically completed the *Tales and Sketches* of the late Professor Mabbott, which made frequent reference to the numerous periodical articles by Poe that I collected into *The Brevities*, issued in 1985. Now, the texts were for the first time objectively determined, edited, and numbered for scholarly purposes (291 of the "Marginalia" and over 600 items, all told). What then should follow this volume, in the sequence? The answer was readily determined: the largest body of uncollected, undetermined and unedited material lay in the *Broadway Journal*, the weekly magazine of one year's extent, which involved Poe from the first to the last number. The history of his relations with the varying staff of the magazine is complicated and has long needed a presentation of the authenticated material by Poe. It ranged from many of his reprinted tales and poems and long signed articles and reviews to hundreds of short single-paragraph notices, comments on cultural and social events, surveys of other magazines, drama criticisms and occasional art critiques, editorial dicta, often with autobiographical touches, special notices and headnotes for translations and other features, and responses to contributors and general inquiries. The journal essayed to play the cultural role of an 1845 *New Yorker*, with its varied articles, satirical woodcuts, and contributions from celebrities like Margaret Fuller, W. G. Simms, and Caroline Kirkland. It packed much material into its two-column fine-print sixteen pages each week, and it was noticed by the exchange papers throughout the country. A few Poe scholars have delved into this wealth of material, but never for a comprehensive presentation (Margaret Alterton, Perry Miller, Sidney Moss, and Killis Campbell; see Bibliography for specifics).

As early as 1968 I had devoted a sabbatical leave to exploring this rich lode of Poe writing, examining everything that had been written about the journal and the ascertainable canon of his *BJ* writings, including materials in the Huntington Library and Duke University, but there was insufficient time to organize my findings, inadequate means of authenticating some "knotty" texts (three of my later works on Poe aimed to serve this purpose), and no ostensible means of publishing such bulky materials. The invitation in 1972 to continue Mr. Mabbott's edition, begun at Harvard and now being continued through the Gordian Press as *The Collected Writings of ... Poe*, provided the opportunity to pull together the many "determined" texts and the vast panoply of notes of every type, to fill in the numerous gaps still left for research, and to shape all this into one of

v

the publishable portions of the "edition." Two volumes, one much oversized, would be necessary; and Mr. John Corta, the publisher, proved graciously amenable. The ensuing complications and problems are described in the separate sections of the Introduction, largely to help others with similar projects to see the possibilities in adapting perhaps unconventional responses to most demanding needs.

ACKNOWLEDGMENTS

As in the preceding volume of *The Collected Writings of Edgar Allan Poe*, namely, *The Brevities*, I wish to express my gratitude for the sole use of materials and books collected by the late Professor Thomas Ollive Mabbott and generously put at my disposal by Maureen C. Mabbott and the legatee of the Mabbott papers, the Libraries of the University of Iowa, under the charge of Dale M. Bentz (now emeritus) and, for its Special Collections, of Frank Paluka (now emeritus). For financial aid given for travel for pertinent materials, for clerical and research assistance, for lay-out help with the facsimile text, for xeroxing and purchase of needed materials, I owe thanks to the Research Foundation of the City University of New York. The preparation of these volumes was made possible in part by a grant from the Texts Program of the National Endowment for the Humanities, an independent federal agency.

I have been indebted for research aid and splended facilities to particular libraries in this country: The City University Graduate Center Library, The Columbia University Libraries, The New York Public Library, and for permission to use and cite Poe's markings throughout the "Whitman" copy of the *BJ* to the Huntington Library in San Marino, to Heyward Ehrlich (see p. xi below), and to D. K. Jackson and Dwight Thomas for being able to read and cite the 1845 section of their *Poe Log* in its prepublication form and to Richard Drechsler and Judith Rubin-Spitz of the CUNY Graduate Center Computer Facility for inordinate help and the use of their center in the laser-jet printing of this volume.

My gratitude is owed for varied and indispensable aid and advice, given in person and through correspondence, to the following, listed merely by name: John Corta, Moshe Carmilly, William Dunmore, Milton Hindus, Miriam Korman, Mary Mitchell, Michael Deas, Brenda Newman, and for direct and skilled help to Ira Lukens (the lay-out artist), Margaret Terry (research and clerical assistant), and, chiefly, Dorothy Novak (self-trained expert in "Nota Bene" and every type of complex task involved in the word processing and laser jet printing).

Above all, my profound gratitude is expressed to Alice M. Pollin, so often called upon for counsel, linguistic and literary insights and knowledge, discriminating judgments, most demanding and varied proof reading, and extraordinary patience.

CONTENTS

INTRODUCTION

All students of the life of Edgar Allan Poe know of his difficulties with the proprietors of the three journals which used his editorial skills from 1835 to 1842: the *Southern Literary Messenger*, *Burton's Gentleman's Magazine*, and *Graham's Magazine*. In consequence he resolved to found his own magazine, based on the highest principles of taste and criticism. These were spelled out in the series of prospectuses which he issued from 1840 through 1849, for the *Penn Magazine*, punningly named, and then *The Stylus* (the name of 1843). They were really manifestoes declaring the need of objective, fearless criticism (although less severe than Poe's had been in the *Messenger*) and of fine literary material with numerous "pictorial embellishments" bearing a "continuous, definite character" (see Dwight Thomas, *Poe in Philadelphia*, pp. 142-144). His rebuffs in job-hunting and lack of patronage led him to plan an expanded role for the *Stylus*, which was described in the prospectus of March 4, 1843 (see Pollin [C], pp. 214-229). This is less than two years prior to the founding of the *Broadway Journal* by Charles Frederick Briggs. Certainly Briggs knew the contents of Poe's new prospectus, stressing the need for engravings of outstanding quality illustrating the texts which are, in general, "vigorous, pungent, original" with criticism that is "independent" and always a reflection of the editor-proprietor's primary and sole "intentions." Poe's assumption of his role as an arbiter of American taste and creativity is evidenced at the end in his hope for "a criticism self-sustained, guiding itself only by the purest rules of Art ..., aloof from all personal bias." The journal must discuss "the belles lettres, ... the Fine Arts, with the Drama" and give "a Retrospect of our Political History." Important will be a "series of Critical and Biographical Sketches of American Writers," such as Poe wrote for *Godey's Lady's Book* in 1846.

Meanwhile, despite his unceasing efforts to sign up *Stylus* backers and subscribers, Poe's "imminent" journal failed to appear. He sent fine contributions ("The Tell-Tale Heart" and "Notes on English Verse") to the short-lived monthly *Pioneer* of James Russell Lowell. The latter would have shown the plan for the *Stylus* to Briggs, his close friend. Poe, meanwhile, won fame with the prize-winning "Gold-Bug," and, upon moving from Philadelphia to New York City, with "The Balloon-Hoax," as it was later called. Poe's projected pamphlet series, *The Prose Romances*, came out in July 1843 with critical, but not financial, success. The second number was never issued. At the end of 1843 Poe's provocative lecture on "The Poetry of America" in Philadelphia and Delaware, and early in 1844, in Baltimore, brought him some public attention, but he remained indigent and lacking in patronage for his cherished magazine.

In October 1844 Poe accepted a position as "mechanical

paragraphist" charitably offered by his friends Nathaniel P. Willis and George Pope Morris, the founders and editors of the *Evening Mirror*. This replaced their own weekly *New Mirror*, a victim of high postal charges (see Mott, pp. 320-330). Poe was to be a subeditor, responsible for short articles and reviews. The partners' insight into Poe's genius and originality of ideas and approaches bore abundant fruit with the publication of "The Raven" in the 1/29/45 issue of the *Mirror*, from advance sheets for February of the monthly the *American Review*, to which Poe had sold it. At once, it became a sensational success.

Meanwhile, Briggs had fulfilled his long-planned ambition to issue a New York weekly, called the *Broadway Journal* (Saturday, January 3, 1845). It was not only Poe's widespread reputation as a littérateur and critic that brought the invitation to review the important new book of Elizabeth Barrett's poems in the first two weekly issues and to write a sketch of editor Willis himself for the third. Briggs must have felt a need for some sort of assistant on the densely printed, two-column journal that still had to set its basic direction, format, and policies. In the brief "prospectus" that Briggs printed in each of the first issues, there was little that disagreed with Poe's earlier magazine "platforms." Here is a copy of Briggs' statement:

Prospectus of the Broadway Journal.
To be Published every Saturday.

THE BROADWAY JOURNAL will differ from any of the weekly Periodicals now published in this city, as it will be made up entirely of original matter, consisting of Essays, Criticisms on Art and Literature, Domestic and Foreign Correspondence, and Literary and Scientific Intelligence.

ILLUSTRATIONS will be given as often as good original Designs can be procured, and drawings and plans of all new public buildings that have either elegance or novelty to recommend them to notice. Particular attention will be given to this department, and no pains spared to make it worthy of patronage.

Efficient aid has already been secured in the services of some of the best writers in the country; but it is hoped that a free channel being opened through which true-hearted men may "let loose their thoughts," will be the means of drawing out some of the slumbering talent amongst us which has not yet been seen afloat on the surface of our periodical literature.

THE BROADWAY JOURNAL will espouse the cause of no political party, but will hold itself free to condemn or approve any men or measures, that a patriotic regard for the welfare of the country may dictate. It will be printed on fine paper with clear type, in the Octavo form of 16 pages, double columns.

TERMS $3,00 per annum—Single numbers 6 1-4 cts.

A liberal discount to Periodical Agents.

All Communications for the Editor must be addressed to the EDITOR OF THE BROADWAY JOURNAL, and all letters on business to
JOHN BISCO, PUBLISHER, 153 BROADWAY.

JOHN DOUGLAS, PRINTER, 68 ANN STREET.

We note that the separate departments of the projected magazine correspond closely to those outlined by Poe, with the same stress on originality and independence. It was the latter issue, according to Bette S. Weidmann (see Bibliography), that made the journal "A Casualty of Abolition Politics," since Briggs refused to support the abolitionists blatantly through his columns. More significant, I feel, is the lack of provision for creative or imaginative work, implied only through reference to "illustrations" and also services of ... the best writers in the country" and "slumbering talent." In the third issue of January 18, Briggs as "Harry Franco" sought to supply this missing element through his own absurd tale, "The False Ringlet" (pp. 42-44). Clearly the pressure of editing duties prevented him from turning out more fiction. Surely, this department was ill supplied by the serialized oriental romance "The Great Tower of Tarudant" by Lowell's coeditor on the *Pioneer*, Robert Carter (called "Robert Oliver"). The dreary installments begin on these pages: 117, 137, 170, and 202. Poe, as new associate editor, was almost immediately able to raid his *Tales of the Grotesque and Arabesque* of 1839 for "Lionizing" in the March 17 issue (1:164-66), continuing with "Berenice" (April 5), "Bon Bon" (April 19), "The Oval Portrait" (April 26), and others almost every week. Poe's name, with that of Watson, was added to that of Briggs in the March 8 issue (1:144). Coincidentally, this was also the last to carry the prospectus of Briggs in the advertising section (1:160). It may also be that Poe received extra pay for extra columns of tales or poems, used in the first volume (June 28 issue), but neither the separate contracts among the editorial partners nor any other preserved data throw light on this matter. In the second volume, Poe's inability to pay for contributions and, perhaps, his desire to disseminate tales not included in the twelve selected by Duyckinck for publication (save for "Lionizing") in the *Tales* (June 1845) led him to publish a larger number of his revised works in volume 2. (see lists more complete in Quinn, 456-57 and Woodberry, 2:148-49, TOM, *Tales*, pp. 1396-98 and separate headnotes).

These and other theories about Poe's motives and policies are treated by Heyward Ehrlich in his adroitly condensed and detailed history of the *Broadway Journal*, which he has graciously allowed to be inserted at this point in my Introduction.

The *Broadway Journal* (1):
Briggs's Dilemma and Poe's Strategy

By HEYWARD EHRLICH
Rutgers University (Newark)

THE *Broadway Journal* of 1845, the last of four magazines edited by Edgar Allan Poe and the only periodical he ever owned, failed to measure up to Poe's prediction: "As soon as Fate allows I will have a Magazine of my own — and will endeavor to kick up a dust." [1] The only "dust" raised by the *Broadway Journal* was comprised of such apparently trivial matter as the "Longfellow War" and the Boston Lyceum hoax. But Poe never displayed in public the least disappointment with the magazine; to the contrary, he appeared highly satisfied in his Valedictory to the terminal issue of January 3 1846:

> Unexpected arrangements demanding my whole attention, and the objects being fulfilled, so far as regards myself personally, for which "The Broadway Journal" was established, I now, as its Editor, bid farewell — as cordially to foes as to friends.[2]

Despite its high spirits, the Valedictory remains enigmatic. Poe's new "arrangements" are unknown; his completed personal "objects" are unclear; and his history of the magazine is in conflict with all other evidence. Poe's statement conceals more than it reveals, and a good many questions concerning Poe's connections with the *Broadway Journal* still go unanswered.

If the *Broadway Journal* episode is puzzling in many ways, little illumination may be found in Poe's correspondence of 1845. He is sanguine of certain fame and fortune in letters to T. H. Chivers, R. W. Griswold, or J. P. Kennedy, but he also complains of dangerous overwork, crushing poverty, and a sense of entrapment while communicating with F. W. Thomas, E. A. Duyckinck, and Neilson Poe. The flashes of hope and despair in Poe's letters of 1845 are contradictory and incoherent; nowhere is his role on the *Broadway Journal* elevated above mystery and even obscurity. It becomes evident that Poe's accounts of the *Broadway Journal* do not provide a basis for reconstructing

---

[1] Poe to Philip P. Cooke, Sept 21 1839, *The Letters of Edgar Allan Poe* ed John Ward Ostrom (Cambridge, Mass 1948) 119; cited hereafter as *Letters*.

[2] *Broadway Journal* II (Jan 3 1846) 407; cited hereafter as *BJ*. One biographer comments on the Valedictory: "What other objects Poe achieved, except the republication of much that he had previously written in prose and verse, it is hard to see" (George E. Woodberry, *The Life of Edgar Allan Poe* 2 vols Boston 1909 II 163).

[74]

the story of the magazine. But one continuous record of that narrative does exist. It may be found in the letters of Charles Frederick Briggs, organizer and founding editor of the *Broadway Journal,* to James Russell Lowell, the man who brought Poe and Briggs together at the launching of the magazine. These letters, first studied by George E. Woodberry in 1885, provide an account of the *Broadway Journal* from another viewpoint.[3]

The stumbling block for the historian who might wish to conflate the papers of Poe and Briggs is that after the former succeeded the latter as editor of the *Broadway Journal* in July 1845, a mutual quarrel arose which grew into a lifelong feud. Briggs privately denounced Poe to Lowell in the second half of 1845; Poe openly defamed Briggs in an early number of *The Literati* in 1846; Briggs then replied with a nasty portrait of Poe in his satiric novel of 1847, *Tom Pepper*; and, finally, until his death in 1877, Briggs continued to support the hostile posthumous memoir of Poe by Rufus W. Griswold.[4] While the Griswold controversy polarized Poe studies, no biographer could hope to reconcile the Poe and Briggs accounts of the *Broadway Journal.*[5]

At the nub of the controversy is the question of whether Poe or Briggs was in control of the succession crisis of July 1845. Briggs claimed that he prudently withdrew from the paper after reaching an impasse with the publisher, John Bisco, over the re-financing of the paper; moreover, Briggs insisted that he had intended to dismiss Poe and that Poe had been willing to go. But Poe told the story that by "manoeuvres almost incomprehensible to myself, I have succeeded in getting rid, one by one, of all my associates" so as to become full editor and owner of the magazine.[6] Most Poe biographers dismiss Briggs's testimony and argue that from the start of the *Broadway Journal* Poe was "the boss" while Briggs merely played "second fiddle," so that, in effect, Poe "outwitted" Briggs to wrest control of the paper from him.[7] For example, A. H. Quinn discredits Briggs's story on the evidence of three business contracts of the *Broadway Journal*:

[3] George E. Woodberry *Edgar Allan Poe* (Boston 1885) 226–239; reprinted in Woodberry (1909) II 123–147. The Briggs-Woodberry version is the basis for the entry on the *Broadway Journal* in Frank Luther Mott *A History of American Magazines, 1741–1850* (New York 1930) 757–762.

[4] Perry Miller *The Raven and the Whale* (New York 1956) 156–157, 174–182; Sidney P. Moss *Poe's Literary Battles* (Durham, N. C. 1963) 241–244.

[5] Jay B. Hubbell "Poe" in *Eight American Authors: A Review of Research and Criticism* ed Floyd Stovall (New York 1956) 1–2.

[6] Poe to John P. Kennedy, Oct 26 1845, *Letters* 299.

[7] Mary E. Phillips *Edgar Allan Poe — The Man*, 2 vols (New York 1926) II 1065; Hervey Allen *Israfel: The Life and Times of Edgar Allan Poe* 2 vols (New York 1926) II 638–639; Moss

It is impossible to reconcile his statements concerning his intention to drop Poe with the actual terms of the contracts, for Poe made his with Bisco, and as Poe, Bisco, and Watson went on together, the weight of evidence seems to be against Briggs.[8]

But in refusing to utilize the Briggs materials in any way, Quinn also discarded the only possible context for reaching an understanding of Poe's administration of the magazine, and Poe's management became, on occasion, simply "inexplicable." [9]

Since the publication of Quinn's biography of Poe in 1941, little new information from Poe's hand has emerged to cast additional light on the *Broadway Journal*. Much new material, however, has been unearthed about Briggs, especially since Perry Miller, in his study of literary New York during the 1840s, began the revival of interest in him as a novelist, satirist, and critic in his own right.[10] Furthermore, it is now possible to compare Woodberry's quotations from Briggs's letters against a good many of the originals, thereby revealing the extent of his sweeping dismissal of economic details: "There was from the first some financial tangle between the parties, which, fortunately, there is no need to unravel." [11] It now appears that this very "financial tangle" provides the key to resolving the enigma of the *Broadway Journal*. The vital document, unfortunately omitted by Quinn, is the original contract for the partnership of C. F. Briggs and John Bisco to launch the *Broadway Journal*; all of Poe's subsequent contracts were built upon it. For the first time, enough new information is at hand to attempt again the reconstruction of the story of the *Broadway Journal*; and with more light thrown on the background and context of the magazine, the accounts of Poe and Briggs may be fairly reconciled at long last.

The new findings indicate that the *Broadway Journal* was burdened throughout its short and tortured life by the dual misfortune of utter poverty and hopeless legal complication. The paper lacked the most minimal amounts

---

241. To one anonymous reviewer, Briggs belonged with such enemies of Poe as Lewis Gaylord Clark and Thomas Dunn English: "What a dreary, spiteful crew Poe had to contend with: Clark and English and Briggs . . . characters in search of a *Dunciad*, all!" (*Times* [London] *Literary Supplement*, Jan 23 1964, p 66).

[8] Arthur Hobson Quinn *Edgar Allan Poe* (New York 1941) 463, 751–753 (Henry C. Watson was called "the best musical critic in the country"; Briggs to Mrs Martha W. Jenks, March 4 1845, Miscellaneous Collections, Manuscript Division, The New York Public Library). Acknowledgment is made to the Archives of American Art; The New York Public Library; University of Texas Library; and Harvard College Library for permission to use material quoted here and below.   [9] Quinn 495.

[10] Miller, p 356 and *passim*; see also my "Charles Frederick Briggs and Lowell's *Fable for Critics*" *Modern Language Quarterly* xxviii (Sept 1967) 329–341.

[11] Woodberry (1909) ii 146.

of operating capital, and hence it was organized as a joint-stock improvisation of working partners who ventured their labors for little or nothing. Seven partners are known to have joined the venture; indeed, often the paper operated simply by adding on as yet undisenchanted working shareholders. It is true, none of the partners was economically ruined, but the *Broadway Journal* never attained stability or security, and the paper frequently resorted to desperate measures to remain alive. In turn, Briggs, Bisco, and Poe abandoned their parts of the paper. Each of the participants had good reason to keep secret or at least private the actual condition of the magazine. Hence Poe's Valedictory is a high burlesque transformed from a painful tale of petty debt and legal squabble.

As early as October 1843, when the American Copyright Club was formed, Briggs had hoped to organize an original "weekly of the true stamp" with the help of Evert A. Duyckinck and Cornelius Mathews, but no publisher could be found.[12] Unusual caution was dictated by the recent failures of *Arcturus*, the *Boston Miscellany*, and the *Pioneer* — the last of which cost its editors $1,000 personally — and therefore Briggs spent more than a year working out the details of a joint stock venture of participating partners.[13] In July 1844 Briggs found a printer, John Douglas, but he would not "enter cockily into a speculation" without a satisfactory publisher, and not until December 1844 was he prepared to go ahead with John Bisco, who had issued the *Knickerbocker* in 1841–1842.[14]

The *Broadway Journal* was begun on a shoestring; unhappily, it never raised itself very far above the level of bankruptcy. On December 23 1844, Briggs and John Bisco entered a contract to share equally in both ownership and profits, dividing control of the magazine into editorial and publishing departments.[15] No more frugal arrangement than this could be imagined.

[12] Evert A. Duyckinck to William A. Jones, Oct 1 1843, Duyckinck Collection, Manuscript Division, The New York Public Library.

[13] Instead of salary, members would be "paid out of the profits"; Briggs to James Russell Lowell, March 10 1844 and April 11 1844, William Page Papers, Archives of American Art, Detroit, Mich, cited hereafter as A.A.A.

[14] Briggs to Lowell, July 9 1844, A.A.A.; Mott 757, 606n.

[15] Contract memorandum of Charles F. Briggs and John Bisco to publish the *Broadway Journal*, Dec 23 1844, the University of Texas Library, Austin. This important document, which casts much light on the subsequent contracts of 1845 (see Quinn 751–753), is here published for the first time:

Memorandum of a contract entered into between Charles F. Briggs and John Bisco for publishing a weekly paper, in the city of New York, entitled, the Broadway Journal, on conditions, as follows.

The proprietorship of said paper shall be shared equally between the said Charles F. Briggs and John Bisco.

The expenditures of either participant were to be solely in cash, paid for only out of pocket, and always immediately reimbursed by one-half by the other partner. By prohibiting the use of credit, the economic liability of the paper was thus kept within safe limits. Briggs even went so far as to insist on the right to keep, presumably for resale, "all books, engravings, or other property" submitted as review copies. Although a partner's share in the *Broadway Journal* had little or no transfer value on the market, still, neither participant wished to cope with unacceptable partners in the future; therefore, this mutual legal hold was enforced: "Neither partner shall dispose of his interest in the publication without the consent of the other." Hence the partners were personally protected against an economic catastrophe, but no provision was ever allowed for the possibility of reorganization or recapitalization.

Poe, meanwhile, also had come to place his trust in the joint-stock idea, although for quite different reasons. Cash salary, Poe believed, had deprived him of his rightful share in the success of *Graham's*: "If, instead of a paltry salary, Graham had given me a tenth of his Magazine, I should feel myself a rich man to-day." [16] On March 30 1844, on the eve of his departure from Philadelphia for New York, Poe proposed to Lowell that the "élite of our men of letters" form a magazine intended to reach a circulation of 100,000 by means of a secret "coalition." [17] Lowell did not reply; however, on Octo-

---

The said Charles F. Briggs shall have the control of the editorial department, shall receive and attend to all communications relating to the same, shall solicit contributions, and perform all other duties that may be required of him as editor of said paper.

The said John Bisco shall have charge of the publishing department, shall make all purchases and contracts, collect advertisements, and receive all monies, and pay all bills, due on account of said publication. He shall keep a full and correct account of transactions connected with his department, in books at all times open to the said Briggs' inspection, and perform all other duties that may be necessary in the publication of said paper.

At the end of every four weeks, he shall make an equal division of all profits from said publication then in his possession.

The said C. F. Briggs shall be entitled to all books, engravings, or other property, that may be sent to the office for review or notice in said paper.

In order that said paper may be conducted as economically as possible, all purchases shall be made with cash, and either party neglecting to furnish his share of funds, for more than three days, after being notified of the actual need of the same, shall forfeit five (5) per cent, on the amount required, for the benefit of the concern.

Neither party shall dispose of his interest in the publication without the consent of the other.
Witness   CHAS. F. BRIGGS
GEO. LITTLE   JOHN BISCO
                                                New York December 23 1844

[16] Poe to Frederick W. Thomas, Feb 3 1842, *Letters* 192; see also Poe to Thomas, May 25 1842, *Letters* 197.

[17] Poe to Lowell, March 30 1844, *Letters* 247.

ber 24 1844, Poe amplified his scheme, suggesting that the joint-stock venture would net its writers "$5000 per an: apiece." [18] Again, Lowell ignored the scheme; instead, he sent a letter of introduction which Poe was to present to Briggs: "He will pay & I thought from something you said in your last letter that pay would be useful to you." [19] Thus began the literary acquaintance of Edgar Allan Poe and Charles Frederick Briggs.

Despite Griswold's unfavorable stories, Briggs liked Poe "exceedingly well" in their first encounters.[20] Initially, Poe was only a contributor to the *Broadway Journal* at a dollar a column; Poe's real interest just then was in joining the editorial staff of N. P. Willis' *New York Mirror*.[21] When an unclear passage appeared in Poe's copy for the first issue, Briggs sent it in Poe's absence to E. A. Duyckinck to emend or strike.[22] By January 30 1845 Poe had been paid $18 for nine pages, or eighteen columns, of articles contributed to the *Broadway Journal*.[23] Perhaps this payment was Poe's last from the magazine; no record seems to survive of any subsequent earnings by Poe from the *Broadway Journal* throughout all of 1845.

The early issues of the *Broadway Journal* were greeted with considerable enthusiasm in reviews reflecting virtually every shade of political and literary opinion in New York.[24] But Briggs did not attract the "sixpences" of "the vulgar"; hence he was forced almost at the start to make his paper "more varied and newsy to suit the scrappy appetite of the monster public." [25] Briggs still refused to make a partisan of the *Broadway Journal*, but now he knew that to maintain his neutrality and independence he required the immediate assistance of a popular writer with an assured following — such as Nathaniel P. Willis of the *Mirror*.[26] At the beginning of February 1845

[18] Poe to Lowell, Oct 28 1844, *Letters* 265–266.

[19] Lowell to Poe, Dec 12 1844, Woodberry (1909) ɪɪ 107.

[20] Briggs to Lowell, Jan 6 1845, and Jan 27 1845, Woodberry (1909) ɪɪ 123–124.

[21] Briggs to Lowell, Jan 6 1845, and Jan 17 1845, A.A.A.

[22] Briggs to Duyckinck, Dec 27 1844, Duyckinck Collection. Briggs had previously asked Duyckinck to become a regular contributor and to write for the initial issue, and although Duyckinck wrote the article on William A. Jones in the second number, he became cool to Briggs by the spring of 1845 (Briggs to Duyckinck, Dec 17 1844 and March 26 1845, Duyckinck Collection 15339 and 15341).

[23] *Letters* 521 n 238.

[24] See *Knickerbocker* xxv (Feb 1845) 184; *Democratic Review* xɪv (Jan 1845) 102; *Weekly News* Jan 11 1845; *Weekly Mirror* ɪ (Jan 11 1845) 213; *Morning News* Feb 1 1845; *Daily Tribune* May 13 1845.

[25] Briggs to Lowell, Jan 27 1845, A.A.A.; *BJ* ɪ (Feb 8 1845) 95.

[26] Briggs wrote to Lowell on Feb 1 1845: "I suppose the public would like a Boz or a Sterne to write six pennies worth of fine things for them weekly. . . . If Willis had half an ounce of honesty he were just the man to please the public"; A.A.A.

Briggs sent to Lowell a copy of the *Broadway Journal* containing "The Raven," commending it as a "grand poem" and as "a mere beautiful something entirely free from didacticism and sentiment. . . ." [27] Soon after, when "The Raven" made a lion of Poe, and Poe's relations with Willis' *Mirror* grew unsatisfactory, a new opportunity presented itself to Briggs. [28] Would Edgar Allan Poe do for Briggs as a substitute for Nathaniel Parker Willis?

Briggs's dilemma was that he desperately needed one or two new writers to join the staff of the *Broadway Journal*, but that he could not afford to pay regular salaries. He was therefore compelled to devise a plan, as he explained in self-mockery, to obtain new contributors "free instead of paying them." [29] On February 21 1845 Briggs offered Poe a work-and-share contract; by performing certain editorial duties each week, Poe would receive from Bisco one-third of the profits. [30] A third writer, the music critic Henry C. Watson, joined Briggs and Poe on the masthead at the same time, as Briggs explained, "upon terms similar to those which I offered to Poe." [31] Although Lowell was not content with Briggs's new arrangement, Briggs assured him that "getting the paper into a paying circulation" was urgent and imperative; furthermore, Briggs reminded Lowell that he had been forced "to get the assistance of a printer and a publisher, in the outset, who have a pecuniary interest in the journal as well as myself; I was thus compelled to adapt my means to my ends. . . ." [32] Now five partners shared in the *Broadway Journal*: Briggs, the printer Douglas, the publisher John Bisco, Poe, and Watson. The exact method employed to divide profits remains somewhat unclear; if Poe and Watson were each entitled to primary thirds, then Briggs, Douglas, and Bisco would be left to take secondary thirds of what remained, or mere ninths. This seems unlikely; perhaps some payment went down on the books as reimbursed costs rather than as shared profit, and conceivably, according to the original contract of December 23 1844, Briggs and John Bisco divided profits into halves and then subdivided each moiety themselves among the

---

[27] Briggs to Lowell, Feb 1 1845, A.A.A.

[28] Briggs wrote to Lowell on March 8 1845: "Poe has left the 'Mirror.' Willis was too Willisy for him" (Woodberry 1909 II 126).

[29] Briggs to Lowell, March 19 1845, A.A.A.

[30] Quinn 751. The signatures of Poe and John Bisco on this contract have sometimes been taken to mean that either or both had some authority which Briggs lacked (Quinn 495), but it must be remembered that John Bisco was here acting with Briggs's consent, according to their original contract of Dec 23 1844, to "make all purchases and contracts . . . and pay all bills" (see note15).

[31] Briggs to Lowell, March 19 1845, A.A.A.

[32] Briggs to Lowell, March 19 1845, A.A.A.

remaining partners. In any event, Poe's income was certainly very small if not nil.

When Woodberry published Briggs's letter describing the arrangement with Poe and Watson, the relevant economic details were omitted. Here is the entire passage:

> One of my most reliable sources of profit is from advertising; book advertising in particular. To secure this I must make my paper in some sort a literary oracle, and a mere collection of squibbs and innuendoes at everything would not command that support. Therefore I thought it best to secure Poe's services as a critic, because he already has a reputation for reviewing, and I could gain them by allowing him a certain portion of the paper. He thought it would gain the Journal a certain number of subscribers immediately if his name were published in connection with it. I did not much like the plan, but he had more experience than myself in such matters, so I consented. Music is almost a universal topic, and a certain amount of advertising and subscription being promised on the condition of a certain part of the paper being devoted to musical concerns I engaged Mr Watson who is confirmed on all hands to be the most competent musical critic in the country upon terms very similar to those which I offered to Poe. But I retain precisely the same authority that I did in the beginning, only I get the services of my assistants free instead of paying them, as I should otherwise be compelled to do.[33]

There has been some dispute over Briggs's claim of retaining undivided authority, but Poe himself confessed afterwards that throughout Briggs's regime he remained merely a "contributor" with no editorial voice.[34]

It did not take Poe very long to discover that his partnership in the *Broadway Journal* was profitless. Poe found himself a "slave" to an exhausting "14 or 15 hours a day" of editorial labor without pay in cash:

> I am as poor now as ever I was in my life — except in hope, which is by no means bankable. I have taken a 3d pecuniary interest in the "Broadway Journal", and for every thing I have written for it have been, of course, so much out of pocket.[35]

[33] Briggs to Lowell, March 19 1845; see also Woodberry (1909) II 127–128.

[34] Poe to Laughton Osborn, Aug 15 1845, *Letters* 293.

[35] Poe to Frederick W. Thomas, May 4 1845, *Letters* 286. Poe had been so pressed for income in March that he committed himself to do a monthly column for the *Southern Literary Messenger* and to handle, through Bisco, the New York subscriptions for that magazine, for which purpose he received $18, but neither the articles nor the cash were ever delivered (*Southern Literary Messenger* XI April 1845 256; Benjamin Blake Minor, *The Southern Literary Messenger, 1834–1860*, New York 1950, 139–140; J. H. Whitty, *The Complete Poems of Edgar Allan Poe*, Boston 1911 *xlix-l*; *Letters* 521 n 238.

Four months after Poe became a partner of the *Broadway Journal*, he took stock of where he stood. On June 26 1845 Poe decided to retire from the magazine, to quit New York City, and to take up work on a proposed book, the "American Parnassus":

> . . . I have resolved to give up the B. Journal and retire to the country for six months, or perhaps a year, as the sole means of recruiting my health and spirits. Is it not possible that yourself or Mr Matthews [sic] might give me a trifle for my interest in the paper? [36]

Neither Evert Duyckinck nor Cornelius Mathews could pay Poe for his "interest" in the *Broadway Journal*; for one thing, what Poe owned could not very well be sold. Afterwards, Briggs corroborated Poe's story of intending to leave the magazine, and Briggs also mentioned Poe's request that his name be maintained nominally on the masthead nevertheless:

> I had told P. a month before that I should drop his name from the 'Journal.' He said I might keep it there if I wanted to, although he intended to go into the country and devote his time to getting up books, and would not therefore be able to assist me.[37]

At this time, the economic woes of the *Broadway Journal* were becoming manifest in other ways: on May 3 1845 the office was moved from 153 Broadway to 135 Nassau Street, presumably for economy, and on May 31 1845 the printer John Douglas, one of the original partners of the magazine, quit the sinking ship.[38]

By June 1845 Briggs's initial enthusiasm for Poe had totally evaporated; perhaps one factor was Poe's intoxicated appearance during his first personal meeting with Lowell that spring. In any event, Briggs was faced with a major economic crisis; for the *Broadway Journal* to survive, Briggs would have to start anew with a different investing publisher. Woodberry omitted an important comment by Briggs on Poe at this time when he published portions of the Briggs correspondence; since it indicates Briggs's mind before the crisis of July 1845, it is here given in full:

> I have arrangements on foot with a new publisher for the Journal who will enable me to give it a fresh start; and I trust very soon to be able to

[36] Poe to Duyckinck, June 26 1845, *Letters* 290; for the dating of this letter, see *Letters* 510–511 n 201.

[37] Briggs to Lowell, Aug 1 1845, Woodberry (1909) II 144.

[38] The subsequent changes in the printers of the *Broadway Journal* graphically depict the instability of the magazine after June 1845: J. R. Winser, June 7 1845 to June 28 1845; Douglas again, July 12 1845 and July 19 1845; unknown, July 26 1845 to Oct 25 1845; Office of the Farmer & Mechanic, Nov 1 1845 to Dec 6 1845; and unknown, Dec 13 1845 to Jan 3 1846.

give you an earnest of its profits. I shall haul down Poe's name; he has lately gotten into his old habits and I fear will injure himself irretrievably. I was rather taken at first with a certain appearance of independence and learning in his criticisms, but they are so verbal, and so purely selfish that I can no longer have any sympathy with him. In all that he has ever written there is not a benevolent thought. I think a machine, something like Babbage's[,] might be constructed to write poetry and criticisms like his. I always did hate your mere proof reading critics. I take it for granted that any man who can write at all can write good grammar, and if he choses to write bad it is a business of his own. But he has no right to utter bad thoughts, and it is his thoughts alone that the critic has any right to handle. Poe is a good proof reader and a good scanner of verses, but his merits as a critic hardly reach further.[39]

Briggs was hoping to start the second volume of the *Broadway Journal* on July 5 1845 with a new partner, Homans, who had already "agreed upon terms with Bisco to buy his interest," and who also had made "a very liberal offer" to Briggs himself.[40] Presumably the arrival of Homans would bring an end to the joint-stock arrangement of the magazine; for the first time the *Broadway Journal* would acquire conventional capitalization.

A few days before Briggs's plan for the reorganization of the *Broadway Journal* would begin, John Bisco disrupted matters when he "exacted more" to sell his share than he and Briggs had agreed upon. Since Briggs could not omit Bisco's name from the masthead without his consent, Briggs suspended publication of the issue of July 5 1845, "meaning to issue a double number, not doubting I could agree with him upon some terms" before the next Saturday of July 12 1845.[41] The veracity of Briggs is substantiated by Evert Duyckinck's report of July 8 1845:

> There's trouble in the camp of the Broadway Journal — no number Saturday. Briggs I believe has fallen in love with a new publisher and finds it difficult to be off with the old. I suppose it will work itself clear & that we shall live (at least I hope so) to see another Journal soon.[42]

Thus far, Poe played no known part in the negotiations; to the contrary, Poe may have been too ill at this time to do a great deal, and he had even can-

---

[39] Briggs to Lowell, June 27 1845, A.A.A.; Charles Babbage was the inventor of an early calculating machine; the final six sentences of the passage are omitted in Woodberry (1909) II 141.
[40] Briggs to Lowell, July 16 1845, Woodberry (1909) II 141–142. Homans was probably J. Smith Homans, general publisher and book dealer, who placed advertisements in the paper during this period; see *BJ* I (June 14, 21, and 28 1845) 382, 398, 415.
[41] Briggs to Lowell, July 16 1845, Woodberry (1909) II 142.
[42] Duyckinck to Lowell, July 8 1845, Houghton Library, Harvard University.

celled a scheduled appearance to read a poem before the Philomathian and Euclidian Societies of New York University on June 30 1845.[43] After the suspended issue of July 5 1845, the resolution looked for by Briggs never took place; to make matters worse, John Bisco was now spurred on by unidentified "evil advisers, and became more extortionate than ever." [44] Certainly John Bisco had overestimated the economic extent to which Briggs was "anxious to go on" with the magazine; Briggs now simply withdrew all offers to buy out his partner: ". . . I told him I would not take it. . . ." [45] The effect of this turnabout was to prevent the resumption of publication of the magazine; John Bisco was as powerless to proceed without Briggs's legal consent as Briggs had been the week before without John Bisco's.

For a variety of economic and legal reasons, Briggs elected to break the deadlock; he allowed John Bisco to issue the number of July 12 1845 without his name on it, if only to obtain a legal claim. Meanwhile, Poe recovered his forces and saw the opportunity at his doorstep; according to Briggs, Poe now

> persuaded Bisco to carry on the 'Journal' himself. As his doing so would give me a legal claim upon him, and enable me to recover something from him, I allowed him to issue one number, but it is doubtful whether he issues another.[46]

Briggs's withdrawal left the *Broadway Journal* in a sad economic condition, as C. F. Hoffman reported on July 12 1845:

> The Broadway Journal stopped for a week to let Briggs step ashore with his luggage and they are now getting up steam to drive ahead under captains Poe & Watson — I think it will soon stop again to land one of these.[47]

As Briggs summarized it, John Bisco, "thinking to spite me, and Poe, thinking to glorify himself in having overmastered me, agreed to go on with it." [48]

[43] *Morning News*, July 3 1845.

[44] Briggs to Lowell, July 16 1845, Woodberry (1909) II 142.

[45] Briggs to Lowell, Aug 1 1845, Woodberry (1909) II 144; Briggs had previously warned John Bisco of such a possibility: "I had also told Bisco that I would have nothing more to do with him after the close of the first volume, and that I would not carry it on unless I could find a publisher to my mind" (II 144).

[46] Briggs to Lowell, July 16 1845, Woodberry (1909) II 142.

[47] C. F. Hoffman to Rufus W. Griswold, July 11 1845, Homer F. Barnes *Charles Fenno Hoffman* (New York 1930) 263.

[48] Briggs to Lowell, Aug 1 1845, Woodberry (1909) II 144; it must be remembered that the *Broadway Journal* was not Briggs's only magazine connection during 1845, for he wrote for others and was even approached to commence a new weekly, which he considered naming *The Balance* (Briggs to Lowell, Sept 29 1845, Houghton Library).

The magazine resumed publication on July 12 1845; two days later, Poe and Bisco signed a contract which made Poe "sole editor" of the paper, put him in possession of one-half of the profits, and gave him an "absolute lien" for the first time.[49] It may be of significance that the document was witnessed by Cornelius Mathews, Duyckinck's constant associate and the leading spokesman for "Young America." It must be kept in mind that the original contract of Briggs and John Bisco was still not abrogated, and Briggs had the power to present John Bisco and Poe with a legal suit for publishing the issue of July 19, as he had threatened he might do. Hence, there was genuine relief on July 18 1845, when Evert Duyckinck reported from within the *Broadway Journal* office: "Mathews out of town — No news of Briggs." [50] For his part, John Bisco threw a cloak of secrecy over all the proceedings, insisting, perhaps for legal reasons, that they were matters "in which the public have no interest." [51] In the end, Briggs succumbed to prudence and discretion, and his threatened legal action was never taken:

> I laughed at their folly, and told them to go ahead; but I still hold the same right that I ever did, and could displace them both if I wished to do so. But seeing so much poltroonery and littleness in the business gave me a disgust to it, and I let them alone, hoping to get back from Bisco some money which I had advanced him.[52]

No account by Poe written during the July crisis is known to exist.

But Poe soon found himself forced to say something about the succession which had made him the sole editor of the *Broadway Journal*. On July 30 1845 the *Cincinnati Gazette* ran a paragraph from its New York correspondent — who happened to be Briggs himself — carrying the dateline of July 19 1845 and telling what seemed to be the story of a disinterested person:

> There has been a flare up in the Broadway Journal, which prevented the appearance of one number a week or two since, and may break up the paper. It originated in some difference between one of the Editors and the Publisher. The Editor undertook to get a new publisher on the paper, and so the publisher turned round and put the name of the other editor

---

[49] Quinn 751–752.
[50] Evert A. Duyckinck to George L. Duyckinck, dated Friday and postmarked July 19 [July 18 1845], Duyckinck Collection.
[51] *BJ* II (July 12 1845) 1.
[52] Briggs to Lowell, Aug 1 1845, Woodberry (1909) II 144. When Duyckinck reported the resumption of the *Broadway Journal*, he gave both parties their due; he acknowledged that Briggs's "clear, acute, caustic style was constantly exhibiting various absurdities of social life, clearing away false pretension, and delighting the reader by the humor which enlivened a wide observation and experience," while admitting that Poe's "subtle powers of analysis have been displayed in the work from the appearance of the first number" (*Morning News* July 24 1845).

on his sheet. Where the merits or demerits of the case lie we do not pretend to determine. The Journal has force — some good criticism and a good deal of bad. It needs more catholicity — more liberality and a little less attempt at severity. With its flashy name exchanged for something more dignified, and its main plan retained, it would soon be the most able and entertaining weekly in the country.[53]

Briggs went on — anonymously, of course — to give an account of a similar difficulty aboard the *Democratic Review*; however, he seemed to be offering certain kinds of editorial advice to Poe. When the item was picked up by the New York *Express*, Poe reprinted it for purposes of refutation; in the process, a few typographical changes took place, and the words "and may break up the paper" were either lost or omitted as Poe answered the *Gazette's* correspondent:

> He is right only in the proportion of one word in ten. What does he mean by "catholicity"? What does he mean by calling "The Broadway Journal" "a *flashy* name"? What does he mean by "putting the name of the other editor on the paper"? The name of the "other editor" was never *off* the paper. What does he mean by his pet phrase "a flare-up"? There has been *no* flare-up either in the case of "The Broadway Journal" or of "The Democratic Review." [54]

One week after Poe printed this denial, he reported the resolution of the complication delaying the *Democratic Review*, noting the appearance of a combined July and August number, which happened to contain "a very clever tale" by Briggs; then, in the following issue of the *Broadway Journal*, Poe came to a truce in the dispute: "We thank the New-York Correspondent of the 'Cincinnati Gazette,' for the gentlemanly tone of his reply to some late pettish comments of our own." [55] In effect, Poe had conceded the truthfulness of Briggs's anonymous account.

The irony of Poe's new situation is that he was full editor and half owner of a magazine that he did not esteem very highly. With sarcasm and contempt, Poe wrote to a cousin: " 'The B. Journal' flourishes — but in January I shall establish a Magazine." [56] In August, Lowell noticed that Poe seemed

---

[53] *Daily Cincinnati Gazette* July 30 1845.

[54] *BJ* II (Aug 9 1845) 79.

[55] *BJ* II (Aug 16 and 30 1845) 88, 126.

[56] Poe to Neilson Poe, Aug 8 1845, *Letters* 292. Briggs confirmed Poe's interest in a new magazine: "The last conversation I had with Poe he used all his power of eloquence in persuading me to join him in the joint editorship of the 'Stylus.' " (Briggs to Lowell, Oct 13 1845, Woodberry 1909 II 147).

to have formed an alliance of the *Broadway Journal* and the "Young America" movement, whose leader, Mathews, was sometimes known as the Centurion:

> I am glad to hear that the conduct of Poe and Bisco about the B. J. was not so bad as I feared. I see that the Centurion's industrious laudatory legion got hold of it.[57]

For Poe, there were few grounds for celebration in the declining economic condition of the magazine; not even a month after the resumption of publication, it must have been clear that the future was bleak indeed without fresh capital. Moreover, Poe had no recourse but to begin a series of plaintive appeals for personal loans in August: "Mr Bisco says to me that, with the loan of $50, for a couple of months, he would be put out of all difficulty in respect to the publication of the 'Broadway Journal.' " [58] By October, Bisco evidently abandoned all hope of realizing a profit from the *Broadway Journal,* and Poe was left to continue the profitless magazine on his own.

The *Broadway Journal* had certainly not prospered between Briggs's departure in July and John Bisco's exit in October; yet, Briggs had simply abandoned his moiety while John Bisco insisted on payment from Poe. By borrowing $50 from Horace Greeley, which he turned over to Bisco, and by assuming an aggregate debt of $140 due in January 1846, Poe finally became full owner as well as full editor of the *Broadway Journal* on October 24 1845.[59] Unfortunately, Poe's reign was to endure for hardly more than one month. The problem of the lack of capital, which had plagued each of the partners from the start, was now placed entirely upon Poe's shoulders, and Poe tried to solve it by means of personal appeals to R. W. Griswold, J. P. Kennedy, T. H. Chivers, Fitz-Greene Halleck, and George Poe, between October 26 1845 and December 1 1845, for sums of $50 to $200.[60]

Perhaps the fullest disclosure of Poe's state of mind at this time occurs in his request to John P. Kennedy:

> By a series of manoeuvres almost incomprehensible to myself, I have succeeded in getting rid, one by one, of all my associates in "The Broadway Journal", and (as you will see by last week's paper) have now become sole

[57] Lowell to Briggs, Aug 8 1845, Houghton Library. Much material favorable to Mathews and "Young America" appeared in the *Broadway Journal* under Poe; see, for example, *BJ* ɪɪ (Aug 2 1845, Sept 27 1845, Oct 18 1845, Nov 15 1845, and Nov 29 1845) 60–61, 177–178, 227, 283–284, 325.

[58] Poe to Thomas H. Chivers, Aug 11 1845, *Letters* 292–293.

[59] Mott 761–762; Quinn 752–753; Poe to Thomas H. Chivers, Nov 15 1845, *Letters* 302.

[60] *Letters* 298–305. Evidently Poe's appeal to Briggs himself in October (see note 56) is yet one more indication of his economic difficulties.

editor and owner. It will be a fortune to me if I can hold it — and if I can hold it for one month I am quite safe — as you shall see.[61]

Poe's account of the history of the magazine is thoroughly equivocal; what is interesting, however, is his closing remark, "if I can hold it for one month I am quite safe — as you shall see." Indeed, Poe began to liquidate the *Broadway Journal* about five weeks later; on December 3 1845 he transferred half his interest to Thomas H. Lane, who was brought in to terminate its accounts.[62] Evidently Poe did not even bother to edit the final issue; it was prepared by Thomas Dunn English, who had become a partner of some kind by investing $30 in the paper in October.[63] English and Lane were the sixth and seventh known partners to join the *Broadway Journal* in 1845.[64] The brief but fevered history of the magazine came to an end, celebrated only by Poe's Valedictory, on January 3 1846.

Poe did not pause to lament the passing of the *Broadway Journal*; to the contrary, the hint of satisfaction as to his "objects" in the Valedictory is enlarged upon in a letter written soon afterwards: "The B. Journal had fulfilled its destiny — which was a matter of no great moment. I have never regarded it as more than a temporary adjunct to other designs." [65] But what were Poe's "other designs"? What did Poe mean in speaking of the magazine as a "temporary adjunct" and "a matter of no great moment"? Why, indeed, did Poe change his course so often with regard to the paper — quitting in June, returning in July, buying it all in October, and disposing of half in December?

Perhaps the fullest disclosure of Poe's motives during the *Broadway Journal* period may be found in a lengthy letter of October 1844 written just six weeks before he met Briggs and joined the paper as one of the initial contributors.[66] In a detailed confession to George Anthon, Poe revealed that he was dedicated to his "ultimate purpose — to found a Magazine of my own, or in which at least I might have a proprietary right," but that he also had

---

[61] Poe to John P. Kennedy, Oct 26 1845, *Letters* 299; Kennedy replied: "Good wishes are pretty nearly all the capital I have for such speculations" (*Letters* 300).

[62] Woodberry (1909) II 427; Kenneth Rede, "Poe Notes from an Investigator's Notebook" *American Literature* v (March 1933) 53–54.

[63] Francis P. Dedmond "The War of the Literati: Documents of the Final Phase" *Notes and Queries* cxcviii (July 1953) 303–308.

[64] It is possible that some of the printers who succeeded John Douglas also became partners of the paper in the same way that Douglas himself did at first.

[65] Poe to Sarah J. Hale, Jan 16 1846, *Letters* 312.

[66] Briggs reported that meeting in writing to Lowell on Dec 17 1844: "Mr Poe called upon me with yr. note" (A.A.A.).

in sight for the present an "immediate object," to obtain the publication of a collection of his sixty-six tales in as many as five volumes. Poe hoped that Anthon might obtain the backing of Harper & Brothers for both his collected works and also an elegant magazine:

> In a word, I believe that the publication of the work would lead forthwith either directly through my own exertion or indirectly with the aid of a publisher to the establishment of the journal I hold in view.

Although the Harpers showed no interest in the projects, the two goals were inextricably connected in Poe's mind.[67] What happened in 1845, soon after the furore of "The Raven," was that he was offered a working partnership in the *Broadway Journal* at about the same time that he began to negotiate with another book publisher, Wiley & Putnam. If Poe could not utilize the publication of his collected works as a tactic to bring about his vision of an affluent monthly, then he would employ a precarious weekly, the *Broadway Journal*, to extract as many editions as possible from Wiley & Putnam. Such is the circumstantial evidence of Poe's "objects" and "designs" of 1845; indeed, the two Wiley & Putnam editions of that year were, in fact, the closest Poe ever came in his lifetime to enjoying a collected works.

Wiley & Putnam agreed to issue a collection of Poe's tales in one volume almost as soon as Poe's name appeared on the masthead of the *Broadway Journal.*[68] The edition was already "in press" by March 16 1845 but there was a delay for some reason; as late as June 26 1845, when Poe offered his share in the *Broadway Journal* to Evert Duyckinck, the book had still not appeared, and perhaps Poe had begun to fear that it would never appear.[69] At this time, Duyckinck was in a curious position; he had been among Briggs's inner circle of initial contributors to the *Broadway Journal*, and he was now both house editor of Wiley & Putnam's Library of American Books and literary editor of the New York *Morning News* and *Weekly News*. Upon receiving Poe's letter, Duyckinck appears to have moved very quickly; two

---

[67] Poe to George Anthon, before Nov 2 1844, *Letters*, p 270–271. The Harpers were said to have rejected Poe's proposal, he was told, because of "*complaints* against you, grounded on certain movements of yours, when they acted as your publishers some years ago" in the issue of *Arthur Gordon Pym* (1838) (Anthon to Poe, Nov 2 1844, *The Complete Works of Edgar Allan Poe* ed James A. Harrison 17 vols, New York 1902 xvii 193). At the time of Poe's appeal to Anthon, four years had passed since his last important volume of fiction, *Tales of the Grotesque and Arabesque* (1840), and three years had passed since Lea & Blanchard had rejected Poe's proposal of Aug 13 1841, that they follow it with a second volume (*Letters* 178 and 178n; Quinn 278–279, 336–340, 397–399).

[68] Briggs to Lowell, March 8 1845, Woodberry (1909) ii 126.

[69] Briggs to Lowell, March 16 1845, A.A.A.; Briggs repeated the report in the *Daily Cincinnati Gazette*, April 2 1845.

days later, on Saturday, June 28 1845, which was to have been Poe's last day as a partner of the *Broadway Journal*, Wiley & Putnam suddenly announced Poe's *Tales* as "just published," and the first review, certainly Duyckinck's own, appeared in the *Morning News*.[70] Usually the Saturday *Weekly News* reprinted the week's literary material from the *Morning News* of the preceding week, but the Poe review did not appear in the weekly edition until July 5 1845, one week later, suggesting the possibility of a missed deadline and great haste. In any event, Poe suddenly possessed on June 28 something he had lacked on June 26, namely, a working connection with a book publisher. Indeed, Poe's first action when he returned to the *Broadway Journal* on July 12 1845 was to agitate for a second Wiley & Putnam volume.

Poe probably reviewed his own book, but he did not stoop to self-adulation. He simply complained that Duyckinck's choice of a "mere selection of twelve tales from seventy" displayed "no particular arrangement" and hence failed to give any idea of Poe's "diversity of invention." [71] Afterwards, Poe continued to employ the *Broadway Journal* to provoke additional favorable comment and to maintain his demand for a second volume of tales.[72] Whether or not this sort of literary politicking really mattered cannot be said, but Poe evidently believed very strongly that it did. The *Tales* enjoyed a successful sale of 1,500 copies; during the summer of 1845, Wiley & Putnam agreed to hazard the publication of a volume of Poe's poetry and to allow Poe to select it himself.[73] Hence Poe's decision to go on with the *Broadway Journal* in July, even though he was ready to retire from the paper in June, seems to have been designed largely to put him in the best possible position to negotiate with Wiley & Putnam.

The proofs of Poe's next volume, *The Raven and Other Poems*, were ready about one week before John Bisco's withdrawal from the *Broadway Journal* in October, and Poe could not have been unaware of his partner's discontent with the magazine. Poe read the proofs the evening before his highly controversial appearance at the Boston Lyceum.[74] That lecture, in which Poe attempted to pass off "Al Aaraaf" as a juvenile work, has been taken as a

---

[70] *BJ* I (June 28 1845) 415; *Morning News* June 28 1845; however, the *Broadway Journal*, which published on Saturday, probably could accept material as late as Friday, except when that day was a holiday, as it was on July 4 1845 (Briggs to Duyckinck, Tuesday [July 1 1845] Duyckinck Collection).

[71] *BJ* II (July 12 1845) 10.

[72] See, for example, *BJ* II (Oct 4 1845) 200.

[73] Poe to Duyckinck, Sept 10 1845 and Nov 13 1845, *Letters* 297, 301.

[74] *BJ* II (Dec 13 1845) 358.

sign of "mental disturbance," but Poe's hoax may have been a stunt designed to bring attention to his forthcoming volume of poetry.[75] Wiley & Putnam announced *The Raven and Other Poems* on November 8 1845; the *Broadway Journal* reported it in Books Received on November 22 1845.[76] But during the period between October 25 1845, the day after Poe became full owner of the *Broadway Journal*, and December 13 1845, ten days after Poe disposed of half that ownership to Thomas Lane, he all but gave over the *Broadway Journal* to the airing of the Boston Lyceum hoax, thereby creating fresh interest in himself as a poet and providing invaluable publicity for *The Raven and Other Poems*.[77] Perhaps the coincidence was accidental — perhaps, too, it was fortuitous again that Poe had launched the "Longfellow War" in March just when the *Tales* were in press — but it appears most likely that Poe did utilize the *Broadway Journal* repeatedly as a device to aid and promote the publication of his books. Hence, Poe's remark of October 26 1845 to Kennedy about the *Broadway Journal*, "if I can hold it for one month I am quite safe — as you shall see," apparently reveals Poe's intention of becoming full owner of the magazine to keep it alive long enough to usher in *The Raven and Other Poems*.

The encounter with Briggs and the *Broadway Journal* in 1845 bears a lesson for Poe scholars who have felt the need "to study more closely his policy as editor of four different magazines in three different cities." [78] Poe's strategy in 1845 became a career policy for himself rather than an editorial policy for his magazine, but there is no reason to assume that Poe held to an identical principle on the *Southern Literary Messenger*, *Burton's*, and *Graham's*. Nevertheless, some common attitudes and beliefs run like a red thread throughout Poe's career; even before he assumed his first editorship, Poe saw a parallel between the necessity for the unity and totality of effect in literary aesthetics — for which he was later to become well known — and the necessity for similar unity in literary politics:

> The history of all Magazines shows plainly that those which have attained celebrity were indebted for it to articles *similar in nature* — *to Berenice*. . . . In the ludicrous heightened into the grotesque: the fearful coloured into the horrible: the witty exaggerated into the burlesque: the singular wrought out into the strange and mystical.[79]

[75] Quinn 487.

[76] *BJ* II (Nov 8 and 22 1845), 280, 307.

[77] See, for example, *BJ* II (Oct 25 1845, Nov 1 1845, Nov 22 1845, and Dec 13 1845), 248, 261–263, 309–311, 357–358.

[78] Hubbell *Eight American Authors* 45.

[79] Poe to Thomas W. White, April 30 1835, *Letters* 57–58.

These qualities, needless to say, were also abundantly displayed by Poe in the *Broadway Journal*. Poe's career nearly always rotated around the magazines of his time; even the largely fictional autobiographical memorandum of 1841 concludes with two items pertaining to his magazine exploits.[80] Poe created over the years certain legends about himself as a magazinist; perhaps the best known axiom of his invention is that he could work by force of will five-fold or even ten-fold increases in magazine circulation.[81] Poe tried to invoke his old magic in 1845, and when it did not work, he simply forgot the *Broadway Journal* episode and persisted afterwards in his conviction that a successful monthly still remained "the one great purpose of my literary life." [82] In the last year of his life, Poe steadfastly believed that the magazinist had to be as inventive in practical action as he was in literary imagination; novelty remained a cardinal principle of both politics and aesthetics: "What the public seek in a Magazine is *what they cannot elsewhere procure.*" [83]

The *Broadway Journal* episode might provide grounds to agree with the description of Poe as "a complete product of the publishing world of his time," a literary figure whose main efforts always went "to master a market." [84] Yet Poe never either attained or even aspired to the merely commercial success of such friendly contemporaries as N. P. Willis. It was Willis, of course, who gave this memorable piece of advice upon the times when, after 1845, the Poe-Briggs war finally came into the open: "Notoriety is glory in this transition state of our half-bak'd country." [85] Indeed, Poe's faults, if they were faults, as an adventurous entrepreneur were not his alone; to the contrary, they belonged to his age. Yet the glory Poe sought was never wealth alone, despite the dream of wealth which plagued him. The eventual glory for Poe was literary reputation — both for the moment and, if possible, for a span of eternity.

Although Briggs and Lowell came to be shocked by what Poe did with the *Broadway Journal*, it must be remembered that they began by encouraging him. Briggs gave Poe a relatively free hand in what he wrote for the paper during the first six months, and Lowell, who had some notion of Poe's dream

---

[80] *Works* ed Harrison I 344–346.

[81] Poe to Frederick W. Thomas, Sept 1 1841 and Feb 3 1842; Poe to Thomas H. Chivers, Sept 27 1842; Poe to Charles Anthon, before Nov 2 1844; Poe to Edward H. N. Patterson, April 30 1849; *Letters* 180, 192, 215, 269–270, 440.

[82] Poe to Philip P. Cooke, Aug 9 1846, *Letters* 330.

[83] Poe to Edward H. N. Patterson, April 30 1849, *Letters* 439.

[84] Howard Mumford Jones *Ideas in America* (quoted in *Eight American Authors* 24–25).

[85] Willis to Poe, n d [1846–1847?] Harrison XVII 206.

of a "coalition," spurred him on in an admiring article published in *Graham's* in 1845. By a double coincidence, Poe had to go to Briggs's office in the fall of 1844 to obtain Lowell's manuscript, which had been sent to him for personal approval; and again, the article itself was finally published in February 1845, just three weeks before Poe and Briggs became partners on the *Broadway Journal.* Lowell wrote:

> Had Mr. Poe had the control of a magazine of his own, in which to display his critical abilities, he would have been as autocratic, ere this, in America, as Professor Wilson had been in England; and his criticisms, we are sure, would have been far more profound and philosophical than those of the Scotsman. As it is, he has squared out blocks enough to build an enduring pyramid, but he has left them lying carelessly and unclaimed in many different quarries.[86]

What Lowell said of the criticism, Poe knew, was equally if not more true of the tales and poems scattered in the files of so many newspapers and magazines. Consequently, Poe used the *Broadway Journal* for the final revision of many tales and poems and as part of his strategy for assuring during his lifetime an "enduring pyramid" — the *Tales* and *The Raven and Other Poems* issued in 1845 by *Wiley & Putnam.*

[86] After 1845, of course, Lowell no longer had such high expectations from Poe, and the passage was dropped when the article was reprinted in 1850; the original version from *Graham's* (Feb 1845) and the reprint are conflated in *The Shock of Recognition* ed, Edmund Wilson (New York 1943) 7.

THE BROADWAY JOURNAL.

VOL. I. NO. 10. NEW YORK, SATURDAY, MARCH 8, 1845. Published at
Three Dollars per Annum. 133 BROADWAY, by
Single Copies, 6 1-4 Cents. C. F. BRIGGS, EDGAR A. POE, H. C. WATSON, EDITORS. John Bisco.

Poe's name joins the masthead.
Berg Collection

Mr. Ehrlich's statement of the dilemma of Briggs and the situation of Poe during the year of 1845 is admirably compendious, employing material from varied sources, some of it used for the first time. I have reservations only about a few points. I have seen no evidence that Briggs was the anonymous correspondent for the Cincinnati *Gazette* (see his note 53) nor does the author provide any. In fact, it was Briggs himself who proudly announced the title "*Broadway Journal*" and lengthily justified it in the "Introductory" of page 1 of the magazine. Surely, Poe would have retorted with his own words in article (c), page 210 (facsimile text and notes of August 9) had this been the case. A more important reservation concerns his basic premise about Poe's reasons for seizing increasing control of the *BJ* during the second half of the year, which he calls "Poe's strategy." Poe scarcely promoted his own tales through the brief, low-keyed review that he himself wrote (see note to 167) and waited until very late to cite favorable reviews of the tales or poems (pp. 283, 299; 337 of facsimile text). Poe's sentence "if I can hold it for one month I am quite safe" (Ehrlich, 88) can scarcely relate to the issuance of his book of poems (Ehrlich, 91), which was imminent. Nor can we totally ignore Poe's editorial statement in the December 20 issue (No. 24, p. 347 article d): "A New Volume of the *Broadway Journal*, will commence on Saturday, the tenth of January next." A well-projected "strategy" could not lead two weeks later to the "Valedictory" (p. 360) concerning "objects ... fulfilled." The conduct of Poe's life is better explained by "whim--impulse-passion" as he earlier wrote to Lowell (Ostrom, *Letters*, p. 257). There is also a tendency toward self-destruction rather than self-aggrandizement operating in many phases of Poe's public conduct of 1845--a thesis that has been excellently presented by Sidney P. Moss (see Biblio.).

THE "DEPARTMENTS" AND MAJOR TOPICS TREATED BY POE

The wide scope of Poe's interests--in the arts, science, social events, politics, contemporary personalities--becomes apparent in the many types of articles from his pen, especially as he became first the leading editor, with Watson covering music, and some drama and art, in July, and then the sole editor, in October. Much earlier, however, it was clear that Briggs willingly assigned him more features than long reviews of prominent books. As the fledgling magazine began committing itself to certain types of cultural news coverage, Poe's capacities were called into play. This can be seen, in part, through consulting the topics, prominent names, and works listed in my Index. We shall find Poe engaged in the criticism of art, music, and drama, as well as literature, in writing essays on such specialized topics as "Street Paving," "Anastastic Printing," and the confrontations of the publisher and writer of magazine literature. In his "Editorial Miscellany" columns, he shows his knowledge of trends in many contemporary fields of science and technology and also in social and political happenings. While the format of the magazine became fairly well established by the end of volume 1, Poe experimented with different arrangements for the reviews, in the use of material from exchange papers, and occasionally in the type of material included (e.g., a play by Laughton Osborn, in installments). Of course, he was hampered greatly by his total inability to pay for contributions, as well as by his own increasing depression and instability as subscriptions fell off and debts mounted. While it is obvious that editing the magazine during the last four months was no longer an inspiration or pleasure, some of the material has much biographical interest for us, as at the time of his Lyceum reading in Boston, which Poe developed into a large "bobbery," and all of it continues to show the wide scope of Poe's knowledge and ideas. Only a few categories need any special attention below:

BOOK REVIEWS

Briggs surely offered Poe an opening primarily as reviewer of important new books, such as Elizabeth Barrett Barrett's *Drama Of Exile and Other Poems*, appearing in the first two issues. Also, in accordance with his planned series of biographical sketches, as in Poe's prospectus, he must have had Poe in mind (see the only one by Poe on Willis, in No. 3). Poe did agree to do a journeyman's job on two more books (see pp. 18-23), but he preferred to continue the "Little Longfellow War" which he had started in the *Evening Mirror*. Briggs obviously was willing to gain a somewhat notorious publicity for the *BJ* with the continuity of the planned series, even while disagreeing with the reckless charges of plagiarism against Aldrich and Longfellow. By the end of March, Briggs and probably most of the readers were thoroughly disenchanted with the whole affair. Poe had also contributed a few special short articles on surveying the exchange magazines and other papers, especially when some special topic claimed his attention (see *SLM*). His supplements in the *SLM* had surveyed comments in the press on his own magazine, and in his letters to the *Columbia Spy* of 1844, he discussed current magazines. Certainly Poe knew the contributing writers and nature of the varied publications better than anyone, and seemed to have an amazing capacity to race through quantities of printed matter for relevant, summarizing comments. This was to become his province on the *BJ* after the "War" ended. And since Briggs was evidently overwhelmed by the complications of the editing tasks, Poe's special capacities as book-reviewer were increasingly being used, although without stipulated pay by column, as previously. His early major effort in this field was unquestionably the two-part review of the Barrett book.

After his "Longfellow War" series, Poe was clearly expected to fill up many pages during the second quarter of the year and chose to do so with inglorious repetitions of *SLM* reviews (see those on Hall's *Book of Gems*, Mrs. Child's *Philothea*, and Dalton's *Peter Snook*). His long piece on the detested poems of William Lord had none of the vivacity of his early review of Theodore Fay's *Norman Leslie*. A few of his notices enabled him to clarify principles of criticism or diction, such as those on Leigh Hunt (and imagination) and on Bolles's new dictionary.

In the second volume he alone undertook the important reviews, most of them of volumes of poetry. Under the pressure of editing the magazine alone, he returned too often to his unfortunate habit of the *SLM* days, of including long and numerous excerpts as space-filler, as can be seen in the most sizable of the reviews: the works of Hirst, Hoyt, Chivers, Hood, Mrs. Smith, Hood (again), Simms, Mary Hewitt, and Fanny Osgood (respectively beginning on 162, 179, 187, 198, 221, 228, 265, 288, 328). (See 144/1-7 note, for his new system of dividing long reviews from brief notices.) Yet, despite the secondary importance of most of Poe's *BJ* reviews, there are many fine statements of principle and demonstrations of critical method as well as cross currents of personal and biographical significance that repay study. It has been possible to include all the material of each review save for two or three instances where the article itself is virtually a headnote to the excerpt (see p. 349).

EDITORIAL MISCELLANY

This feature of the second volume of the *BJ* was equivalent to the "Editor's Table" in the *Knickerbocker* and similar "spaces" reserved for the editor of other journals. Briggs was apparently casting about for such a channel of personal opinion or else news oddities, often presenting mixed excerpts from the domestic and foreign press, as in "Varieties" (1.29), "Bits of News" (1.77, 1.94), "General Intelligence" (1.142), "Miscellany" (1.366), "Miscellanea" (1.348), "Miscellanies" (1.381), "Weekly Notes." In the second volume Poe soon hit upon his own phrase, "Editorial Miscellany" (2.60-63), and retained it throughout the volume. Often the first section was his personal comment on statements about the magazine or about himself (as in the Boston press after the Lyceum reading). Often this was followed by adapted or verbatim excerpts from the newspapers and magazines of America or from abroad. The restrictions imposed by limited space have required that those patently copied here without change be eliminated, especially where the topics seem most tangential to the interests of the editor and the readers of the journal, as well as of today. However, relatively few have been dropped in view of the difficulty of ascertaining definitively the verbatim aspect of material from utterly unidentified papers and also in view of the need for showing the full scope of Poe's interests. Often in my notes are cross references to loci in his other works, including fiction, that corroborate Poe's interest in the topic. It is noteworthy that Poe marked with a "P" for Mrs. Whitman many of the "Editorial Miscellany" articles, often thereby defining the section that was of personal or particular interest because of the event or the issue discussed. Harrison, who saw this copy when in the hands of F. P. Halsey, carelessly dropped several from his "collected works" even when listing them in his bibliography, so that some of this important material has escaped the notice of students of Poe (see Hull, p. 519).

Needing a passing mention is the "Box" that Poe addressed "To Readers and Correspondents" or simply to the latter. This often spoke about the need to return an item or the acceptance for publication of a contribution by someone with a pseudonym or specified by initials. Often there are editorial comments of telling effect. R. H. Stoddard is told that his "Ode on a Grecian Flute" was, first, lost; next, plagiarized, on which comments (plus his personal visit) hangs a long tale of Poe's most malignant denigrator and editor after Griswold (see 186, 198 notes). The Della Cruscan flirtation with Mrs. Osgood is archly insinuated in various of the "boxes." Sometimes a familiar name lurks under the letters, such as "W.W."-- "Walter Whitman," being thanked for his essay before its appearance in the *BJ*. All of these receive whatever comment is useful in the notes and are listed in the Index, but many more unknowns should yield their secret to scholarly delving.

Another type of editorial opinion is attached to pieces of printed material--not by Poe, in the main text, but furnished in his footnote or headnote: e.g., his three sentence footnote to Whitman's "Art-Singing and Heart-Singing" agreeing with Whitman's view of music. (See also his headnote to Fuller's satire [220]). Either through an excerpt from the text or a summary in my notes, the reader is apprised of the connection of Poe's comment and the text.

The articles in the *BJ* of an essay nature rather than in the form of editorial opinion are important in that they include the five long installments of "The Little Longfellow War" (q.v. in Introduction) and deal with plagiarism, imitativeness, and originality. While lacking cogency, balance, and effective rhetorical development as a whole, and being obsessively hostile to Longfellow's works, they raise basic issues both on the broad topic of what is meant by artistic composition and on Poe's relations with contemporary writers. Tangential to these are his several short statements on copyright, encouragement of native American talents, publishers' payments and standards of criticism in the other arts as well. (The article, "Some Secrets of the Magazine Prison-House," 1.103-4, appears in TOM's *Sketches*, pp. 1206-1210). There are a few short articles on non-literary themes, resembling in style and development several essays that he inserted into *BGM* in 1839-40; these relied upon sedulous notetaking from other sources, especially encyclopaedias. "Street Paving" is to be assumed of this nature (94-96), while "Anastatic Printing" utilized a contemporary British magazine (83-86; also, 135-36). A third area began with his sketch of Willis--of the type that he developed into the accounts of the "literati" in *Godey's*, the next year; we remember Poe's stress on such biographies in his prospectuses. The short satire on Margaret Fuller, with its picture, also underscores his wish for meaningful illustration, which the indigence of the magazine soon terminated.

THE DRAMA

While it had long been customary for weekly journals to review the current drama, Briggs himself was hostile to that field of criticism as he stated in *BJ* (1.30), giving some highly prejudicial arguments about typically poor acting and imitation of the British stage. He would have minimized the amount, but Poe must have prevailed, through his respect for the theatre, as N. Bryllion Fagin has well shown. He started with a long review on "The New Comedy," *Fashion* by Anna C. Mowatt, whom he greatly admired, and continued with occasional reviews and short references that may be followed in my Index, under "drama," "theaters" (such as the Park, Niblo's New Bowery, Palmo's) and specific actors and also elocutionists (Mowatt, Murdoch, Vandenhoff); see also, Dinneford, the manager (anent honest dramatic criticsm, 96-98), and Shakespeare for the stage and its literature. Sorting out Poe's dramatic criticism apart from that of Watson, in the second volume, has been difficult because some of the review material is obviously dependent upon the accounts of the daily press. Moreover, James E. Murdoch, Poe's friend, was obviously used for filling out empty pages during the last few difficult months of the journal. Watson also contributed unsigned reviews, which I have had to eliminate. Poe's genuine articles serve well in clarifying phases of his thought about imitation, parallel progress in the different arts, and stage intrigue or plot.

MUSIC

As early as March Briggs seemed willing to accord a prominent role to music criticism and offered Henry Cood Watson (1818-1875) terms similar to those of Poe (see Ehrlich's account at note 33). Yet he surely had to contribute in other fields to justify an equal share in the income--small as it proved to be. Even the brief *DAB* article shows him as of high reputation and considerable versatility in journalistic writing. We should note that for the 10/11 *BJ* Watson wrote a tale, "The Falling Star" (2.208-210) and a column on the "National Gallery at the Rotunda" (signed "W." right over Poe's on "The Ivory Christ," signed "P." in print [2.213-14]). Watson's "appreciation" is extremely literal and gauche. This is a sequel to one of 9/20, unsigned but mentioning "much familiarity with the galleries of England" (169), with an overblown essay on his trip to an art auction at Bordentown (194-196). Apparently he worked also for the British New York weekly, *The Albion*, and Willis's *New Mirror*, earlier. He was always on good terms with Poe, but was diverted from the *BJ* by his many musical activities, such as lectures, music composition and teaching (see 264 of facsimile text), and the organization of music groups, including the Philharmonic Society of New York. Hence, his name was dropped from the masthead of the 10/25 issue, although traces of Watson's presence still can be found later, in music references and in "Editorial Miscellany" borrowings from the press abroad. For example, the first paragraph of the last "Fine Arts" column in the 1/3/46 issue (2.406) mentions "Chapin [*sic*], the celebrated composer and pianist"--the man whom James Huneker regarded as Poe's musical parallel. Poe's intense interest in music, both as performed and as basic to prosody must also be noted (see Pollin, [H]). Occasionally but rarely here he felt qualified to comment on Mendelssohn's music for *Antigone* or the quality of performances (see Index for "music," Alpers, *Antigone*, Donizetti, and Loder).

ART

Poe's keen interest in the graphic arts was manifested in his attention to details of illustration, binding, cover decoration, and paper quality in his reviews, as well as in his frequent references to renowned artists of the present and past, reflecting his reading and visits to galleries (see Pollin, [I] Part I). A partiality for woodcut illustrations marked the plans of both Poe and Briggs and while the funds permitted, Briggs managed to have this feature in volume 1, but volume 2 has only a steel plate of the organ of Trinity Church, described in the text of 10/11, 214-217. Briggs himself often discussed art gallery exhibitions and invited his friend William Page, an artist whom Poe himself admired, to contribute a series of six very technical and very dull articles on "The Use of Color in Imitation in Painting" (see the pages in Poe's Index under "Paintings"). Evidently both Poe and Briggs shared many views about the role of art in the magazine, and Poe even lent his letter press to a wood cut caricature of Margaret Fuller. The use of Gavarni sketches was apologetically acknowledged by Briggs (see notes to 44/19). After the departure of Briggs, Poe was probably unhappy with Watson's coverage of art and essayed to review exhibitions of two pieces of sculpture; see "The Ivory Christ" and "Sortie du Bain" in the Index. His use of source material and the terms employed were rather interesting than enlightening. See also, in the Index, pages given for other Poe art discussions under C. E. Lester, Hiram Powers, *Harper's* ... *Bible*, *Martin's* ... *Bible*, Titian, Raffaelle, and art.

The following are titles or subjects of the illustrations above vignette size printed in volume 1 (with their original pages), some of which are reproduced in my facsimile text on the pages given in parentheses: 8: Woman with Bustle (1); 57: Morris and Willis before the Mirror (44); 89: A Suspended Bishop (143); 105: Horace Greeley (119); 136: A Man of the Upper 10,000 (15); 153: Caricature of Margaret Fuller (34); 168: A Stock Speculator; 200: The Devil (102 and 108); 216: Mr. Hudson (76); 232: Presentation at a Literary Soire (82); 248: Paul de la Roche (vignette portrait); 289: Union Square.

Illustrations Reproduced in the Facsimile Volume

Page in Facsimile Edition

1   *"The Bustle"
15   *One of the "Upper Ten Thousand"

MISCELLANEOUS SUBJECTS

ADVERTISEMENTS AND PUBLICITY NOTICES

Occasionally, Poe inserted advertising copy into his editorial columns to cultivate favor with advertisers (see 227/54 note) or as a favor to a friend (see reference to Watson's Glee Class, 264). In a sense, many of the short references to new book projects by Wiley and Putnam or the other publishers are an attempt to please real or potential advertisers. These notices are inserted only when they appear to be in Poe's words. The advertisements themselves did not seem to be diminishing in total number, Hull observes (p. 508), during Poe's sole editorship, and with the 9/27 issue the format was changed from two column to three column pages (with smaller print, of course). Yet much of the material was probably gratuitously inserted or paid for at reduced rates. On 11/1, the format reverted to two-column pages. It has been impossible to insert this material, even when Poe may have composed the copy, save for his own pseudonymous investment offer of a share in the *BJ* (see 220/29 n).

Another broad category included in my facsimile text relates to notices for and about the journal itself. These are sometimes Bisco's announcements of a change in the editorial personnel (see p. 160 [facsimile text]), office changes (as when the *BJ* moved next door to Thomas Dunn English, editor of the *Aristidean*, to save expenses [see P36/38n]), or lists of the designated agents for the magazine, with their communities indicated--at the end of the advertisement page (311). The last have not been reprinted, but sometimes excerpted names have been mentioned when relevant to Poe's main text (see TOM, 82/18n, for example).

ARRANGEMENT OF THE MATERIAL

Poe's prose writings in the *Broadway Journal*, save for his fiction, was to comprise the basic text of this part of the edition of his *Collected Writings*. The great quantity and variety of this material posed a problem. It was issued chronologically and was often tied to a succession of events, both personal and public, such as his relations with Briggs and Bisco, editor and proprietor, or his quarrel with Longfellow or his Lyceum lecture-reading in Boston. Internally he sometimes made cross references to a book reviewed earlier in a later review or promised to talk about a topic or a book in a later issue of the magazine. Hence, it seemed imperative to offer all the material chronologically, in the order of its original presentation, and in a form as close as possible to the original. Since all the authenticated Poe material would require at least two volumes of the print used for the previous volumes of the series, with no room left for the copious notes required for this edition, a separate volume would have to be added, making three in all. From any realistic publishing point of view this would be unfeasible. A composite facsimile edition for Poe's text, in one oversized volume, seemed to be the solution. The difficulties about textual inaccuracies in a hastily produced weekly magazine could be solved, as I shall indicate. There are great advantages to having a separate volume of pages of annotations and comments, keyed to the text itself, that can be held next to the first volume; no awkward thumbing through separately for the notes and flipping of pages back and forth!

This having been determined, the first task was the authentication of all the material by Poe that must be included--a lengthy process outlined below. After the "true" Poe text was checked off in the two volume set of a facsimile reprint of the *BJ*, I made excellent copies of all the pages of the journal with this material. One set was for my "dummy," pasted up on large notebook sheets into which all my notes of explication, cross references, comment, etc. would be kept after determining the "shaping-up" of each page of the text-volume. As far as possible, I tried to keep the columns separately on each page, but this was scarcely possible for many of them, and composites of several different part columns, shorter than the full ones, often had to be added together. The full column length of the *BJ* page is nine and one-quarter inches, the outside book page size of my own volume being eleven inches. Since a double column page, as in the magazine, would leave too little room for margins, especially with line numbers added, the columns had to be made single in all cases. Moreover, space was required for adding Poe's markings in the Whitman copy (see below for "Poe's Markings"). Not all columns approximate nine inches, of course, and frequently they had to be "joined" with added headings always prepared (in bold face type print). These showed the exact source of the article in the magazine itself: the date, page of location (volume included), and whether in the left or right hand column (designated by "L" or "R"). The original heading of the column, if any, was also transferred with the column to indicate the nature of the material (review or "editorial miscellany" or "drama criticism"). Once the page had been "composed" a folio number was assigned to it, which was always used henceforth for cross references and discussions. In the left hand margin printed numbers (in ascending fives) were affixed to designate the exact line being sought or being explained. A full column, in the tiny print of quoted material, might extend from lines 1 to 95. Each page was regarded as a continuous column, even though spliced together from a few separate pages. In the right hand margin were placed two types of material: occasional phrases for items that were less than certain as to Poe's authorship or included because of Poe's footnote or headnote comment or later reference so that the reader could follow his "argument." Also, that margin was reserved for Poe's markings in the Whitman copy, reproduced here in my facsimile.

After the working copy of the composite text had been made up, a very careful duplicate was prepared, using a clean set of xerox copies. A set of special mats had been ordered with guide lines for laying out the columns and various heads very exactly. A lay-out artist worked under my direct and constant supervision, employing a special wax process that allowed items to be moved long after the page was completed. More recently I found it necessary to shift items on occasion and used rubber cement to the same purpose. Aside from the preparation of the annotations and commentaries for the second volume of the set, the major task was correcting Poe's text for typographical or other errors, all of which editorial alterations, of course, had to be recorded and listed in the Introductory special section. I shall leave a full description of this lengthy process for later. The text itself also had to be analyzed for the Index at the end. A working index, of course, had to be developed, especially since cross-references to all sections of the Poe columns were being made in the notes. There were also the "buried" items, such as books implied in the text, the authors of titles mentioned, the filling out of initials, especially in the responses to contributors and correspondents. Major subjects not stated in the text but needed for index purposes also had to be inserted into the cards being filed for the final index.

About a year before the final form of the books was in hand, a new element for this editor arrived with the use of a word processor and a laser jet printer. Although all my notes and index cards had been hand written or typed, and filed and alphabetized manually, I decided that for many good reasons, I would use the aid of a personal computer for putting my notes together and in the format for printing. A major reason was to escape the "dominance" of the printer over the text in the sense that one is always apprehensive about a long text with complicated subject matter, many foreign phrases, and differentiated type. Experiences with many books in the past had taught me about the unexpected intrusions into a nearly perfect text that can be introduced by ingenious or careless typesetters. To free myself from seemingly endless proof-readings of galleys and page proofs, I decided to word process the entire text, especially after realizing that the printer of *The Brevities* had sent me word processed galleys. I was fortunate to be able to devote part of a small grant from the City University of New York, Research Foundation, to the acquisition of an IBM personal computer (XT, two diskette-drive model). My part-time helper was enabled to input the entire text through a soft ware program entitled Nota Bene, which is published by Dragonfly of Brooklyn, and promoted by the Modern Language Association. It did everything needful for my rather simple text (of volume 2).

My final decision to simplify the process of seeing the book though the end of the text and printing stage was to take advantage of the kind offer of the Computer Facility of the Graduate Center of the City University to allow me to print it out on the Hewlett Packard Laser Jet Printer. One of the cartridges for printing gave me a type font fully compatible with the Baskerville type of the previous volumes of the series of the *Collected Writings*. My secretarial helper and I were able to format each of the pages with the heading in differentiated type, with the right dimensions and, fortunately, with proportionate spacing for the letters and micro-spacing between the words and, of course, with right margin justification. The clever spacing capacity of the printer made hyphenations at the end of a line unnecessary. It is true that the Nota Bene program did not access the proportionate spacing (the new version will have that capacity, I am told), but the Facility made XY Write available as an intermediary soft ware program between the diskettes, prepared with Nota Bene, and the Laser Jet cartridge F. Hence, I was able to run off the entire book in about two hours of actual printing time. Only the accents could not yet be managed (the new Nota Bene, version 2, will access that present feature of Cartridge F on the printer). An artist-friend was willing to follow my model and inserted about 150 foreign accents and diacritical marks, such as the dieresis. The present text is the result. The pages were used for the "repros" or plates needed for the printing press, and the final print is without printers' errors and is quite presentable in appearance.

AUTHENTICATING THE POE PROSE
IN *THE BROADWAY JOURNAL*

The process of authenticating the Poe materials in the magazine, was begun in 1968, during the course of a sabbatical leave intended for this purpose. Various other projects intervened, fortunately, since I was aided much later by a riper acquaintance with Poe's life and works and by the development of three instruments that shed considerable light on various phases of his content and style. All but a dozen small articles and a few columns of "Miscellany" which Poe borrowed from other journals, have been positively verified and are here presented. The methods used for culling approximately 350 equivalently full columns from about three to four times that amount of printing (since all his reprinted poetry and fiction are excluded) are based on the following factors:

1. Some of the items are signed by Poe with his name or initials in print.

2. Many were signed by Poe in pencil in the copy of the two-volume set that he gave to Sarah Helen Whitman in 1848 and which is now in the Huntington Library in San Marino (see the special section below on "Poe's Markings"). I studied the "printed out" frames from the Duke University Library microfilm of the "Whitman" copy for its added initials, underlinings, sidelinings, and small corrections--as clues to his authorship.

3. Previous scholars have studied particular articles to allocate them to the canon, and have briefly published their findings (see the Bibliography below): Margaret Alterton, Killis Campbell, Heartman and Canny, T. O. Mabbott, Perry Miller, J. W. Robertson. In addition I have weighed the evaluations in the theses of James Reece and, above all, William Doyle Hull, III. This last unpublished work has been particularly helpful, although it addressed only the canon of review material. Originally I prepared a scale for each item of "positively, probably, or possibly by Poe," taking into account all previous views on the subject for each article or set of reviews. Ultimately, I relied on my own judgment and, occasionally, intuition. The doubts and problems are recorded and discussed in the related notes.

4. Poe's characteristic or habitual vocabulary can be studied through my *Word Index* (1983) which is virtually a concordance to all his tales and sketches in the Mabbott-Pollin edition. This sometimes helps to decide stylistically upon an article that may be by Briggs or Watson or Poe. Along with this, and even more useful, is an instrument that lists his word coinages together with all their loci in the Harrison edition. Since there are over 1,000 of these in my updated, revised *Poe, Creator of Words* (1976; 1981), more than one article can be determined by the coincidence of a Poe creation elsewhere.

5. Poe's allusions to various persons, sometimes obscure, in his present or past associations, along with reference to titles, sometimes very arcane, need to be traced from columns of the *BJ* into other

works. My *Dictionary of Names and Titles in Poe's Works* (1968) for all volumes of Harrison's edition grants ready access to such names for this sort of checking.

6. Biographical data, often tied to other contemporaneous writings and actions by Poe, shed light on his content. Sources of these are Poe's letters (Ostrom, ed.) and biographical works by A. H. Quinn, Hervey Allen, George Woodberry, and T. O. Mabbott, and the forthcoming *Poe Log* by D. K. Jackson and D. Thomas.

7. Parallels for style, rhetoric and content in other Poe works can be derived through studies with onomastic and thematic indices or lists, such as *An Index to Poe's Critical Vocabulary* (1966) by Cauthen and Dameron, or the extensive index in the *Tales* (Mabbott ed., 1978).

8. A useful tool also has been my own edition of his many short pieces subsumed in *The Brevities* (1985), since many of his columns in the *BJ* found their way into the "Marginalia" in an abridged or modified form, this fact occasionally determining it as in the Poe canon. It may be well to mention here that there are no manuscripts for Poe's writings in the *BJ* and there are no variants as there would be for a tale or poem reprinted later. However, to the extent that a modified article in a *BJ* column is a variant, the elements that both have in common have been discussed in my notes and if there is a close proximity, collations have been given.

TYPOGRAPHICAL ERRORS: EDITORIAL CORRECTION
OF THE TEXT OF VOLUME 1

The 800 pages of the *Broadway Journal* were not, by any means, models of printing accuracy and care. A weekly magazine, densely printed on its sixteen pages, in two columns, can scarcely be expected to be punctilious and sedulously proofread. These and other factors, such as the lack of an adequate, full-time staff, guaranteed a large number of errors, both in the quality of the editor-contributor's copy and in the page proofs. Moreover, the changes in the printer were not helpful to high standards. Finally, the deterioration of the type itself, apparently not consistently replaced for worn letters or other equipment, led to an increasingly defective letter press, as the list below indicates. Rather than present Poe's text in this difficult, even distracting guise, I felt it necessary to make basic editorial corrections, always recording the original form for the scholar. The determination of an error needing correction is sometimes a problem, of course, since an apparent error may really be an author's idiosyncrasy which needs annotation rather than correction. This is true, for example, of Poe's use of the dieresis over the first rather than the normal second of two sounded vowels. I have discussed this fully in *The Brevities*, pp. xxxviii-xi, and leave this odd usage unchanged, according to Poe's preference. On the other hand, although the digraph is often misused, as in "coesura" for "caesura" I have changed it to the normally preferred form because I feel certain that the typesetter has misread Poe's style of writing (see *The Brevities*, pp. xxxvi-xxxviii).

In general, in the absence of manuscripts, no attempt could be made to differentiate between the errors of Poe the author and those of the typesetter. In large measure, any formal distinction between errors in accidentals and substantive matters has been blunted or lost. My effort has been to present a text that would create as few difficulties for meaningful reading as possible. Needed changes have been made and have been recorded below for reconstruction of the text or for specific scholarly purposes. In general, punctuation has been preserved as printed, based on the usage of that time (e.g., commas within parentheses, quotation marks in the place of italics, commas separating subject from verb in a sentence). Only end-sentence punctuation errors have been clarified (and recorded). Accent marks, even in foreign-tongue words, have been corrected and recorded, especially since they sometimes enable us to read, sound out, or understand a word, sometimes changing a word into a totally new one. Spelling has been checked for contemporary usage and preserved, if then valid, despite our present usage (see Apalachia in 56/58 and 67). On the other hand Poe's common misspelling of "parrallel" being unsanctioned is corrected. Sometimes a name may be deliberately misspelled, for ironic or rhetorical purposes (146/34) ("Clarke" for "Clark"); this is retained with a note. Sometimes a word may be erroneous in the quoted original. In that event, it may be preserved with a note (as in 18/57: "Alcolyte"). Hyphenations, of course, need not enter into any type of alteration or listing in this volume, for a facsimile text. However, if there should be any doubt about Poe's use or printing, as when he is rewriting an excerpt quoted, the *Word-Index to Poe's Fiction* can settle some problems.

"Broken letters" and low-placed hyphens or dashes have been corrected without being recorded. However, an upside-down letter ("u" for "n") is corrected and recorded. Some very obvious errors had to be left, without change, simply because of lack of space to make the correction (e.g., "emation / emanation" across two lines, 14/31-32).

This raises the question of the manner of correction. For a facsimile text, one cannot retypeset an incorrect line; one can merely splice in a letter or letters, substitute extra ones, or erase or whiten out surplus letters. All these methods were used by the lay-out artist, my helpers, and myself, after all proposed changes were shown on the mock-up pages, recorded in my lists, and verified before being changed on the facsimile pages intended for the printer. Various means for changing were employed: eradicating, cutting away letters, pasting better copy over the word or words. Letters were glued onto the text, if possible and needed; small slips with words were sometimes found elsewhere or reconstructed from other letter press and inserted; and spaces between letters and between words were altered if useful. But none of these changes has been made silently--that is, without appearing below. In the following errors, listed by page and line, the original word is placed before the slash and the correction or action (or else "stet") taken afterward.

TYPOGRAPHICAL ERRORS

1/12: Royal / Royall *stet* (see n); 2/48: experiment / experience *stet* (see n); 8/2: Rosarie / Rosary *stet* (see n); 9/43: Ambrosianians / Ambrosians; 14/31-32: emation / emanation *stet*; 16/28: qnite / quite; 17/9: thamselves / themselves; 18/57: Alcolyte / Acolyte *stet* (see n); 21/60: have been / (repeated); 23/64: wll / will; 24/10: guurd / guard; 30/6: covict / convict; 30/14: those / these; 30/79: specially / specifically *probably wrong, but stet*; 30/93: madam / madman; 31/9: Pinckney / Pinkney *uncorrected* (Poe's habitual error); 33/3: "the" missing at end of line *uncorrected* (see n); 35/15: panygeric / panegyric; 35/56: villifier / vilifier; 37/25: Petameter / Pentameter; 37/46: do'nt / don't *uncorrected*; 43/10: practicul / practical; 47/12: anapoest / anapaest; 53/16: occuring / occurring; 54/27: èlite / élite; 54/33: It / Its; 56/58, 67: Apalachia / Appalachia *stet* (see n); 57/13: air / hair; 60/42: parrallel / parallel; 63/63: Siil / Still; 63/94: Re uge / Refuge; 64/25: urgentt / urgent; 66/45: genera(X) / general; 69/11: gettlng / getting; 69/23: anapoestic / anapaestic; 75/9: SOMEBOBY / SOMEBODY; 77/26: Truman / Trueman; 80/44: Mr. I / Mr. J; 82/10: benefitted / benefited; 83/19: Kuhner / Kühner; 84/60: aud / and; 85/26: desiarble / desirable; 88/33: cathedrá / cathedrâ; 89/8: *Merchant's / Merchants'*; 91/18: chorusses / choruses; 91/30: chorusses / choruses; 92/14: Cleaveland / Cleveland (?); 92/21: Waverly / Waverley; 92/28: Meravingian / Merovingian; 93/5: *Assemblee / Assemblée*; 93/20: to to meet / to meet; 93/50: last. / last,; 94/20: parrallel / parallel; 96/49: Diuneford / Dinneford; 98/29: crèation / création; 98/30: on / ou; 98/48: he / the; 98/64: cords / chords; 104/47: Francois / Francois; 104/64: n est / n'est; 105/4: Rose / Ruse; 105/29: althougH / although; 106/3: Snapp / Stapp *stet*; 107/4: Snapp / Stapp *stet*; 107/68: niaseries / niaiseries; 107/70: nearly / newly; 108/1: nnmber / number; 110/48: in(X)roduction / introduction; 111/10: Quincy / Quincey; 112/19: Ethioipan / Ethiopian; 114/14: rusteling / rustling; 115/32: hvae/have; 117/21: Pease / Pearse *stet* (see n); 118/32: Aud / And; 120/47:

Claiments / Claimants; 121/46: (form)ng / (form)ing; 122/23: innoculated / inoculated; 122/50: recgnised / recognised; 123/27: Aroundt hee / Around thee; 126/55: anapoest / anapaest; 126/56: Jambic / Iambic; 126/66: coesura caesura; 126/68: excessive and say / excessive, say,; 126/43: effects / affects; 127/4: offspriug / offspring; 128/21: Zchokke's / Zschokke's *uncorrected* (see n); 129/1: Philoemon / Philaemon; 129/37: Philoemon / Philaemon; 130/27: Clazomenoe / Clazomenae; 130/50: Troponius / Trophonius; 131/40: Clazamenoe / Clazomenae; 131/45: hows / shows; 131/48: (narra)____ / (narra)tive; 131/62: Philoe(mon) / Philae(mon); 132/1: Philoemon / Philaemon; 132/48: intreaty / entreaty; 133/22: (Phi)loemon / (Phi)laemon; 133/50: "Anarcharsis" / "Anacharsis"; 139/55: andmuslin / and muslin; 140/26: havn't / haven't *stet*; 142/28: harrangues / harangues; 144/28: Abreviations / Abbreviations; 146/8: Lausaune / Lausanne; 146/34: Headly / Headley; 150/33: Waverly / Waverley; 152/22: guilatining / guillotining; 152/23: simillar / similar; 156/11: palacial / palatial; 156/18: a / at; 156/25: I / It; 156/50: on / in; 162/65: Moneddo / Monéddo; 163/22: swept / slept *stet* (see n); 165/24: coesura / caesura; 165/44: anapoest / anapaest; 165/49: coesura / caesura; 166/39: too / two; 166/61: Scoevola / Scaevola; 167/61: speeimens / specimens; 167/69: as ... as / as ...; 169/40: Clarke / Clark *stet* (see n); 169/45: critick / critique (see n); 171/48: Aenone / Oenone; 171/63: bnt / but; 173/4: dilligent / diligent; 174/68: bnt / but; 174/72: Gotzebue's / Kotzebue's; 175/3: Edmont / Egmont; 176/17: berself / herself; 178/22: Chatam / Chatham; 179/29: Profonnd / Profound; 179/38 te / to; 182/60: O'er_all / O'er all; 183/6: pamplet / pamphlet; 183/56: róle / rôle; 185/1: Nothig / Nothing; 185/31: so / to; 185/36: breack / break; 188/37: my / thy *stet* (see n); 190/56: himsel / himself; 191/29: ard / and; 192/1: *Encyclopoedia* / *Encyclopaedia*; 193/33: intellectnal / intellectual; 194/56: thanin / than in; 195/3: lofyt / lofty; 196/27: reduced / seduced; 196/27: to / into (see n); 197/38: Athenoeum / Athenaeum; 197/53: Lwei Frauln / Zwei Frauen; 197/53: Wa- / Ha-; 197/60: Daguerreotype / Daguerreotype *stet* (see n); 204/63: did'nt / didn't; 205/38: Massino / Massimo; 206/8: *Cyclopoedia* / *Cyclopaedia*; 207/45: ommissions / omissions; 211/24: dissappear / disappear; 211/66: Qnarterly / Quarterly; 212/10: a critic a / a critic-; 213/14: phrophseied / prophesied; 213/23: Renssellaer / Rensselaer; 213/28: Factary / Factory; 213/32: ii / it; 14/1: T(X)e / The; 214/20: milions / millions; 214/20: *milllion* / *million*; 214/37: establisment / establishment; 215/3: aristing / arising; 217/9: for / For; 217/11: Chippendale / Chippindale (see n); 218/52: beiefly / briefly; 219/20: (publish)rs / (publish)ers; 219/23: Kettel's / Kettell's; 220/53: intentiou / intention; 221/51: gullty / guilty; 222/55: upsn / upon; 223/37: I. S. / J. S.; 225/59: mentlon / mention; 225/62: aurograph /

autograph; 226/57: d(X)testable / detestable; 229/44: reedy / weedy; 234/8: *Encyclopdia Encyclopaedia*; 234/47: rôles / rôles; 235/4: uneqaul / unequal; 235/57: Senors / Senores(?) *stet*; 237/53: 1887 / 1837; 237/55: 76 / 74; 242/14: Hall / Hale; 242/28: *Merchant's / Merchants'*; 242/44: be-(because) / be-(cause); 242/55: Huntingdon / Huntington *stet* (see 243/9); 245/55: issne / issue; 247/19: Humbolt's / Humboldt's; 247/20: fist / first; 247/47: Soireé / Soirée; 248/22: Tne / The; 248/26: *Cyclopoedia / Cyclopaedia*; 249/41: oe'er / o'er; 250/53: bsen / been; 251/10: Bhagoat Geeta / Bhagvat Geeta (see n); 251/30: crlour / colour; 251/66: we / ye; 251/69: onr / our; 252/1: Murdock's / Murdoch's; 252/3: Rroken / Broken; 253/22: /whlch / which; 259/9: naratives / narratives; 259/14: Eaery / Every; 262/5: Wheewell / Whewell; 264/31: Embarrasment / Embarrassment; 265/17: Lopez / Lope *stet* (see 279/12); 269/3: explanatian / explanation; 269/6: Syntatical / Syntactical; 269/40: *Cyclopoedia / Cyclopaedia*; 269/44: Nnmerous / Numerous; 272/38: Aud / And; 273/1: Ditsen / Ditson; 274/57: cotinuation / continuation; 276/50: Glacono / Giacomo; 278/13: Schlemil / Schlemihl; 279/12: Lopez / Lope; 279/45: beantifully / beautifully; 279/53: ure / are; 279/62: aud / and; 280/15: repeatrng / repeating; 281/7: cordailly / cordially; 281/50 papet / paper; 283/21: millionare / millionaire; 285/13: idiosincratic / idiosyncratic; 285/29: could'nt / couldn't; 286/14: reccollected / recollected; 286/16: reccollect / recollect; 286/23: Willlam's / William's; 287/27: Wilhelmmeister / Wilhelm Meister; 287/29: Bensenerto / Benvenuto; 287/33: compldte / complete; 288/45: Lrom / From; 289/49: Cleonoean / Cleonaean; 292/37: orsginality / originality; 294/12: Benevenuto / Benvenuto; 295/45: ttreatise / treatise; 300/27: Poettical / Poetical; 301/36: earried / carried; 302/8: Rusehenberger / Ruschenberger; 303/30: *Merchant's / Merchants'*; 303/43: *Merchant's / Merchants'*; 303/50: anthor / author; 303/53: *Merchant's / Merchants'*; 304/9: *Merchant's / Merchants'*; 305/15: sculptnred / sculptured; 307/55: Monkton / Monckton *stet*; 312/66: comliest / comeliest; 313/2: cirtical / critical; 320/19-20: plan, produced (repeated) / deleted *uncorrected* (see n); 320/28: and (and) / and *stet*; 320/31: father / farther; 320/36: mo(X)e / more; 320/42: (com-)yositions / (com-)positions; 320/45: Mouths / Months; 320/45: Prorpietor / Proprietor; 323/4: hut / but; 325/12: in future / in the future; 325/51: timeto / time to; 331/35: anapoestic / anapaestic; 331/35: anapoests / anapaests; 333/43: Chiropedist / Chiropodist; 333/48: Chiropedy / Chiropody; 339/27: Lucitania / Lusitania; 345/21: Huntingdon / Huntington *stet*; 346/31: *Cyclopoedia / Cyclopaedia*; 347/20: *anapoestic / anapaestic*; 349/33: plgrims / pilgrims; 351/53: Worsdworth / Wordsworth; 359/38: Salamanaca / Salamanca; 360/8: Herrman / Herman; 361: Babarities / Barbarities; 361: Elenora / Eleanora; 362: Monseur Eduart's / Monsieur Edouart's;

364: The Ravens / The Raven; 364: The Pilgrimage to Keolaar / ...
Kevlaar

(End)

THE "LITTLE LONGFELLOW WAR"

Poe carried over from the *Evening Mirror* a campaign against
Longfellow, begun in January and encouraged apparently by Willis,
for the sake of the nearly scandalous publicity, that Briggs uneasily
tolerated. Poe's hostility to many aspects of Longfellow's writing was
five years old, commencing with his charge in the 10/39 *Burton's
Gentleman's Magazine* that *Hyperion* was a tasteless, careless farrago
of very mixed elements. Opposing the widespread acclaim of the
poems in *Voices of the Night*, Poe had declared them lacking in unity
and originality in 1840. He roundly attacked also the obvious and
inartistic didacticism of Longfellow's works in reviews and in
lectures, while yet conceding him a very high place for his felicitious
diction, clever handling of commonplace ideas, and occasionally
graphic or affecting details. His acerbity increased as Longfellow
acquired new honors, enjoyed large receipts from sumptuously bound
and illustrated volumes, and received the post of Professor at
Harvard, while he was luxuriously ensconced in Craigie House (see S.
Moss; also, Pollin [G]). It was no more than critical justice for Poe
to tell the "truth" about a man of talent who was too popular a model
for the creative writer in a developing America; he waged a
campaign of bravado and contumacy in crude terms and sarcastic
arguments. Thereby he dissipated much of the credit that "The
Raven" had brought him early in 1845. For the items relating to the
material in the *BJ*, listed below, please see the commentary-notes in
volume two giving details and cross-references for many of Poe's
points.

Chronology of the "Little Longfellow War" (Poe's title, see p.
28)

1/13-14/45) Poe's criticism of Longfellow's anthology *Waif*
appears in the *Evening Mirror* (hereafter *EM*).
1/15) "H." (George Stillman Hillard) writes from Boston to
defend his friend Longfellow.
1/18) Willis, in the *EM*, promises "an argument" on the
subject of the attack on the book.
1/20) Hillard's letter, accompanied by a biting reply from
Poe, appears in the *EM* (also the *Weekly Mirror* of 1/25)

1

1/25) The Buffalo *Western Literary Messenger* publishes an attack on Longfellow's "Good George Campbell" as a plagiarism or distortion of a Scottish ballad, not an alleged translation from the German.

2/5) A second defense of Longfellow, by Charles Sumner, is sent to *EM*, and appears with a humorous reply from Willis.

2/8) The New York *Rover* repeats the charge by the *Western Literary Messenger*, adding a reference to Poe's first article.

2/14) Willis, in the *EM*, states that he disagrees with all disparagement of Longfellow (also in the *WM* of 2/22).

2/15) Briggs publishes a paper against Poe's attacks, called "Thefts of American Authors," in the *BJ*, 1:109.

2/19) Longfellow writes a reply to the "George Campbell" accusation for *Graham's Magazine*, published only in the May issue.

2/28) Poe lectures on the "Poets and Poetry of America," at the New-York Historical Society, alluding to Longfellow's plagiarism. The lecture was widely reported in the press (see also *BJ*, p. 35).

3/1) The defense of Longfellow by "Outis" (almost certainly Poe himself) appears in *EM*.

3/8) Poe replies to "Outis" in the *BJ*, including the whole of the 3/1 article of the *EM* (*BJ*, 28-33).

3/15) Poe's reply is continued (*BJ*, 37-41).

3/22) Poe's reply is continued (*BJ*, 45-53).

3/29) Poe's reply is continued (*BJ*, 58-65).

4/1) Poe reviews Longfellow's *Poems* in the *Aristidean*, in the same strain (pp. 131-142).

4/5) Poe's reply concluded (*BJ*, 73-74).

POE'S MARKINGS in *THE BROADWAY JOURNAL*

During the fall of 1848 Poe was courting the widow Sarah Helen Whitman of Providence (see Quinn, 572-592). On a brief visit to Providence, late in October, as a sort of pre-engagement present, he offered her a copy of the two volumes of the *Broadway Journal* with his own marginal and intertextual notations. On the top of the Index to volume 1, then bound at the front of the first volume, she wrote the following: "Given to S. H. W. by E. A. P. / October 1848." In the upper right-hand corner of the first page of volume 2, she wrote: "From S. H. Whitman. / March 27, 1874." The documents in the Ingram collection, now in the University of Virginia, explain her annotation, concerning her sending the volumes to John Ingram in England for his life of Poe and edition of his works (see Hull, p. 518-19). Somewhat inaccurately, she wrote: "Every anonymous article or paragraph written by him has the pencilled letter P. appended to it. He added these letters in giving me the volume."

The last sentence may explain numerous omissions--or else he ignored articles that did not seem important or even tactful three years later. Harrison explains the further fate, their being owned by F. R. Halsey by 1902 (*Works*, 12: vii-ix) who enabled him to use the markings--rather carelessly, we think now. Finally, they were sold to the Huntington Library of San Marino, California, which has made photostats of the autographed pages available to the University of Virginia and a microfilm to Duke University. My study-copy of all the notations comes primarily from the Duke University microfilm; the Huntington Library has responded to queries about obscure markings. Apparently Mrs. Whitman sometimes strengthened the penciled marks of Poe, but the letters of his name and his writing in general are consistent and undoubtedly authentic.

The markings are of several types as appear in my reproduction of all of those occurring in the text of my own composite volume 1. There is, first, the initialed identification of articles with a printed "P" through an inserted "P" or "E.A.P." (twice). These are frequently added after long reviews or the "Editorial Miscellany" feature of each week's issue. Sometimes, one should note, the "P" is not placed at the very end of the article or after a section of it; occasionally this may imply that another hand finished the article or the column, but this is rare. In volume 2, Poe had almost no coadjutor for any of his columns, save for music, drama, and art (i.e., Watson).

Other marks were made by Poe either over the text or in the margins: sidelinings of a portion of the text, underlinings, and, occasionally, an "x" in the margin or a large "X" over a portion of the text (202). The last one I have inserted only over the margin at that point, since I did not wish to interfere with the reading of the text, indicating the matter in the related note. Sometimes Poe pointed Mrs. Whitman's attention to another part of the text by a cross reference (see p. 28). He sometimes wrote a short message concerning the text (see p. 23) and in a few places inscribed a hint of some opinion, through a question mark (pp. 21, 157). Finally, he occasionally corrected a blunder in the margin or wrote a word of explication or substitution (pp. 2, 244). There are many more markings that appear in the texts that are excluded from my composite volume: all the tales and poems by Poe and all of the material written by others, especially Briggs. It is true that Poe rarely notates other writers' material, but occasionally he singles out a passage for sidelining, and these must be omitted. One comment in Poe's autograph, at the top of the first page--entirely by Briggs, perhaps deserves to be recorded here: "N.B. It was not until No. 10 that I had anything to do with this journal as Editor."

The method of inscribing the Poe markings on the facsimile

text needs mention. The lay-out artist and, occasionally, I too reproduced the initials as closely as we could, in the same "spot" on the column. This would also be true of all comments, single words, and phrases. The few underlinings and the various "x" marks we drew in. The sidelinings we "traced" from special sheets of prepared "rules" together with the brackets that ended these lines, so that their blackness and "frame" would cause them to stand out on the page.

Below are the pages on which there are one or more Poe markings in my composite text. Wherever the page has at least one initial for Poe's name, I have added an asterisk to the page number. Otherwise, most of the unstarred numbers designate sidelinings only.

Volume 1: 2, 8*, 15*, 18*, 21*, 23, 28, 29, 34*, 37*, 41*, 54, 57*, 60, 69, 70*, 74, 77, 78*, 81*, 83, 86*, 88, 91*, 96*, 98*, 105, 111, 115*, 116*, 117*, 123, 127*, 134*, 135, 143*, 154, 155*, 157.

Volume 2: 164, 167*, 169*, 170, 171*, 177, 178*, 182*, 184*, 189*, 190*, 202, 205*, 206*, 210*, 211*, 212*, 218*, 219, 222*, 223*, 224*, 229, 230*, 231*, 232, 237, 240*, 241*, 244*, 250, 251*, 253*, 254*, 256, 257*, 258, 263*, 264, 267*, 271, 275*, 276*, 277, 278*, 279, 280*, 283, 284*, 290*, 294*, 295, 297*, 299*, 300*, 312, 313, 315*, 318, 319*, 321*, 324, 325*, 326, 332*, 334, 335, 336, 337, 338*, 339*, 340*, 344, 347, 348*, 351, 355, 356, 357, 358*, 359.

A SELECTED BIBLIOGRAPHY OF STUDIES ON POE, CHIEFLY FOR THE INTRODUCTION

The following list of books and articles relates primarily to citations and references in the Introduction. The text of the annotations comprising this volume has adequate bibliographic data, save for a few often cited books which are included in the list given here. The letters before the multiple items are used in the reference parentheses of the Introduction.

Allen, Hervey, *Israfel* (New York, 1926; rev. ed., 1934).
Briggs, Charles, F. *Independent*, "The Personality of Poe," December 13, 1877, 1-2.
Alterton, Margaret B., *Origins of Poe's Critical Theory* (Iowa City, 1925).
Campbell, Killis [A], *Cambridge History of American Literature* (New York, 1918), 2:55-69, 452-468.
Campbell, Killis [B], *The Mind of Poe* (New York, 1933), pp. 187-238.
Campbell, Killis [C], "Bibliographical Notes on Poe," *Nation*, 1909, 89: 623-624.
Campbell, Killis [D], "Who was 'Outis'?" *University of Texas Studies in English*, 1928, No. 8, pp. 107-109.
Ehrlich, Heyward, "The *Broadway Journal* (1): Briggs's Dilemma and Poe's Strategy," *Bulletin of the New York Public Library*, 1969, 73: 74-93 (reproduced in my Introduction).
English, T. D., "Reminiscences of Poe," *Independent*, October 15, 22, 1896; 48: 1382, 1415-1416.
Harrison, James A., *Complete Works of ... Poe* (New York, 1902), 12:viii-ix.
Heartman, Charles F. and Canny, J. R. *A Bibliography of First Printings of ... Poe* (Hattiesburg, 1940, rev. ed., 1943).
Hull, William Doyle, "A Canon of the Critical Works of Edgar Allan Poe with a Study of Poe as Editor and Reviewer" (Dissertation, University of Virginia, 1941), especially pp. 398-693 (on the *Mirror* and the *Broadway Journal*).
Jackson, David K. and Thomas, Dwight, *The Poe Log* (to be published, Boston, G. K. Hall, 1986).
Mabbott, Thomas Ollive, *Collected Works of ... Poe*, Vol. I, *Poems* (Cambridge, Mass., 1968); especially useful for the "Annals," pp. 529-572; *Tales and Sketches*, II-III (1978), especially useful through the Index items.
Moss, Sidney P., *Poe's Literary Battles* (Durham, 1963), Ch. 5 especially, 132-189 ("Poe and Longfellow").

Mott, Frank Luther, *American Magazines* (Cambridge, Mass., 1957), 1:757-762.

Ostrom, John Ward, *The Letters of ... Poe* (1948; rev. and augmented ed., New York, 1966), 2 vols., paged continuously.

Penner, John Talbot, "Edgar Allan Poe and the *Broadway Journal*" (Master's Thesis, Columbia University, 1965).

Phillips, Mary, *Edgar Allan Poe, The Man* (Philadelphia, 1926), 2 vols. paged continuously, pp. 987-1082.

Pollin, Burton R. [A], *The Brevities* (New York, 1985).

Pollin, Burton R. [B], *Dictionary of Names and Titles in Poe's Collected Works* (New York, 1968).

Pollin, Burton R. [C], *Discoveries in Poe* (Notre Dame, 1970).

Pollin, Burton R. [D], *Poe, Creator of Words* (Baltimore, 1974, rev. ed., Bronxville, 1980).

Pollin, Burton R. [E], *Word Index to Poe's Fiction* (New York, 1982).

Pollin, Burton R. [F], "Poe as Edward S. T. Grey," *Forum*, 1973, 14:44-46.

Pollin, Burton R. [G], "Poe and Longfellow," *Mississippi Quarterly*, 1984, 37:475-482.

Pollin, Burton R. [H], "Poe and Music," *Die Musik in Geschichte und Gegenwart* (supplementary volume), 1978, 16:1504-1507.

Pollin, Burton R. [I], "Poe and His Illustrators," *American Book Collector*, 1981, NS 2:2-17, 33-40.

Quinn, Arthur Hobson, *Edgar Allan Poe* (New York, 1941), pp. 451-496, 751-753.

Rede, Kenneth, "Poe Notes," *American Literature*, 1933, 5:53-54.

Reese, James B. "*The Broadway Journal* with Special Reference to Poe," (Master's Thesis, Duke University, 1948), Appendix A, pp. 170-179.

Robertson, John W., *A Bibliography of the Writings of ... Poe*, 2 vols. (San Francisco, 1934), 1:175, 191-196; 2:223, 234, 241.

Stedman, E. C. and Woodberry, G. E. *Works of ... Poe* (Chicago, 1894-95; rep. 1914).

Weidman, Bette S., "*The Broadway Journal* (2): A Casualty of Abolition Politics," *Bulletin of the New York Public Library*, 1969, 73: 94-113.

Woodberry, George E. *Life of Poe* (Boston, 1909), 2:114-185; 368-390.

SPECIAL ELEMENTS IN PARTS 1 AND 2

1. Every page of volume 1 is given a folio page number next to the heading and has been given line numbers in the left margin, in an ascending series of fives. The notes, reflecting this treatment, are all given a number cluster, divided by a slash: to the left of which is the corresponding folio page number of Poe's text (in the facsimile of volume 1) and to the left, the line or lines discussed in the note. A modified right-hand bracket sign always separates the number from the text of my note in volume 2. Cross references to these number clusters designate the note volume, in general, unless a bracketed "Facsimile text" is included. In that case, the reference is to Poe's words in volume 1. Please do not confuse the indicated original pages of the *Broadway Journal* with my numbered folio pages; the former are given next to the dates in boldface print at the top of each separate part of Poe's original columns simply to indicate the continuity and chronology of his articles.

2. As is explained in the Introduction: "Typographical Errors in the Main Text," Poe's text has been reproduced with minimal changes, and these are invariably recorded in the Introduction.

3. The spellings of English words are not changed unless there is clear warrant for listing the words as "typos." British or uncommon spellings, allowed in the period, are retained. Allowed forms, although inconsistent, are retained without change. Some seeming errors in proper nouns, such as "Pinckney" and "Clarke," are kept unchanged, but discussed in the related note. For Poe's peculiar handling of the dieresis and, to a smaller extent, of the digraph (sometimes called diphthong), see Introduction, under "Typographical Errors" and *The Brevities,* Introduction, pp. xxxvi-xi.

4. The system of multi-volume or periodicals/volume/page citation is uniform, with arabic numbers for both, separated by a period, not by a colon. Thus, for a volume of Harrison's set of Poe's works, 10.135 means volume 10, p. 135, and for *Poe Studies,* 15.7-13, means volume 15, pages 7-13. Where the topic of the reference is clear, the title of the article cited is often omitted. In general arabic rather than roman numerals are used for all act/scene/line citations of plays and for (poetic) book/stanza/line citations.

5. Pages are frequently cited without "p." or "pp." especially for basic texts, such as TOM's *Tales* or A. H. Quinn's biography of Poe or Pollin's *Dictionary of Names* or *Word Index to Poe's Fiction.* Note that TOM is often used for the text of *Tales and Sketches,* sometimes

alone, without the book title. This does not refer to TOM's comment, only to the text, which is regarded as definitive. For other Poe texts, especially of reviews, besides the reference to the original magazine loci, the Harrison text is given simply as "H" without any period. For a newspaper, (e.g., *Evening Mirror*), "2/4" means "p. 2, column 4." For a tale "364/13" means "p. 364, line 13."

6. Space is saved and unnecessary clutter avoided through the use of obvious abbreviations (all listed) and through dropping the month of most periodical publications in cited criticisms. Almost all dates are cited in arabic numerals, with slashes, thus: month/day/year: e.g., 6/13/36 = June 13, 1836. A two-digit figure for the year is, assumedly, 18--. All other centuries require a four-digit figure, i.e., 1756 or 1910.

7. A reference to the composite facsimile text of the *BJ* uses solely my folio page number (without a volume number). Any reference to the *BJ* using a volume number (1 or 2) plus a page number implies the text of the original two volumes only. The articles by Briggs, Watson, and other contributors--not printed in my volume--can be consulted in the two-volume facsimile reproduction published in 1965 by AMS Press (New York) in an edition of 500 copies, and not as yet exhausted. Less convenient but found in more libraries is the microfilm of the *BJ* which is part of the American Periodicals series. The catalogue, *Union List of Serials* (1968), locates original two-volume sets in eleven major libraries (two of which are, in reality, facsimile copies); Brown University also owns a set. All are deemed "rare books."

ABBREVIATIONS AND SHORT TITLES

AL
Am.: American
BJ: *The Broadway Journal*
Br.: *The Brevities of Poe*, Vol. II of *The Collected Writings* (1985), Burton R. Pollin, editor
BGM: *Burton's Gentleman's Magazine*
Ch.: Charles
CS: Chapter of Suggestions, in *Brevities*
DAB: *Dictionary of American Biography*
DNB: *Dictionary of National Biography*
DP: *Discoveries in Poe* by Burton R. Pollin (1970)
EAP: Edgar Allan Poe
ed(s).: editor(s) or edition(s)
EM: *Evening Mirror*
En. Brit. or *En. Br.*: *Encylopaedia Britannica*, 11th edition, of 1911, unless another edition is specified
FS: Fifty Suggestions, in *Brevities*
Godey's: *Godey's Lady's Book*
Graham's: *Graham's Magazine*
H: Harrison, James A., ed., *The Complete Works of Edgar Allan Poe* (1902), 17 vols.
Letters: see Ostrom
L.: London
LC: Library of Congress
Lit. or Lit. in a title: literary or literature, but "Lit." always means "Literati" (sketches of 1846 by Poe, printed in *Godey's Lady's Book*)
"Lit.": "Literati" sketch (or sketches) of 1846
Log: *The Poe Log*, D. K. Jackson and D. Thomas, editors
LST: Literary Small Talk, in *Brevities*
M (or MM): Marginalia (one or several articles), in *Brevities*
mag.: magazine
Mi Q: *Mississippi Quarterly*
Moss, *PLB*: see *PLB*
OCAL: *Oxford Companion to American Literature*
OCEL: *Oxford Companion to English Literature*
Odell: *Annals of the New York Stage*, Odell, ed.
OED: *Oxford English Dictionary*, a reissue of *New English Dictionary* (1884-1928; new ed., 1933)
Ostrom: *Letters of ... Poe*, J. W. Ostrom, ed. (1948, rep. 1966)
para(s).: paragraph(s)
PCW: *Poe, Creator of Words*, Burton R. Pollin, ed. (revised and

augmented edition, 1980)
PD: *Dictionary of Names and Titles in Poe's Collected Works*, Burton
    R. Pollin, ed. (1968)
Pin: Pinakidia, in *Brevities*
PLB: *Poe's Literary Battles* by Sidney P. Moss (1970)
PMLA: *Publications of the Modern Language Association* (the journal)
PN: *Poe Newsletter* (later *Poe Studies*)
Poems (or TOM, *Poems*): *Poems of Poe*, ed. Mabbott, see TOM
PPA: *The Poets and Poetry of America*, R. W. Griswold, ed. (1842)
PS: *Poe Studies*
pseud.: pseudonym
pub.: published; occasionally, publisher
Quinn: *Poe: A Critical Biography* by A. H. Quinn (1941)
ref(s).: reference(s)
rev(s).: review(s), occasionally, reviewed
ROP: Poe, *The Raven and Other Poems* (1845)
SAR: *Studies in the American Renaissance* (an annual)
SLM: *Southern Literary Messenger*
SM: Supplementary Marginalia, in *Brevities*
TOM: Thomas Ollive Mabbott, ed., *Tales and Sketches* (1978), or
    simply his name alone; also TOM, *Poems*: vol. 1 of the
    Harvard ed. (1978)
U.P.: University Press
Wm.: William
WM: *Weekly Mirror* (based on the *Evening Mirror*)

1/1} This two-part review is Poe's major essay in the whole *BJ* for many reasons: It displays major critical principles about the language, construction, and suitable topics of writing; his attitudes on contemporary authors, such as Tennyson, and observations on many of the past, such as Homer, Aeschylus, Aristotle, and Milton; and it offered Poe a chance to discuss the poem by Elizabeth Barrett which supplied so much to "The Raven." Elizabeth Barrett Barrett, who was to be married to Robert Browning in 1846, had many literary ties to America (q.v. in Elizabeth R. Gould, *The Brownings and America*, 1904, Boston, *Poet Lore*, especially pp. 12, 18, 20, 24). The "learned poetess" mentioned in *Graham's* Editor's Table saw four of her sonnets published in the 12/42 issue of that magazine. *Graham's* offered four more in 1843, and three in 1844. Other periodicals offering her work were *Arcturus* of 2/41 (from which the four sonnets of *Graham's* 12/42 were transshipped), *NAR* 7/42, *Democratic Review* 7 and 10/44, and the *Mirror* 12/7/44. In the *Pioneer* of 4/43 can be found letters of praise from Lowell and Mrs. Sigourney. She had also a keen interest in international copyright laws, as did Poe and Mathews, who long nurtured her reputation in America. From the 10/39 *BGM* printing of "The Exile's Return" and her appearances in *Graham's*, Poe must have formed some idea of her importance. He also knew of her friendship with the British poet and journalist R.H. Horne (cf. 105/31), whose good offices he wished to engage for British publication of his tales (see Pollin, *AL*, 1965, 38.185-90; also, Poe *Log* for 1/25/45). Both Brownings were aware of Poe's efforts to cultivate their favor (see his dedication of the *ROP* to Elizabeth Barrett Barrett) and often discussed Poe in letters and conversations (q.v. in *Letters of Robert Browning and Elizabeth Barrett Barrett, 1844-45*, Harvard U.P., 1969, 2 vols., E. Kintner, editor).

Poe's criticism of this, the major poem of the volume (published as *Poems* almost simultaneously in England, with the proof sheets used for the American copytext, the volume being issued early in 10/44) was kinder than that of posterity, as Gardner B. Taplin indicates (see *The Life of Elizabeth Barrett Barrett*, Yale U.P., 1957, pp. 124, 126, 130, 132-3, 135, the British press being rather sharper than the American). Elizabeth herself noted the oddly uneven, variedly pro and anti comments of Poe in her later remarks to Robert Browning (q.v. in Taplin, pp. 137-8; Kintner, 297-8).

Even before this review, Poe recognized the importance of her volume in America, and gave it two short notices in the *Evening Mirror*. His earliest remark on the book (which was published early in October) was in the 10/7/44 issue, deeming the work superior to that of Tennyson and Motherwell, with three poems quoted, two *in toto*. In the 11/7/44 issue, Poe defends Miss Barrett from an anonymous detractor as not "disordered or mad," reprinted in the *Weekly Mirror* of the same date (noted by Woodberry, 2.102).

1/5} For James Puckle (1667?-1724, not a "Sir") and his work, see M 23, which uses this quotation, and note b which follows.

1/8} G_____ must stand for Rufus W. Griswold (1815-1857), eventually Poe's literary executor and author of the large best-seller, *The Poets and Poetry of America* (1843). For Poe's regular derision of him, see MM 82, 101, 123.

1/9} Mary Wollstonecraft (1759-1797), author of *Vindication of the Rights of Woman*, was attacked by Horace Walpole as a "hyena in petticoats," perhaps Poe's sole knowledge of her importance to the female movement.

1/12} Anne N. Royall (1769-1854), began by writing of her travels over the United States in 1824. As a critic she was noted for her liberal spirit and reformer's zeal, as well as her indiscretion and amateurish nature. She displayed an uncanny ability to uncover graft, making her an object of fear in Washington. Aside from her books, which serve as a valuable source of social history, she also edited several papers (*DAB*).

1/13} Zoilus: For Poe's extensive use of the 4th cent. B.C. rhetorician, known for his witty, spiteful criticism, see LST 1 a.

1/14} Salic law: laws of the Salian Franks (on the Sala or Yossel) erroneously thought to establish exclusion of women from the thrones of Europe.

2/4} puffery: undue praise, used often by the journals of the day. For the first episode in Poe's campaign against it (promotion of *Norman Leslie*) see S. Moss, *Poe's Literary Battles* (1963), ch. 2, and Pollin, *Mi Q*, 1972, 25.111-30.

2/11} The American is Cornelius Mathews (1817-1889), ed., with Duyckinck (q.v.), of *Arcturus*, the organ of the Young America movement (for this nationalistic reaction to British supremacy in letters, and Poe's advocacy of it, see Claude

Richard, *Studies in Bibliography*, 1968, 21.25-58). Although friendly at first, Poe came to vilify Mathews and his work in later years (cf. MM 269, 270, 278).

2/16} "Beersheba to Dan": see *Judges* 20.1, "From Dan even to Beersheba."

2/17-20} *Democratic Review*, 10/44, 15.370-7, review of *A Drama of Exile*; "...nor will she fail to speak her mind, though it bring upon her a bad rhyme." Contrary to Poe's statement, the context is complimentary (p. 377). J. and H. G. Langley was the firm publishing *both* the Am. edition of her poems and the *Democratic Review*.

2/21} Poe refers here to the *American Review, A Whig Journal*, 1/45, 1.38-48, which begins: "Miss Barrett's new book...is published simultaneously with the English edition, under the care of an American author* [*Mr. Mathews] to whom Miss Barrett pays a delicate compliment in her preface, and whose volume of Poems she praises...'as remarkable in thought and manner, for a vital, sinewy vigor, as the right arm of Pathfinder.'" First sentence (p. 38): "...there are but 2 poets ...[in] the new generation--Alfred Tennyson and Miss Barrett." Page 39: 2 methods for the critic, the synthetic and the analytic. First, for the greatest poets--"take the poet's own word, and proceed with him in the development of his work."

2/39} For Elizabeth Barrett Barrett's grateful response to Poe's critique, expressed in her letter to R. H. Horne (who sent it to Poe in 5/45), see A. Quinn, *EAP*, 451-2; also the Poe *Log* for 1/25/45, and Pollin, "The Spectacles," in *AL*, 1965, 37.185-90, specifically, 185, 189. Poe exaggerates about the "long published" and "universally read" volume, out only four months, obviously because of her popularity and influence in England. For his own slavish reading of "Lady Geraldine's Courtship" as reflected in "The Raven" see TOM, *Poems*, 356-7.

2/48} experiment/experience (in Elizabeth Barrett Barrett)

2/43} "I decided on publishing it after considerable hesitation and doubt," p. vi; implies *here* for the first time.

2/59-68} The errors are (in vol. 1) 23 worldless; 26 split/spilt; 37 ?; 45 forgone (this spelling is found in an instance from 1849, by M. Arnold, *OED*); 53 ?; 56 communicable; 80 curse-mete/cruise-mate?; 166 steads/steeds; 174 chambere/chamber or ladye/ladye; 180 steal /steel; (last line faint and missing many letters); 185 "were it found her"/"were it to find her"; 251 wordly/worldly.

In vol. 2: 109 "The Last Bower": astonied/astonished (Poe ignores its being an archaic form of "stunned"); 114 faries/faeries or fairies; 240 "Catarina to Camoëns": Drop/Dropped (?); 247 "Sleeping and Watching": reveillie/reveille (?); 253 "Wine of Cyprus": T ese/These; 272 "The Dead Pan": Frore/Froze (the former is an archaism, probably deliberate, of the latter).

3/35} James Silk Buckingham (1786-1855) was a British journalist and politician who travelled a great deal in the Orient. In his retirement he lectured on his travels (see M 288). It was perhaps his temperance pamphlets which, at least in part, earned him Poe's enmity (see Pollin, "Poe's 'Some Words with a Mummy' Reconsidered," *Emerson Society Quarterly*, 60.60-7).

Lectures on Egypt and Palestine, D. Fanshaw, NY, 1837, 8p. *Notes of the Buckingham Lectures: embracing sketches of the geography, antiquities, and present condition of Egypt and Palestine...* (Leavitt, Lord and Co., NY, 1838), 266p.

3/37} For Blitz, see 41/20 [facsimile text] below.

3/40-51} On pp. 127-28 (with no substantive changes).

4/14} *bull*: a self-contradictory proposition (*OED*).

4/31} For "fire and brimstone," see *Psalms* 11.6, *Luke* 17.29, *Rev.* 14.10.

4/33} See *Drama of Exile*, p. 21: "When countless angel faces, still and stern / Pressed out upon me from the level heavens, / Adown the abysmal sphere;"

4/42} *niäiseries*: foolishness; silly things (actually spelled *niaiseries*, Spiers & Surenne, 1852) or *niaiseries* by Poe, who liked the word (see *Br.* xxxvii-lx, M 291e).

4/48} For Poe's knowledge of Milton, see Thomas P. Haviland, "How Well Did Poe Know Milton?", *PMLA*, 1954, 69.841-60.

4/54} See *Paradise Lost*, Satan's speech, book 6.

4/59} Puff-paste refers to a light, fluffy dough (*OED*).

4/61} *reveillé*: not a typo, but uncommon now (reveille or reveille). From the French *réveillez*.

5/9} For Poe on allegory, see Pollin, "*Undine* in the works of Poe," *Studies in Romanticism*, 1975, 14.59-74.

5/16} Cf. Poe, "The Power of Words," *Democratic Review*, 6/45; TOM 1215: "This wild star--...I spoke it--with a few passionate sentences--into birth." The sequence of dates is significant. Lines 15-27 are lines 1053-66, 1.68.

5/65} See M 201 for quotation and ref. to Homer. These are on *Br.*, pp. 82-83.

5/77} For Poe's possible coinage of "Art-product" see *PCW*, p. 41.

6/8} On 1.39.

6/18-20} The poem is on 2.7-63; the rest is from Pref. 1.ix. For the "heresy" of didacticism according to Poe, see "The Poetic Principle" (q.v. in H 15.271-2, and *IV*, pp. 11-12).

6/24} Jean Louis Guez de Balzac (1597-1654), prominent French essayist. See Pin 154 for Poe's ascription to him of Bouhours' book.

6/25} *angélique* (more correctly). No French phrase book has yielded this quotation.

6/30} For "under current" and its relation to "Allegory" see M 98n.

6/37} "Chris North" in *Blackwood's* of 11/44, 55.621-39, specifically, 635, *Drama of Exile*, 2.24.

6/44} The actual quotation is, "...syntax of the passage will puzzle future..." Poe's change or the typesetter's?

6/57-67} In 2.24.

7/22} Cf. the legend concerning Oedipus and the Sphinx.

Also "Thou Art the Man": "I will now play the Oedipus to the...enigma (TOM 1044)." The lines are on 2.28.

7/35} *Blackwood's* writes, "We shall commence (after reviewing *A Drama*) with her sonnets; for these appear to us to be by far the most finished of her compositions in point of style; and in depth and purity of sentiment, we think that they surpass any thing she has ever written, with the exception of the poem entitled 'Bertha in the Lane'" (p. 622).

The magazine prints in entirety "Discontent," "Futurity," "Comfort," "The Meaning of the Look" and "Patience Taught by Nature."

The actual quotation concerning "Bertha," paraphrased by Poe, runs thus: "But the gem of the collection is unquestionably the poem entitled 'Bertha in the Lane.'"

7/42} Note Barrett's success with the sonnet in later years, and their popularity at the time of this review (cf. 1/1). Poe himself rarely used the sonnet form (TOM, *Poems*, 323, note to line 9). For her sonnets see pp. 135-62.

"The Prisoner," 1.161, reads thus: "Nature's lute / Sounds on behind this door so closely shut, / A strange, wild music to the prisoner's ears, / Dilated by the distance, till the brain / Grows dim with fancies which it feels too fine; / While ever, with a visionary pain, / Past the precluded senses, sweep and shine / Streams, forests, glades,--and many a golden train / Of sunlit hills, transfigured to Divine."

7/46-61} "The Romaunt of the Page," 1.167; "The Rhyme of the Duchess May," 2.65; "The Poet and the Bird, a Fable," 2.102; "A Child Asleep," 2.127; "Crowned and Wedded," 2.140; "Crowned and Buried," 2.146; "To Flush, my Dog," 2.156; "The Fourfold Aspect," 2.163; "A Flower in a Letter," 2.170; "A Lay of the Early Rose," 2.184; "That Day. For Music," 2.207; "L.E.L.'s Last Questio," 2.223; "Catarina to Camoëns," 2.233; "Wine of Cyprus," 2.248; "The Dead Pan," 2.266; "Sleeping and Watching," 2.245; "A Portrait," 2.241; "The Mournful Mother," 1.214; "A Valediction," 1.218; "The House of Clouds," 2.227; "The Lost Bower," 2.104.

8/2} "The Lay of the Brown Rosary," 1.183-213 (Elizabeth Barrett Barrett's spelling).

8/18} The actual phrase from Aristotle is *dio kai philosophateron kai spoudaioteron poiesis historia ta kath'hekaston legei* ("Thus poetry is superior to and more philosophic than history; poetry treats more of the general, history of the peculiar" [*De Arte Poetica*, Vahlen's Text, Edward R. Wharton, tr., 1890], p. 28.)

Poe's misquotation betrays an ignorance of Greek confirmed by the same corruption of this phrase in his 1836 "Letter to B____." (H 7.xxxvii) and an 1842 review of *Stanley Thorn* (H 11.12).

8/21} To provide an example, the first stanza of "The Cry of the Human" (2.177) runs thus: "'There is no God,' the foolish saith,-- / But none, 'There is no sorrow,' / And nature oft, the cry of faith, / In bitter need will borrow: / Eyes which the preacher could not school, / By wayside graves are raised; / And lips say, 'God be pitiful,' / Who ne'er said, 'God be praised.' / Be pitiful, O God!"

arabesquerie: Poe coinage (cf. *PCW*, p. 23).

8/22} "The Cry of the Children," 2.131-39.

8/25} "Bertha in the Lane" (cf. 7/35), 2.195-206.

8/27} *Democratic Review*, 10/44, p. 376: *"Bertha in the Lane,"* pastoral, tender, and well wrought out, but perhaps not one of the best."

8/28} For *Blackwood's Edinburgh Magazine* (p. 626) in Poe's works, see *PD*, 110; also SM 1n.

8/32} "Lady Geraldine's Courtship," 1.221-264.

8/40-43} N. B. Poe's use of the language and meter of this poem (q.v. in 2/29 above).

9/11} On 1.224, st. III. This popular gift book poem was revised in later editions.

9/18} *Blackwood's*, p. 638.

9/19} Christopher North: pseud. of Professor John Wilson (1785-1854), M.A., Oxford. Summoned to the bar, 1815; he joined the staff of *Blackwood's* in 1817, becoming the magazine's chief supporter with John Gilbert Lockhart (cf. H 9.171, 10.213). In 1820 Wilson was elected professor of moral philosophy at Edinburgh on the strength of his Tory convictions. It was in *Blackwood's* that he wrote, under his pseudonym, *Noctes*

Ambrosianae (1822-35, cf. 9/43). See *PD*, p. 99; cited as critic SM 1, SM 7.

9/30} *Blackwood's*, p. 637.

9/31-32} On 1.261. The italics are from *Blackwood's*, indicating dissatisfaction.

9/35} Poe's pun (-um equaling -us) in the Latin ignores Frederic's penchant for French (therefore "Chacun a son goût").

9/43} Ambrosians: the conversations of North's circle, which make up *Noctes Ambrosianae*, supposedly took place in Ambrose's Tavern (OCEL).
Saint Ambrose (340-397 A.D., bishop of Milan from 374) greatly influenced church music (hymnody and antiphonal psalmody). Ambrosian liturgy and music at Milan long resisted the trends of the Church at Rome. The term "Ambrosian" was early applied also to any Latin hymn sung at the Hours. Poe's obscure allusion may be to any of these elements.

9/47} This image may derive from Lucian's statue, used by Poe thrice (cf. FS 21).

9/54} J.P. Pritchard, *Classical Weekly*, 26.132, sees a ref. to Horace, *Carmen*, III, st. XXX, 1-5: "Exegi monumentum...fuga temporum."

10/5} "blé": "A Drama of Exile," 1.33; The Romaunt of the Page," 1.73 (without accent).
"chrysm" (chrism): "A Drama of Exile," 1.68, 1.118, 1.121; "nympholeptic": "The Lost Bower," 2.117; "oenomel": "Wine of Cyprus," 2.256.

10/6} "chrysopras": "A Vision of Poets," 2.51.

10/8} "'ware": "A Drama of Exile," 1.75-6; "The Romaunt of the Page," 1.177; "Crowned and Buried," 2.148; "A Rhapsody of Life's Progress," 2.218.

10/9} "'bide": "Crowned and Buried," 2.152; "A Rhapsody of Life's Progress," 2.218; "'gins": "The Lay of the Brown Rosary," 1.201.

10/10} "'las": "Rhyme of the Duchess May," 2.85; "The House

of Clouds," 2.231; "oftly": "Catarina to Camoëns," 2.238; "ofter": "The Mournful Mother," 1.215.

10/11} "oftest": no entry

10/12} "erelong": "Futurity," 1.146.

10/18} "Dew-pallid": "A Drama of Exile," 1.75; "Pale-passioned": "A Drama of Exile," 1.56; "silver-solemn": "A Drama of Exile," 1.53.

10/19} "drave": "A Drama of Exile," 1.68; "The Romaunt of the Page," 1.166; "A Vision of Poets," 2.30; supreme: "Crowned and Buried," 2.149; lament: "A Drama of Exile," 1.33.

10/22} "L.E.L.'s Last Questio": title, 2.223

10/23} "The Cry of the Human": title, 2.177; "Leaning from my human": "To Flush, my Dog," 2.161.

10/24} "Heaven assist the Human": "A Drama of Exile," 1.42;   "the full sense of your mortal": "The Fourfold Aspect," 2.166; "a grave for your divine (Divine)!": "The Dead Pan," 2.273.

10/25} "falling (Falling) off from our created (Created)": "A Drama of Exile," 1.45; "(my master) sends this gage, (Lady,) for thy pity's counting!": "The Romance of the Swan's Nest," 2.261.

10/27} "they could not press their futures on that present of her courtesy": "Lady Geraldine's Courtship," 1.245.

10/28} "Could another fairer / Lack to thee, lack to thee?": "A Drama of Exile," 1.55.

10/30} "Hope withdraws her peradventure": "Catarina to Camoëns," 2.233.

10/31} "And deal in pathos of antithesis": "A Drama of Exile," 1.84; "Wherein I, angel, in antagonism to God and his *reflex beatitudes*": "A Drama of Exile," 1.88.

10/33-34} "Then a sough of glory shall your entrance greet / Ruffling round the doorway": "A Drama of Exile," 1.121; "God's possible": "The Cry of the Children," 2.138; "rule of mandom": "A

Drama of Exile," 1.105.

10/35-69} These lines were used almost verbatim in M 222.

10/40-46, 49-59, 73-74, 77-78} These are to be found on the following pages: 2.157, 1.29, 2.127, 1.30.

11/3, 5} From 1.19, line 98; 1.39, line 502.

11/8-10} From "Cry of the Children," 2.139.153-56.

11/13-15} 1.103.1749-51.

11/15} abasement / debasement

11/24-27} 1.98.1653-56, and see 11/44 below.

11/43} *Graham's Magazine*, 1/45, 27.46-47; passage (by E. P. Whipple?) quoted in entirety plus previous line: "Shall I be mother of the coming life?" It is set down, along with four other excerpts from "A Drama of Exile" under the sentence stating, "The following we cut from their connection with the Drama, for their independent beauty."

11/44} Nat-Leeism: Nathaniel Lee (1653-1692), English playwright famed for the bombastic style of his *Rival Queens* and *Sojourn in Bedlam* (*DNB*). The critic in *Graham's* was Edwin P. Whipple, Poe tells us in a late essay (see H 13.201). The four lines are collected by TOM (*Poems*, 377-78) as Poe's adaptation of Barrett's lines.

12/3} "A Drama..." 1.34: "Is God's seal in a cloud. There seem to lie / A hundred thunders in it, dark and dead; / The unmolten lightnings vein it motionless;" and "The House of Clouds" 2.228: "Of a riven thunder-cloud, / Veined by the lightning!"

12/3-4} "A Drama..." 1.53: "And silver-solemn clash of cymbal wings." and "The Dead Pan" 2.269: "And your silver clash of wings."

12/6} "A Drama..." 1.27: "Of spirits' tears." and "A Drama..." 1.131: "as of the falling tears of an angel."

12/8} "Lady Geraldine's Courtship" 1.244: "When we drive

out, from the cloud of steam, majestical white horses," and "The Cry of the Human" 2.179: "The rail-cars snort from strand to strand, / Like more of Death's White Horses!"

12/20} no entry in concordance

12/21} "Perplexed Music," 1.144/14.

12/22} "Lady Geraldine's Courtship," 1.245/222.

12/23} "The Cry of the Children," 2.137/123.

12/24} "Lady Geraldine's Courtship," 1.223/2.

12/25} "A Lay of the Early Rose," 2.194/199-200.

12/26} "Catarina to Camoëns," 2.234/18.

12/27} "Catarina to Camoëns," 2.237/84.

12/28} "A Drama...," 1.26/227-8.

12/29} "Perplexed Music," 1.144/11.

12/30} "A Drama...," 1.59/892.

12/31} "The Romaunt of the Page," 1.167-36.

12/32{ "The Lay of the Brown Rosary," 1.186/21.

12/33} "The Lay of the Brown Rosary," 1.193/130.

12/34} "Lady Geraldine's Courtship," 1.223/1.

12/35} "A Vision of the Poets," 2.43/653.

12/36} "A Child Asleep," 2.129/31.

12/37} "The Cry of the Children," 2.131/3.

12/38} "Catarina to Camoëns," 2.239/127.

12/39} "Catarina to Camoëns," 2.235/69.

12/40} "To Flush," 2.161/90.

12/41} "The House of Clouds," 2.231/79.

12/49} The *OED* gives "far-fetchedness" to Poe as the first user.

12/58} "A Drama...," 1.43/583-4: "Think how erst your Eden, / Day on day succeeding";   "A Drama...," 1.44/601-3: "While our feet struck glories / Outward, smooth and fair, / Which we stood on floorwise";   "A Drama...," 1.45/618-20: "Then in odes of burning, / Brake we suddenly, / And sang out the morning..."

12/59} "A Drama...," 1.45/627-8: "All disparted hither, thither, / Trembling out into the aether,--"
"A Drama...," 1.70/1089-90: "Filtered through roses, did the light enclose me; / And bunches of the grape swang blue across me--".

12/60} "A Drama...," 1.71/1114-6: "Thou man, thou woman, marked as the misdoers, / By God's sword at your backs! I lent my clay / To make your bodies, which had grown more flowers"; "A Drama...," 1.72/1131-2: "I was obedient. Wherefore, in my centre, / Do I thrill at this curse of death and winter!--"; "A Drama...," 1.89/1477-9: "And we scorn you! there's no pardon / Which can lead you aright! / When your bodies take the guerdon..."

12/61} "A Drama...," 1.95-6/1600-2: "Strong to struggle, sure to conquer,-- / Though the vessel's prow will quiver / At the lifting of the anchor"; "A Drama...," 1.101/1708-9: "As the simoom drives wild across the desert,-- / As the thunder rears deep in the Unmeasured,-"; "A Drama...," 1.101/1710-1: "As the torrent tears an ocean-world to atoms,-- / As the whirlpool grinds fathoms below fathoms,--".

12/62} "A Drama...," 1.120/2079-81: "Through the door of opal, / We will draw you soothly / Toward the Heavenly people"; "A Drama...," 1.121/2087-9: "Then a sough of glory / Shall your entrance greet; / Ruffling round the doorway...";   " A Drama...," 1.122/2116-8: "To the thick graves accompted; / Awaking the dead bodies, / The angel of the trumpet..."

12/63} "A Drama...," 1.126/2183-5: "Blind the beast shall stagger, where It overcame him,-- / Meek as lamb at pasture-- bloodless in desire-- / Down the beast shall shiver,--slain amid the taming,--"; "Lady Geraldine's Courtship," 1.251/277-9: "*He had left her,--peradventure, when my footstep proved my coming-- / But for her--she half arose, then sat--grew scarlet and grew pale: / Oh, she trembled!--'tis so always with a worldly man or woman*";"The Lay of the Brown Rosary," 1.185/6-7: "*She looks down the garden-walk caverned with trees, / To the limes at the end, where the green arbour is--*".

12/64} "The Lay of the Brown Rosary," 1.187/41-2: "*The old convent ruin the ivy rots off, / Where the owl hoots by day, and the toad is sun-proof.*"; "A Drama...," 1.118/2030-2: "*By the desert's endless vigil, / We will solemnize your passions; / By the wheel of the black eagle...*"; "Lady Geraldine's Courtship," 1.227/41-3: "*Quite low born! self-educated! somewhat gifted though by nature,-- / And we make a point of asking him,--of being very kind; / You may speak, he does not hear you; and besides, he writes no satire,--*".

12/65} "Lady Geraldine's Courtship," 1.239/157-9: "*There, obedient to her praying, did I read aloud the poems / Made by Tuscan flutes, or instruments more various, of our own; / Read the pastoral parts of Spenser--or the subtle interflowings / Found in Petrarch's sonnets...*"; "Lady Geraldine's Courtship," 1.244-5/213-5: "*She was patient with my talking; and I loved her--loved her certes, / As I loved all Heavenly objects, with uplifted eyes and hands! / As I loved pure inspirations--loved the graces, loved the virtues*".

12/66} "Lady Geraldine's Courtship," 1.258-9/353-5: "*Oh, of course, she charged her lacqueys to bear out the sickly burden, / And to cast it from her scornful sight--but not beyond the gate-- / She is too kind to be cruel, and too haughty not to pardon...*"; "The Lost Bower," 2.124/334-5: "*The young children laughed thereat; / Yet the wind that struck it, riseth, and the tempest shall be great!*"; "The Cry of the Children," 2.133/34-5: "*Ask the old why they weep, and not the children, / For the outside earth is cold,-- / And we young ones stand without, in our bewildering*".

12/67} "Wine of Cyprus," 2.250/41-3: "*Do not mock me! with my mortal, / Suits no wreath again, indeed! / I am sad-voiced as the turtle,*"; "A Flower in a Letter," 2.174/67-9: "*Before the priestly moonshine! / And every wind with stolèd feet, / In wandering down the alleys sweet, / Steps lightly on the sunshine;*"

13/6-13} "Lady Geraldine's Courtship," 1.251/281-4.

13/30-39} "Lady Geraldine's Courtship," 1.238-9; line 34: "a brown partridge."

13/51} psychal: for Poe's coinage and frequent use see *PCW*, p. 35.

13/52-64} "Bertha in the Lane," 2.201-2.

13/67-76} "The Lost Bower," 2.115.

13/77} See Pin 14, 33; MM 7, 139A for Poe on Dante.

13/80-87} "The Cry of the Children," 2.135-6.

14/3-8} "Crowned and Wedded," 2.144-5 (with "glory and degree" in her poem).

14/11} In the forties Poe liked to cite the witticism ascribed incorrectly to Hierocles of Alexandria (ca. A.D. 430) as one of a collection of 260, concerning the "scholastikos" who offered a brick as a sample of a house that he wished to sell (see Poe's rev. of Brougham's *Writings* in the 3/42 *Graham's*, H 11.101), his rev. of Dawes' poetry in the 10/42 *Graham's* (H 11.145); and his letter to Charles Anthon of 11/2/44. Poe apparently could not decide upon the spelling for the Greek "chi" (second letter) and used "h" and "k" and "ch".

14/13} The word "constellatory" has 3 *OED* instances: 1650, 1823, and Poe's.

14/24 ff.} The next two paras. were reused as the first of ten articles (Marginalia 213 ff.) in the 5/1849 *SLM*, q.v. in the *Br.* for glosses on all questions below save one in 14/62. Except for this and one in 15/1-3 (below), no changes of significance were made by Poe--sharpening of the rhetoric here and there for small substantive matters and improvement of the pointing. Since M 213a contains a collation it is here omitted. Note c treats of Poe's love of Shelley and offers material from other Poe texts, especially for "The Sensitive Plant."

14/25} *Childe Harold* III, xcvii. See M 213 for full glosses on Poe and Percy Bysshe Shelley and his "Sensitive Plant"--a Poe favorite.

14/47} Francis Bacon, first baron Verulam (1561-1626), philosopher, lawyer, essayist. Poe often refers to his *Essayes* and borrows from them--but later he deprecates his philosophy. See Pin Intro.; SP 29; FS 3; MM 147, 213, 183, 196, 262.

14/57-65} The importance of this passage and the variation of Shelley's work in the 1849 text warrants a similar note. Poe here combines a Tower of Babel with a Chinese pagoda with bells derived from the mad Ophelia, "Like sweet bells jangled, out of tune and harsh" (*Hamlet*, 3.1.166). *Alastor: The Spirit of Solitude*, about the quest of a doomed youth for the visionary ideal is somewhat more suitable than *Prometheus Unbound*; Poe's sole ref. to these two works in this passage suggests his better acquaintance with Shelley's short lyrics. Poe seems to consider "glare" as equivalent to "*bizarrerie*," which he used often. For "spectrum" he is apparently going back to the root, meaning "image."

14/70} Samuel Taylor Coleridge (1772-1834), leading English Romantic poet, later known for his interest in esoteric metaphysics, which Poe deplored. *PD*, p. 22; MM 109, 133, 193, 213, SM 19. Poe slightly reduces his scorn for him in M 213.

15/1} In the 1849 text Poe adds one small word of significance in his evolving theory of composition: "the most profound Art (based both in Instinct and *Analysis*) and the sternest Will"--the italics and capital being Poe's own. Since he had written the "Philosophy of Composition" and the essays on prosody by then, the deliberate sedulous working out of the Art-Product has become fundamental.

15/7-35} The last para. was not used by Poe for M 213, perhaps because he had realized (by 5/1849, date of the article) how specious was much of the talk about her imitating Tennyson. A little older (1806-61) than he (1809-92), she had been writing poems before his *Poems, chiefly Lyrical* (1830), and while she avowed her love of Tennyson in 1842, her style and themes derived much more from Byron, Shelley directly, Landor, Greek drama, et al. than from Tennyson. Her fame has sadly declined from then, with her verse considered "too fluent and undisciplined, despite her theoretical excuses for slack rhymes and her intense social protest" (Baugh, *Lit. History of England*, p. 1403; Sampson, *Concise History of English Lit.*, 583). It is curious that Poe acknowledges her forthright independence and liberal tendencies toward human rights, product of Shelley and other Enlightenment writers, but he refuses openly to discuss the themes, in part because of his elevation solely of lyrical poetry, from which his antididacticism would exclude the message. As for her insistence upon the Tennyson influence--she did not start out with his "works beside her" and between the midthirties and 1845 Robert Browning, soon to be her husband, was providing a series of poems and verse dramas counting for far more influence over her style and form. Poe knew about the marriage and about Robert's poetry, but probably indirectly (*Letters*, 320, 329). The profusion of images and the complicated comparison of Tennyson and E. B. B. as to health and imagination lead to confusion, not clear conclusion.

16/5} Nathaniel P. Willis (1806-67), editor, journalist, poet, graduated from Yale, 1827, edited *American Monthly Magazine* in Boston (1829-31), with reasonable success, despite notoriety as a poseur and dandy. In New York, he became associated with George P. Morris and went abroad as the *New York Mirror*'s foreign correspondent. Despite indiscreet dispatches, he again met with success, social and professional. Back in New York (1836) Willis began writing for the theater. In 1839-40 he published the weekly *Corsair*. He again, with Morris, became co-editor of the *New Mirror*, the daily *Evening Mirror*, and in 1846, the long-lived *Home Journal*. Willis defended Poe against later calumnies, and has a place of importance in the development of the American short story (*DAB*). See *PD*, p. 98; M 192.

16/10-11} Bryan Waller Proctor (1787-1874), English poet. Intimate with Hunt, Lamb, Dickens. Reginald Heber (1738-1826), popular poet and hymn writer. See SM 23; H 9.198, 12.36. Fitz-Greene Halleck (1790-1867), American poet, featured in Griswold's *Poets and Poetry of America*. See *PD*, p. 41, for numerous articles and comments. Henry Neele (1798-1828), solicitor, poet, and misc. writer, contributed to periodicals and pub. his collected poems in 1827. Willis reviewed his *Literary Remains* in 4/29, in the *Am. Monthly Mag.*, 1.33, as "boarding school poetry, and lack-a-daisical prettyisms" (see Auser, *Willis*, 1969, pp. 28, 151). James Henry Leigh Hunt (1784-1859), English essayist and poet. Intimate with leading literary figures, especially the poets. See *PD*, p. 47; M 179. Charles Lamb (1775-1834), English essayist and humorist, see *PD*, p. 53; M 109. Washington Irving (1783-1859), the first characteristically American author, who established his reputation while American letters were in the formative stage of independence from British domination. See *PD*, p. 48; MM 156, 102.

16/14} "in fee simple impartite": held in his own right, unconditionally, and not parted or divided.

16/38} Coleridge (q.v. 14/70) authored *Aids to Reflection* (C. Goodrich, Burlington, 1829, lxi [2] 399p.) and "Genevieve" (first published in the *Cambridge Intelligencer*, 11/1/1794 [pp. 19-20, Oxford ed., Coleridge]).

16/54-61} Poe's passage on this distinction became part of the 5/46 "Lit." sketch of Willis and also comprised FS 41 (q.v.), with the opinion on Thomas Moore.

17/12-36} These lines became M 220 (q.v.), just as the lines above. This entire section on Fancy was derived by Poe from Coleridge, as he admits (cf. M. Alterton, H. Craig, *EAP*, NY, 1935, rev. ed. 1962, p. xxvii; Floyd Stovall, *EAP*, 1969, 156-60). For collations with M 220 see the note, which discusses Hugo's *Cromwell* as a source, and R. Jacob's different view.

17/26} However, in "Philosophy of Composition" (para. 18, H 15.201), Poe denies this "neutrality" of topic by opting for "the death of a beautiful woman" as "the most poetical topic." Cf. Ivor Winters in *AL*, 1937, rep. in E. Carlson, *Recognition of Poe* (1966), pp. 184-90.

18/9-10} The final phrase may strike us as an instance of Poe's allowing the sound of an alliterative pair of words to determine the thought, such as it is; it yields very little significant meaning.

18/11} For Poe's follow up of this rev., see p. 35 (a). Although Poe labeled this important article (from which he derived M 221) with a "P" and it was listed in the bibliographical index by Harrison, it was omitted in his ed. and in every other compilation. For Bulwer Lytton (1803-73), popular English dramatist, political figure, historical and romance novelist, see *Br.* Index, and M 221 specifically, since that article is closely adapted from this (19/46 through 20/43 [facsimile text]).

18/12} Actually, the only publisher was James W. Judd & Co., 1845, v-xi + 143 p. No other publisher was listed, in any of the catalogues consulted, as having anything to do with this ed.

Cf. 18/34 below.

18/13} C. Donald Macleod (1821-65), prominent Presbyterian minister and writer, who studied for the ministry at Columbia College, took orders as an Episcopal priest at 28, and became a country rector; following this he left for Europe in 1850 for travel and study. After conversion to Roman Catholicism (as Xavier) he became editor of the St. Louis *Ledger* in 1857. Later professor of *belles lettres* and rhetoric in Ohio, he wrote histories of Mary, Queen of Scots, et al., a volume of poems, and a great deal of fugitive verse. See Francis S. Drake, *Dictionary of American Biography* (J.R. Osgood, 1872), p. 578; *Nat. Cyclopaedia of Am. Bio.*, (J.T. White, 1891, 1907), 5.421.

Poe's assumption of Macleod's fame must be a result of Macleod's work having been published in the periodicals. There is no reason to assume much notoriety at this point. Cf. 54/55 below.

18/26} Intro. by Macleod, p. vii.

18/34} Poe is correct. Macleod must have used a comprehensive edition of 1836, published in Paris by Galignani (and probably not edited by Bulwer), for the English community there, as there exists no British collection prior to 1845.

Poe's cited edition of Macleod's collection is a mystery. The only traceable edition is not by Farmer & Daggers (see 18/11 [facsimile text]). He must have possessed a special issue released in the U.S. Its existence is verified on 35/19-20.

18/35} The statement concerning Macleod's age supports his identity as belonging to the man described above. Macleod's misspelling of "Alcolyte" for "Acolyte" on p. xi (q.v. on 18/57), followed by Poe or his typesetter, suggests his immaturity. Also note Macleod's arrangement of the collection:

I. Ballads and Descriptions (10 poems); II. Philosophical and Religious (18 poems); III. Songs and Lyrics (20 poems); IV. Misc.

The listing of Category II (above), highly unlikely for the worldly Bulwer (q.v. in *DNB*), points to the editorship of the Rev. Macleod.

18/50} This is a mere, brief selection, compared to the fullness of the Paris ed. (cf. 18/34}.

18/57} Acolyte: typo is from the original Preface.

19/8} Actually, at this point there was no London edition of a collection by Bulwer (see 18/34).

19/26} This appears on p. v, with italics added.

19/28} *Tremaine*: L.: H. Colburn, 1852, 3 vols.; Phila., 1852, 3 vols., no pub. given. The author is Robert Plumer Ward (1765-1846), q.v. in M 221.

19/34} *De Vere*: L.: H. Colburn, 1827; Phil., 1827, Carey, Lea & Carey (see M 221).

19/46-58 [and 20/1-45]} This whole passage was adapted very closely for M 221, q.v. for explication of almost all names and titles given here (in notes c-f).

19/50} Jane Porter (1776-1850), author of romantic novels in the style of Scott. After her success in her native Scotland with a first novel, *Thaddeus of Warsaw*, 1803, her fame spread throughout the Continent in 1810 following the publication of *The Scottish Chiefs*. Her attempts at composing drama met with failure, however.

19/52} Benjamin Disraeli (1804-81) had already published *Vivian Grey* and *The Young Duke* among other novels.

20/10} *Athens. Its Rise and Fall with views of the Literature, Philosophy, and Social Life of the Athenian People* in 2 vols., 1837; vol. 1, vii-ix + 484 p.; vol. 2, xxx + 596 p. (cited in MM 117, 221).

20/19} Claude Adrien Helvétius (1715-71), Parisian gentleman and liberal philosopher (the name is the Latinized form of Schweitzer, not a Swiss reference), who sought to rival Montesquieu. It is doubtful whether Poe actually studied his works. See M 221f for the Bulwer source of this quotation from *De l'Esprit*.

20/32} James Crichton (1560?-82?), Scottish scholar credited with copious learning. His reputation supposedly rests on his travels to the Italian universities, where he discussed Scholastic doctrine and demonstrated great linguistic ability. It is speculated, however, that his accomplishments are largely invented by Thomas Urquhart (q.v., *DNB*). See MM 207, 221.

20/33} Harrison Ainsworth (1807-1896), British historical novelist, friend of Dickens and Thackeray, detested by Poe. See MM 12, 221.

20/54} "The Ill-omened Marriage," pp. 33-76.

20/64-65} John Philpot Curran (1754-1817), Irish lawyer and judge. In spite of his Protestantism, he defended Irish radicals, advocated Pitt's measures limiting power of the regent, and refused intimidation with the aid of sarcastic wit. See M 95. For metaphor run mad see *PCW* for two more uses, one in *BJ*, 2.404.

21/5} Seigneur Guillaume de Salluste Du Bartas (1544-1590), French poet, author of *La Semaine* (1578). This work, a biblical epic on the Creation, was influential and popular primarily abroad, where translations revealed a grandeur of range and vision, while omitting newly coined words, and mitigating his bizarre metaphors (*En. Brit.*, 13th ed.). Cf. Pollin, "Du Bartas in Poe's Criticism," *Mi Q*, 1969, 33.45-55; H 4.112, 9.67, 11.159, 259. Poe's view of him was consistently limited and unjustified.

21/12} *ars celare artem*: ars est celare artem--(true) art is to conceal art--a Latin proverb.

21/21} "Mazarin," pp. 1-3, 42 lines. "André Chénier," pp. 4-5, 44 lines (for A. Chénier, see Pin 64). "The Last Crusader," pp. 97-9, 14 stanzas.

21/26} These lines appear on p. 5.

21/30} P. 5, collated thus: would/*could* prophet,

21/31-37} See "The Rationale of Verse" (1848), H 14.210, for a discussion of "acatalectic." The first draft of "The Rationale" was published as "Notes on English Verse" in the 3/43 *Pioneer*. The first two paras. correspond exactly to the section above in the 1848 article, which describes "acatalectic" as mentioned in the *BJ* in 1845.

21/39} A song from George Colman the Younger's (1762-1836) *Love Laughs at Locksmiths*, act II (Bartlett).

21/47} P. viii. There is not a word about "Miss Bailey." It is Poe's joke.

21/48} *niaiseries*: A Poe favorite, from the French (see too 4/42 above).

21/63} No Intro. or Preface, pages are numbered 5-84; title page also has quotation from La Bruyère in French. It is interesting to note that Poe's long analysis and condemnation of the book was observed scoffingly by *The Town* of 2/22/45 (see Poe *Log* for the date).

21/64} According to Hull, not one of Briggs' articles in the *BJ* concerning drama suggests imitation of the Elizabethans as a problem in American drama. Poe's article, "Does the Drama of the Day Deserve Support?" clearly helps to determine authorship of this piece. In the 1/9 *Evening Mirror*, Poe identified this type of imitation as an impediment to the development of an American drama, and that attitude is evident here (cf. 23/56-64 [facsimile text]).

22/7} P. 27.

22/11} P. 45.

22/14} Poe's mixed views on the Irish appear in M 102 and "Why the Little Frenchman" (TOM 462-70).

22/24-37} Found on p. 11. Poe makes minor changes (i.e. corrections).

22/43-50} From p. 14.

22/52} Found on p. 15.

22/69} Pp. 22, 23. Concerning J.T. Headley: See p. 206 [facsimile text] and Headnote to "The Cask of Amontillado" (TOM 1252).

23/29-30} Pp. 45-46.

23/42} Pp. 49-50.

23/44-55} From pp. 49-50.

23/60-64} From p. 52.

23/67} Chapter IX, pp. 61-69. For Poe's keen interest in this topic see 86 and 103-104.

23/75} Pub. of "The Raven" in *American Review* and *Mirror* (q.v. in TOM, *Poems*, 360).

23/81-82} "He hath not fed of the dainties that are bred of a book" (*Love's Labour's Lost*, 4.2.25).

24/1} Not totally by Poe, who probably wrote paras. 4-6, possibly also para. 3.

24/31} See "Anastatic Printing," pp. 83-86.

24/44} See 84/55 for data.

24/51} This para. alone is probably by Poe. In the 2/15 *BJ*, 1.103-104, appeared Poe's bitter attack on publishers, "Some Secrets of the Magazine Prison-House." It has been omitted from my text solely because it was included by TOM in his *Tales* (1205-10) as having "fictional narrative." The Philadelphia *Sun* of 2/19 published a reply, obviously with the data on Graham and Cooper that Poe mentions in the para. See also 27/65-67 (for a further apology) and M 74c. Clearly Briggs regarded these two passages by Poe as inadequate, for he himself responded rather sharply to Poe's "Magazine Prison-House" article with a satirical sketch entitled "The American Authors' Union" (*BJ* of 4/12, 1.233-34), concerning effective measures to take against "publishers ... fattening on the heart's blood of authors." The major personage is a "pale" poet whose "stylus" is an icicle, and whose speeches are full of typical Poe phrases. Although fairly good-natured, it could not fail to arouse some resentment in Poe himself.

24/59} See *PD* 23 for Poe on Cooper, for comments often unflattering.

24/60} See 27/64-9 for Poe's apology on this remark.

25/1} This is the source of M 182 (q.v. for notes to details of para. 1) and is much like part of Poe's 2/12/45 review in the *EM* on English's *Aristidean*. The *EM* is the source of M 143 (q.v.).

25/6} "Magazine-ward" is Poe's coinage. For the topic, see Ostrom, *Letters*, pp. 247, 270.

25/10} *caviare*: *Hamlet*, II.ii.465.

25/19-20} The compound word is Poe's coinage (*PCW*, p. 34), also in *EM*. The hyphen is missing in the listing in *PCW*, p. 34, (q.v.).

25/26} *currente calamo*: with a running pen; fluently; offhand.

25/36} Poe's coinage of "belaud" dates from 1841 (see *PCW*, 23).

25/45-46} Plates: *Dacota Woman and Assiniboin Girl*, Carl Bodmer, pinx ad nat[.], engraved by Rawdon, Wright and Hatch, 1st plate; *View on the Delaware, near Bordentown*, engraved by Smillie and Hinshelwood, artist appears to be Ch. Rodmer, but perhaps Carl Bodmer; *The Love Letter* (q.v. on p. 26), engraved by Illman and Sons. For Poe's earlier refs. to Dakotas and Assiniboins, see *Julius Rodman*, pp. 550-1, derived from Lewis and Clark's journal. For Poe's interest in Indians, see M 184a, and 55-56 [facsimile text].

26/2-3} Poe's decided opinion about magazine art helped to drive him from *Graham's*, or so he claimed (see Pollin, *AL*, 1968, 40.164-78).

26/6} Found on pp. 97-103.

26/7} Catharine M. Sedgwick (1789-1867), novelist, sister of Theodore and author of popular romantic domestic novels with realistic details. Poe often reviewed her works, and usually favorably (see *PD*, p. 83 for loci). "An Incident at Rome" (corrected from text) is on pp. 104-8.

26/9} Found on pp. 109-120.

26/14} The story is divided into nine chapters. For William Gilmore Simms, see Index of *BJ* and *Br*. Is it coincidental that two weeks later (3/15) Simms wrote on the "remarkable" Mr. Poe to Evert Duyckinck (see Poe *Log* for the date)?

26/15-17} "Serenading," prose, pp. 121-2; "Lucy Dutton," prose, pp. 125-7; "Foreign Mysteries," prose, pp. 132-5.

26/17-19} Pp. 128-30 contain a few stanzas and "The Lay of the Lady Corinne," "The Wild Wood Rose," "The Lord of Delmaine," and "The Fairy in the Shell," plus untitled ballads. Frances Sargent Osgood (1811-50) was a minor poet, author of mediocre sentimental verse of varying popularity. She wrote under the pseudonym "Kate Carol" (cf. 69/25 [facsimile text]). For her close relationship with Poe, see M 209; also 54/53 for her magazine publications.

26/20-24} Pp. 142-44. See M 122, for Lowell's book defended against Wilson's criticism. See also *EM* of 1/11/45 for Poe's review showing his present partiality to a man later abhorred for his abolitionist views. Even now Poe tempers his praise with "peculiar abilities" in mentioning the review of *Conversations on Some of the Old Poets* by James Russell Lowell.

26/25} Pub. 1845, Pref. iii-iv, Intro. v-viii + 797.

27/35} From Longfellow's "Psalm of Life": "We...leave behind us / Footprints on the sands of time."

27/40} Such a comparison via the Egyptian mummy is the theme of "Some Words" (TOM 1175-1201).

27/44} This chapter is found on pp. 752-85.

27/45} Robert Henry (1718-90), of Scotland, pensioned for his *History of England* (eventually 6 vols., 1781-93).

27/48} "During the last session of congress, Mr. Tyler communicated to the senate a treaty formed with the republic of *Texas*, by which that state was to become a member of the Union. The treaty was not ratified by the senate" (p. 784).

27/49} 1st part, "Ancient History," 1-323; 2nd part, "Modern History," 327-797.

27/63} The letter is printed in the 3/8 *BJ* (pp. 158-59) with no comment.

27/69} Poe's apology for his sharp remarks (24/60 [facsimile text]) confirms the good relationship with Graham, who handsomely defended Poe's posthumous name in the 3/50 *Graham's*.

28/1-7} It is Poe, not Briggs, who assigns the term "Longfellow War" to this unfortunate series of articles in the *Mirror* and *BJ*, as the denial of editorial "we" shows. Briggs disaffiliated himself from all of it in his column "Thefts of American Authors." in *BJ* of 2/15, mildly reproaching the *Mirror* for publishing Poe's initial attack (BJ 1.109, not included in my facsimile volume), but not mentioning Poe's name. Notice Poe's side-marking ref. to this page, probably for Mrs. Whitman's benefit. Since Poe here gives, very cursorily, the "history" thus far, I refer the reader to my account in the Intro. for details of the continuity of the episodes in the "War."

28/21} *EM*, 1/14/45.

28/24} *EM*, 1/25/45.

28/29} *EM*, 1/20/45.

28/30-33} The friend was George S. Hillard (1808-79), lawyer, orator, intimate with Northeast literati, q.v. in R. B. Shuman, *PMLA*, 1961, 76.155-56. See also Moss, *Poe's ... Battles*, 157n, 158-61. The 1/15 letter from Boston was published by Willis in the 1/20 *Evening Mirror* with a headnote about Poe's *Waif* notice as "written in our office by an able though very critical hand, and we give the following reply to them from as able a friend of Longfellow's in Boston. We add also the *reply* to the '*reply*,' and declare the field open. We judge the poet by ourself when we presume that he prefers *rubbing* to *rust*--sure of being more brightened than fretted." With the title "Post-Notes by the Critic," Poe's "Postscript" followed immediately after the letter--proof enough of Willis' participation in the "War": "If ever a man had cause to ejaculate, 'Heaven preserve me from my friends!' it is Mr. Longfellow. (para.) My 'literary strictures' on the poem consisted, generally, in the assertion, that it is the best of poems, one of which, at least, should have been received with acclamation. (para.) I defy Professor Longfellow and his friend conjointly to say a rational word in defence of the 'identical illustration' to which, as gently as possible, I objected. (para.) I defy that I misconceived either rhythm or metre--call for the proofs--and assert that Professor Longfellow knows very little about either. If the proofs are called for *here* I will give them. (para.) Mem: it is by no means impossible, however, that on the points, I may err. I may know nothing about rhythm--for I remember (with regret) that it was precisely the *rhythm* of Mr. Longfellow in the proem, which elicited my unqualified applause. (para.) I did not dispute Mr. Longfellow's 'right' to construct his book as he thought proper. I reserve to myself the right of thinking what I choose of the construction. (para.) I mentioned my idea that the anonymous contributions were perhaps, in general, Mr. Longfellow's, because I thought so, and because every body thought so. If they are not--what then? Does the friend, however, mean to persist in the assertion, that not one of them is Mr. Longfellow's? (para.) As 'the charge of habitually imitating other American poets requires no especial reply'--it shall surely rest undisturbed by any reply of mine. (para.) It seems to me that the whole state of the case may be paralleled thus: / A accosts B, with--'My dear friend, in common with all mankind, and the angels, I regard you as a demi-god. Your equal is not to be found in the country which is proud to claim you as a son...but permit me! there is a very--a *very* little speck of dust on the extreme end of your nose--oblige yourself and your friends by brushing it away.' 'Sir,' replies B, 'what you have asserted is wholly untrue....I consider you a malignant critic, and wish to have nothing further to do with you--for know that there *are* spots upon the sun, but my proboscis is a thing without spot!'"

28/34-36} Poe's allegation of Longfellow's prodding his second friend, i.e., Charles Sumner, into writing a protest has no factual basis. The poet tried to remain above such brawls (see Moss, 164-65; and Pollin, *Mi Q*, 1984, 37.4, 475-82).

28/42} The negative "not" belonging before "accessible" was inadvertently omitted from the *WM*, 1.287; but not from *EM*, 2/5/45 (and also dropped from the *BJ*, Harrison and Shuman's article). Lowell unfortunately was dragged into the controversy over Longfellow's originality, but nevertheless helped Poe to secure the Lyceum lecture invitation.

28/52} It was not only other friends of Longfellow but also his very partial magazine publisher, George R. Graham, who extracted from Willis an avowal that "he dissented from *all* the disparagement of Longfellow" in the rev. of *The Waif* (*EM*, 2/14; *WM* 2/22, 1.317). Surely Poe is joking about "the satire...in Mr. Willis' manifesto," especially since he had just complained about the letters of two of Longfellow's "coadjutors."

28/61} From *Hamlet*, 1.2.185 ("In my mind's eye, Horatio"), and interesting as insight into Poe's behaving like a stage director, manipulating his dramatis personae for a spectacular public effect. (See also 29/4: "If I die for it"--pure melodrama!)

29/8} This is Jupiter the Thunderer, a standard Latin epithet as in Ovid's *Metamorphoses*, 1.170. Poe's allusion is clearly stimulated by a remark made by Willis in the 2/5 *EM* (*WM* of 2/8, p. 287) in his apology for the fracas over Longfellow and Poe (p. 2, cols. 2-3), stating that he had expected better replies from the Boston papers, but only the letter from Sumner came. "Thunder was sometimes 'out to pasture.'" Willis again shows (see n. to 28/30-33 above) his hopes of creating a newspaper ruckus that will attract readers; he also here leads the way for disrespectful language--a way taken up by Poe vehemently. Poe's tacit joke here is that through the Outis letter he has become a Grace (or Fury) himself.

29/19-20} Poe so particularly alludes to Briggs' defense of James Aldrich, then inscribing the page at the side for Mrs. Whitman's benefit, that we must transcribe the burden of the article in the *BJ* of 2/15, 1.109; the poems compared are "The Death-Bed" by Thomas Hood and "A Death-Bed" by James Aldrich (q.v., below): "We can discover no resemblance between these verses, sufficient to warrant the charge of plagiarism, excepting the measure and the subject, which are certainly not peculiar to Hood; the thoughts are by no means identical. We are very sure that the Mirror would not be guilty of accusing any one of a literary theft without good reason, but we do not perceive the warrant for the accusation in this case. Mr. Aldrich is the last man in the world to be guilty of so disreputable an artifice, and certainly would never have committed a theft of this kind, which would have been certain to meet with instant detection. The truth is, that his lines appeared in the New World in 1840; and two years afterward, when Hood's lines first appeared, he copied them himself into the same paper of which he had become an assistant editor. There is certainly a curious coincidence of feeling between the verses of Mr. Aldrich, and those of Hood; but such things are very common in all the poets, from Homer downwards. There is no such thing as originality of sentiment; expression is all that any poet can claim as his own. There is hardly a name in Mr. Griswold's catalogue of American poets, less obnoxious to the charge of plagiarism than that of James Aldrich." The final two paras. of Briggs' article very reasonably speak about the universal charges of plagiarism leveled against popular and great authors, citing the *Rover*'s attack upon Longfellow concerning the Motherwell-Wolff poem and the charge against Mrs. Ellet. It may have been Briggs' remarks which gave Poe his striking notion of the "poetic sentiment" as making the artist so sensitive to the excellences of others that he unconsciously incorporates merits that he perceives into his own work. Curiously, in his "Lit." sketch of James Aldrich (1810-56) he offers this excuse for the "*poetical* thefts" for which he again arraigns him (H 15.62-64). Considering the small talent of this magazinist, minor editor, and poetaster, this is too generous on Poe's part, but even his newly found parallel, between "Molly Gray" and Tennyson's "Airy, fairy Lilian!" seems far-fetched. Briggs was mistaken, in the para. given above, about the primacy of Aldrich's lines, for Hood's poem first appeared in the 8/36 *Englishman's Magazine*, supposedly on the death of his sister, while Aldrich's appeared in the 5/19/41 *New World* and in Keese's 1842 anthology.

29/40} The original *EM* article included "the" just before "poems" as is needed by the sense.

29/82} It would be easy to compile a longer list of the differences in language between the two poems--surely no inconsiderable factor in judging the equivalence of both on such a commonplace theme. It is noteworthy that the singularity of Poe's ideal "poetical topic"--"the death of a beautiful woman"-- condemns all well-read authors of aspiring genius to a uniformity that easily might be considered imitative ("Phil. of Composition" para. 18). Poe himself, as "Outis," in the 3/1 *EM*, acknowledges this element in his first para., reprinted below.

30/2 ff.} This article on "Plagiarism," by "Outis" (Greek for "no man"; cf. Odysseus' trick played on the gullible Polyphemus) appeared first in the *EM*, 3/1, and, soon after, in the *WM*, 3/8, 1.346-47. As one of the central documents in the "Longfellow War" it deserves attention. To my mind it is unquestionably Poe's hoax contribution, aiming to preserve interest in the controversy in both the *Mirror* with Willis' connivance and in the *BJ*, probably without Briggs' awareness (since he would have subsequently revealed the truth after falling out with Poe). Mary Phillips, in working on *Poe--The Man* (Phila., 1926) felicitously decided that the MS. of "The Reviewer Reviewed" showed the same tactics as the "Outis" defense of Longfellow--a clever hoax in which Poe, the anonymous author, sedulously attacked Poe the author for detailed faults (pp. 956-96). Killis Campbell, on the basis of the incomplete document, instead proposed C. C. Felton, the entirely inappropriate friend of Longfellow as "Outis" in *University of Texas Studies in English*,

1928, No. 8, 107-109, repeating this in *The Mind of Poe* (229). TOM "inclined to believe" him to be Poe in his 1969 *Poems* (557), and in his *Tales*, which includes "A Reviewer Reviewed" complete by "Walter G. Bowen," concludes that "Outis" is Poe (1378-79). Sidney Moss (*Poe's Lit. Battles*, 169 and 170n), following Campbell, thinks otherwise. My major points are these: a) It is written in a clever imitation of Poe's manner, as Quinn (454) admits, although he does not think it to be Poe. Yet why should any friend or defender of Longfellow and Aldrich ape Poe's manner and introduce such dubiety into the dispute? How could he be so clever about tricks of phrasing and even the slight misquotation of Gray's line (lines 60-61), typical of Poe? b) This parallels Poe's attack on his own methods in tale-writing presented in "The Reviewer Reviewed" (TOM 1377-87, especially n. 17), a manuscript that convinced Mary Phillips and TOM. c) Why otherwise should Poe so promptly and completely reprint so long an attack on himself? It makes good points, shows much information, and would be worthy of suppression, rather than exposure, were it not Poe's. See Poe's letter (Ostrom, 282-84) to Jeremiah Hunt, Jr., who, as ed. of the Ithaca *National Archives* of 3/13, had criticized this very "Outis" reply in the present issue of the *BJ*. Poe casuistically explains his reprinting the "letter of Outis itself, to which I wish to give all the publicity in my power ... [for] the more thorough refutation.... There will be *four* chapters in all" (of reply). Does not this sound like a preplanned campaign of essay-responses? d) The joke about Poe's name, taken almost verbatim from an 1839 Philadelphia paper would be unknown to a Boston friend of Longfellow and not quoted even if known (see 31/24, repeated 60/1). e) The picturesque instance about a letter matching a phrase by Whittier is basically inapposite and unverifiable; why not use instances drawn from the works as published of two separate known poets? Moreover, why be so vague about the date, the title of "the splendid annual" and the title of the poem (see para. 2 below)? f) The half-truth about the similarity of the use of the repetend is most unlikely to occur to any ordinary observer, but not to Poe, who loved that poem and knew it well (*PCW*, 106). g) The exaggerated denial in the last para. of knowledge of Mr. Aldrich, sufficiently known for his editorial work on the *New World*, and included in a brief biographical sketch in Griswold's *PPA*, is the unrealistic opposite of the awareness of journalistic chitchat hinted immediately before. h) And why should a defender of Longfellow go out of his way, in the penultimate para., to praise "The Raven" for its "power," etc.?

30/13-37} As is indicated in (e) in the above note, there are truly absurd elements about this whole comparison, so vaguely presented as to be unverifiable. Why not name the writer of the letter, especially if it has been published? What is the annual containing the poem and what is its title? The biographies of John Greenleaf Whittier (1807-92) and the bibliographies fail to evidence early contributions to "splendid annuals." Whittier often revised his reprinted poems, of which the editions are lacking critical apparatus. Closest to the cited line is a section of "The Pageant" in *The Complete Poetical Works* (Boston: Osgood and Co., 1876; collected at intervals from 1848 with "Note by the Author to the Edition of 1857"), pp. 263-64, "The gleaming tree-bolls, ice-embossed, / Hold up their chandeliers of frost" (st. 4) and "The flora of the mystic mine-world / Around me lifts on crystal stems / The petals of its clustered gems!" (st. 7). Unfortunatley, untenable is the theory that "The Pageant" is the later form of an earlier poem with the sought-for line, since Thomas Franklin Currier, *A Bibliography of J. G. Whittier* (Harvard UP, 1937), p. 318, establishes its printed date as 1871 in *Winter Poems by favorite American Poets*, p. 13. This shifts the identification to the vaguer possibility of an uncollected poem on a wintry scene with this image from his early years which was noted "by every reviewer in the land, for the exceeding beauty of the imagery" (Outis' letter, 30/28-29) but was never reprinted or recorded! We must assume then that the germ of the image or description stayed with Whittier for 40 years, until 1870. How much more likely that the whole matter is a "confirmatory" spoof devised by Poe?

30/26} The word "is" (rendering the sentence meaningless) does not appear in the *Mirror* texts, but is reprinted in the Harrison volume.

30/45-49} See 29/19-20 for the true dates of both poems.

30/60-61} The quotation, slightly modified as was often Poe's habit in quoting, comes from Gray's "Progress of Poesy," 3.4: "Thoughts that breathe, and words that burn."

30/74-75} The biblical text is Gen. 32:26, whatever the poem to which "Outis" refers.

30/94} The word "madam" is an obvious typo for "madman." The other substantive changes in the *BJ* from the *Mirror* texts (with the *BJ* line shown) are as follows: 14 those / these; 63 on the / on to the; 79 specially / specifically.

31/5} John Neal (1793-1876), prolific ed. and author, early and late of Portland, intermediately of London and Baltimore, was one of Poe's staunchest defenders, even after his death (see MM 197b, 216 for data). Early he and Tobias Watkins largely wrote Paul Allen's (1775-1826) two-vol. *History of the American Revolution* (1818) and revised his narrative poem *Noah* (1821). The three were members of the Baltimore literary Delphian Club, which published the monthly *Portico* (1816-18).

31/6} Richard Henry Dana Jr. (1815-82), famous for his *Two Years Before the Mast* (1840) was author of the popular "The Dying Raven" which may have contributed hints to Poe's "Raven" according to TOM's ambiguous suggestion (*Poems*, 372 for lines 38-47). In general Poe was indifferent or even hostile to Dana (q.v. in M 290 and loci in *PD*, 25) but surely borrowed from "The Buccaneer" (1827) for "Metzengerstein." There is no record that I have found of Neal's charging Dana with "pirating upon" Bryant for his poem "The Dying Raven." In fact, Dana had sent his first poem, "The Dying Crow," to editor Bryant for the first issue of the *New-York Review* in which it appeared (5/1825) under its new name, with advised changes. Bryant never wrote on such a topic, unless Poe is implying that his "To a Waterfowl," a totally different bird-poem, furnished some ideas. It is all the type of nonsense that evidences a hoax-letter written by Poe himself, playing the role of "Outis."

31/9} Poe was very partial to the poetry of Edward Coote Pinkney (1802-28), whose name he always misspelled as here. TOM thinks his poetry influenced by that of Pinkney. As the son of the brilliant and haughty lawyer and diplomat William Pinkney (1764-1822) he was reared in Baltimore and London. The father was posthumously attacked by John Neal for his arrogance in the novel *Randolph* (1823), for which the son vainly sought a duel, but the gossip about Willis' plagiarizing from the son's poetry is unsubstantiated. Later Poe traces a close connection between his celebrated "Health" and a poem by George Hill (see M 208a for this and other details about Pinkney).

Lydia Maria (Francis) Child (1802-80) was very early a popular (and prolific) writer of periodical tales, novels, and poems, and prominent too as an abolitionist ed. Poe reviewed her *Philothea* (128-34) and cites a poem in his "Lit." sketch (H 15.105-107), Poe's allusion here to Neal's charge that Willis had borrowed something from her poem is either spurious or lost in the labyrinth of rumor.

31/20-22} These comprise lines 43-45 of "Sea Weed."

31/24} This proves Poe's authorship. See *Alexander's Weekly Messenger*, 12/18/39, 4/1-2, Poe's article, "Enigmatical and Conundrumical," #25: "Why ought the author of the 'Grotesque and Arabesque' to be a writer of verses? Because he's a poet to a *t*. Add *t* to Poe makes it Poet."

31/52-53, 55-56} Lines 52-53 are 93-96 in "The Rime of the Ancient Mariner" and 55-56 are 99-102. The first word of line 55 should be "Then" and not "They."

31/67} "went on a-warbling" in the *EM*.

31/79-83} Two non-Poeian touches occur here: "hereafter" used adjectivally and "dosing." *Word Index*, 102 gives 3 instances with "z" spelling, none with "s" for "sleeping"; but these are weak counter arguments.

31/91} Surely, if the poem cited by "Outis" enables him to make fifteen parallels or similitudes with lines in "The Raven" we must conclude that it too has been created by Poe for this occasion and for its use in the following episodes of the "Longfellow-War." Since Poe has planned the whole campaign for reasons of publicity, first for the *Mirror* and next for the *BJ*, which he had just joined, it would be easy to speak of an "anonymous poem" seen "some five years ago." Totally unknown and totally third-rate, it could contain all the cues that he needed for his argument. Writing a cliché-ridden set of verses was child's play for the versatile Poe, who easily wrote parodies and take-offs (see *Poems*, 485-90, "Comic Rhymes"; "Don Pomposo" 7, "O Tempora" 8, et al., q.v. on pp. 150, 219, 328-29, 339, 340, 382, 424, 449). There are strange elements in his explanation and shaping of the three stanzas that can only thus be explained. For example, he says "it is too long," but all the needed elements for his analysis and analogy of the two poems are here in the three stanzas. He could have made this point himself, but instead speaks of it as potentially very long (51/10 [facsimile text]), despite his habit of analysis. The material of the stanzas is too apt for Poe's purposes and even employs three lines of his own verse, modified: Line 1 savors of "Thou wert my dream" of the 1831 Intro. to "Al Aaraaf" (line 2) and line 4 sounds much like "A Dream" (written for Mrs. Jane Stanard's death, in 1827): "But a waking dream of life and light / Hath left me broken-hearted" (3-4; *Poems*, 79). Line 7 echoes "Al Aaraaf" (1.20): "Away--away--'mid seas of rays that roll" (p. 100); and lines 1, 6 of "The Valley Nis" (p. 191): "Far away--far away...." The first stanza too and the general title and theme are reminiscent of Shelley's "To a Skylark" which Poe had been reading in 1830 just before writing the new Intro. to "Al Aaraaf" (*Poems*, 159-60, note to lines 20-21). Other phrases remind us of the "cento-like" composition of this "poem," such as Shakespeare's "Unto the sweet bird's throat" (*As You Like It*, 2.5.4) and "give me excess of it... / That strain again!" (*Twelfth-Night*, 1.1.2, 4), and Milton's "Sweet bird" in *Il Penseroso* (1.61). The name Clare would readily spring to the mind of an idolator of Tennyson, whose poem "Lady Clara Vere de Vere" (1832) probably entered into Poe's "Lenore" of 2/43 in Lowell's *Pioneer* (see Pollin, *Names*, 1975, 23.1-5). And all of these main subjects were departed, much-mourned beloved maidens. The medial rhymes were a favorite device of Poe's but unlikely for another writer in three stanzas so otherwise banal as these. All told, these factors and others that might be detailed make this sentimental parody eligible for entrance into the canon of poems of Poe, who naturally could never acknowledge them in the fixedly anonymous "Outis" article.

32/10} The reference is to the parody on "The Raven" entitled "The Owl" in the 2/17 *EM* (1/6) and in the 2/22 *WM*, p. 311, signed "Sarles." For line 11 the *EM* reads "any other."

32/29} *ex-parte*: in the interests of one side only.

32/35} See M 191b for this, and other loci, taken from "Le Belier" in A. Hamilton's *Contes de Féerie*.

32/67} For Poe's stress on "the Calculus of Probabilities" see "Marie Rogêt" (TOM, 724, 774 n2; also *Letters*, 385).

32/74} See Thos. Haynes Bayley's (*sic*) *I'd be a Parody* (lines 1, 3 garbled), first pub. in Sharpe's *London Mag.*, 1829. The poem is, of course, itself a parody on Bayley's own "I'd be a Butterfly": "I'd be a butterfly; living a rover, / Dying when fair things are fading away!" (st. 3). Bayly--the correct spelling--(1797-1839) produced songs, 5 novels, 36 stage pieces, quickly and popularly.

33/3} typo: "the" is missing at the end of the line.

33/34} See Pin Intro. for Poe's error about "André" (really Andere, others) as coed. with Suard of the 1803 *Mélanges*. See Pin Intro. for Isaac D'Israeli's *Curiosities of Lit.*, which Poe plundered for the items in *Br.*

33/44} For Poe's full use of *Joe Miller's Jests* (1739), probably J. Mottley's work, in "Autography" see TOM *Tales*, 259-286; also 307 n26, for Poe's mixing Miller and J.S. Mill. See note b for his use of these comestibles and Bentham's disciple for his attack on illogic.

33/58} Q.v. *Thessalonians* I.5.2: "The day of the Lord so cometh as a thief in the night." See *PD*, pp. 86-7 for this in "Masque."

33/59-61} This sentence is quoted by Poe in para. 1 of M 198, a discussion of plagiarism.

34/1} Although marked with a "P" in the Whitman copy, this sketch has never before been included in a collection of Poe's writings. Other marks of Poe's style show in the ridicule given to the term "authoress"; the mention of "the New-York Katy-Did, and the Bunker- Hill Katy-Didn't" from "Thingum Bob, Esq."; the allusion to autographs (cf. "Autography," H 15.139); and the reference to "too blue" ink, in relation to Fuller, shows Poe's prejudice against professional blue-stockings (cf. FS 1).
   Sarah Margaret Fuller (1810-50) edited the *Dial* as a member of the Transcendentalist circle (hence the ref. in the last phrase). In 1844 she accepted Horace Greeley's invitation to become literary editor of the New York *Tribune*. It was probably with Greeley in mind that Poe mentioned Hoboken, as it was a notorious setting for duels, and as Fuller's employer he might have taken offense.
   It was from Fuller that Poe derived the expression "A Dream Within a Dream," which appeared in his "Literati" sketch of her in 8/46. Poe was reportedly seen with her in the company of Mrs. Osgood, and it was under his instructions that the caricature by Samuel E. Brown of Boston was done (the features fitting descriptions by contemporaries).
   For a full account of this sketch, cf. Pollin, "Poe on Margaret Fuller in 1845: An Unknown Caricature and Lampoon," *Women and Literature*, Spring 1977.

35/3} See sequel on 57/42 ff. [facsimile text].

35/8} See Mott, *Am. Periodicals*, 1.358-63, for the popularity then of the mammoth weekly papers, which have deteriorated and shredded out of existence, as with this one (no copy is left in NYC). Others were the NY *World* and the Boston *Notion.*

35/11} poppyish: q.v. *PCW*, p. 34.

35/20} See Poe's review (p. 18) for confirmation of his statements, which verify his critical honesty, as did his reviews in the *SLM* a decade earlier. NB: Poe did not review the "*Minor Poems*" and carelessly, it seems, accepts the *Emporium's* error.

35/31} Delivered at the New-York Historical Society, 2/28/45.

35/35} No full detailed account of Poe's hopes and efforts to join the profitable American "lecture circuit" has been presented, nor can it be here. Following the 1842 publication of Griswold's *Poets and Poetry of America*, very soon reprinted and then revised frequently, Poe developed a talk on major poets in the volume and on his views of poetry, given in Phila., 11/21/43; Wilmington, Del., 11/28; and Newark, Del., 12/32; Baltimore, 1/31/44; Reading, Pa., 3/13; and now New York. Accounts from the press inform us of the content (Phila., *Sat. Museum*, 11/21; *Del. State Journal*, 11/28 and 1/2/44; Baltimore *Sun*, 3/21/44; q.v. in J.B. Nolan's *Israfel in Berkshire*, pub. in Reading, 1948). Fullest are the New York papers, some cited below. Poe also wrote rather smugly and exaggeratedly about the lecture in letters (q.v. that of 3/17/45 to J. Hunt, Jr., in *Letters*, 283-4; see also Quinn, *EAP*, pp. 457-8 for a summary).

35/47} For Poe's long-fought battle against the "puffing system," which favored mediocre books if written in America or by close or influential friends, see Sidney Moss, *Poe's Literary Battles* (Durham, 1963), pp. i-62. The bluntness of his attacks upon Theodore Fay's *Norman Leslie* (1836) certainly undermined his relations with the chiefs of literary journalism early in his career.

35/51-52} N.P. Willis' account, typically laudatory of Poe, began with an announcement in the *Evening Mirror* of 2/27, and anticipates "Damascene slicing" and "fine carving" by Poe's "critical blade." The report of the 3/1 issue of the *Evening Mirror* praises the acidic style with which certain authors were attacked, and mentions an audience of two to three hundred. It was reprinted in the *Weekly Mirror* of 3/8, I.347 (see *The Prose Works of Nathaniel Parker Willis*, 1845, p. 775).

In the New York *Daily Tribune* Margaret Fuller (q.v. in 34/1 note) gave a well-balanced, articulate report of Poe's lecture, disparaging Poe's reading. The piece ends thus: "We are rather ashamed to add that this Lecture by a Poet and critic of genius and established reputation was listened to but by some three hundred...people. Any dancing dog or summerseting monkey would have drawn a larger house."

A terse, well-balanced summary in the 4/45 *Democratic Review* (16.413) mentioned the need for a just and independent criticism as his main topic, his deprecation of puffery and derogation of "popular idols," his recitations of Bryant, Willis, and Halleck, his disapproval of Dana as favored by the *NAR*. It advocated publication of the lecture, revised and augmented. Very likely this was by Evert A. Duyckinck (1816-78).

A small "report" objected to his remarks on New England poets in the Boston *Atlas* of 3/4, and the NY *Herald* condemned his censure of all and implied self-superiority as a poet (see Poe *Log* for 3/2/45).

John Louis O'Sullivan (1813-95), lawyer, journalist, diplomat, helped found and edit the *United States Magazine and Democratic Review* (1837-46). In his *Morning News* of 3/1/45 appeared a long "rave" review of the lecture.

35/70} See 42 [facsimile text] for his quoting in full "Florence Vane," recited at the lecture.

36/1} This represents a summation of Poe's views on American satirists and their role, which were presented at intervals through reviews: first, in a rev. of Wilmer's *Quacks of Helicon* in the 9/41 *Graham's* (H 10.182-95) and last in 1849. He uses the same refs. and ideas to introduce each one, in almost identical terms: the clumsy mock epic, *M'Fingal* (1782) of the Connecticut wit John Trumbull (1750-1831); the *Croaker Papers* (1819) by Fitz-Greene Halleck (1790-1867) with the aid of J.R. Drake; and *The Vision of Rubeta* by Laughton Osborn (1809-78), q.v. in MM 133, 215, and "Lit." sketch (H 15.44-9). The so-called sequel is *Arthur Carryl* (1841). Newly introduced is the sarcastic ref. to W.E. Channing (1818-1901), friend of Emerson, who was savagely derided in the 8/43 *Graham's* (H 11.174-90). The names and major ideas of the first three paras. of the present essay are reshaped or adapted for the start of Poe's rev. of Lowell's *Fable for Critics* in the 3/49 *SLM* (H 13.165-7).

36/15} The friend is most likely Willis at the *Evening Mirror*, who knew England and its aristocracy well.

36/34} A buried ref. to the panorama from Aetna (TOM 1278/4) and also a legend about Empedocles (see Pollin, Pin 151, and *PS*, 1978, 11.21-6).

36/45} See *Letters*, p. 197 for his noted scorn of this quality.

36/49} Pub. by the Association, 1844, 31p.

37/5} Poe often cites the satire *Hudibras* of Samuel Butler (1612-80), as in *Br.* (8 loci, q.v. in Index) and *Tales* (q.v. in Index, 1417). He may have used the notes to the 1744 ed. of Grey (Pin 94).

37/6} For Laughton Osborn and his works in relation to Poe's views see M 133 (plus Index entries); also, on this passage, see Poe to Osborn, 8/15/45 (*Letters*, 293-5 and Supple. 4 of *AL*, 1974, 45.527-8).

37/14} Park Benjamin (1809-64), abandoned law for journalism in 1834, worked as editor for the *New England Magazine*, Greeley's *New Yorker*, the *New World*, and the NY *Evening Signal*, and wrote much mag. verse. His criticism was noted for its acidity (*DAB*); q.v. in *PD*, p. 9.

37/15} Cf. *prononcés* in "Thingum Bob, Esq." (TOM, 1137).

37/25} Poe noted the misprint of "Petameter" himself.

37/29-45} Page 11/209-26.

38/13} *mutate nomine*: under a changed name.

38/20} Poe's penchant for the theatrical scene set-up, as here, is basic, says N.B. Fagin, *The Histrionic Mr. Poe* (Balt., 1949).

38/27} A personal hit here--Longfellow was a great dandy of his time (see Simms' ed. ref. in the *Patriot*, quoted by Poe, 38/45; also 38/51 below).

38/28} A Poe coinage from "Beau Brummel."

38/30} An allusion to the fable of the jay who dressed up in peacock feathers.

38/42} Could the "foreign count" be the Count D'Orsay, London's leading dandy (see preceding para.) and a chief figure in Willis' reports to the press from London (collected in *Inklings*)?

38/45} See 312/64-5 [facsimile text] for Simms' attack on Longfellow's dress.

38/48} "upper ten thousand": An expression for the cream of society, created by N.P. Willis, here used facetiously (see illustration, p. 15).

38/50} *bon ton*: good style, fashionable taste.

38/51} Longfellow was noted for his impeccable dress and propriety. See H. S. Gorman, *A Victorian American ... Longfellow* (1926), pp. 54, 77, 156, 163, 210.

38/53} Poe uses this as "whole cloth" or without basis, i.e., a lie.

39/1} Poe ascribed to Griswold's *PPA* the phrase "gentleman of elegant leisure" and often used it depreciatively (see M 158a).

39/39} Used in Poe's *Wakondah* (rev., H 11.25), derived from Hugo's *Notre Dame*, VI., vi, q.v. in *Discoveries in Poe*, ch. 1.

39/43} Proof conclusive? Poe was born in Boston.

40/3-13} A passage of inexcusable vulgarity, says Quinn, *EAP*, p. 455.

40/12-13} Lines from *A Drama of Exile* (1.98) cited on p. 11 are somewhat reminiscent of this.

40/20-48} See p. 30 above for this passage.

40/61} Note Poe's 38 compounds ending in "looking" (*PCW*, pp. 17-18).

40/69} Poe deplores the "rage for glitter" in "Phil. of Furniture" (TOM 499).

41/3} *nil admirari*: to be astonished at nothing (Horace, *Epodes*, 1.6.1).

41/12} For this alleged reply of Talleyrand see FS 28c.

41/21} Signor Antonio Blitz (1810-77), magician and ventriloquist. He came to America in 1834 and made his début at Niblo's Garden in 1835. Blitz later settled in Phila., leasing the Phila. Museum lecture room for his winter performances. One of his most popular acts was with trained canaries.

Prof. Rogers is either Henry Darwin (1808-66) or his brother William Barton (1804-82), who advanced in 1842 highly abstruse theories about the origin of mountains.

41/24} Pentateuch: the first five books of the Old Testament.

41/51} For Poe's other uses of Laplace's theory see CS 2n.

42/2} See 35 (b) for the lecture.

42/4} Poe knew this poem well, for it varies only in accidentals (save for "hope" in line 7). Poe praised the poem (which he, as ed. of *BGM* printed) in his "Autography" of Cooke (1816-50), poet, lawyer, and frequent correspondent with Poe (H 15.234). For their close lit. relations, see TOM, *Poems*, 211, 323, 480, 560, and *Letters* as indexed on 646. The theme here suits Poe's prescription in the "Philosophy of Composition" Poe intended to have Cooke (and Lowell) write a preface for his critical account, "Literary America" (see Quinn, 561).

42/5} From *Froissart Ballads and other poems*, Phila., Carey and Hart, 1847, pp. 171-73.

43/2} *Inaugural Address*, delivered Tuesday evening, Jan. 7, 1845, before the Mechanics Institute of the City of New York. Meetings were held at City Hall (the Institute is now located at 20 W. 44th St.). *Address* pub. 1845, 23p.

James J. Mapes (1806-66), agriculturist and chemist, applied scientific principles to farming, later developing successful chemical plant foods.

43/3} The reasons for assigning this to Poe are inferential: the lively style, different from that of Briggs (as Hull asserts) and Poe's interest both in the topic--the "arts of design" and the sponsoring agency. For the latter see the transcribed speech on "aerial navigation" (in this very issue of the *BJ*, pp. 169-70, not reprinted in the present text) with many side-linings in the Whitman copy, as though Poe is confirming scientific data already used in his "Balloon Hoax" of 1844.

43/23} Perhaps the passages on "Caryatides" here eventually led to Poe's use of them very integrally in "Hop-Frog" (1849; see TOM *Tales*, 1351, 1353).

43/31} Charles L. Barritt, actuary. Name signed after announcement of meeting dates. See no. 8 (2/22), 1.115-7 for his article, "Why Are Not the Sciences Better Understood?"

43/34} *George Cruikshank's Omnibus; a vehicle for frolic and fun*, 1845, 72p. See Poe's 1/42 comment on the artist (H 11.15). See M 291a and f for the lack of humor and melancholy in Hood.

43/40} Vol. XVI, no. LXXXI.

43/43} The editor was J.L. O'Sullivan (q.v. in 35/52 [facsimile text]). Poe always lauded this journal, which published the first two installments, and later, in 1846, nos. VI and VII of the "Marginalia" (see *Br.*, XV, XXIV).

43/44} *The Late Acting President*, pp. 211-4.

43/51} *The Presidents of Texas*, pp. 282-91, by C. Montgomery.

43/53} This is *The Devotional Family Bible*, ed. by Rev. Alexander Fletcher, containing the Old and New Testaments, published by R. Martin and Co. of NY, with notes, marginal refs. and a steel engraving in each part (priced at 25 cents). Briggs had reviewed part I in no. 8 of 2/22 (1.125), and in no. 15 (4/12), 1.226-7, he would rev. III, both revs. being much longer than this one. The terseness of this and the small space allotted it make it possible, if not likely, that Poe wrote the rev.; Hull thinks not.

43/58} *The Literature of Fiction*, pp. 268-82, by Auguste D'Avezac (1780-1851), New Orleans lawyer and diplomatic officer in Europe.

44/5} "[Park] Benjamin and his colleague James Aldrich left

it in March, 1844, being succeeded by Henry C. Deming and the Rev. James McKay, and later by Charles Eames. There is no doubt that it was much tamer in its last two years--more like the old *New-Yorker*--and it was merged in 1845 into the *Emporium.*"-- from Mott, *A History of American Magazines*, (1957), 1.361-2. See a letter of 2/14/49 from Poe (*Letters*, 428) proving Poe's personal acquaintance with Eames, who had written a flattering headnote for the 2/1/45 reprint of "The Haunted Palace" and for the 2/15 reprint of "Ligeia" (see Poe *Log* for those dates).

44/12} Perhaps in reciprocity, the *New World* soon published a kindly parody of "The Raven" in three stanzas about Poe as the bold warrior of the *BJ* defending truth, reprinted as "A Gentle Puff" in the 4/26 *BJ* (see p. 102, art. c).

44/18} Both editions published in 1845 by the same publisher, xii, (13)-396p. The promised rev. did not appear, but see M 161a-c, and the sketch of George Bush (1796-1859) in "Lit." of 5/46 (H 15.6-7).

44/19-35} It is likely that Briggs was largely responsible for writing this article, but with some help from Poe concerning his tale and the general issue of originality. Since Poe was also much concerned over the issue of woodcuts as illustrations for journals, this is included. For the issue of plates in the *BJ*, as promised in the "Prospectus" and embodied in vol. 1, see my Intro. to this vol. Illustrations can be found on these pages with those bearing traces of Gavarni's original design starred: 8*, 57, 89, 105, 136*, 153, 168, 200, 232*, 289; the vignettes are all typical of satirical Gavarni sketches (216, 232, 289). A few plates seem to be by a "Rodman" while many are marked with the name of Samuel E. Brown (of Boston) who seems chiefly to be responsible for the plates. Neither has any distinction or lasting reputation. Gavarni was the very well known name of Sulpice Guillaume Chevalier (1801-66), who early became renowned for his lithographed sketches of the fashions, types, characteristics, foibles and habits of Parisians of all ages and classes. First through *Les Gens du monde* and then *Charivari* his fame spread, and he was sought after for illustrations of books by Sue, Balzac, et al. It is perhaps his *L'Oeuvre Célèbre de Gavarni* (Paris, 184-) that this article designates in line 23 as the source of several of its sketches (see next para.). Its statement "in regard to the first one" is this: "We give an instance of the present taste, which every body will see has not been exaggerated, as the fashions usually are in the fashion plate, of ladies' magazines" (1.8, the article on "Fashion" and its gross distortions). The promise in line 33, to begin a series of "original drawings by artists of genius," was not kept and one suspects the same inept artist (Rodman) in the rest save the Gavarni print on 1.232 (82 [facsimile text]). While Poe mentions Gavarni no place else, we know his strong admiration of the French school of illustration, and partiality for such sketches (see his refs. to Grandville, e.g., *Letters*, 224, 232, 247; see also *Discoveries in Poe*, ch. on the "Stylus"). The plates clearly proved too costly to be continued by the impecunious editor of vol. 2--Poe himself.

Four of the drawings in the first part of the *BJ* are taken directly from *L'Oeuvre Celebre de Gavarni*, which has the subtitle of "479 original sketches," of which three are reproduced in my facsimile-volume. They are all included in sections, rather than on numbered pages, sometimes with different titles and details. I am listing them in the order of their appearance in my text: A, on 1 [facsimile text]) originally on 1.8 of 1/14-- for "The Bustle"-- Section 19, "Exposition des produits de l'Industrie" (with the placard in the window originally saying, in French, "petticoats and crinolines"); B, on 15 [facsimile text]) originally in 1.136 of 3/1, for "One of the Upper Ten Thousand"-- Section 3, entitled "Freshly decorated"; C, on 82 [facsimile text]) "A Presentation at a Literary Soirée," originally on 1.232 of 4/12-- section 30, with the title "Presenters and presented"; D) originally on 1.168 of 3/15, in a letter describing a typical "Speculator in Stocks" (not reproduced in my facsimile)-- from section 15. It may be assumed that other plates in the *BJ*, as suggested above, are taken from other Gavarni sources, by Briggs and Poe. As for "the Life of a Lion" (i.e., "Some Passages in the Life of A Lion"-- the new title in the *BJ*, 1.164-66, for "Lion-izing")-- Poe here refers to his 1839 *Tales of the Grotesque and Arabesque*, reprinting the tale from the 5/1835 *SLM*. It could scarcely be called "an originality." It would also be included in his forthcoming *Tales* (pp. 58-63) of 1845.

44/38} Clearly Poe was being attacked for republishing his old tales, even though "Lionizing" of *Tales of the Grotesque and Arabesque* was much revised for its appearance in this number (1.164-6).

44/41} The essay by Hertzman, "Thoughts of a Silent Man, No. 2" on pp. 163-64, is a laudation of T. Nichols' *Vestiges of Creation* for controverting modern skepticism; it ends with a sonnet to the author. This is one of five inspirational essays by Hertzman beginning on *BJ*, pages 151, 184, 212, 227. No major

American catalogues list any books by Hertzman.

45/4} For the letter of Outis, and its role in the "saga" see pp. 30-32 above.

45/6} Poe a little reluctantly complied with the popular American voice, acclaiming Wm. Cullen Bryant (1794-1878) as our greatest living poet. Two dozen reviews, articles, passages, etc. on Bryant show his admitted merit and importance (*PD* 14 for loci), although his 1/37 *SLM* rev. of his poems (H 9.268-305) offers reservations about his skill in versification, the range of his subjects, and his freshness of language. Yet he praises even the "beauty" of his "didactic conclusion" occasionally (H 9.300).

45/43-45} He quotes Outis, 31/3.

46/29-31} See line 2: "Over many a quaint and curious volume of forgotten lore" and Poe's stress on "the fantastic" aim in "Philosophy of Composition" (paras. 29-32; H 14.205-206).

46/61-62} See 126/31-35 for Poe's alteration in citation of the format of "Raven" lines.

46/70} Again, as in 31/55, 46/27, Poe substitutes "they" for "then."

47/24-32} See "Rationale of Verse," based on the 3/43 "Notes on English Verse" for Poe's views on meter and "equivalence" which Lowell mocked in "A Fable for Critics." See this also in MM 133, 147 with refs. to Gay Wilson Allen and J. A. Greenwood, but Poe's whimsy here is clear.

48/25-27} This seems a very good clue to the truth--that the three stanzas are really by Outis, that is, by Poe. He complains about not being shown them and suspects them to be "falsified, for...forcing a similarity." Surely, the "raven" and "dream-bird" coincidental similarities are otherwise too many!

48/55} For this private spelling of Arabic Aden or Adn or Eden (as in "Raven" line 93) see *PCW*, 83, which traces it to Bulwer's novel *Leila*.

48/62-63} Poe refers to M 104 concerning Amelia Welby's poem of "the class *passionate*."

49/35-36} This is close to the last sentence of "Philosophy of Composition" in the 4/46 *Graham's* and, embedded in this sequential analysis of his intentions and meaning for various lines, it reveals the genesis of his essay of the next year. At the very end "the intention of making him emblematical of *Mournful and Neverending Remembrance* is ... seen" (plus quoted lines).

49/41} See 31/91 (middle of note) for this as being in an early poem by Poe.

50/15-17} See the headnote to the *American Review* first printing, of 2/45, 1.143-45, "in which it is thought Poe had a hand" (*Poems*, 360-61), which states: "In regard to its measure, it may be noted that if all the verses were like the second, they might properly be placed merely in short lines...but the presence in all the others of one line--mostly the second in the verse...give (*sic*) the versification an entirely different effect." In confirmation, Willis praised its "masterly ingenuity of versification" and Brooks, ed. of the NY *Express* of 2/5, praised its "originality of versification"--an opinion quoted by the 3/45 *SLM* (q.v. in *Poems*, 361-62).

51/16} See this possibility refuted from the nature of the 3 stanzas provided in 31/91 note *ad in.* In line 13 above, "so long" should be "as long."

51/58-61} Poe is being disingenuous here, since he knew very well that Thomas Hood (1799-1845) was 11 years older than James Aldrich (1810-56) and had begun publishing at an early age; this poem, said to be on his sister's death, had appeared in the 8/31 *Englishman's Mag.* while Aldrich's first came out in the 5/29/41 *New World* of which he was associate ed. Poe's "Lit." sketches are full of just this sort of detail, which he sedulously researched and stored when suitable. See M 160 for his use of Aldrich as imitator. Significant is the fact that eight poems by J. Aldrich are included by Griswold in the *Poets and Poetry of America* (1843 ed., pp. 383-84), including this and the "Lines" of M 160, whereas Poe had only three (pp. 387-88)--a disproportion distasteful to the poet.

52/12-13} This must have been the germ of or a stage in the evolution of para. 18, epitomized in "The death, then, of a beautiful woman is, unquestionably, the most poetical topic in the world" (H 14.201).

52/43} See 32/67, 41/51.

54/2-10} Thomas Willis White (1788-1843) was a successful printer of Richmond who founded the *SLM* in 8/34 (not 1835) to give a cultural or literary voice to the South, as his Prospectus stated (see it reprinted in D.K. Jackson, *The Contributors ... to the SLM* [Charlottesville, 1936], v-vi. Poe became ed., contributing also revs. and creative works, late in 1835 to the beginning of 1837, when he left for NYC. For White see D. K. Jackson, *Poe and the SLM* (Richmond, 1934), 16-18; also, TOM, *Poems*, "Annals," 545-47. The clear error in dating needs explanation-- perhaps that Poe supplied Briggs with details of the whole article, patently known only to Poe--and left it to his write-up, as Hull suggests. However, the style is more that of Poe than of Briggs; I suspect a rewrite by Poe and an oversight concerning the date, for Poe had even reviewed the *SLM* for the Baltimore papers, late in 1834 (see Jackson, *Poe and the SLM*, pp. 5, 30). Likewise, the pro-Southern slant of the whole article and inordinate praise of the *SLM*'s influence betokens Poe rather than Briggs, friend of the abolitionist Lowell. See Poe *Log* for 3/28 for Briggs' epistolary defense of the *BJ* on the issue against the abolitionist attack by Robert Carter in his paper *The Liberator*. Yet Briggs was publishing, in 5 installments, from 2/15 to 3/29, on 106, 117, 137, 170, 202, the inept, tedious "fairy tale" derived from Irving's *Alhambra*, "Great Tower of Taradant" by "Robert Oliver."

54/13} James Ewell Heath (1792-1862), author of the novel *Edge-Hill* and an anonymous play, and the state auditor of Virginia (1819-49), served as unpaid ed. until 5/1835, when he handed the *SLM* post over to Edward V. Sparhawk (1798-1838). The latter, who had published poetry and been a NY newspaper reporter, issued three numbers before he and White apparently had a clash over editorial policies; this led to Poe's taking over, after White, on his own and with the help of friends, rather ineffectively edited the *SLM*.

54/19} "Secession" is not a very accurate word. It was a complex situation of mutual ill-will and dissension between Poe and T.W. White, partly caused by White's disapproval of Poe's dissipation (he was supposedly drinking heavily at times during the early period of his marriage in Richmond). See Quinn, pp. 258-60.

54/22} Benjamin Blake Minor (1818-1905), lawyer and

educator (L.L.B., William and Mary, 1839) who practiced mainly in Richmond, edited the *SLM* 1843-47. He served as president of the University of Missouri, 1860-62.

54/47} This and lines 13-15 above show the desire to promote Poe's name for gaining subscribers.

54/50} *The Columbian Lady's and Gentleman's Magazine, Embracing Literature in Every Department: Embellished with the Finest Steel and Mezzotint Engravings, Music and Colored Fashion,* vol. I.

54/52} "The Children of Mount Ida," pp. 145-54, prose with poetic introduction, by Lydia Maria (Francis) Child (1802-1880), author and abolitionist, q.v. in *PD*, p. 20.

54/53} "A Flight of Fancy," p. 185, poem. "Our Engravings" (John Inman and Robt. West, eds.): "The Infant St. John and the Lamb"--Johnson Sc. The title of the second plate was not reproduced, but there is a short description of both at the end of the magazine "Franklin--the Man in the Boy"--(name of artist not given), tells the story of Franklin giving up a loaf of bread to feed a woman and her children.
This issue also contained a piece by C. Donald MacLeod (see 18/13 and 54/55), "Myrrha of Ephesus," p. 167, a prose tale, with poems, of Christian conversion in classical times.

54/55} *The Columbian* was important to Poe for a number of reasons. Mrs. Osgood, an important figure in Poe's life (q.v. M 209; Quinn, *EAP*; TOM, "Annals" in *Poems*.), also had poems placed in the 1/45 and 3/45 issues. Poe overestimated MacLeod's renown (q.v. 18/13) owing to his works' appearances in the mag. Volume II (1/44-12/44) contained three tales by him: "Lucia Norea: A Tale of the Days of Sallust," p. 80, with 2 poems; "The Prisoners of Chios, A Legend of the Greek Isles," p. 154; "Truce unto Death: A Romance of Athens," p. 245.
Volume II is also noteworthy for its relation to Poe's tales. It contained the first appearances of "Mesmeric Revelation" (8/44), "Angel of the Odd" (10/44), and "Byron and Miss Chaworth" (12/44). The 8/44 issue also contained J.T. Headley's "A Sketch. A Man Building a Wall," the source of Poe's "The Cask of Amontillado."
"The Domain of Arnheim" found its first publication in *The Columbian* 3/47 issue.

55/1} See p. 80(c) [facsimile text] for the follow-up, and M 184 for Poe's adaptation of the last paragraph on p. 56. The type size of para. 3 is misleading, for everything that follows is by "a correspondent of valued opinions" until the last para. (q.v.).

56/7} David Dudley Field (1805-94), a lawyer long active in politics as an Anti-Slavery Democrat. He was instrumental in reforming penal, political and civil procedural codes in New York. Many of his codes were adopted elsewhere in the USA and abroad (*DAB*).

56/58-77) Poe's misspelling of Appalachia corresponds to that of the pamphlet of the NYHS committee (for the report, see 80/30).

56/71} Poe elsewhere is not concerned to do justice to the American Indian as "despoiled" and "killed," as we see in his treatment of the Missouri Basin savages in "Julius Rodman" (see chapters 3-5 and notes thereto, on pp. 621-32, and his frequent derisive use of "Kickapoo"--loci on p. 191 of *Word Index*). On the other hand, Dirk Peters, a half-caste, is a demi-hero in *Pym*.

56/75} See M 184b for Irving's role in the naming movement, and the note to 80/30 [facsimile text] for a quotation in the committee's report.

57/1} Rebecca Shepard (Reed) Nichols (1819-1903); the stanzas appear in a poem called "Lament of the Old Year" in her collection *Songs of the Heart and the Hearth-Stone*, Thomas, Cowperthwait and Co., Phila., 1851, pp. 271-5.

57/36} dactyllic: see his correction, 69/23 [facsimile text].

57/50} Coverlid is an accepted variation of coverlet (cf. 35/7: counterpane).

57/60} See 35/1 [facsimile text] for Poe's rather adversarial comments on this weekly, of which no extensive file exists available to me. This helps to prove the fragility of the "mammoth" papers, poor in fiber quality and bound to shred from the numerous foldings required for storage. See p. 244 for Poe's report of a less unfavorable comment on him in the *Emporium*. In M 35 Poe similarly jokes about the long ears of a fabled cat.

57/63} For "P. P. C. of Va." see Philip Pendleton Cooke, in 42/4 n.

57/66} This appeal came early in the Poe-Osgood relationship, for "Ellen" was an occasional pseudonym of Frances Osgood, used for "To the Evening Star," a poem in the March issue of the *Columbian Magazine* (i.e., the *C. M.* here). The apparent response was quick, for in the 4/5 *BJ* appeared "The Rivulet's Dream" (1.215) by "Kate Carol," in the 5/12 *BJ* (231) "Love's Reply" (by Osgood) plus "Spring" by "Violet Vane," and in the 5/31 *BJ* (347) "Lenore" by "Clarice" reprinted in Poe's review in 12/13 *BJ* (2.354)-- all the authors being F. Osgood under pseudonyms.

58/3-7} This comes from the last para. of Outis on p. 32.

58/12} The meaning of "Outis" in Greek is, of course, Nobody.

58/16-23} The fault of Outis in the poorly placed modifying phrase, giving Poe a chance for humorous attack, is a slight reason for ascribing it to another writer, save that Poe, in the haste and stress of the whole campaign, the "Longfellow War," may have produced sentences that he could justly emend later, such as 51/13 [facsimile text] above. Whether inserted carelessly or even deliberately as part of the whole joke, his criticism of his own style, as here (and as he did in "The Reviewer Reviewed"), makes the hoax even more convincing.

58/36} Poe's coinage (*OED*).

58/44} The phrase, meaning "hither and thither," coming from old tennis court usage for the banging of balls, was originally in this style, not the modern "from pillar to post."

58/52} Wm. Gifford (1756-1826), prominent Anti-Jacobin critic and ed. of the *Quarterly Rev.*

58/55} For John Wilson (Christopher North, q.v. at 9/19 [facsimile text]), see SM 1 and 7. For Thomas Babington Macaulay (1800-59), historian, see *Br.* Index.

59/7} Cf. 54/17.

59/9} The 12/41 issue said "from 5,500 to 25,000 subscribers" and by 5/42, to 40,000 according to Poe and Sartain (Quinn, pp. 330, 342).

59/34} Poe is correct about the "ten years," which began with the 1835 *SLM*. See his published defense against the charge of "slashing and cutting" in the letter to the Richmond *Compiler* editor of 1836 (*Letters*, 100-2, and the note thereon).

59/60-69 & 60/1-21} See pp. 31-2, above, for this passage with the notes. The cited lines comprise 43-45.

60/6-7} "The Haunted Palace" (lines 26-29) reads: "Through which came flowing, flowing, flowing / And sparkling evermore, / A troop of Echoes..." (p. 316).

60/27} For 4 more loci of this Poe coinage see *PCW*, p. 37.

60/32-34} See M 147, especially note g, for Poe on age-old love of rhyme.

60/57-80} Much of the following, even in wording, comes from Poe's rev. of Longfellow's *Voices of the Night* in the 2/40 *Burton's* (H 10.71-80, specifically, 76-80). See especially the last para. transferred to 61/67-82 (q.v.).

60/59-60} In the *BJ* of 4/26/45, renamed "To F_____" (lines 8-10).

60/78} *Poems*, Henry Wadsworth Longfellow, with illustrations by D. Huntington (Carey and Hart, Phila., 1845), is used for collations on pp. 60-61 [facsimile text], but no accidentals are recorded.

61/11} Christie Eleyson / Christe, eleyson!; also 61/15, low / slow; also one / twelve.

61/67-82} Poe transcribed from his 2/1840 rev. of *Voices*, in order to support his current charge of Longfellow's "imitation" (called "plagiarism" in 1840), the two poems by Longfellow and Tennyson and the final paragraph (shorn of its last sentence) with very few substantive changes (H 10.76-80).

61/68} See Mrs. R.S. Nichols, "Lament of the Old Year" (cf. 57/1) and Miss E.J. Bayard's "Funeral Chant for the Old Year" (Griswold, *Female Poets of Am.*, p. 357).

61/82} See two poems on the same topic in the 2/45 *Graham's*: "Dirge for the Old Year" by Wm. Hosmer (p. 74) and "A Requiem for the Old Year" by T.B. Read (p. 56).

61/85} *Lear*, 5.3. See the same point made in a long review (probably largely by Poe) in the 4/45 *Aristidean*, reprinted in *American Library*, p. 768.

62/31} Poe learned of this from Lawrence Labree's NY mag. *The Rover*, 2/8/45, p. 336, which derived its data from the Buffalo *Western Lit. Messenger* of 1/25/45, p. 336. Longfellow sent an explanation of the affair, 2/19/45 (obviously after *The Rover*'s charge but before Poe's), to Graham, whose magazine published the letter on 5/45. It is given in H 17.382-5, without the German text of Wolff. Longfellow denies having read Motherwell's 1827 poem before seeing the German, and explains that the translation was part of Karl Gollmick's *Der Sangersall*, offered as original compositions in 1842 (see Moss, *Poe's Lit. Battles*, 162-64, for fuller explanation). Properly it is Gollmick, and Mary Phillips, 975-77, erroneously gives it as Gollmich.

62/58} "Toom": empty.

62/60} Pp. 80-3, Act 2, Cambridge 6th ed. (1844). See Poe's long rev. of this in "The American Drama," *American Whig Review*, 8/45 (H 13.54-73), in which he charges plagiarism from Cervantes, not himself, as here.

62/86-8} Properly, *Halle der Völker: Sammlung vorzüglicher... grösstentheils zum erstenmale metrisch... übertragen*, meaning, *Hall of the people: a collection of excellent folksongs of the major nations, most of them translated for the first time into metrical German.*

64/31} A pious vow? / A vow--a vow?

64/49} This spelling is given only for an 1867 entry, among many others in the *OED*.

64/60-70} Collated with Bryant's *Poems* (NY, 1843), p. 33: no substantive changes seen.

64/72} To / For (on p. 106)

64/82-86} Used also in M 138.

65/5} Sharpe was the publisher, Henry Kett was the editor, of this, the 2nd edition.

65/27-28} From *Politian* by Poe (*Poems*, 272/11).

65/38} See *American Library*, 502 (757.32) and Moss, *Poe's Lit. Battles*, 176, 193-95, for the "epigrams" of Cornelia Wells Walter, ed. of the Boston *Transcript*.

65/41} Longfellow's aloof stance relating to the literary battles of the day makes it seem unlikely that he instigated anyone to do any thing. There is no evidence that he knew Cornelia Walter, although it is likely that, being a hack, she fulfilled her position by seeking some sort of introduction and making even occasional distant contact with the celebrity.

65/42} Poe gives a finely discriminating evaluation of Anna Cora Ogden Mowatt (1819-70), later Mrs. Wm. F. Ritchie, as magazine poet, playwright (*Fashion*), pamphlet novelist (*Evelyn* and *The Fortune Hunter*), and elocutionary reader and actress (as of 1845), in a long "Lit." sketch (H 15.27-32), embodying material from these two *Fashion* revs. and that on 177-78. She continued writing romantic narratives, theatrical accounts and an autobiography, etc. after 1846, when she withdrew to live in Europe in 1861. For the published play see 76/6 [facsimile text].

66/42} *haut ton*: high social standing.

66/69} *Macbeth*: 3.4.109.

67/2} An allowed variant of accessory.

67/22} *Hamlet*, 5.1.261.

67/47} A cant name for a Frenchman (Brewer).

67/57} hackneyism: a Poe coinage.

67/61} For Poe's use of Sheridan, see Pin 50, M 112, FS 32 and H 9.178, 12.117, 125.

67/67-8} The lounge for the actors once normally provided by theaters.

68/24} inartisticalities: Poe's coinage.

68/35} Cf. *EM*, 1/9/45, *WM*, 1/18/45, "Does the Drama of the Day Deserve Support?" adapted to MM 131, 171, q.v. for discussions.

68/47} Poe's views on the Am. stage plays of the period are discussed by N.B. Fagin, *The Histrionic Mr. Poe*, 107-24, and by Robert Jacobs, 382-87. Poe derived the idea of intrigue in Spanish drama from A.W. Schlegel, q.v. above and M 186d. Odell remarks on this rev. and that of 4/5 of *Fashion*, finding this one far less perceptive and pointed than the second (5.100).

68/59} London, 1841. Dion[ysius] Boucicault (1820-90), skilled adapter of plays from novels (originally Bourcicault).

68/64} In a letter from the Griswold MSS., the photostat of which is in the U. Va. Library, it is found that Mrs. Mowatt wrote to Poe on a Thursday evening:
"(I regret that) I have not a more legible manuscript of the Comedy to submit to your perusal--...your criticism will be prized--I am sorry that they could not have been made before preparations for the performance of the Comedy had progressed so far."
At the end of the review Poe acknowledges that the criticism was based on the MS. After he saw the play several times, Poe wrote another review, in a more sympathetic vein (p. 76). Fagin notes (107) his claim to seeing it 10 times.

68/79-81} Poe comments on several actors in the 2nd rev., p. 78.

68/95} Note that many auditors of Poe's poetic readings complained of his sing-song delivery (e.g., Margaret Fuller in the *Tribune*, 3/1/45).

69/22} See 57/36, also her stanzas in *BJ* 1.248.

69/25} Pseudonym of Frances Osgood, q.v. in Index. See p. 75 [facsimile text] for her poem and p. 205 for Poe's four line response, "Impromptu," discussed in TOM, *Poems*, 379-80. See *BJ*, 1.231 for her "Love's Reply." (However, according to J.G. Varner, "Note on a Poem Attributed to Poe," *Am. Lit.*, 1936, 8.66-8, Kate Carol, that is, Mrs. Osgood herself, was author of these lines. The confusion arose, he claims, from the couple's habit of addressing poems to one another in the *BJ*.) See also Poe *Log*, entry for 3/1/45 for Mrs. Osgood's account of Poe's effort to invite her interest and judgment during March.

69/27} "Violet Vane" is another of Osgood's pseudonyms, used for her "So Let It Be" in the 4/5 *BJ*, 1.217, to which Poe replied in "To____" on 5/24 (*BJ* 1.325); see TOM, *Poems*, 381-2. Cf. "Violet Vane's" poem "Spring" in *BJ* 1.231.

69/30} This issue contains two long Briggs revs., a "Longfellow War" installment, much on the drama, music, and art, but no short revs. See below and 78-79 [facsimile text] for Poe's promised revs. of 4/5.

69/31} M 180 is derived largely from this article, q.v. for collations with the book of Wm. Newnham, and for full notes on Newnham (1780-1865). For Poe's changing views on hypnotism, or mesmerism, see M 180a-b.

70/26} For Townshend (1798-1868), English priest and friend of Dickens, see M 180d.

70/31} See M 180a.

70/40} Poe dropped, from M 180, this ref. to Harriet Martineau (1806-76), celebrated miscellaneous writer of philosophical bent and friend of many literary celebrities, who visited America, 1834-6, and wrote on it. She became ill after a trip to Venice from which she recovered, so she claimed, through mesmerism (1844). Newnham gives her own account in App. A and alludes to her on p. 138.

70/47} Poe cites an American reprint of this prominent British journal on 71/5 [facsimile text].

70/50} 400 p. + lvi.

70/57-8} This is verbatim from p. vi.

70/61} Publishers of Poe's poems and tales in 1845.

70/64} Vol. 57, no. 358, 369-400.

71/4} Poe is surprisingly mild toward John Wilson

("Christopher North") here, q.v. in *Br.* (SM 1, 7) and *PD*, p. 99 (7 loci). See *BJ* 2.406 for English's squib on Kit North.

71/9} Burgess and Stringer.

71/10} Poe uses this for 70/45 [facsimile text].

71/20} Pub. 1845, no preface, 252 p.

71/22} For John Henry Mancur (1774-1850) see M 129.

71/23} For the prolific historical novelist George Payne Rainesford James (1801-60), see FS 6, SM 5a, the second of which points at Poe's 10/36 rev. of James' *Lives* (including that of Mazarin).

71/27} Both names are mentioned in the introductory first chapter. The setting is Paris, 1650.

71/30} Thomas Low Nichols (1815-1901), journalist, hydrotherapist, pioneer dietician.

71/34} 32 p., double column.

71/35-38} David Lee Child (1794-1874), lawyer, journalist, anti-slave reformer.
Naboth's Vineyard: The possession of another coveted by one who will use any means to acquire it (*Kings*, I.21). Child's name was associated with Texas through one of his previous books, *The Texas Revolution*, Washington, D.C., 1843.

71/40} Pub. 1845, 125 p., double column.

71/44} H. Didimus: pseud. of Edward Henry Durell (1810-87), a linguist and jurist who practiced in New Orleans. As a federal judge, he was active on behalf of the Republican party in Louisiana (*DAB*).

72/9} Pub. 1846 (1845), 446 p.

72/12} Poe knew Frost, editor and high school teacher in Phila., and speaks well of him in the "Autography" of 12/41 (H 15.242-3). Cf. *Letters*, pp. 125, 148; TOM, 921, for his tale as a source of Poe's "Oblong Box."

73/6} Lane, publisher, 1842, (v)-viii, 9-344 p.
Thomas H. Lane was to become co-pub. of the *BJ* with the departure of Bisco.

73/10} Pub. 1845, x, 7-121 p. These elementary texts in many sciences have virtually disappeared from all libraries.

73/12} This appears on the cover.

73/13} "from the text of Milne Edwards and Achille Comte" (*sic*; quoted from the title page).

73/15} Pub. 1845, vi, 8-143 p.

73/18} Poe claimed that the increasing "namby-pambyism" of *Graham's* spurred his departure (see Pollin, *AL*, 40.164-78).

73/20} Sarah Josepha Hale (1788-1879), author, editor. Edited the *Ladies' Magazine* in Boston from 1827. When Godey bought it in 1837, she became literary editor of his *Lady's Book*. She was a leader in the movement for women's education, and an arbiter of American female tastes, however, she is best known as the author of *Mary's Lamb* (1830). She figures largely in the works of Poe (H 8.117-8; *BJ* of 11/1), who always tactfully praised the editor of *Godey's*.

73/26} Pub. 1845, xxii, 394 p.

73/27} Poe usually notes format details of books under review but rarely so exclusively.

74/2} Poe's coinage (from French and English forms) often used through the *Eureka* period (see *PCW*, p. 37).

74/22} The interrupting comma must be purely rhetorical.

74/30} Perhaps from *John*, 3.3: "I say unto thee, Except a man be born again, he cannot see the kingdom of God."

74/39} Poe's rather casuistical exoneration of true poets who unconsciously plagiarize is belied by most of his charges against the "arrant" borrowings of Longfellow and Aldrich earlier. In the *BJ* of 9/20 (pp. 252-53) is Poe's editorial against Whittier for "pick-pocketism" from Bulwer, implicitly conscious. The heart of his attack became SM 11; see Index for numerous other attacks against plagiarists in the *Br.* for wilful theft. Poe's campaign against Longfellow continued throughout his life and greatly harmed his reputation (see Moss, *Poe's Lit. Battles*, ch. 5, and Pollin, *Mi Q*, 1984, 475-82). There were many good reasons for dropping the "War" at this point: the increasing distress of Briggs, who had reluctantly agreed to the series for publicity value, Lowell's objections to the treatment of Longfellow, sent in letters to Briggs (see Woodberry, 2.125-31), the exhaustion of the topic itself, plus admonitions even from such friends as Duyckinck that he was exaggerating and overdoing the basically sound cautions about imitating (see the *Democratic Review*, "Plagiarism," 4/45, 16.413-15).

75/1-9} Surely the *BJ* ed. who wrote this headnote is Poe alone, using a sentimental suggestiveness of phrasing that is derived from the Della Cruscan verses of Robert Merry and his followers. This is one of several exchanges between Poe and Frances Osgood ("Kate Carol"), succinctly discussed in TOM, *Poems*, 556-58 (for other *BJ* items see 78, 105, 118, 209, 328-32 et al., in Index).

It is likely that Kate Carol deliberately borrowed ideas and even words from poems of Poe, such as "Evening Star," (*Poems*, 74-75), "A Dream" 79-80, "To the River" 134-35, "Fairy Land" 161-62 and especially "Israfel" 173-75. The poem's title and subtitle obviously show Poe's personal knowledge of its source; in Mrs. Osgood's *Poems* (1850) it was collected (pp. 449-50) solely under its first line as title. We wonder what was the alternate last line that Kate Carol vouchsafed to Poe, who was playing the starry "Israfel" to her lowly "rill." We must note TOM's conviction of the affair's Platonic nature after his considerable study of it, despite this exchange and many flirtatious meetings, 1845-47, approved by Virginia.

75/38} Note Frances Osgood's popular book, *A Wreath of Wild Flowers from New England* (1839), first pub. in London, and reviewed by Poe (H 13.105-25, and mentioned in 13.186-7, 15.96-100). Poe loved to dwell on Fanny's "grace," charm, and affinity to "dance"--all of which play a role in this poem as in many others (st. 3-4).

76/4} For Poe's *BJ* rev. of that opening night, see 65 ff.

76/6} *Fashion* was the most important imaginative work of Anna Cora Ogden Mowatt Ritchie (q.v. in 65-69 [facsimile text]), who wrote it following an aborted career as a public reader of poetry (1841-42), when she had turned to journalism. Subtitled *Life in New York*, it was a farce ridiculing the *nouveaux riches* of the period. The play was published in 1850.

"*Fashion* was published in London in 1850, and was reprinted, with *Armand*, in Boston, in 1855. The present edition is based upon a collation of these two texts, which differ very slightly. The play was revived at the Provincetown Theatre, New York, Feb. 3, 1924, and after moving successively to the Greenwich Village and Cort Theatres, ran for 235 consecutive performances, until August 30." From *Representative American Plays*, A.H. Quinn (1938, 5th ed. of 1917 ed.), p. 280.

76/11} See 65-69 above.

77/6} In Sheridan's *Rivals*.

77/9} See 67/67.

77/21} At the end of Act 5, p. 311.

77/37} Sir Philip Sidney, *Astrophel and Stella*, Sonnet 1: "Look, then, into thine heart and write." See *PD* for other Sidney refs.

77/40-78/20} Poe's ideas on drama having been aired in the *EM*, are here (and on p. 68) further developed and will be repeated in MM 131, 171, 186; q.v. for details and other texts.

77/45} Poe's coinage.

77/66} See 19-20 [facsimile text] above and M 177.

78/9} Goldsmith's *Vicar of Wakefield* (1766), ch. 9: "They would talk of nothing but ... Shakespeare and the musical glasses."
For Poe's views on Shakespeare see N.B. Fagin and Pollin, *SAR 1985*, a comprehensive survey.

78/25} See M 186.

78/27} 1 *Cor.*, 15.28: "That God may be all in all."

78/40-53} The cast is the same as on p. 68.

78/57} Although unsigned by Poe, this long series of Poe's

revs. is full of the names of his friends, with characteristic Poe commendations (see especially Osgood, R. Morris and G.P. Morris, and S.J. Hale).

78/59} For Mrs. Osgood, see note, 75/5 and 78/62. Her poem "The Fan" is on p. 166 of this issue.

Lydia Howard Hunt Sigourney (1791-1865), poet and essayist. Although conventional and imitative, she was held in high regard in her own day. The primary theme of her 67 books is death (*DAB*). Her poem "Sudden Death" is on p. 167.

Emma Catherine Embury (1806-63), author, conducted a literary *salon*. Her work was characterized by vagueness and conventionality. Poe knew her from *Graham's* as an assistant ed. (see Pollin, *AL*, 1968, 40.164-78). Her "True Love a Hundred Years Ago" is on p. 171.

Seba Smith (1792-1868), journalist, political satirist. His wife, Elizabeth Oakes Prince Smith (1806-93), a novelist, Lyceum lecturer and women's rights reformer, was known through her contributions to the popular periodicals (*DAB*). See loci in *PD*, 86. Her "The Rustic" is on p. 156.

78/60} "Fanny Forrester": pseud. of Emily Judson (1817-54), wife of Baptist minister Adoniram Judson. Wrote several popular moralistic works. Her "Nickie Ben" is on p. 151.

Francis Joseph Gründ (1798-1863), Austrian journalist, traveller, politician, acquaintance of Poe (cf. Quinn, 399). His "Monologues Among the Mountains by 'A Cosmopolite'" is on p. 168.

"Wm. Landor": pseud. of Horace Binney Wallace (1817-52), brilliant lawyer and misc. writer from whom Poe borrowed greatly (see Index of *Br*. and refs. in M 10b). His piece, "The Masquerade," is on p. 176.

Robert Morris was highly praised as a poet in "Autography" (H 15.211) and also by R.W. Griswold (Boston *Notion*, 8/7/41). Cf. 270c.

78/62} Hull notes Poe's use of "grace" in every rev. concerning Mrs. Osgood, specifically "Literati," *Godey's*, 9/46, and "Marginalia," *SLM*, 4/49. See M 209 for more on Mrs. O's "grace."

78/64} "The Toilers," p. 156, note before poem: 'I saw a widow who was yet young--perhaps forty--but whose form, once fresh and healthful had become exactly the reverse. It was now nothing but skin, sinew, bones and no flesh. She had three sons at work in the mills, and although they toiled incessantly, they could scarce earn enough to keep the fiends of famine from the door.'--English Factory Report

"Again--the bell rings out / Upon the morning breeze-- / And see the toilers rushing forth / Like startled human bees-- / Like startled human bees, alas! / The honey of the hive / Is often rung from youthful hearts / That wither as they strive." (Excerpt from middle.)

79/4} See *Letters*, 179, referring to "contemptible pictures, fashion-plates, music and love tales" in *Graham's*.

79/7-50} For Poe's regard for Morris, co-ed. of the *Mirror*, as a song-writer, see M 202 and note k; also Pollin, *Prairie Schooner*, 1973, 46.223-35.

79/8} On pp. 145-50.

79/28-44} On p. 149.

79/45} On p. 148.

79/46} "Woodman" not copied, mentioned p. 147.

79/47} The actual title is simply "Near the Lake," p. 149.

79/52} Engraved by Welch and Walters, artist's name looks like "Bagg" or "Hagg."

79/61} Drawn by Smillie from a sketch by T. Addison Richards.

79/66} Louis Antoine Godey (1804-78), founded it in 1830, and Sara Josepha Hale (q.v.) was editor 1837-77. In 1898 it was absorbed by another magazine. Its appeal to wealthy ladies was through fashion, sentimentality, moralism, and illustrations.

79/72-76} Leslie--p. 149; Hale--p. 163; Embury--p. 164; Anna Mowatt--"Helen Berkley; or, the Mercenary Marriage"--p. 170.

80/1-7} A. Mowatt--p. 184; S. Smith--p. 145; Gould--p. 181.

80/6} See 78/60 for Francis Gründ.

80/10} The artist was H. Corbould, the engraver, A.L. Dick.

80/17-21} There seems to be no trace of this publication.

80/22} See Mott, *American Literary Periodicals*, 672, for an earlier (but still published) *Ladies' Garland, Devoted to Lit.* etc. (1837-47 and 48-49 under a new name).

80/25} The first may have been the last, for no data on this is available.

80/26} See 55-56 [facsimile text] for the start.

80/27} See 56/7 for Field.

80/28} For Hoffman (1806-84), varied author and ed., see M 202k. For Schoolcraft (1793-1864), eminent ethnologist, especially of Indian lore, see "Rodman" 1.18A. His article on Indian names is in *BJ* of 3/1, 1.138.

80/30} "National Nomenclature"--Report of the Committee of the New-York Historical Society, 3/31/45, 8 p., offered by a resolution of 3/4/45 on the subject.
Pp. 4-5: "We'll quote a letter of *W. Irving* of some years ago, 'We want a national name. We want it politically and poetically.'" (This followed by 3 full paras.)
P. 6: "Duly proposed: Apalachia or Alleghania."
P. 8: "Favored name: Allegania [*sic*]"
signed: "David Dudley Field, Henry R. Schoolcraft, Charles Fenno Hoffman, NY 3/31/45"

80/37} The joke? James Harper (1795-1865), reform mayor of 1844, was head of the firm J. & J. Harper, John being one of four brothers. Poe felt little gratitude to the firm after the 1838 *Pym* was issued.

80/40} For Porter see 19/50 [facsimile text] and M 221.

80/44} Joel Tanner Hart (1810-77), self-taught portrait sculptor.

80/48} Shobal Vail Clevenger (1812-43), self-taught Ohio sculptor, who took Hart as his inspiration. The word "ideal" means imaginative, as here.

81/1} After leaving the *SLM* in 1836, there appeared no revs. from Poe until 5/45. In that issue, there appeared a rev. of

the *Dictionary of ... Antiquities* which incorporated the following notice in the *BJ*:
"The *SLM* rev. contains two introductory paras. of background material (characteristic of Poe in revs. of this sort) not found below. Hull notes occasional verbal parallelism, and believes that the changes wrought in the *SLM* serve to improve the piece."
Elements of the two revs. appear in the Anthon articles of "Autography," *Graham's*, 11/41 (H 15.179-82), and "Literati," *Godey's*, 6/46 (H 15.34-6).

81/6} Pub. 1845, lx + 1124 p. (NY). Sir Wm. Smith (London), 1842, 1st ed.

81/8} John Potter (1674?-1747), Regius Prof. at Oxford, ed. of classic texts, pub. *Archeologica Graeca* (1647-98).
Alexander Adam (proper spelling, 1741-1809), teacher and writer on classics and for schools. The sentence is adapted from line 8 of Anthon's preface.

81/11} There are 11 headings.

81/18} Charles Anthon (1797-1867), most influential classical Am. scholar of the century. See MM 115, 168, 175.

81/20} E.g., botany, minerology, and zoology.

81/22} See Preface, p. v.

81/30} For revs. of Anthon's other classical texts see 23, 110, etc. (in Index), and *PD*, 4. Poe relied much on Anthon's translation of a Hebrew passage (MM 115, 175) and was helped on the *NY Rev*. The hue and cry over Anthon's "adaptations" of classical, edited texts and compendia enters the Anthon discussions of Poe, often facing the same issue.

81/41} Is Poe facetious in the notion of such an application of the term?

82/4} This second ed. of the 1845 "reader" had the distinction of including "The Raven" before its appearance in Poe's book, as TOM noted in *Notes & Queries*, 1943, 185,225; *Bulletin of the New York Public Library*, 1943, 47.581-84; *Poems*, 556. George Vandenhoff (1813-85) was a transplanted English actor, lawyer and public reader (see p. 90 for his acting). For details of his life to 1839, when he came to America, see *BGM*, 2/40, 6.59-62, an article by Burton, during Poe's editorship. His *System* was well advertised in the *BJ*, 1.240, 256, 272, 398, 415; 2.16, 32, 48. In the collective rev. in the 9/15 *Aristidean*, 240, Poe again revs. the book and says "Mr. Poe's 'Raven' is shamefully mangled" through typographical "blunders."

82/13} This demonstrates Poe's deep interest in good voice projection and fine reading of poetry, often shown in his own lectures and private readings (see TOM *Poems*, 559), although there were many dissidents about his "sing-song" style. Note the objective of recitation as the inspiration of "Ulalume" (*Poems*, 409-10), under the stimulus of Prof. Bronson.

82/18} This was a pamphlet (Phila.: Lyceum Press, 1843; not extant) of John Tomlin (1806-50). See discussion of Elizabeth C. Phillips, U. of Kentucky. Poe exchanged several letters with Tomlin (see *Letters*, Index); see Tomlin's close imitation of "To One in Paradise," in his "To Helen" in the 12/43 *SLM*, and, was involved in a case of ill-will at Jackson, Tenn., 1840-47, and figured in *Holden's Dollar Magazine*, 1848, 2.644. See "Autography" (H 15.231) for Poe's sketch. N.B.: Tomlin is listed in the advertisements of *BJ* 10/11-1/3/46 (2.218-412) as local agent for the magazine.

   In the 6/21 *BJ*, on 1.398, is printed Poe's note, which includes acknowledgment to "J.T." and also to Chivers ("T.H.C."), as follows:

   TO CORRESPONDENTS.-- We are greatly indebted to the author of the Correspondence between a Mother and Governess-- also to A.M.J.-- to J.T. of Jackson-- to T.H.C.-- and to F.W.C. of Boston. We are forced to decline "The Heart Unshared." We are anxious to hear from Ellen of N., in D.

82/33} For Poe's adulation of Shelley, see M 213 and especially note c; also p. 14 [facsimile text].

83/2} Gerardus Johannes Mulder (1802-80).

83/6} James Finley Weir Johnson.

83/7} Benjamin Silliman (1779-1864), prominent chemist, geologist, naturalist, at Yale, founded and directed the foremost *Am. Journal of Science and Arts*, mentioned in "Von Kempelen" (see TOM, 1355; Pollin, *Discoveries in Poe*, 186). The London ed. had 184 p.

83/15} For Anthon see 81/18.

83/17} Pub. 1844, xii + 536 p.; the same for the 1845 ed.

83/19} Raphael Kühner (1802-78), pub. many eds. of Greek grammar. "Compend" is an accepted variant of "compendium."

83/29} See p. 101 for notes and a variant review, and 111 for a long quotation.

83/34} Pub. 1845, [7]-566 p. Poe is wrong about the pages here, on p. 101, and in the *SLM* rev.

83/35} This notice and the one on page 101 (April 19) correspond to a rev. in the *SLM*, 5/45 (362-28). Hull suggests that, pressed for time, Poe met the May deadline by combining the *BJ* notices into a two and one-half column rev. for the *Messenger*. Tone, matter, and attitude show no discordance.

83/42} Poe's usual wording (sans "of"). For this phrase, probably derived from *Stanley*, see M 160c.

83/52} This far-sighted essay of enlightened views, although derivative in its data, was first reprinted by Harrison (14.153-9) and, as a separate edition (badly printed "limited" ed., 150 copies) by the Silver Quoin Press, Chicago, 1946, 5 p. (said to be "completed" Jan. 1947). Its brief Intro. asserts: "It is, perhaps, a little unkind to revive an article such as this; for the author might now be somewhat embarrassed by his enthusiasm and his optimistic predictions for a method of printing which is now so completely obsolete." Others, such as Briggs, shared this fervor. See note to 84/29 for a modern study of the topic.

83/54} The process was discussed on 24/31-36 [facsimile text], 2/22. See also insertion in "Varieties" by Briggs of a description from the London *Art Union* in *BJ*, 1/11, p. 29 and 2/8, p. 88 (neither reprinted here); and also a technical description quoted below, pp. 135-36 [facsimile text].

84/1} This misquotation from Francis Bacon's *Essays*, no. 43, "Of Beauty," was a Poe favorite (see MM 147c, 213e).

84/20} Poe's heroine, unfortunately, forgot this human tendency in the tale of this period, "Scheherazade" (TOM 1149 ff.).

84/24} *OED*: Anastatic (from Gr. for resurrection, or causing to stand). Of the nature of revival; specifically applied to a printing process in which facsimiles of writing, drawings, or letter-press are produced by a transfer process from zinc plates.

84/26} Alois Senefelder-- the correct spelling-- (1771-1834), accidentally invented lithography or printing from a stone "plate." His handsome pension proves it was not a "frivolous invention" despite the circumstances. Senefelder wrote a full account of his discovery in *Vollständiges Lehrbuch der Steindruckerei* (1818).

84/27} Poe is using an obsolete sense ("innovation") for the noun "novel" if the definite article is intended and not a blunder.

84/29} The topic has been studied and presented by Geoffrey Wakeman, *Aspects of Victorian Lithography: Anastatic Printing and Photozincography* (Wymondham: Brewhouse Press, 1970; 63 p.). He traces it from its "discovery" by M. Baldermus of Erfurt, its exploitation in England by the German steam engineer Wm. Siemens and by Joseph Woods, who named it, through its publicity in various journals including the *Art-Union*, and through Faraday's lecture-demonstrations, into its various commercial applications for antiquarian journals and books, map-copying, and limited reproductions of graphic sketches. By 1895 it had lost favor because of the need for better quantity-duplication, the advances of photographic printing processes, and the unreliability of the chemical processes involved.

84/52-58} *The Art-Union* of London, 2/1845, 7.39-40, contains, on both the ample leaves (2 columns), illustrations done by the anastatic printing method, with a text about the process interspersed. Illustrations include "The Nurse" and "The Revelry," woodcuts from *The Book of British Ballads*, plus new amateur drawings. Poe's facts, details, and explanations are taken or closely adapted from the tiny print of the magazine article.

84/58} Actually two leaves, entirely set anastatically.

85/6} Poe's enthusiasm for this soon outmoded process was excessive, but how social-minded it was!

85/19} Poe's "circular letter of 11/1845," inviting subscription to the *BJ*, exists in the LC, and Morgan and Huntington Libraries (*Letters*, Check List 587-90). In a rev. of *Putnam's Am. Facts* in *Aristidean*, p. 239, Poe notes that the plates "are produced anastatically."

85/24-30} The points about one remaining copy and warehousing expenses are in the *Art-Union* (p. 40).

85/55} Poe's writing is outstandingly neat, elegant, and legible, and often miniscule (see MS. of "Hans Pfaall" reproduced in *Imaginary Voyages* between 386 and 387). This is Poe's original point, not in the magazine.

85/58} Poe objected to typographical blunders, especially when the author was deprived of proof-reading. See his 1842 letter to R. Hamilton of *Snowden's* in Moldenhauer, *Poe MSS.*, 55.

86/1-19} All these points are Poe's, including the relegation of women to the post of scribe.

86/29} Poe's animus against these gentlemen was often thus expressed although the Griswold source seems to be an error (see M 158a).

86/31} Poe applies "poor-devil" hyphenated to "authors" elsewhere: "Thingum Bob" and "Magazine Prison-House" (TOM, 1140/31, 1207/26); also an uncollected rev. of Mathew's *Memoirs*, *BGM*, 6.57.

86/46} For Poe's keen interest as an author, see 23, 103, and M 103c. See also *BGM*, 1840, 6.202, for five paragraphs by Burton on the link of mammoth papers to international copyright.

87/4} Daniel Webster, Mass.; John Berrien, Georgia; Willie Mangum, N. Carolina; George Evans, Maine; James Morehead, Kentucky; John Crittenden, Kentucky; William Archer, Virginia; John Clayton, Del.

87/7} For the political orientation of the *Whig Review* by George H. Colton, ed. '45-'47, see Mott, 750-1.

87/14-20} The respective pages are: 341-61, 371-83, 413-23, 424-32.

87/21} Pp. 363-70. This magazine also printed "The Raven" and "Valdemar."

87/25} Pp. 405-12.

87/27} The adjective for "savans" also (TOM, 1312/26).

87/30} The critics are not "asses" but "apes" (p. 407).

87/31} This is on p. 405.

87/32} Kilkenny Cats: The phrase "To fight like Kilkenny cats" comes from the practice of Hessian soldiers occupying Kilkenny during the rebellion of 1798. They would tie the tails of two cats together, then drape them over a clothes-line. The cats fought until one or both died (*OCEL*). Cf. *N and Q*, series V, 3.433. The expression was used by Poe in "Why the Little Frenchman..." (TOM, 468). Also in Ostrom, *Letters*, 212.

87/35} Poor form of "nosce te ipsum" (Latin, "know thyself").

87/40-53 ff.} On p. 412.

87/53} Poe omits: "the third, the Great Traitor;".

88/40} The famous Washington, D.C. "chit-chat" mag. of Mrs. Anne Royall running from 1831 for 5 years (see Mott, 356).

88/46} *SLM*, pp. 202-11.

88/52} L. and NY, Wiley & Putnam, 1841, viii + 266 p. On p. 221 of this number of the *BJ* Briggs cites Catlin's Indian sketches as the historical model.
George Catlin (1796-1872), painter of NY notables, successively portrayed Indians and their customs.

88/54} Last sentence of "Vindication" article: "For our humble selves, we frankly declare we have no respect for a philanthropy confined to only one color, and which embraces every country but its own. Whether eagle, or cormorant, jack daw, or owl, we hold to the old proverb, It is a base bird that befowls its own nest."

88/56} Pp. 235-43. Poe says this on 14/15-24.

88/60} On pp. 281-87.

88/64} On 252-53. Interesting is the announcement on p. 256 of *SLM* under "Literary criticism: E. A. Poe, Esq." that he will contribute monthly "a critique raisonnee" of the most important new works. Perhaps it was his awareness of the new burdens of the *BJ* that caused him to omit mention of this abortive plan.

88/67} P. 201.

88/68} "The Poet," pp. 212-3.

88/69-71} Pp. 253-56, "Holgazan."

88/71-74} *SLM*, p. 255. For example see *Eureka*, H 16.222-3, and 297-8, for favor toward Nichol. (Poe usually drops "of" after "worthy.") J.P. Nichol (1804-59) wrote *Views of the Architecture of the Heavens* (1837); see *Eureka*, para. 156. The anonymous author was Robert Chambers (1802-71), author of many books on Scottish history and literature, and a partner in the publishing firm of W. & R. Chambers of Edinburgh. *Vestiges* came out in 1844.

In a letter to George E. Isbell, dated 2/29/48 (H 1.277), Poe wrote, "'The Vestiges of Creation' I have not yet seen; and it is always unsafe and unwise to form opinions of books from reviews of them." However, this comes almost three years after the remarks here in the *BJ*, which imply a knowledge of the work. This not being definite proof of previous familiarity, one may look to Carol Madison's article (*Texas Studies in Literature and Language*, 1960, 2.350-67) positively identifying *Vestiges* as an important source for *Eureka*, especially n. 17, p. 365, and n. 5, p. 352. See also three revs. of *Eureka*: Decius (*New World*, 2/12/48, p. 2) on the lecture; the Boston *Transcript* (6/20/48) and Willis' *Home Journal* (8/12/48) on the prose poem, all of which mention *Vestiges* as a likely influence. In the 3/45 *Aristidean*, ed. by T.D. English (q.v.), Poe again attributes the work to Nichol in the column (probably his) "In Our Bookshelves" (specifically 82-84).

Poe's uncertainty was shared by the rest of the literati; cf. *The New World*, 2/15/45, where the reviewer announces the work to be by Sir Richard Vivian, Baronet, a member of various Natural History societies and a known book collector, and states the thesis in terms close to *Eureka*'s "argument." See also 234 and 327 [facsimile text].

88/75-76} "P.'s Correspondence," pp. 337-45. Hawthorne presents Byron, Moore, Shelley, Keats, etc. plus Willis, Bryant, Neal, et al.

89/5} Pp. 413-5, re Poe's articles in the *BJ*.

89/6} Pp. 376-84; pp. 387-400.

89/7} Lewis Cass (1782-1866), statesman and soldier. Engraved by J.B. Forrest, from a daguerreotype miniature.

89/8} For relations of Poe and Hunt, see Pollin, *Texas Studies in Literature and Language*, 1974, 16.305-13. Modestly, Poe omits Hunt's high praise of the tone and criticisms of the *BJ* (q.v. in Poe *Log* for April *ad. init.*).

89/13} Rev. of *Essays on the Principles of Morality, and on Private and Political Rights and Obligations of Mankind* by Jonathan Dymond, NY: Collins, Brother and Co. For several other laudatory revs. of Hunt and his work see the Index and Pollin, *Texas Studies in Literature and Language*, 1974, 16.305-13. For Poe's brief notice of Dymond's book and a note thereon see 115/34-41 and n.

89/15-24} The source of this is an excerpt from the book in review, not given verbatim by Poe.

89/28} This comes from p. 354 of the *Merchants' Mag.*

89/35} There is an engraving of the jail opposite page 44 in Henry Dawson, *Reminiscences of the Park and its Vicinity* (NY, privately pub., 1855). The building was on the N.E. edge of the park next to City Hall, also known as "The Common." It was built in 1756 and later converted to a hall of records. It was torn down in 1903 to make way for the first subway. (Information from pp. 24-25 of Meyer Berger, *The Eight Million* [NY, Simon and Schuster, 1942].) Poe's expressed interest springs from his own condition of perennial indebtedness.

89/40} This article furnished M 186 (see para. 2 below). Note also Dinneford's irate response to this rev. (96-98). See also the musical background, causing these performances (91/7-25 below).

89/49} Pliny, *Natural Hist.*, XXIII, 77, "with a grain of salt or with reservations."

89/62} For Schlegel's *Dramatic Lectures* (London, Bohn, 1846 ed.), on *Antigone*, see pp. 100, 101, 104-7, in ch. 1 (first British ed., 1815; Phila., 1833). See Pin 105 for Poe's use of the book.

90/2-31} These lines, with the para. indentation canceled, comprise M 186, q.v. for fuller glosses and for the minor variations.

90/14} Through a forged Renaissance inscription, he was considered to be sculptor of Venus de Medici (as in "Assignation" and "Ligeia"--M 186b).

90/18} *Hamlet*, 4.4.66: "My thoughts...be nothing worth."

90/43} For Dinneford see pp. 96-98 [facsimile text]. Poe's remark on the size of the Greek theatre is not very clear, since the three dimensional hill-side structure could scarcely have a diameter. According to J. M. Walton, *Greek Theatre Practice* (1980), pp. 88-89, the circular orchestra space of the Athenian structure under Pericles was reduced from a diameter of 90 to 72 feet, but this did not comprise the hillside seats. All told, 17,000 persons could be accommodated, rendering Poe's notion of 700 feet tenable, whatever his meaning.

90/48} Wm. Mitchell (1798-1856), who ran the Olympia Theater, 1839-50, devised a topical burlesque entertainment.

90/59} See 82 (a) for Vandenhoff's book on elocution with "The Raven."

91/1} The expression for secret derision with both "in and "up" derives from the large, loose sleeves once suitable for concealing the face.

91/7-25} Considering the great stir in Berlin and London caused by Felix Mendelssohn's music to *Antigone* for male voices and orchestra, Poe is correct. Recently appointed Kappellmeister to Frederick IV of Prussia, who desired to revive Greek tragedy, Mendelssohn followed Tieck's advice eagerly. His composition was at once put into production at the royal theatre, 10/28 and

11/6/41, was given again in 1842 (also in Leipzig) to crowded houses (also 1843), and finally was played 45 times at Covent Garden in 1-2/45, while the composer was in London. He enjoyed the write-up and caricature in *Punch* (1/18/45), and spoke also about the ballet-girls in the Bacchus chorus (see *Groves Dictionary of Music*, 1927 ed., reissued 1939, 3.410 for an account with the picture). The manager of Covent Garden also sent for his *Oedipus*, which had come out of the Greek "period" after the *Antigone*. Poe surely had read some of this critical acclaim in the recent British press--which had led to the American performances. Poe is wrong about the lack of great "success" abroad (89/50 [facsimile text]).

91/13} The spelling of unisonious is acceptable (*OED*).

91/17} Poe must have meant "though" but the "to" is not impossible.

91/28} Poe did not resume this critique.

91/39} Sir Richard Jebb, *The Tragedies of Sophocles*, Cambridge U. P., 1912, pp. 153-4:
"*Chorus*: Love, unconquered in the fight, Love, who makest havoc of wealth, who keepest thy vigil on the soft cheek of a maiden; thou roamest over the sea, and among the homes of dwellers in the wilds; no immortal can escape thee, nor any among men whose life is for a day; and he to whom thou hast come is mad."

91/43} George Loder was highly reputed for his playing on piano and double-bass and his conducting. Odell records many of his performances (see Index, vol. IV) and a lecture on music on 5/26/43 (see pp. 679-81, 685-86). His wife was often featured as a concert singer. For a long rev. by Watson of Mendelssohn's *Lobegesang* see *BJ* of 3/1, 1.140-41.

92/3} Josiah T. Marshall, [title correct] 2nd ed. rev., NY, Appleton, 1845, 492 p. (there is no data for the 1st ed.). The promised rev. was not inserted.

92/5} Henry Hope Reed (1808-54), professor of rhetoric and English literature at the University of Pennsylvania from 1835 until his death. In addition to Arnold's *Lectures* he also prepared editions of Wordsworth, Gray's *Poetical Works*, George Frederick Graham's *English Synonymes*, and other works. His main preoccupation was Wordsworth.

92/6} Translated by Henry Francis Cary, *The Vision ... of Dante Alighieri*, 1845, 587 p.; illus. by John Flaxman.

92/7} Protestant Episcopal.

92/8} There is no record of any work of Wordsworth's being published by Appleton until 1850, when the firm published *The Prelude*, which was a reprint of the 1850 L. edition.

92/9} Felicia Hemans, *The complete works of Mrs. Hemans*, 1845, 2 vols.

92/10} J. Liebig, 1845, 546 p. Appleton's issued Liebig's letters in 1843 (Mansell) and 1848 (Roorbach).

92/11} Alexander Reid (1802-60), *A Dictionary of the English Language ... with an introduction by Henry Reed*, NY, 1845, 564 p.

92/12-13} All large catalogues consulted show the English translations (including Appleton's) to have been executed by Wm. Hazlitt. Michelet's *History*, which appeared in Paris, 1832, was translated first in a London ed. of H.G. Bohn's Standard Library (given as 1846 in British Museum Catalogue, but still Hazlitt's source, and perhaps actually pub. 1845, early enough for the American piracy). This probably accounts for Poe's erroneously attributing the translation to a "Victor G. Benné," but it must also account for the 6/45 *SLM*'s ascribing this ed. to "Victor G. Benné" (11.391).

92/14} This item by Briggs is in the 3/1 *BJ*, 1.143, stating that *Saul*, sketched six or seven years ago and now carefully revised, will soon appear through Wiley and Putnam of NY.

92/15-19} Heinrich Friedrich Theodor Kohlrausch (1780-1865), *A History of Germany*, trans. by J.D. Haas (NY, Appleton, 1845), 487 p.

92/20-22} This too is publicity for an advertiser; see 1.256 of the same *BJ* number, announcing "3340 pages [in 5 volumes] for $2.50" and listing the first eight of the "Waverley" novels (correctly spelled); also see announcement on 150/33-44 [facsimile text].

92/22-25} The series included: Thomas Macaulay, Archibald Alison, Sydney Smith, John Wilson, Thomas Carlyle, Francis Jeffrey, Sir Thomas Noon Talfourd, Sir James Stephen, Sir James Mackintosh.

92/27} Brougham and Vaux, Henry Brougham, 1st baron. *Lives of men of letters and science, who flourished in the time of George III*, 1845, 295 p.

92/28} *The Historical Essays, published under the title of "Dix Ans d'études historiques," and Narratives of the Merovingian Era*; by *Augustin Thierry*, 1845, 204 p., double column.

92/31} No. 11 consists of Poe's *Tales* (see p. 167).

92/35} Poe's confirmed opinion; cf. 71(a).

92/37} See Poe's rev. (H 10.195-96).

92/43} Pp. 428-30, excerpt from 429-30, in the English ed. of 3/45.

93/5} See Poe's use of a tale in *La Belle Assemblée* for "The Spectacles" (Pollin, *AL*, 1965, 38.185-90).

93/16} "battles for them with"

93/35} See Poe's rev. (H 10.195-96).

93/42-51} For the great popularity of Barbara Hoffland (1770-1844) and her possible influence on Poe, see *Imaginary Voyages*, p. 6.

93/55} See 80 (d) for another squib at J. Harper, the leading publisher.

93/64-86} Of these three paras. (and articles) probably only the first is by Poe, here again in pursuit of an evasion of true "originality" of material. The other two are, first, a statement of Briggs' insistence upon neutrality in political issues and a response to "R.C." or Robert Carter, editor of the abolitionist Boston *Liberator*'s attack on the *BJ* of 3/28/45, which had ascribed to Briggs, as the author, Poe's laudation of the *SLM* (p. 54 above) and attacked Briggs for numerous "sins" against the cause of Abolition. These are briefly indicated by Bette

Weidman in the *Bulletin of the New York Public Library*, 1969, 73.109-110, in her broad argument that the *BJ* was a "casualty of abolition politics."

94/1} This essay closely resembles a long editorial in the *Mirror* entitled "Try a Mineralized Pavement" using much of the same material differently arranged and worded (*EM*, 2/8/45, 2/1; *WM*, 2/15, p. 296). The *Mirror* article was the sequel to one called "Wood Pavements" in the 1/31 *EM* (2/8 *WM*) issue, but this merely reports on a "scientific English Gentleman's" description of the widely used wooden blocks of London streets, and bears no traces of Poe's style. That of 2/8 by contrast introduces the system of "overlapping and riveted roads, called stereotomic," to which Poe makes prominent ref. in "Murders" (TOM 536; also Pollin, *SAR 1977*, 235-59). Poe's interest in the general subject may be linked to his alleged work in 1834 in a brickyard (see *Scribner's Monthly*, 1875, 11.142-43 and *American Notes & Queries*, 1943, 3.36). More significant is his evident interest in technological advance (cf. "Scheherazade," "Mellonta Tauta" and "Mummy") and also his sensitivity to the "nuisance of street-noise." The last five paras., on Kyanizing and wood-preservation, use Poe's presentation of the topic in Letter 5 of *Doings of Gotham*, 6/12/44 (1929), 61-3, as well as in four paras. of the *EM* article (2/8). The data on Roman roads of the first four paras. comes, unquestionably, from an encyclopaedia or "school-boyish" textbook (as Poe hints in para. 3), but skimming through likely articles in *Rees's Cyclopaedia* and the *Americana* (of Lieber) has not revealed the source. Poe's disavowal of having books before him and being accurate in details (in the last para.) is almost a guarantee of his copying--although carelessly perhaps--large swatches of material, especially in view of the technical material included. Mary Phillips, *Poe*, (p. 1007) cites the 1/15/1914 *Engineering News*: "Poe was fairly well informed on at least one branch of engineering."

94/5} New Yorkers, as in his 1844 letters, "Doings of Gotham."

94/6} This parallels the germ of "Mellonta Tauta" set in 2848, with Manhattan obliterated and transcontinental railroads showing only faint traces (TOM 1291-1305).

94/13} The fourth road named perhaps is intended to prove Poe's writing "from memory" since it was not well known and could scarcely ever have been, for Tusculum was a city near

Frascati, 15 miles S.E. of Rome, famous for early allegiance to Rome and later as a resort for Romans, not likely to give its name to a road. The *Enc. Brit.* (11th ed., 23.588) lists the chief roads radiating from Rome, as does the article on "Roads" in the *Oxford Classical Dictionary*, without mentioning a "Tusculana." The Via Appia went to Capua and later to Brundisium, the Via Flaminia to Ariminum in the north, and the Valeria to Aternum due east, on the Adriatic.

94/17} This is the basis of the "Mummy's" argument about non-progress.

94/18-50} The style of this para. is not that of Poe, and the technical information is far beyond his province, in fact, beyond that of Lewis and Short, *Latin Dictionary*, which does not give these technical meanings of "fistucationes" and "nucleus." Poe's informant is correct about the general procedures and materials (cf. "Roads" in *En. Brit.*, 23.388). John L. McAdam (1756-1836) became internationally famous for his advocacy and promotion of compacting into a solid mass a layer of small broken stone on a convex, well-drained earth roadbed (see his *Present State of Road-making*, 1820).

95/15} For other loci of this archaic word, see M 2b and letter V of *Doings of Gotham*, all showing Poe's hatred of street noises.

95/21} This is Poe's adjective-coinage derived from the expression, "spare at the spigot and spill at the bung": To be parsimonious in trifles and wasteful in great matters, like a man who stops his beer-tub at the vent-hole and leaves it running at the bung-hole (Brewer).

95/44-7} Poe suggests that baleful "vapor" is ruining the Ushers' health and home (TOM, 400); see Ian Walker, *Modern Language Review*, 1966, 61.585-92.

95/48} John Howard Kyan (1774-1850) worked on this process, 1812-28, as reported by Faraday and Birkbeck (see *DNB*, 11.348). Poe used this for his "Mummy" tale (TOM, 1186 at n. 18). No one seems to question Kyan's claim, as does Poe, but the *DNB* calls his process "superseded."

96/41} A Poe coinage.

96/44} In 1835 wooden pavements had been experimentally laid on Broadway in NY. Poe's final words come from Daniel 5:27, "Thou art weighed in the balance and found wanting."

96/48} The Despatch Post was established early in 1842 privately, with thrice daily deliveries of letters and packages. In 8/42 this was expanded and made part of the government Post-Office establishment with 100 stations for the deposit of letters, costing three cents for delivery. The spelling of "despatch" was an acceptable variant.

96/54} Poe's note of 4/2/45 and Dinneford's reply, here given, of 4/15 should be inserted into the Check List of Ostrom's *Letters*, which now lacks it, even in the revised form of *SAR 1981*. A response communicated to me indicated that he must have thought of it as "outside the friendly letters" category, but there are more formal or professional letters included in the Check List. This should assume the numbers 533a (by implication) and 533b on p. 221.

97/5} Poe facetiously repeats the misspelling at the end.

97/17} This is an obsolescent term for exclamation points.

97/53} Altering contemptuously the letter of a successive name is Poe's method in "Autography" I (q.v. in TOM, 261-91; also H 11.13ff.).

98/20} Not a typo (caterer), but a "repeat" of Dinneford's error.

98/22} [Rev. Ralph Hoyt], *Night: a poem* etc.

98/24-31} "It is men as individuals and not mankind who invent. Each one arrives on earth in his due turn and at his own time, masters the things known to his fathers, embodies them in new combinations, then dies after having added some small particles to the sum of human knowledge. As for the total creation of an entity--I believe it impossible. God himself, when he created man, could not or dared not invent him; he made him in his own image."
Despite Hull's wish to assign the rev. to Briggs, this quotation and also the emendation of a poetic line below, plus the stress on plagiarism clearly assign it to Poe. Even in the 4/36 *SLM* rev. of Drake's poems, Poe spoke of the distinction between

God's creative power and man's (H 8.283), as also in the 1/40 *BGM* rev. of Moore's *Alciphron*: "All novel conceptions are merely unusual combinations" etc. (H 10.61-2). Whether or not Dumas contributed language and ideas to Poe, this extensive citation avows Poe's leading interest.

98/39} As in Edward Young's *Night Thoughts* (1742-5), cited by Poe at the end of "Premature Burial" (TOM, 969).

98/53} Poe's alteration (of a line on p. 10) might entitle it to enter Appendix III, "Collaborations" in *Poems*, 491 ff.

98/57} Poe devotes two articles to the Rev. Ralph Hoyt (1806-78): a long rev. of his *Chaunt of Life* in the 7/26 *BJ* (179-82, below) and a "Lit." sketch closely adapted from the former (H 15.37-38). Amusingly, Poe there also praises the "physique" of the book and individual stanzas and lines, but deprecates poor phrases and wording, citing many excerpts.

99/3, 4, 6} nature / nation; And makes / Need make; others'.

99/8} This is an 1845 reprint of the 1844 L. ed., 255 p. + vii-x. See M 179 for Poe on Hunt as critic.

99/13} This alludes to Lockhart's attack on the "Cockney School of Poetry" in the 10/1817 *Blackwood's*.

99/29} Cf. another Poe rev. of Hunt below (230-31} signed "P" and wholly consistent with this, unaccountably unsigned. See also p. 347.

99/49} A Poe habit in criticism (see 11/55-59 and 98/54).

99/52} *The Story of Rimini* (1816; later revised; xix, 111 p.; L., 1819; 111 p.).

99/55} See "Rationale of Verse" (H 14.220) for Hunt's floundering in his "Principle of Variety in Uniformity."

99/67} Surely a plural (times) is intended.

100/13} See CS 11 for Poe's groundless charge against Thomas B. Macaulay on the *Novum Organum*. For Poe on Macaulay see *Br.* Index. Macaulay wrote: "The inductive process is not likely to be better performed merely because men know how they perform it" (rev. in *Edinburgh Review* of 7/1837).

100/22} For Macaulay's *Lays*... (1842) see p. 212 [facsimile text].

100/44-77 + 101/1-37} Given as *Essays and Letters*, I, 16 (on next page).

101/23} Cf. Poe's coinage of "one-idead" for *Eureka* (H 16.191).

101/28} See George Colman's *Sylvester Daggerwood* (1795): "My father was an eminent button-maker ... but I had a soul above buttons."

101/32} Phrase deleted: "It was a nobleman who first thought of this most poetical bit of science."

101/37} See 83 and 111 [facsimile text] for more on this. Fauvel-Gouraud (he used a hyphen) had coined the word in 1844 from "mnemonics" plus "phreno" (mental) and now explains the "difference" (see line 55). There are six "Lectures" with many inserted tables of varied "learning" to sharpen the memory. In the *SLM* rev. Poe speaks as though he has met the author, or at least attended a lecture.

101/55} Dr. Richard Grey, Rector in England, pub. *Memoria Technica* (L. 1730), the basis for Gregor von Feinagle, *New Art of Memory* (L., 1812) as the author recounts (60-83). Joseph Lalande (1732-1807), eminent astronomer, could have praised the system but not the book.

101/56} Comparison is *Hamlet's*, 1.2.140, a Poe favorite.

101/69} 492 p.

101/75} Poe is careless about this; the bread is made from dried and ground beech or other wood without turpentine (pp. 128-29 [facsimile text]).

101/79} See 122/5 for Poe's satirical ref. to this pamphlet.

101/84} Henry Champion Deming (1815-72), lawyer and politician of Connecticut, translated Sue's *Mysteries of Paris* and *The Wandering Jew*. *Mysteries of London* is mentioned in passing by Francis Gründ in "European Correspondence," an article in the 5/45 issue of *Godey's*, p. 183, as an imitation of Sue, as is *Mysteries of Berlin* (see 145, 213 [facsimile text]). See Poe's *Letters* (316) requesting a Deming autograph.

102/4} 168 p. H.W. Herbert (1807-58), published much sport oriented fiction and essays; also military history. This was one of his first books. See M 116a.

102/14-38} This is Poe's title for a short section of a long installment poem in the *New World* of 4/15/45, 10.250, which is significant enough for explanation. The weekly, once a mammoth paper, but still very sizable, had been edited by James Aldrich and Park Benjamin until 3/44, and now by Charles Eames. Poe enjoyed excellent relations with the journal, which reprinted "The Haunted Palace" (2/1/45) and "The Raven" by "Quarles" in the 2/22/45 issue (10.120) parallel to a take-off on the city government in the "Raven" meter, called "The Veto" by "Snarles." The same pseudonym, with a subtitle "The Corporation Poet," was used for "Songs of the Suburbs" in the 3/8 issue containing two stanzas in the "Raven" meter with several phrases and ideas therefrom and a footnote alluding to Poe's poem. This led to a Spenserian mock-epic about the various papers of the city in a nightmare combat, recited for the benefit of Mrs. Snarles, whose apple dumplings have given Snarles dyspepsia. Various meters are used. The title is "The Pressgang," the subtitle "A Vision"; "Fytte the First" is in the 3/29 issue. "Fytte the Second" of 4/19 (10.250) contains the three stanzas cited by Poe, immediately followed by "Then came a knight / Up through the fight, / With new and shining armor on," etc. The meter is that of "The Man for Galway" (see *Poems*, 462-63), often used by "Snarles" with many other suggestions of wording that bear comparison with Poe's "Eldorado." To continue--"Fytte the Third" in the 4/26 issue ends the piece, with no further take-off on "The Raven." Other Poe related items insured Poe's close reading of this important paper, such as an announcement of his lecture (3/1) and indirect review on 3/8, a reprint of "Ligeia" in the 2/15 issue and an admiring para. on "The Raven" (2/15) a week before the reprint. Only the absorption of the paper by the *Emporium* in 4/45 precluded many more "gentle puffs" for Poe, one assumes.

102/10-13} The respective pages are: 1-39, 40-77, 104-148, 149-162, 162-192, 193-227 + appendix; 228-243, and editor's section--257.

102/16} Poe was either forgetful or disingenuous here, for "The Raven" occasioned numerous parodies, as he knew; he himself refers to C.C. Cooke's "The Gazelle" (112) printed in the *WM.* Earlier the 2/17/45 *EM* had printed "The Owl" and that of 2/22 "The Craven" by "Poh!" while later the 6/7 *WM* would print "The Whippoorwill" (ref. in *Poems*, 352 n. 4).

102/21} A ref. to Col. James Watson Webb (1802-84), diplomat and journalist, ed. of the paper until 1862.

102/28} A large double-edged broadsword, formerly used by Scottish Highlanders.

103/3} Francis Gründ (see 78/60 [facsimile text]).

103/6} Cf. Gouraud's book reviewed above, 83, 101 [facsimile text].

103/14} The customary adj. is "Herodian" for Herod, King of Judaea (40-4 B.C.).

104/13-22} The respective pages are: 197-200 (Eliza Leslie), 178-180, 237 (Hannah F. Gould), 201.

104/18} H.S. Sadd.

104/19} Probably Wm. Sidney Mount (1807-68), genre and portrait painter of honesty and craftsmanship; see his genre pieces on Long Island country life.

104/20} G.B. Ellis.

104/21} "Editor's Book Table," p. 239-40.

104/22} "Our Copyright," p. 240.

104/30} A good example is Poe's selling "The Raven" to the *American Review* for 2/45, but arranging for its publication in the 1/29 *EM*, with Willis (*Poems*, 360-61).

104/35} For this favorite theme see "Copyright" in Index. In its issue of 6/45, *Godey's* acknowledged Poe's kind words by reprinting the para. (lines 21-35) with a designation of "some very just remarks on the subject" (30.284).

104/37-38} The respective pages are: 205-15 (Edward Preble), 193-200, 236-37.

104/46-47} mois, Français

104/76-78} J.T. Headley, "The Music of Italy," pp. 202-204; Caroline Butler, "Emma Alton," pp. 216-218; Henry Tuckerman, "The Profession of Literature," pp. 220-222; Fanny Forrester, "Blanche de Nouville," pp. 223-232; and Elizabeth Smith, "The Rustic," a poem, p. 232.
This magazine number (p. 240) also contains Longfellow's letter refuting the "Good George Campbell" plagiarism charge.

104/81-84} To the poem, on p. 201, Poe adds the italics and drops a comma after "then:" There is no warrant for the terminal "h" of Hamburgh in *Graham's.*

105/2-3} James Smillie (1807-85); C.H. Bodmer (see Mott, 548).

105/3-9} F. Forrester, "Nancy," pp. 193-98; Tuckerman, "Thoughts on the Poets," pp. 227-34; Mrs. Ellet, "The Klobotermann," pp. 205-207; John Brougham, "Tales of Irish Superstition," pp. 200-204; Miss Brown, "The Musicians' Adventure," pp. 235-36; T.S. Arthur, "The True Friend," pp. 210-14; Miss Brawner, "The Truant," pp. 215-17; E.J. Porter, "The Gipsy Bride," pp. 219-22; Robert A. West, "I've Thought of Thee, Dearest," lyrics, pp. 239-40; Mrs. Osgood, "Golden Rules in Rhyme," pp. 208-209.

105/18} Poe's correction is verified in Osgood's *Poems* (1846), pp. 56-57.

105/19-22} The three plates are at the start of the May number (p. 193), two relating to later articles as follows: "The Wedding" by J. B. Forrest (with no printed ref. to Morton) for Robert A. West's poem, "The Wedding" (p. 236), "The Idle Servant," engraved by H.S. Sadd, from a painting by N. Maes, for a prose sketch (p. 226). The two-page song by Herman S. Saroni sets "I've thought of thee, Dearest" by Robert A. West (239-40). Saroni published the *Musical Times* later (1849-52).

105/23-33} See Mott, 721-24 for this serious, important Charleston monthly, ed. by David K. Whitaker, aided by James

DeBow. In the 4/45 issue the articles cover: Union of Races, pp. 372-448; Hoar's mission, pp. 455-78; S.C. politics, pp. 479-526; general literary interest (rev. of *A Drama of Exile*), pp. 300-12; rev. of "Spirit of the Age," pp. 312-49.

105/30} See Poe's rev. (H 11.266) for more of this laudation.

105/29-31} Poe wrote of "Orion" in *Graham's*, 3/44, that it is "one of the noblest, if not the very noblest poetical work of the age" (H 11.275). In fact, it was Poe's heresy of preferring "Orion" to many classics that partly turned Briggs against him (cf. Woodberry, 2.145-46). Horne was E.B. Barrett's friend and important in London literary journalism (see *PD*, 46 for numerous Poe refs.).

105/32-33} Richard H. Horne's *A New Spirit of the Age* was published as "edited" by Horne, in the NY reprint of 1844, with no indication of separate authorship beyond this: "It will be sufficiently apparent that several hands are in the work" (p. viii). The biographical sketches are of individuals, such as Dickens, W.S. Landor, Robert Montgomery, and Carlyle or of pairs, such as E.B. Barrett and Mrs. Norton. Poe's omitting an "of" after "worthy" is characteristic (see note on p. 1 for E.B. Barrett and Horne).

105/36} For Poe's love of puns see M 87 (and the *Br.* Index).

105/46} By coincidence, this is the story point of Poe's 1839 tale of "The Little Frenchman"--therefore a reason for his choosing this as filler.

105/48} See TOM, *Poems*, 379-80; and 69/25 above. This is included to fill out editorial material on Mrs. Osgood.

105/52} The implicit pun of the fourth line accords with the Intro. Misc.; it also implies Poe's pronunciation habits.

105/63} For many items on James Edward Murdoch (1811-93) see Index and p. 175 for Poe's rev. of *Orthophony: or Vocal Culture in Elocution*. Poe, whose lectures often had small audiences, appreciated such ovations. He lectured 2/28 at that place.

106/4} The author, more correctly, is Stapp; the book has 164 p. and was republished (Austin, 1935).

106/9} Collations are made from the Phila. ed. (G.B. Zieber and Co., 1845), pp. 145-47.

107/2} B. Mayer (1804-79), founder in 1844 of the Maryland Historical Society; *Mexico As It Was and As It Is* (1844), is cited in the *Weekly Mirror* of 5/3, p. 63 (opposite "The Gazelle" on p. 112 [facsimile text]). The author of the rev., not Poe according to the style, says that his purpose in speaking of the book is "to gibbet literary thievery." He gives a list of 21 widely separated passages with the pages of their parallels in Mayer. Right below this article is an interesting "review" of the *Aristidean*, mentioning Poe's "savage, merciless, bitter and unjust" attack on the "Waif" of Longfellow, who will not "let judgment go against him by default!"

107/6} Pub. 1845, 23 p.

107/9} Marsh (1801-82) was a lawyer, diplomat, scholar in many fields.

107/17} Marsh's oration to the New England Society was about the Goths and their descendants, the Puritans of New England. Marsh is attacked for floridness of language, imprecision and fanaticism. The remarks contained in the pamphlet originally appeared in *The Churchman* newspaper of NY.

107/19} The following rev. was synopsized by Poe for his 9/45 article XIX, "Our Bookshelves" in *The Aristidean* (234-42), specifically no. 6, on 235-36; one sentence from the *BJ* is quoted verbatim.

107/20} This information was gleaned by Poe from the publisher's ed. For part 1, "Second Series," see the rev. or rather long excerpt in 10/11/45 *BJ* (278 [facsimile text]).

107/28} For Macaulay see Indexes of *Br.* and *BJ*, and for Wm. Cobbett see SM 18.

107/34} Essay II, para. 3: "I went to the Louvre to study, and I never did anything (in painting) afterwards."

107/44} "On a Landscape of N.P."--a scene with Orion setting out on a journey.

107/49} "On the ignorance of the Learned," pp. 45-54.

107/51} The last para. discusses the fresh insights of men and women of "good sense" and little learning.

107/57} Pub. 1845; 292 p.

107/60-69} Poe either misunderstands Putnam's explanation of the provenance of this anonymous article (249-92 in his vol.) or chooses to do so. The original article, deliberately hostile to the British, is a mock review of the most recent productions of Griswold, Longfellow, Bryant, Colton, and one anonymous author of *Washington (a poem)*. It first appeared in the *Foreign Quarterly Review* (London) of 1/44 (pp. 291-324). Thence it was copied by the *North American Review*, vol. 59, 7/44, 1-44, which explained at the very end that it came from the British journal, which "pretended it came from the *North American Review*." Putnam merely transferred this concluding remark to the headnote of his reprint. Poe seems to have overlooked this statement, although he is right in questioning the motives of Putnam, for long a resident in London as spokesman for the books of Wiley and Putnam.

The French word "niaiseries," here misspelled, is one of Poe's favorites to designate "trifles," "foolishness," "nonsense." It is one of his "hall marks."

107/71} The publisher apologizes for the poor quality of the plates, presumably made by anastatic printing (see pp. 83-86 [facsimile text]).

108/4-17} "Texas," pp. 90-104; "Widow," pp. 111-14 (by Walt Whitman); "Hans Spiegen," pp. 127-29; Longfellow commentary, pp. 130-42 (by Poe himself, with a mention of the *BJ*); "Shood-Swing," pp. 146-52 (a "Tale of China," by English); "Notes," pp. 153-55 (Poe is the first entry); "Strangling," p. 89; "Polly Bodine," p. 156; "Heart-Burst," p. 104. For a good analysis of the article on Longfellow see Moss, *Poe's Lit. Battles* (176-78), who judges this attack as deliberately more "devastating" so as to make those in the *BJ* seem comparatively mild and balanced.

108/36} Although not a French usage, Poe seems to mean "moral tone" here as he did "physical appearance" by "physique" in 86/44 [facsimile text]. The woodcuts (decorated initials and vignettes) by the young, highly competent F.O.C. Darley (1822-

88), later under contract for Poe's abortive *Stylus*, insured some artistic merit.

108/38} For Poe's general opposition to namby-pambyism see 36/44-47.

109/1} Although probably not by Poe, this is included to show Poe's continuing interest in the subject (see 55, 80 [facsimile text]).

109/12} See M 28n for the origin of the basic adage.

109/24} See Poe's verse "nutmegs out of a pineknot" (*Poems*, 394).

109/50-68} "Caudle lecture. A curtain lecture." Term derived from a series of papers by Douglas Jerrold, "Mrs. Caudle's Curtain Lectures," which were pub. in *Punch* (1846). These papers represent Job Caudle as a patient sufferer of lectures from his nagging wife after they draw the curtains of their bed.

109/64} Laman Blanchard died in 1845; see 92-93 above.

109/68} Dionysius Lardner (1793-1859), scientist and editor of the *Cabinet Cyclopaedia* (133 vols.) and *Cabinet Library* (1830-44), lectured in U.S. and Cuba (1840-45) as well as the British Isles.

109/73-77} William Howitt (1794-1879) was author of *Visits to Remarkable Places: old halls, battle fields, and scenes illustrative of striking passages in English history and poetry*; pub. in London, 2 vols., 1840-42, and in Phila. by Carey and Hart, 1841. The book here promised is not listed in catalogues.

110/5} "Homeric Glossary" is correct.

110/7} Pub. 1844 and 1845, viii + 599 p.

110/20ff.} This comes from p. vi.

110/24-34} Richard Payne Knight (1750-1824): "In 1808 he printed privately fifty copies (London) of his 'Carmina Homerica, Ilias et Odyssea.' This consists of Prolegomena, the text being added in the later edition of 1820, 8vo. His object was to restore the text to its supposed original condition and he introduced the digamma and various earlier forms" (*DNB*, 11.259). Poe's source is Anthon's Preface. For Poe's great respect for Anthon, often diplomatically displayed, see my Index for other reviews.

110/42-43} Correctly spelled Buttmann, Nägelsbach.

110/52-54} The same words appear on p. vii of the book.

110/58} As usual, Poe lauds Anthon, America's leading classicist, as in other articles (see Index).

111/2} *Blackwood's*, 4/45 (British ed.): "Virgil, Tasso and Raphael" (401-414); "Ping-Kee's View of the Stage" (415-423); "The Midnight Watch" (424-447); "Vestiges of the Natural History of Creation" (448-460); "Marston: or, the Memoirs of a Statesman, part XVI" (461-473); "Bentham's Etruria Celtica" (474-488); "Suspiria de Profundis: being a sequel to the Confessions of an English Opium Eater" (489-502); "North's Specimens of the British Critics. No. III, Dryden" (503-528).

111/6} Thomas De Quincey (1785-1859) published the first version in 1822. For Poe's use of De Quincey see TOM 199, 207, 339, 880 and *Letters*, 58. The side line is probably Poe's--for emphasis, but an illegible word (not reproduced) has the general style of Mrs. Whitman's writing.

111/11} See 83, 101 [facsimile text] for revs. of the embodying book.

111/14} Author's preface, "Ante-Praedictum."

111/17-59} From "The Rising Sun," pp. 451-53.

112/3} More properly Linz on the upper Danube in Austria.

112/6} See Poe's fondness for puns in 105(a) and the *Br.* Index.

112/10} Shakspeare: Poe's regular spelling.

112/12} James E. Murdoch gave a series of five readings on Shakespeare at the Society Library beginning on April 18. The plays selected were *Macbeth*, *Hamlet*, *Henry IV*, and *Othello*. See

105(c).

112/16-18} Palmo's was established in 1844 as an Italian opera house by Ferdinand Palmo. November and December saw operas by Rica and Donizetti, followed by Rossini's *Semiramide* in January. *Antigone* was presented on April 7, and the Ethiopian (i.e. Negro) Serenaders began on May 1.

112/21} May 6.

112/28-32} After several delays Griswold finally delivered his paper, "Literature and Art in America," at the NY Historical Society on May 6. The lecture took about two hours and was well received by the audience (Joy Bayless, *Rufus Wilmont Griswold* [Nashville: Vanderbilt U. P., 1943] pp. 98-99). See Index for Griswold entries.

112/33-40} W. Alpers was linked as pianist and organist to the inception of the Philharmonic Society (12/42; see Odell, 4.679-80, 684) and he is most active in the accounts of concerts as instrumentalist until close to his death on 5/3/45.

112/41-45} This appears in the 5/3 *Weekly Mirror*, 2.62, with this caption (probably by Willis): "The following, from our new-found, boy-poet of fifteen years shows a most happy faculty of imitation" and, under the title, "after the manner of Poe's 'Raven.'" The end of every one of the 12 stanzas of 6 lines each has the refrain "Fare thee well." It ineptly tells of Isabel, now an angel, who appears to the poet as an evanescent gazelle. One suspects that Cooke is somehow related to Philip Pendleton Cooke of Virginia, who contributed to the *BJ*, exchanged letters with Poe, and perhaps influenced "Annabel Lee" (see Index of *Letters* by Ostrom).

112/45} Samuel Carter Hall (1800-89); the excerpts are from only vol. 1 of the 3 vol. set (Chaucer to Prior). "Old English Poetry" is not part of the title. This rev. of the NY ed. (304 + vii-x p., Saunders and Otley, 1836) originally appeared in the 8/36 *SLM*. It was rewritten for the *BJ* with the omission of the first 1 1/2 columns (see H 9.91-103, especially 94ff.), and comprised also SM 3 and SM 9 in *Br*. See the extensive notes of commentary for both articles and the collation for the passage from the *BJ* article, changed from that of the *SLM*, in SM 9b. No ed. of 1844 or 1845 warranted this article, showing Poe's desire to express or reaffirm his views on the British poets.

Hall's book was reprinted in 1848.

112/55-60} For this early (1836) statement of the "indefinite" and its link to both arts see SM 3n and M 44.

112/62} "Ideality" for "beauty," a phrenological term, is common in Poe's work (see M 20).

113/8-37} For the *Davideis* (or *Creation*) of Abraham Cowley (1618-67) see Pin 48, MM 75, 202, SP 36. For John Donne see M 202 (and loci given there). In M 202 he links these two through "fervid, hearty, free-spoken songs" but here through Samuel Johnson's application of "metaphysical." He often opposed Coleridge's "anomalous metaphysicianism" (see M 202g) and, usually, Wordsworth's "didacticism" (M 202). Poe seems confused about the different British schools, their aims and methods, perhaps through his confinement to anthologies. In the initial para. of the rev. (omitted here) Poe instances the poets of 400 years in the book, ranging from Chaucer and Lydgate to Dryden and Matthew Prior (1664-1721), evidencing the looseness of Poe's designation of "school" for this "entire class of writers."

113/45-50} Samuel Carter Hall (1800-89) had a splendid career in journalism, literature, and art criticism, with many books in varied fields and some recognition. Poe's deprecation seems unwarranted. The 1836 ed. of this volume (p. 114) shows no differences from Poe's transcription save for the accidentals, Poe having modernized spellings. Sir Henry Wotton (1568-1639) addressed "On his Mistress, the Queen of Bohemia" (*Gems*, 116-17) to Elizabeth, the daughter of James I.

114/1-2} The word "art" here seems to contradict 113/9, save that there too he speaks of the artificial verse of Cowley, apparently meaning here that art is equivalent to elaborate technique, overwrought perhaps rather than with well-applied or "adapted" principles leading to a successful "Art-Product" as he says in *Eureka*. It is still a fuzzy distinction which ignores the aims and standards of the period itself in imposing a strait-jacket of criticism.

114/9-12} George Wither (1588-1667) wrote the five pastorals subsumed under this title in the Marshalsea prison, to which his satires of 1613 brought him; after a series of publications and further trouble with the government he became a convinced Puritan--perhaps the link which caused Poe's comparison with the youthful Milton's invocation to the goddess Melancholy (1632). The excerpt cited from *Gems* (pp. 166-70) has been modernized in spelling by Poe.

114/39-42} Bishop Richard Corbet (1582-1635), a decidedly minor poet, whose poems were collected in 1647. Poe cites "Farewell to the Fairies" (*Gems*, 143-45) by the first line (which needs a comma after "Farewell") rather than its given title.

114/42-76} This comes from "The Nymph Complaining for the Death of her Fawn" as in the *Miscellaneous Poems* (1681) of Andrew Marvell (1621-78) and thus titled by Hall in *Gems* (63ff.). Collation shows changes only in accidentals save for 72: On / With, here and in *SLM*.

114/77-87} This section begins SM 9, which continues to the end of the *BJ* and *SLM* article, save for not incorporating the relatively minor substantive changes introduced into the *BJ* text (see SM 9c for collations). See SM 9a for comments on Poe's keen interest in pet animals in life and in his fiction.

115/1-26} In his paraphrase of Marvell's 30 lines Poe is not entirely faithful, for he inserts "nest-like bed" and the "head turned back" (of the fawn) as well as the link of the winds with the four feet. The plural of "delights" enables him to list the "graces" in the poem, while the fawn of the poem had one delight, to fill itself with roses.

115/26-33} These are not "concluding lines" for the poem, which continues with the actual death and final tears of the animal. The sentimentality of Poe's analysis apparently leads to his own word "hyperbole" (with absurdity added in SM 9 or copied from the *SLM* version). The speaker clearly is not a "child" but a maiden to whom the suitor Sylvio had given the deer before he proved "false." The wanton "Troopers" casually shot the deer which dies, and the "nymph" promises to erect a Niobe-like statue of herself with the deer at her feet.

115/34-41} This short notice may be assigned to Poe as the sort of work that Briggs would scarcely assign himself, even to skim through, while the reviewer's singling out "the one chapter" sounds characteristic. It came out posthumously in 1829 in London, in 2 vols., the American edition having vi plus 569 p. in one vol. Dymond (1796-1828) was writing against Paley's Utilitarianism and veering towards that of Godwin and the

English liberals; hence, his disparagement of "Legal Practice." The essay, "The Morality of Legal Practice," is on pp. 154-68. For a fuller treatment, from the discussion in Hunt's *Merchant's Magazine*, see 89/13-24 [facsimile text].

115/42-53} This is a mere announcement of the book and an unfulfilled pledge of a future notice. The singling out of the subtitle is typical of Poe's interest and method. Curiously, the word "chronothermal" meaning pertaining to time and temperature did not enter the language until 1881 (*sic*) in the *OED*. The American editor, Samuel Henry Dickson (1798-1872), was prominent, having founded the Medical College of South Carolina, and becoming professor at NYU and elsewhere after 1850.

116/1-3} M. Alterton first attributed this to Poe; see *The Origins of Poe's Critical Theory*, U. of Iowa, 1925, p. 84. Cf. 304/53 [facsimile text] for a cross ref. The article, signed "P" but not printed by Harrison, is important; it shows Poe's keen interest in the graphic arts, as also in "Assignation," "Philosophy of Furniture," "Oval Portrait," and "Oblong Box," and in his close attention to the illustrations of the books reviewed. It also demonstrates the limitations of him and others of his day in judging works of art (see the last para.). We are hampered in assaying this rev. by not having the material that probably was distributed or posted at the exhibition, which cannot now be traced. The original by Titian may be "Venus and Cupid" at the Uffizi Gallery of Florence, ca. 1545, or "The Venus of Urbino" (Uffizi, ca. 1538), the latter a celebrated nude. For Poe's second thoughts about "Venus" see 304/53-59 [facsimile text].

116/4} Sir Thomas Lawrence (1769-1830), noted portrait artist, formed a renowned collection of drawings by Michael Angelo and Raphael.

116/5} Washington Allston (correctly) (1779-1843), American painter and poet, pupil of Benjamin West in London and much influenced by the Venetian school of painters. Poe mentions the apostrophe to Allston in his rev. of the poetry of Rufus Dawes in the 10/42 *Graham's* (H 11.136).

116/32} This common spelling of Raffaello Santi or Sanzio (1438-1520) was used by Poe (in regard to his "Venus") for his obscure, inexplicable joke in "L'Omelette" (TOM 35). The "Madonna of the Chair" is in the Pitti Palace, Florence.

116/37-40}   Poe's statement about the hedonic purpose of art is basic to his aesthetics, which held that didacticism or the promotion of morality should have nothing to do with literature.

116/41-46}   Poe alludes to a sexist principle for exhibition-visits as though it was not then unusual. In 1806 the Pennsylvania Academy of Fine Arts (Phila.) displayed plaster casts of nudes, presumably male, from the Louvre *draped* on a Monday visiting day "for women only." This custom persisted into the 1840s and 1850s, q.v. in M. A. Hallgreen, *Landscape of Freedom* (1941), 177, and Helen W. Anderson (1911), *The Penn. Academy of Fine Arts* (1911), 1, 13. Poe's statement about women is fine, but he somewhat attenuates it with his rather gauche joke about the response of the very young and old at the end-- the sort of joke that is rare in Poe's chaste writings. The question of nudity in art was rife in Victorian America, and it erupted over the exhibition at the time of Hiram Powers' nude female statue of "The Greek Slave" (q.v. in 282, 287, 304; see also "La Sortie du Bain," 297 [facsimile text]).

116/47-55}   Poe was a strong adherent of Jeremiah Reynolds, proposer and proponent of the U.S. government expedition to the unknown South Pole area, and deeply resented the appointment of Charles Wilkes (1798-1877) to head the six-ship four-year expedition, presented in *Narrative of the U.S. Exploring Expedition* (1844); in his uncollected, brief rev. of preliminary activities in the 9/43 *Graham's* Poe explained that future glory would accrue to Reynolds, not Wilkes. For this partiality and for his many debts to Reynolds for ideas, language and general stimulus in *Pym* and the tales, see the many notes (listed in the Indexes) and for two reviews see *PD*, 78 (7 loci), also *Discoveries in Poe*, ch. on "Poe as Miserrimus." It must be said that Reynolds was an enthusiast and something of a scientific quack. The *SLM* article is on pp. 305-22.

117/9}   The examples are on p. 316.

117/19-20}   Pp. 281-87.

117/20-25}   Pp. 295-99. See "Literati" sketch of 7/46 (H 15.69) where he likewise misspells Pearse. For the Barrett article see 4/45, 235-43.

117/26}   Cf. 88/55-59 for his earlier response to this article and 14/15-24 for Poe's views.

117/36} Poe's strange oversight! There are 8 poems on 266, 278, 287, 294, 299, 303, 305, unless he means nothing worthy of the designation.

117/39-53} Of all these, only F. O. C. Darley's name is signed. The pages of the contributions are, respectively: 243-47; 261-65; 269-70; 271-75; 276-77; 266-68; 279-80. Nathaniel P. Willis, Poe's very good friend, in 1835 married Mary Stace, who died in childbirth in 1845.

117/55-61} The "View of Rock Mountain" is the second plate, with the other two being the first and third, all preceding the text of the number.

117/62} Harrison prints from the Griswold 1850 *Memoir* (p. vi) a letter from Poe to Griswold containing an apology for being "offensive" to Griswold (in Poe's lecture) and ending: "See my notice of C. F. Hoffman's sketch of you" (H 17.170). Killis Campbell (*Mind of Poe*, 91) compared the original with that printed by Griswold, italicizing passages forged and inserted by Griswold, including the ref. to "my notice" (also Quinn, 449). Griswold describes the letter as "without date," but Campbell cites the post mark "New York, April 19," which is 1 month before the appearance of this notice. Ostrom completely omits this end-section in *Letters*, 284-85.

117/63-67} This is one of the most generous and favorable statements on Griswold made by Poe. Charles F. Hoffman's sketch is on pp. 241-43; for the author see 80/28 above.

118/1-2} *The Prose Writers of America with a survey of the history, condition, and prospects of American Literature* (Phila., Carey and Hart, 1847), 552 p.

118/3-9} These are the "papers" in the 6/45 *Graham's* by title, author, page and genre: "The Trial," W. H. C. Hosmer (244), poem; "Poor Benny," Joseph R. Chandler (245-50); "Forgive the Doubt," Henry Tuckerman (250), poem; "Little Harry's Dream," Ann Stephens (251-54); "Ho-Ta-Ma," Charles Hoffman (261-63); "Dante," Longfellow (264); "Sketches of Naval Men," Edward Preble Cooper (265-76); "Laura, or the Veiled Maiden," Caroline Butler (277-80), prose; "Wayfarers," Elizabeth Smith (280), poem; "The Flowers," Fanny Forrester (281), poem; "May," Alfred Street

(244), poem.

118/13} An understood "looking" can easily justify the "like."

118/14-16} See 78/62 [facsimile text] and note for a similar comment on her 4/45 *Graham's* poem; "Lulu" is on p. 281.

118/38} deeper / deepen; this is the only variant, perhaps showing Poe's great care in this transcription and printing.

118/48-51} See 162-67 [facsimile text] for the rev. of the book by his former friend of Phila. For a possible (and amusing) cause of the rupture see TOM *Poems*, 317/12.

119/59-62} The adulation by the British Establishment and general populace of the military hero and Tory statesman, Field Marshal Arthur Wellesley, first duke of Wellington, distressed Poe, now veering toward the Young America (and anti-British) movement; hence his mockery of this half column in the *Albion*, the weekly long publication in NY for the resident British and their entourage, in the number for 5/10/45, p. 288 (col. 1). It starts thus: "By the late arrival we learn that the Morning Post of the 18th ult. contained two paragraphs stating the Duke was taken suddenly ill in the House of Lords, and was obliged to quit the house leaning on the arm of another peer. The Duke contradicted these reports in the following characteristic manner." There follows his letter of 5/18/45 denying this, claiming that he stayed to the end of the session and took part in the discussion, that he told a caller that he was well the next day and not "convalescent," and these facts should be stated in the paper. The rest of the article is the quoted passage. Poe wishes to show the pomposity of the man and his admirers and deprecate upper-class English style.

119/65} Col. John Gurwood (1790-1845), private secretary to the duke of Wellington (Arthur Wellesley, 1769-1852), was editor of the *Wellington Despatches* (1837-44).

120/14} Poe scorned the works and views of William Cobbett (1766-1835), very varied author (known also as "Peter Porcupine"), and especially detested his *Grammar* (1817, pub. in America first). See SM 18b for treatment.

120/80} Poe is humorously alluding to Falstaff's account to

Prince Henry, in *King Henry IV* (I), 2.4, of his brave resistance to assailants who grow in number from 2 to 11, but he skips from 4 to 7. Is this Poe's joke?

121/1-2} Poe often berates authors for this "fault"; his deliberate use of the device of polysyndeton at the end of "Masque" is famous.

121/29} William Wilberforce Lord (1819-1907), *Poems*, 1845, 158 p. (ed. by TOM as *Poetical Works*, 1938). See M 169a for a brief account of this poet, minister, and friend of the *Knickerbocker* group.

121/32} In fact, Lord studied at the University of Western NY, then at Princeton Seminary and Auburn Theological Seminary, was made a fellow of Princeton College (1845), took orders in the Episcopalian Church (1847), etc. In 1845 his verse won praise from Wordsworth (says *National Cycl. of Am. Biog.*, 3.516; see also 126/46 below).

121/35-45} Poe obviously treats Lord here as a new be-puffed darling of the above group, just as he had Theodore Fay, praised in advance for *Norman Leslie*, which Poe "exposed" in the 12/35 *SLM*. See Moss, *Poe's Lit. Battles*, and Pollin, *Mi Q*, 1972, 25.111-30. This may explain Poe's vituperation of Lord as poet and overlooking of his playfulness.

121/45-46} Charles King (1789-1867), ed. *NY American* (1823-45), assoc. ed. of NY *Courier and Enquirer* (1845-48), president of Columbia College (later Col. University, 1849-64).

122/4-5} See 101/79 for mention of this 12 1/2 cents edition. *The Voices of the Night* first came out in 1839 as the principle poem in a collection (Cambridge: J. Owen), xv + 144 p. By 1843 it was in its seventh ed. at Cambridge and was being published in London. In 1845 the poem was brought out with a few others (Boston: Redding and Co.), 32 p.

122/18-19} See *The Book of Common Prayer*: "O God, when thou wentest forth before the people: / when thou wentest through the wilderness, / The earth shook, and the heavens dropped / at the presence of God" (*Oxford Dictionary of Quotations*, 396).

122/37} This is an accepted variant of "doggerel."

122/51} In "The Poetic Principle" (1850; in his earlier lecture of the late 1840s), para. 16, Poe says that this "sentiment" inspires the "soul" to create "supernal beauty," especially in music.

122/54} Poe, with his preference in subject matter for the death of a beautiful woman ("Phil. of Comp." para. 18), often alludes to Juliet's death (see "Poe and Shakespeare" in *SAR 1985*, by Pollin).

123/1-3} "Worship," lines 47ff. (above 2 lines included). The italics are Poe's.

123/11} Ibid., 94ff.

123/15} See "King Pest" (TOM, 253) for a situation using similar terms. Poe's "Burton's" should be "Burton," since the ale comes from an English brewery town named Burton, not a proprietor of that name.

123/20-33} Lines 132ff. (Poe's italics).

123/45} "To My Sister" is the title.

123/53} Poe adds "(wilt)" and italics.

123/68-76} This is on p. 131.

124/2-18} This is on p. 134.

124/14} This is on p. 63.

124/25-33} This, on p. 60, is clearly meant as a burlesque of Poe (e.g. Poe's word "Aidenn" ends line 4, q.v. in *PCW*, 83). See more on this, 126 below.

124/35-39} Obviously in ref. to Fuseli's famous "Nightmare" picture.

124/49} This is on p. 81 (p. 50 in the 1938 reprint of the *Complete Poetical Works*); TOM adds the distich to Poe's "Comic Rhymes," *Poems*, 488-89.

124/57} On pp. 32-38. See the "Lit." sketch on M. Fuller (H 15.76) for a use of this passage.

124/59-67} Poe ridicules Lord's poems again in M 169, for being borrowed. Poe greatly admired the swirl and roar of Niagara (TOM 387, 580, 862, 1017).

125/1-2} The excerpts are from p. 351.

125/13-25} These are lines 61-73.

125/46} "Calliope," line 76.

125/47-48} *Merry Wives of Windsor*, 5.5.77. Poe is unjust; there is no link.

125/50} From "Worship," lines 193-94.

125/53} The novel of 1828 by Edward Bulwer Lytton (q.v.).

125/57} "Ode to England," lines 207-208.

125/56-62} This charge plus that anent "Haunted Palace" (126/1-24) is used for M 214, q.v. for analysis. See also notes for 126.

125/64} "Worship," line 244, which reads: "And ere beheld on earth, did garden heaven!"

125/67} A variant of other texts, this is recorded (1.50-52, 54-56) by TOM in *Poems*, 99, 101, as Version *H*.

126/1} Poe here and below is quoting from Lord's "The New Castalia."

126/14-24} Lines 1-12 of this poem of 1839 and also used in M 214. TOM's note on line 12 (*Poems*, 317) is interesting, especially for the Hirst parody; TOM contended that this *BJ* attack on Lord is "an ironic jest. Lord's poem was a deliberate parody, which Poe pretended to take seriously." This is undermined by Poe's excerpting the charge for M 214 as one of his many anti-plagiarism passages. The parody is obvious to us, but possibly not to Poe. Unfortunately TOM, more knowing about Lord than anyone else, did not see fit to report Lord's response in letters to Poe's attack. See M 214b for Poe's later borrowing from "New Castalia" for "The Bells." Several revs. call it a "burlesque" without mentioning Poe however, e.g., *SLM*,

6/1845, 11.641-45: "a miserable parody," and *Godey's*, 7/45, 31.47: "A Tennysonian travesty ... full of melodious jinglings and tinklings of words."

126/25-30} Lines 67-70.

126/31-35} These comprise lines 3 and 4 in the octameter version of "The Raven," and are treated by TOM as variant *G* which differs from the established version in wording and in meter: "While I nodded, nearly napping, suddenly there came a tapping, / As of some one gently rapping, rapping at my chamber door--." (See *Poems*, 363, 369.) Did Poe genuinely wish to change these elements or merely write carelessly a poem that he was to recite so often?

As to the conversion into tetrameters--here so much easier to contain within the narrow columns--the headnote in the 2/45 *American Review* printing, in which Poe clearly had a hand, explains why other lines in each stanza could not be halved this way--not to mention that "Philosophy of Composition" (para. 10) sets "about 100" lines as the ideal length of a poem--therefore of "The Raven" (108). More important--could Poe imagine Lord's parody to be a deliberate "theft"? Notice how Poe insinuates himself amongst the admired great ones at the end of the para.

126/46} Lord had been tutor at Amherst College, and see 121/32n. Poe, who left college so early, often lashed out at "Professor" Longfellow.

126/58-62} The six lines from "Worship" come from these pages: 2, 3, 8, 12, 15.

127/4-8} On p. iii.

127/14-16} From "Worship" (238), Poe's italics, and omission of exclamation point.

127/17-29} From "Hebrew Hymn" (1 ff.). Poe adds italics and changes "more glorious."

127/30-34} From "To a Lady About to Take the Veil" (st. 11).

127/35-37} "Saint Mary's Gift."

127/38-40} "Sonnet: Birds in Winter" (7 ff.).

127/41-44} "Sonnet: My heart built up a palace."

127/45-47} "To an American Statesman" (st. 5, lines 7-8).

127/48-49} Poe here exaggerates (see "didst" at p. 128).

127/54-57} See *Godey's* laudation of Lord (7/45) for a sample. See *The Town* for a humorous rejoinder to the rev. by Poe (in the Poe *Log* of 5/31).

127/58-59} Poe here puns on *The Litany* of *The Book of Common Prayer*, as above.

127/60-63} Wm. Trotter Porter (1809-58) was the popular, sizable editor of the varied sports and cultural journal *Spirit of the Times* in NY (from 1831-1844). Poe was friendly enough to attempt to place a sketch by P. P. Cooke (1846, *Letters*, 313-15) in the weekly.

127/64-69} Poe was partial to the folk-humor style of such sketches, as in A. B. Longstreet's "Georgia Scenes," which he had praised in the *SLM* (H 8.258-65). The two "tales" were "The Big Bear of Arkansas" by T. B. Thorpe and "Jones' Fight" by "an Alabaman." For a laudatory judgment of the ed. see Mott, 480-81.

128/2} James Field, ed. of *St. Louis Reveille*, was a friend of Poe and often supported him in his paper (see Ostrom, *Letters*, 318-20, 324, 327).

128/5} Poe had become friendly with the young Felix Octavius Carr Darley (1822-88), who was to become one of America's greatest illustrators, first, through his contract to furnish plates for *The Stylus* (1/31/43) and next, for his two woodcuts for the "Gold-Bug" (6/7/43), q.v. in Quinn, 369, 392.

128/6} NY: Saxton and Miles, 1845, 15 p.

128/12-13} Misprint for *The Dorsay Portraits* (Phila.: Carey and Hart, 1845, 128 p.). These seem to be caricatures or take-offs on satirical sketches dealing with the portraits by the notorious Count Alfred D'Orsay, member of Lady Blessington's coterie in London (described by Willis in his "reports" from London), soldier, spendthrift. The sole copy of the book has not been available to me for examination. Perhaps Poe's orientation toward British novels by Disraeli (*Vivian Grey*) and Bulwer Lytton (*Pelham*) motivated his remark at the end.

128/17-20} No copies of this "pamphlet" are reported by the LC catalogue. It was first pub. in London: H. Clarke, 1845, 74 p.

Johann Heinrich Daniel Zschokke (the proper spelling, 1771-1848) was reared in Prussia before becoming a strolling actor, then a serious student at Frankfort, and finally a teacher and novelist. He moved to Switzerland where he held a high post in the government educational system and published, most prolifically, histories, historical and moralistic fiction (collected writings pub. 1825-28 in 40 vols.). See 150/45 ff. for a less favorable notice of this author.

128/26} This rev. first appeared in the *SLM*, 9/36, almost exactly as it is here. Poe's opinion appeared in condensed form in "Literati," *Godey's*, 9/46.

Lydia Maria Francis Child (1802-80) was a prolific writer of novels, tales, essays, and occasional pieces in journals and separately published. In the "Lit." sketch (H 15.105-107) Poe commends her work for its "purity, chastity and ease" of style, imagination and vigor--the last evident especially in her novel of 1836, *Philothea*. The *BJ* article is a virtual reprint of Poe's rev. in the *SLM* of *Philothea: A Romance* (Boston: Otis, Broaders; NY: George Dearborn, 1836), 2 vols., 234 p., now published again (Boston: J. H. Francis, 1845, 290 p.). The only significant changes are at the beginning (see below, 33n). All collations and refs. to the text are made to the 1836 ed. The book initially and in its reprint and also Poe's long, enthusiastic revs. evidence the intense interest of the time in historical fiction and in classical history, also shown in Poe's works, such as "To Helen," "The Coliseum," and "Shadow."

128/27} For Poe's views of Eugene Sue's style, see MM 176, 181. The designation itself is Poe's coinage.

128/33} The first seven lines of this rev. differ from that in the *SLM* of 9/36, 2.659-662, para. 1 (two sentences of which are adapted to the beginning of the "Lit." sketch):

"Mrs. Child is well known as the author of 'Hobomok,' 'The American Frugal Housewife,' and the 'Mother's Book.' She is also the editor of a 'Juvenile Miscellany.' The work before us is of a character very distinct from that of any of these publications, and places the fair writer in a new and most

favorable light. Philothea is of that class of works of which the
Telemachus of Fenelon, and the Anarcharsis of Barthelemi, are
the most favorable specimens. Overwhelmed in a long-continued
inundation of second-hand airs and ignorance, done up in green
muslin, we turn to these pure and quiet pages with that species
of gasping satisfaction with which a drowning man clutches the
shore.
        The plot of *Philothea* is simple...."

   128/38}   *Both* texts misprint "Clazomenea" which is correct in
Pin 72.

   129/55}   denied / introduced

   129/56}   should be tried

   129/64}   and is condemned (*SLM*)

   130/5}   is also adjudged (*SLM*)

   130/17}   already done (*SLM*)

   130/19}   It is done / They are

   130/27}   Not a typo in *SLM*.

   130/41}   On pp. 141-42.

   130/66}   The most special (*SLM*)

   130/71}   with his now (*SLM*)

   131/1-39} On pp. 152-54: Charities / Gharitioe (line 25) and
bounty / blessing (line 37).

   131/46}   This is in ch. XIII, near the end.

   131/52-54}   are pictures whose merit will not fail to be
appreciated by all whose good opinion is of value. (*SLM*)

   131/57}   soul-directing (*SLM*). Although an obvious "typo" I
leave it for its many interesting implications.

   131/61}   at Corinth (*SLM*)

131/70} Ch. XIV, p. 182.

131/73} In the novel the name is "Pandaenus" but in both revs. it is thus.

132/4-8} Ch. XV, p. 192. *SLM* (also the original) has "in the fountain" and "is then rejected." Cf. "the waters" in the original.

132/14-16} In place of "The subject ... Newnham" the 1836 text has: "It will be seen that even the chimeras of animal magnetism were, in some measure, known to the ancients." For Wm. Newnham, author of *Human Magnetism*, with its discussion also of Chauncey Hare Townshend, see Poe's *BJ* rev., 69-70, used also for M 180 (with commentary notes on the book and both men). Poe's keen interest but skeptical views helped to produce the hoax-tale "Valdemar," later discussed in the *BJ* (see 355-56).

132/21} of the events which befell (*SLM*)

132/22} On pp. 194-96 of Ch. XV.

132/48} The word "intreaty" is probably a deliberately used old-fashioned form, actually given by the *OED* for the 17th and 19th centuries.

132/72-73} again said / had spoken (a line deleted here)

133/7} It may be that Poe derived a slight stimulus for his three dialogue-in-heaven sketches from this passage quoted in 1836--as well as an idea used in "Valdemar," completed 11/45.

133/19} slaves, Mibra and Geta (*SLM*)

133/25-55} *Collations*-- 25: is no ignoble specimen / 26: not any powers on the part of any author / 27: an evidence / 29: and this little ... is greatly weakened / 30: the constant necessity of / 31: costume, habits / 32: It should be borne in mind that the "*Pompeii*" / 33: this species / 36-37: an event so far from weakened in interest by age, ... thrillingly exciting / 51: the mere vehicle for bringing forth / 53: which we have mentioned as at variance / 54: shall be justified in declaring the book / 55: a signal triumph /.

133/50} Both the 1699 *Telemachus* (*Télémaque*) of Bishop François Fénélon (1651-1715) and *Anacharsis* (*Voyage du jeune*

Anacharse — 1788) of the Abbé Jean Jacques Barthélemy are mentioned in the unrevised first para. of 1836, as setting the frame and tone for *Philothea* as a favorable educational novel. The favorable citing of Edward Bulwer Lytton's *Last Days of Pompeii* (1834) earlier in the para. is a rare instance of approval of Bulwer, much discussed and often exploited for curious bits of learning and *bons mots* but rarely praised. For Poe's adverse views of this very book see M 49, CS 6 and, especially, LST 4.

133/57, 58, 61, 62-63, 64, 65-67 & 134/1-8} *Collations*-- advantageously / Its purity of thought and lofty morality are unexceptionable. It would prove ... / with whose spirit / for when we know that the fair authoress disclaims any knowledge of the ancient languages, we are inclined to consider her performance as even wonderful. / at which a scholar / (and ... teachers [end]) = the trial of Aspasia and her friends for blasphemy should have been held before the Areopagus, and not the people. and we can well believe that an erudite acquaintance of ours would storm at more than one discrepancy in the arrangement of the symposium at the house of Aspasia. But the many egregious blunders of Barthelemi are still fresh in our remembrance, and the difficulty of avoiding errors in similar writings, even by the professed scholar, cannot readily be conceived by the merely general reader.

On the other hand, these discrepancies are exceedingly few in Philothea, while there is much evidence on every page of a long acquaintance with the genius of the times, places, and people depicted. As a mere tale, too, the work has merit of no common order--and its purity of language should expecially recommend it to the attention of teachers.

134/8} One notes that Poe has trimmed up his language a bit and has eliminated a few unnecessary phrases and technical points which, he may have realized, were shaky in the first rev., such as the Areopagus formality. He still leaves the deliberate impression that he has newly read Barthelemy's book, probably never even conned. It is noteworthy that he seems to exempt, totally, this class of fiction from his growing conviction about the harm done to art through didactic objectives, probably because the purpose and the method are so overt and the artistic aims so secondary.

134/9-18} Although this is probably by Briggs, as Hull asserts, the material is so intimately connected with the end of "Literary Gossip" on p. 346, which has much in Poe's vein of thinking and received numerous side linings from him in 1848, that I include it for overall interest and relevance. Moreover, Charles Astor Bristed (1820-74), friend of G. H. Colton, who published "The Raven," was richly attractive to Poe as an independent thinker and scion (see M 191a). Certainly, Poe rarely is even this favorable to the hostile *Knickerbocker Mag.* Bristed's rev. of *English Poetry and Poets of the Present Day*, is on pp. 34-46, in "Literary Notices," while the "original poem" is on 487-88 (q.v. below).

134/19} Article (b) on this page is actually the third of a group marked "Literary Gossip," the first two of which are undoubtedly by Briggs. But they are all separated by rules and it is barely possible that Poe, with his intense admiration for Tennyson might have executed this one, especially in view of his sidelining the whole discussion that precedes the poem and even portions of the verse. The text itself is based on the *Knickerbocker*, reason for denying it at all to Poe. Poe's obvious attention to the article subsequently makes it worthy of reprinting, with a very great caveat as to authorship.

134/29-30} Tennyson used as a motto for his 1830 "Mariana" poem "Mariana in the moated grange," an adaptation of *Measure for Measure*, 3.1.279.

134/35-39} A similar anecdote appears in the London *Mercury*, 1921, 5.144-55, "Memories of Tennyson" by Mrs. W. Cornish.

134/40 ff.} The "American gentleman" was misleading the *Knickerbocker* and therefore the *BJ* concerning the provenance of this, for it was a most interesting poem printed in a "collection of miscellaneous poems by various authors, edited by Lord Northampton, *The Tribute* of 1837. The *Edinburgh Review* of 10/37 said: "We do not profess to understand the somewhat mysterious contribution of ... Tennyson, entitled Stanzas ... which describe the appearance of a visionary form, by which the writer is supposed to be haunted amidst the streets of a crowded city" (The Cambridge ed. of Tennyson's *Poetic and Dramatic Works*, Boston, 1898, 832-33). Interestingly, the great poem *Maud; A Monodrama* (1855) grew out of this poem, which was included as the 4th section of Part 2, with many changes. Tennyson later said that it should be called "'Maud, or the Madness' ... slightly akin to 'Hamlet,'" one of the two "finest things I've written." Our specific interest is the closeness in manner, mood, and even theme it bears to typical Poe productions, with some hints too for Poe's "Ulalume" of 1848. Tennyson summarized it to Dr. Van Dyke: "It is dramatic; it is the story of a man who has a morbid nature, with a touch of inherited insanity, and very selfish. The poem is to show what love does for him ... the man with the strain of madness in his blood and the memory of a great trouble and wrong that has put him out with the world" (Riverside ed., p. 198). The two editors responsible for this period in *A Literary History of England* (1948, Baugh, ed.), Chew and Altick, keenly say about the poem: "The plot, with its poor but proud lover pitted against the heroine's wealthy family and his haughty rival, and leading to death and madness, is quite commonplace. The self-revelations of a speaker of abnormal mentality owe something to the scenes of madness in prose fiction" (1387). There is something of "Lenore" and "The Man in the Crowd" and, especially, as this section was reshaped in the final publication (pp. 214-15), of "The Raven" and "Ulalume" so that the cross currents between the two poems are worth exploring, although not here, as an instance of the "spirit of the age" as it affected both master poets.

135/46-47} memorial / manorial; heats / beats

135/57-59} In the 6/45 issue, front page. Poe's growing enthusiasm over this "new" process (as in 83-86) makes insertion of this technical explanation likely.

136/14} See 223 (8/23/45).

136/15} Willis was Poe's truest and staunchest friend.

136/16-18} See 118 for another announcement and poem from this work and the rev. (162-67).

136/19} *Democratic Review*, 5/45, "On Writing for the Magazines," 16.455-60, by Evert A. Duyckinck.

137/4-5} This typical view is developed in his essay on Willis; see 17/12-36nn and also reprint in M 220.

137/7} See "Magazine Prison-House" in 2/15 *BJ* (in TOM, 1205-10; note his "Preface"); also 24/51-60 [facsimile text].

137/12} Poe was then developing this view in the *EM* as well as the *BJ*. See MM 143 and 182, based on cols. there.

137/24} T. B. Macaulay's 7/37 *Edinburgh Review* notice of Basil Montagu's *Works of Francis Bacon* was gathered into the *Critical and Misc. Essays* of Macaulay which Poe reviewed in the 6/41 *Graham's*, q.v. in CS 11. For other, less favorable comments on Macaulay see *Br.* Index.

137/27} This is Poe's coinage.

137/37} For Nathaniel Hawthorne, Wm. Gilmore Simms, and Nathaniel P. Willis see Index of this vol. and of *Br.*

137/45} Poe's original 1836 version of this essay laid no stress on the capacity "to construct"--now become his major critical tenet.

137/52} The name probably suggested to Poe his derisive parody "Snook Farm Phalanx" for "Brook Farm" in the 12/13 *BJ* (see 338 below).

137/55} This rev. originally appeared in the 10/36 *SLM*, 2.727-30. Poe provided a new Intro. (paras. 1-4) to replace the original one (paras. 1-2). He used the earlier piece with no changes beyond occasional minor verbal ones, a few of which are annotated below, new para. indentations, and, in the final para., the omission of the last sentence.

In 1836 he was reviewing a reprint pirated by Carey, Lea and Blanchard, Phila., under the title *Peter Snook, a Tale of the City; Follow your Nose; and other Strange Tales. By the Author of 'Chartley,' the 'Invisible Gentleman,'* &c. &c. (1836). This must have been drawn from the 1834 London reprint of the 1831 *The Old Maiden's Talisman and other Strange Tales* (Bull and Churton) in 3 vols. (In the *Am. Mag.*, 5/1836, is an announcement of *Peter Snook and other strange tales*, 2 vols., surely the same as that above, as appears from the LC catalogue). "Peter Snook: a tale of the city" is the longest, occupying 2.157-296 and 3.3-146. The author, James Forbes Dalton, is unmentioned in the London and American vols. and, probably for that reason, by Poe, who calls him simply the author of "Chartley" and of "The Invisible Gentleman"--said to be "exceedingly popular, indeed, unrivalled save by Boz and a few others. Poe even implies that he is Dickens himself; by 1845, he had dropped this notion. Dalton has managed to escape every major history or dictionary of British literature and even the *DNB*, but he still retained Poe's favor after ten years as this long reprint shows. Poe's lack of information about the reprint of the original rev. and a certain vagueness in the whole Intro. led L.G. Clark of the *Knickerbocker* for July to condemn *Peter Snook* "as an article from an old English Magazine" which the editor "lauds without stint." (See 169/31-40 [facsimile text] for Poe's comment.) Collations for cited passages below are being made from one of the very few copies extant in the USA, the British 3 vol. 1834 edition; borrowed from the Midwest--a scarcity which shows the great decline of this "Magazinist" in popularity.

137/56 ff.} This section is on pp. 161-63.

137/59} Here and on the following pages are the loci of citations (in Poe) in the 1834 London ed.: 59:161; 61;162; 65;163; p. 138/52:259; 138/62:261; 64:263; p. 139/13:264; 18-48:269-73; 139/73-140/45:281-84; 141/14-18: vol. 3, 61; 45-57:75-76; 142/6-26:90.

138/47-58} On p. 259.

138/59-66 + 139/1-3} On pp. 261, 263.

139/8-17} On p. 264.

139/19-47} On pp. 269-73.

139/25} waiting / standing

139/34-35} Here a page and a half, deleted, contains inquiry and answer about Margate and Clarinda.

139/35-40} Some of the "punny" names for business firms and balance sheet details in two of Poe's tales may have been suggested by such passages in Dalton's work: "The Business Man" in the 2/40 *BGM*: TOM, 484-85 and "Diddling": TOM, 879.

139/55} The separation into two words, "ware house", is not authorized in the *OED* save that two 16th century instances are spelled thus. It is left uncorrected in the text.

139/73 + 140/1-45} On pp. 281-84.

141/14-18} Vol. 3, p. 61.

141/45-57} On pp. 75-76.

141/52} from business / from my business

142/6-27} On p. 90.

142/45} *SLM*, 2.730: Poe first wrote "in petto"--his customary error for "in brief" (which in Italian means "in the chest" or "in secret, in reserve"), by confusion with the French "petit," one imagines (see *Letters*, 148, TOM 365/V 870/9 1017/29).

143/19} Originally Poe printed "each in their own way."

143/26} The last sentence of the 1836 rev. is omitted. It reads: "We will venture to assert that no painter, who deserves to be called so, will read 'Peter Snook' without assenting to what we say, and without a perfect consciousness that the principal rules of the plastic arts, founded as they surely are in a true perception of the beautiful, will apply in their fullest force to every species of literary composition."

144/1-7} This new heading and the concept of dividing brief notices from longer revs. must have been a joint idea of Briggs and Poe, which prevailed for the rest of vol. I before Poe's assumption of complete control in vol. 2. Hence we find the new classification plus the old "REVIEWS" as follows: 6/14 (1.379 and 376 ff.); 6/21 (1.395 and 392 ff.); 6/28 (1.410, under "BOOKS LATELY RECEIVED" and 408 ff.). In vol. 2 the distinction of short notices and long revs. is dropped and the new department becomes "CRITICAL NOTICES" on 7/12 (2.7 ff.) and for the rest of the vol. The new title reflects Poe's views of what a rev. should be, despite the curt treatment given to most of the books noticed.

144/8-14} This large work by William Bolles (1800-83) apparently had wide circulation for the decade, came out in an abridgment (New London, 1846 and Phila., 1846), and was reprinted in 1848. Poe's views changed, q.v. in the rev. on p. 148. The 1845 ed. had 944 p.

144/33-41} This is one of the many competitors of the reprint journals, often devoted to the latest British novel, such as the *New World*. It was pub. by Lloyd Smith, vol. 1 comprising the nos. of 1-6/45. "The Eventful Life of a Soldier" by Joseph Davidson is printed in triple columns, pp. 348-92. In style, this is the only one of the notices that does not sound like Poe's ordinary reviewing approach (e.g. "matter given very liberal," "very beautiful," and "only object"), but it seems unlikely for Briggs to be responsible for one out of the entire number. Hence it is here included.

144/42-51} This *Manual* of 211 + xii p. was published in 1829 by H. J. Bigelow (1818-90), who had just been elected president of the Boylston Medical Society, a group of Harvard medical students. The assertion about Strabismus is verified in Wm. Bigelow's *Memoir of H. J. Bigelow* (Boston, 1900), p. 29. Poe undoubtedly derived this "fact" from the Intro. (no copy has been available to me for verification).

144/52-58} Article (d) concerns a reprint of a 40-page pamphlet, dating from 1841. The two anonyms ending Poe's list are "G. T." and "S. E. J." on 31-33 and 37-40. Poe was fond of *Rejected Addresses* by Horatius Smith and his brother (q.v. in Pollin, "Figs, Bells, Poe, and Horace Smith," *Poe Newsletter*, 6/1970, 3.8-10) and in general liked satirical verse and parodies (see *Br.*, articles under Laughton Osborn).

144/59-60} *The Bustle*; *a Philosophical and Moral Poem*, by the Most Extraordinary Man of the Age; Boston: Bela Marsh, no. 25 Cornhill, 1845, 82 p.

145/1-3} For Poe's derision of the bustle in America, see the end of "Scheherazade" (TOM, 1169); cf. also the first woodcut in the *BJ*, 1.8 (used as my first illustration, on p. 1). The accompanying text is not by Poe, but it well states the case against such deforming dress. The only copy of the book that I managed to consult (in the Harvard library) does not support Poe's charge of poor verse, but the frankness was "gross indecency" for the time--perhaps accounting for its disappearance from public libraries. The Preface explains that Eve kept sexual love (lust) alive in Adam by subtlety of dress. She extended the fig concealment to a sort of kilt and then she died. Examples of the text are these: St. 37, p. 23, "And drawn from her high destiny by lust;--/ Seduced her husband, and returned to dust."; St. 50, p. 30, (They always used dress) "to recruit / Their sexual influence."; St. 60, p. 35, (*re* bodice) "The very chinks / Twixt certain parts, are easily espied."; St. 93, p. 51, (The bustle) "was seen / More ... to ape / The natural parts of woman; till between / Enormous buttocks of enchanting shape, / Appeared, like life itself, a deep ravine!"; St. 103, p. 56, "Why do you make your rump appear so furious--/ So meretricious? and seem so salacious?"; St. 114, p. 62, (She is) "a living sexual volcano."

145/4-10} This book, of 226 p. (1845), is by the "dictionary man" of p. 144.

145/12-19} This lurid, highly satirical exposé of Phila. (494 p.) by his old friend Lippard (1822-54) was never reviewed in the *BJ* despite the asterisk. For their close relations see *Letters*, 242-43, 455-56, and Pollin, *PS*, 1974, 7.22-23. For Darley and Poe see my Index. Darley's frontispiece consists of two separate drawings, the top, a man with a lamp looking into an open grave, the bottom, a man floating in a coffin on some fairly large body of water.

145/20-22} This must be one of the many crude, seamy imitations of Eugene Sue's inordinately popular *Mysteries of Paris* that poured from the press in cheap newsprint, leaving no trace today.

145/23-28} This 1845 novel of 108 p. has disappeared from available library collections. The terms used and the question at the end (see M 52, para. 1 for a similar instance) bespeak Poe. He did not "recur to it" afterwards.

145/29-52} This poem of 1845, of 71 p., has become extremely rare (Harvard copy used). Poe's transcription of the conclusion is accurate. It supports his views of the adverse effect of an obvious, overriding "message" as he explains in his diatribes against Longfellow.

145/53-61} It behooved Poe to support the Wiley and Putnam's Library (his 1845 books being published also by W. and P.) with a strong commendation, although no further rev. appeared. These two vols. were 768 + xiv and 242 + vii pages. The author, although known as Eliot W. (1810-52), was Bartholomew Elliot George Warburton, miscellaneous Irish writer and traveler; the 1845 *Crescent* related his 1843 Eastern tour. Typical of the response was a glowing rev. in the *Dublin University Mag.*, 1/45, 25.116-26.

146/1-5} This is included as an example of the types of reasons for eliminating entries from the canon, although Hull says, "Poe, I think, is the author." In language it has the rhetorical exaggeration of Briggs: "of necessity" and "every thinking person must read"; "pretending to acquirement can remain quietly in ignorance of what is written" and "Most sincerely do we rejoice"--all foul flourishes to Poe! In content Poe would repudiate such regard for Brougham and for Voltaire (*"the most powerful who ever existed"*!). Of this, there is no doubt, but less extreme instances where doubt should exist occur in this section of the journal, where Poe and Briggs were sharing management, perhaps uneasily.

146/6-17} The style and information of the last sentence cause an ascription of this to Poe. The book, of xxii + 33-355 p., is a selection of essays from *Discours sur Quelques Sujets Religieux* and from *Nouveau Discours* by Alexandre Vinet (1797-1847), Swiss litterateur and theologian, who taught at Basel, with great repute, and wrote prolifically on behalf of liberty of conscience and separation of church and state. Poe alludes to Thomas Chalmers (1780-1847), teacher of theology and chemistry, who wrote numerous treatises on the first, and on philosophy et al.

146/20-28} No traces of the first two have been found in lists and libraries consulted. *The Comic English Grammar* (1845) is a 144 p. reprint of an 1840 work by Percival Leigh, illustrated by John Leech, who also did work for *Punch* and was to illustrate *Mrs. Caudle's Curtain Lectures* in 1846 (see 109 above). In his 1/42 *Graham's* rev. of *Stanley Thorn* (at the end), Poe sets Leech above Cruikshank as an illustrator (see H 11.15), but acknowledges the latter's greater reputation. It was Poe's contention that all previous writers on grammar were misleading, with Lindley Murray as perpetuating ancient errors (see "Rationale of Verse," para. 5). For this school textbook writer (1745-1826) see FS 33c. Poe seems a bit confused about the role of the illustrator as "author." The fault in "best work of the two" is exceptional in Poe's writing--perhaps a typesetter's gaffe left uncorrected.

146/30-31} Mirabeau Buonaparte Lamar (1798-1859) was the second president of the Republic of Texas. He also wrote poetry in the Byronic fashion (*DAB*).

146/32-35} "The Oregon Question" (523-33) by David Dudley Field (see 56, 80 [facsimile text]); "The Bridal of Pennacook" (537-55) by J. G. Whittier; "Emerson's Essays" (589-602) "by a disciple"; "How to Purchase Old Italian Paintings" (576-578) by J.

T. Headley.

146/36-39} Vol. 12, no. 6, essay on pp. 499-520. For Poe's many flattering refs. to the mag. and its proprietor, Freeman Hunt, see this Index plus Pollin, *Texas Studies in Literature and Language*, 1974, 16.305-13. For the banker, poet, essayist, and traveler, Henry Cary, see the "Lit." sketch (H 14.67-68) and M 158. Cary translated this article by Charles Coquelin, in the 7/43 *Revue des Deux Mondes*.

146/40-49} "Mystery of Iniquity" (551-74) by D. F. Bacon; "American Letters" (575-80) by "Il Secretario" (E. W. Johnson).

146/50-51} Poe adds "daily" and "dispute" for "a dispute."

146/59-61} George H. Colton (1818-47), author of *Tecumseh*, glorifying Gen. Harrison, q.v. in "Lit." sketch (H 15.9).

146/63-64} "Let not the cobbler (criticize) beyond his last" (Pliny on Apelles' remark about a cobbler critical of shoes in a picture).

147/1-19} This is drawn from the Wiley and Putnam first vol. in the new series, by Horatio Bridge, ed. by Nathaniel Hawthorne. Poe was very fond of the sentimental verse and "romances" of Letitia Landon (1802-38) and probably wrote a rev. of Laman Blanchard's *Life and Literary Remains of L. E. L.* for the 8/41 *Graham's*. This article helps to establish Poe's writing that rev. (in H 10.195-96), which is somewhat too gushy for his normal pen. Her inordinate popularity led to a host of rumors about the marriage to Captain George McLean (Governor of the Gold Coast colony), and her death from prussic acid, perhaps from an overdose of her "medicine," perhaps a suicide, perhaps murder through her husband or a "discarded mistress" (*DNB*).

147/20} On pp. 137-39.

148/8-14} For data about this and other eds. see 144 [facsimile text].

148/15-18} Poe demonstrated his own need for such a dictionary by citing that of Bolles in a letter to T. H. Chivers of 11/15/45 (*Letters*, 302) and in his 1846 "Lit." sketch of Margaret Fuller (15.79), although there it sanctioned a usage that he wished to condemn as "vulgar." Despite the "need" and the several eds. of the work, it has disappeared from all large libraries in NYC (being consulted in the Harvard U. copy). All the important details and most of the language of this long rev. are borrowed from the Prefatory material of the dictionary, very slightly adapted.

148/18-22} Here and below Poe is borrowing the names cited by Bolles, so that it is scarcely necessary to try to sort out which of many dictionaries of the late eighteenth century were intended. Thomas Sheridan (1719-88) issued *A General Dictionary of the English Language* (1780). John Walker (1732-1807) projected his "Pronouncing Dictionary" in 1774 but published it in 1791, apparently basing it partly on Sheridan's.

149/14} While Poe merely seems to affirm the approach and principles of Bolles throughout this rev., it is important to note the conservative position he takes about spelling save for the Noah Webster "thrust" against the "our" ending. This rev. of 1845, a kind of midpoint in Poe's critical output, might well serve as a guide for a thorough analysis of his spelling habits and practices, not only as author but also as editor. The variants for the tales provided by TOM and Pollin provide materials hitherto discouragingly scattered, and the Ostrom *Letters* are another large source. Yet there is still no study of Poe's presentation of the language throughout his two decades of authorship--an analysis much needed. (For a small beginning to two spelling elements of this topic, see *Br.*'s Intro. "On the Digraph and Dieresis in Poe's Texts," pp. xxxvi-xl.) This is one of the few wholly favorable refs. to Dr. Samuel Johnson, who seemed too verbose and oratund to Poe, and who represented the oppressive hand of England on American culture, especially at this period of Poe's veering toward the "Young America" movement. For numerous refs. see *PD*, 49 and note his derogatory coinage (actually an abridgment) of Johnsonism (*PCW*, 30).

149/35} It is important to note Poe's approval of the sanction of obsolete words, since his own habits in both creative and critical work led to a merger of the old-fashioned and the modern, despite his inconsistent condemnations of style in his revs. Again, one notes no thorough or even partial study of the whole matter, save for the cursory treatment in the Preface to the Booth-Jones *Concordance* to the poetry (1941). My *Poe, Creator of Words* (1974; revised edition 1980) and *Word Index* (1982), virtually a concordance to all the creative prose, furnish much more material for a systematic and thorough study of such matters as his inclusion of rare words: "tantalistical," "ebon," "litten," "nare," "tintimarre," "moss-y-mantled," and "Aidenn" or his new coinages such as "tintinnabulation" and "marginalic."

149/36-37} This abridgment came out in 1846 (see 144 [facsimile text]).

149/51-57} These are given as follows: Directions to Foreigners (Particularly the French) (pp. 12-14); Rules to be Observed by the Natives of Ireland and Wales, in order to attain a just pronunciation   of English. Mostly extracts from Mr. Sheridan's Works (15).

149/65-68} It is likely that this small item was inserted by Poe, friend of William Gilmore Simms, whose "Magazine" paralleled the *BJ*, *The Southern and Western Monthly Magazine and Review*, 1-12/45, in its lifespan and its being almost totally written by the ed. himself. The May issue attacked the *North American Review* for provincialism. Poe's data are somewhat confused here, suggesting that he did not see the article (pp. 297-311) itself. Simms, the author, complains that the *North American Review* has recently issued a circular appealing for funds to continue the journal, maintaining that for nearly 30 years it has "represented" the taste, science, and literature of America. In rejoinder Simms avers it has forwarded the interests solely of New England, excluded Southerners, and ignored the greater cultural importance of NY. Abroad it is given far too much credit, alas. The sentiments are generally those expressed by Poe in his frequent attacks.
The source of Poe's information must have been Simms or Mathews, whose book Poe was about to rev. (193-95). See also Briggs' article, "The North and South," citing the *North American Review* in *Simms' Magazine* (1.337-39, 5/31/45).

150/1-6} This 1745 reprint has 176 p. Mrs. Catherine Grace Frances (Moody) Gore (1799-1861) pub. over 70 works of fiction, drama, and song lyrics over her long career as author, very popular in her day and parodied as such by Thackeray. Her genre is accurately given by Poe who clearly knew her *Cecil*, of which he satirically speaks for its borrowed learning in "Thou Art the Man" (TOM, 1051). Benjamin Disraeli and Bulwer Lytton, authors of the two novels mentioned, have worn much better, to this day: *Pelham; or the adventures of a gentleman* (L., 1828; 3 vols.); *Vivian Grey* (L., 1826; 5 vols.).

150/26} The "well-known scholar and *litterateur*," on the previous page, is specified in the above ref. as William Beckford, author of *Vathek*, an opinion that Poe borrowed from R. H. Horne's *New Spirit of the Age*, q.v. in TOM, 1060 n10.

150/27} Robert Southey's *Doctor* was to Poe still an anonymous work, stuffed with curious learning and whimsical sallies, which he reviewed in the 6/36 *SLM* and used for SM 2, about which see SM 2a, e, f, for full discussion. For Poe and Southey, see Pollin, *Wordsworth Circle*, 1976, 7.101-106. Hull indicates here echoes of a passage that Poe had used three times before, in reviewing *The Doctor* (*SLM*, 7/36), *Canons of Good Breeding* (*Burton's*, 11/39), and *Guy Fawkes* (*Graham's*, 11/41).

150/33} Poe uses here a characteristic device which Hull labels "the title trick," a means of economizing time and including the maximum number of books noticed in an issue. The method becomes habitual in the second vol., when Poe is sole ed. and reviewer.

150/33-44} For earlier announcements (and spelling correction) see 92/20-22.

150/46} Am. ed. published 1845, 111 p. in double columns. Trans. by Samuel Spring. *Giafar Al Barmeki*, a tale of the court of Haroun al Raschid (NY, 1836, 2 vol.), is sometimes ascribed to Gardiner Spring, a prominent NY minister.

150/55} Samuel Spring (1746-1819) was a Congregationalist minister, prominent in the foreign missionary movement and a founder of Andover Theological Seminary.

151/1-11} Mordecai Noah (1785-1851), lawyer, playwright, journalist, U.S. Consul to Tunis (1813-15), ed. of *National Advocate*, *Enquirer*, *Evening Star*, and the NY *Sunday Times*, invariably elicited friendly comments from Poe, as in both sets of "Autography" (H 15.110-11, 207) and even in *BJ* 11/1/45 below when reprinting the Lyceum report of the adversary of the Boston *Transcript* (p. 297 [facsimile text]). Poe had worked on his *Times* in 4/1844 (*Poems*, 332) which had immediately reprinted "The Balloon Hoax" (TOM 554). There is reason to believe that he had contributed ideas to Pin 23 and *Pym* (Note for 5A). Unfortunately there is no file of the *Times* extant, only a fragment of one issue; this source cannot be traced. Poe's love of

flowers is demonstrated clearly in several sketches, such as
"Eleonora," "Domain of Arnheim," and "Landor's Cottage," and in
such poems as "To Helen" (of 1848-49) and "For Annie."

151/12-19} The large size, lavish format, and generous
emolument of this book must have augmented Poe's resentment
against Longfellow, q.v. in S. Moss, *PLB*, 184, and Pollin, *Mi Q*,
1984, 37.475-82. The book was *The Poets and Poetry of Europe*
(Phila., Carey and Hart, 1845), 779 p.

The ornamental title page consists of 17 little scenes of
Europe set in a circle around the title, the author and the
publisher, signed: G. H. Cushman / J. Warr. There is a second
title page, which gives date of publication and a sub-title ("with
introductions and biographical notices") and a quotation from
Gray. Some translators to whom Longfellow gives special thanks
are John Bowring, trans. Dutch, Spanish, Portuguese; W. Herbert,
trans. Icelandic, Danish, Spanish; Louisa Stuart Costello, trans.
French; Edgar Taylor, trans. German, French, Spanish; Robert
Jamieson, trans. Icelandic, Danish; Charles T. Brooks, trans.
German; John Adamson, trans. Portuguese; Benjamin Thorpe,
trans. Anglo-Saxon.

151/20-29} Anna Charlotte Lynch (later wife of Vincenzo
Botta, scholar and prof. of Italian at NYU) (1815-91), set up an
important literary salon that included Poe, Greeley, Margaret
Fuller, et al. Poe explains in the "Lit." sketch (H 15.116-18) that
her many poems in journals and annuals did not warrant a vol.
in 1845 (but *Poems* came out in 1849, these two poems being on
93-98). The two poems were later to be reprinted in the 6/20/46
Harbinger, 3.28-29. Poe adapted sentences from this headnote for
his sketch of Anne Lynch (15.117) as follows: The "two noble
poems ... should be considered as one, for each is by itself
imperfect. In modulation and vigor of rhythm, in dignity and
elevation of sentiment, in metaphorical appositeness and
accuracy, and in energy of expression, I really do not know
where to point out anything American much superior to them,"
etc. The rest of his sketch is so effusive as to indicate a more
personal involvement, in 1846--if only in gratitude for her
tribute and support--than he usually had with the "literary
ladies." Miss Lynch and her circle of poets are interwoven into
Poe's life intimately and crucially from 1845 (see all the Index
refs. in Quinn, *Poe*, and TOM, *Poems*), leading me to conjecture
that the two poems reprinted by Poe conceal her picture of Poe
himself, charged with a cold indifference to the poetess. Poe
had done the same with the poetic addresses of Mrs. Osgood, who

was a more attractive member of the "circle." Many of the terms reflect Poe's works and the themes are intrinsic to his orientation; e.g., "The Ideal" (11.1, 5-6): "A sad sweet dream! It fell upon my soul / Darkening the fountain of my young life's stream, / It haunts me still and yet I know 'tis but a dream." See her letter to Poe (dated by Ostrom as 6/27 in Check List, and given in H 17. 258-59) thanking him for this "notice" and exhorting him to endeavor to rally from the despondency manifested in his recent letter to her (now lost). No one else has drawn this inference, to my knowledge. See also 282/30 for her poem on "The Ivory Christ" and 326 for "Farewell to Ole Bull."

152/1-5} There is no evidence that this is by Poe rather than by Briggs, save for the Poe-oriented topic, the style of the three short discussion-paras. and the likelihood that Poe had more access to the exchange papers, such as the Charleston *Mercury*. We note the coinage of "word-spilling" (line 57). Poe was especially sensitive to abusive and florid language; his discussions of these matters and grammatical faults were hallmarks recognized by all readers. Moreover, from his soldiering days ('27-'28) at Fort Moultrie in Charleston Harbor, Poe displayed interest in the cultural activities of the city--an interest unlikely in Briggs. Since there is a kind of irony usefully pointed out by the editorial writer here, I assign this to Poe.

152/56-57} The practice of alliteration, usually within limits, as in the two "b's" and two "w's" of this sentence, betokens Poe rather than Briggs, whose style is more heavy-handed and whose sentences normally ramble tediously or awkwardly. Poe was also becoming more attached to the city, and would be more likely to defend it against such aspersion, especially in a journal named after its main thoroughfare (see 1/3 *BJ*, 1.1).

153/1-7} Tayler Lewis (1802-77) was lawyer, educator, Orientalist, and at this time taught Greek at the Univ. of the City of (not in, as Poe gives it) New York. In 1850 he was to shift to Union College, his alma mater. This 1845 book of 378 p. was intended as a college text despite Poe's final paras.

153/10-11} Lewis makes this point in his first para.

153/14-28} These lines are a paraphrase of the Statement of the Argument, pp. xxi-iii.

153/21-24} This topic is basic to *Eureka*, as in H 15.210-11, 310-11.

153/29-33} This para. is, almost verbatim, from the first sentence of para. 2 on p. xxi.

154/21-24} The information is from the Statement of Argument, on p. xxii.

154/25-33} Poe synopsizes fairly, with stylistic improvement, the argument of Lewis, pp. xxi to xxiii.

154/35-40} The material here is from the Statement of Argument, p. xxiii.

154/46} By the obsolescent term "converse" Poe seems to mean any interchange of ideas, not merely through oral speech.

154/49} Curiously, the word "Platonian" is given as a substantive for "Platonist" (1569, 1611) but not at all adjectivally.

154/53} It is noteworthy that this harsh generalization by Poe is sidescored by him in the 1848 markings.

154/57-66} These two quotations (with Poe's small "caps") come from pp. xii-xiii. Poe himself, in *Eureka*, which says much about "nebular star-dust," was accused of "a subtle pantheism" (q.v. in Pollin, "Contemporary Reviews of *Eureka*," *Am. Transcendental Q.*, 1975, 26.26-30).

154/67-69} In *Eureka* Poe carefully notes that John Pringle Nichol--Poe erroneously gives him a terminal "s"--(1804-59), prof. of astronomy, writer on science, and lecturer in 1848 (just in time to influence *Eureka*), has been abandoning his "nebular star-dust" views (H 16.222-3, 262, 297-98). George Combe (1788-1858), leading spokesman and writer for phrenology, lectured in America (1838-40). Poe knew his *Elements of Phrenology* (q.v. in M 12b; see also *PD*, 23). Poe liked essays of Francis Bacon but was becoming ever more dissatisfied with his writings on the methodology of science, most demonstrably at the beginning of *Eureka*.

155/1} The quotation ending at the top is from p. xii.

155/3-5} Poe cited this sentence by Gottfried Wilhelm von

Leibnitz (1646-1716) five times, beginning with 1831 ("Letter to B_____"), after taking it from Coleridge, without knowing its original source. He had just learned this from Charles Briggs' rev. of Mackie's tr. of J. E. Guhrauer, *Life of ... Leibnitz* in the 5/26 *BJ* (1.328-31). The full account is given in M 161b; see also MM 38, 87, for more on Leibnitz' role in Poe's works.

155/6-11} Lewis, Intro., ix-xi, frankly avows one intention to be producing a textbook for college seniors. Clearly Poe was limited to his Intro., despite numerous quotations elsewhere in Greek, frequently incorrect.

155/15} The "modest" book had 128 p.

155/17} The author was Charles Edward Anthon, son of Charles Anthon's brother, John, who was an educator and numismatist (1823-1883). The mistake, while trivial, proves that although Poe gave the impression of a close acquaintance with this noted scholar, whose letter on biblical Hebrew he exploited repeatedly (see MM 115, 175), he had little or no personal contact with him. Indeed, the length of this rev. of so slight a book also implies an attempt to curry favor with the "wrong father." See the *BJ* Index for numerous refs. to Charles Anthon. On the other hand, it is possible that the entire article is ascribable to Briggs, who had less reason to claim any knowledge of Charles Anthon the uncle. Hull believes that the ref. to "the Rev. Dr. Anthon," being unique with regard to all of Poe's statements on Charles A., certifies the non-Poe provenance. On the other hand, if it were a mistake by Briggs, about the uncle (as father) and if Poe knew the facts, would he not have corrected the error in proof sheets before it might be ascribed to the wrong one of the "*BJ* editors"? Also, the interest in palace furnishings (p. 156) and the language of "floating palaces" sound like Poe's work. I include it with a very firm caveat.

155/39-43} He begins his book with an anecdote about Charlemagne and the founding of Aix-la-Chapelle (pp. 13-21). The mid-point is p. 76.

155/51} Throughout the article the accents over French names are left omitted: Trèves, Liège.

156/4} On p. 78.

156/17-36} This is on pp. 105-106.

156/38} This quotation is on pp. 109-10.

156/43} travelled / traversed

156/69} "thoughts of all"

157/1-13} Hull assigns this and also the next article somewhat tentatively to Poe. The style is not that of Poe: e.g., "by no means as good" where Poe would invariably write "so good" and the lack of a comma after "devotion," rendering the sentence meaningless at first reading (but this could be poor typesetting and proof-reading), and the ambiguity about a "giant and buffoon" (is this one character or two?). The volume appeared both in London and, probably typeset from the copy sent by ship, in NY (153 p.). Sue's *Mysteries* had led to a host of so-called Sue novels, some of them apocryphal, such as *Mysteries of Berlin.*

157/14-22} Like many juvenile works, this has become impossible to examine over 100 years later, but it is listed in Roorbach. Hull believes that Briggs gave himself the two leading revs. and assigned the other trivialities to Poe, to follow in sequence; hence, meriting little space and probably a most casual glance.

157/23-29} The Wiley and Putnam origin of this work probably required this terse, unthoughtful laudation of the book and author. William Howitt (1792-1879) was early a published author in journals as well as books. He and his wife Mary used their extensive travels as source of many works of description and experience (see 109 for an earlier notice of another work).

157/30-38} Most of this vol. of 1845, of 222 p., was a reprint in large measure; the first three stories were pub. in 1838 (Harper) under the title *Constance Latimer or The Blind Girl.* Emma Catherine Embury (1806-63) was a prolific writer of verse, tales, and novels, from childhood. From 1828, as Mrs. Embury, she established a literary salon and was much sought after by journal editors, sometimes serving as a nominal one herself (cf. Mott on her role in Snowden's *Ladies' Companion,* 627). She contributed many items, as a kind of assistant ed., to *Graham's* during Poe's editorship (see *AL,* 1968, 40.164-178). Her sentimental, cliché-ridden, obviously contrived works signally show the claims demanded on Poe's patience and tact. Her being a "female writer" made the last easier for him.

157/39-47} This is the fifth ed. of a work first pub. in 1831, by the greatly admired writer James Kirke Paulding (1778-1860). Poe had sought his influence with the Harpers for earlier publication of his tales (and also for his *Penn* magazine venture; see Index to *Letters* and H 17.31-32; also Quinn, 249-51). This novel, set in upper New York during the French and Indian Wars, was one of his many historical pieces, often deprecating the English and current romantic approaches. The last sentence neatly suggests Poe's probable view of the work itself.

157/48-55} For rev. see 167 [facsimile text].

157/56-61} This was by Mrs. Elizabeth Caroline Grey (1845), 155 p. Surely Poe's sentence is ironic.

160/1-18} The failure to publish, on 7/5/45, evidences the managerial, editorial, and financial crisis of the magazine at the end of June: the growing dissension between Briggs and Poe, the latter's return to his tippling habits under strain, the decline in subscriptions, and Bisco's growing impatience with the lack of profit. For details on these factors and on Briggs' efforts to replace Bisco with J. Smith Homans and surprising withdrawal, himself, from the *BJ*, see H. Ehrlich's survey, reprinted in my Introduction (text at footnote 36 through 52). Without question Poe played a role in the writing of Bisco's statement.

162/1} Poe's copy has survived. See M Intro., note a.

162/4} Henry Beck Hirst (1817-74), an eccentric bird-seed store-keeper, poet, and lawyer, of Phila. was Poe's intimate friend during his residence there (see Woodberry, *Life of Poe*, 2.419-200). He helped Poe write the biting rev. of Griswold's *PPA*, for the Phila. *Saturday Museum* of 1/28/43 (H 11.220-43) with an unquestionably Poe content and style, and he wrote the biography of Poe in the same journal of 3/4/43, crammed with the ana and poems supplied by Poe himself. Despite Poe's later cooling to Hirst because of his parody of "The Haunted Palace" (see TOM, *Poems*, 317, and Quinn, 354-55), Hirst wrote a moving, sympathetic obituary notice in the Phila. *Courier* of 10/20/49 (Quinn, 653-54). In 1848 appeared his *Endymion* in 4 parts. He died insane.

The first para. of the rev. is a combination of Poe's personal knowledge and material from the Preface: that "Most of the following poems were written" during "preparation for the Bar," that some had been published in magazines anonymously, and that the book's "uncouthness" is due to the subject rather than the author. The pages are v-vi + 168.

162/7-8} This compound is a Poe coinage.

162/21} Poe means any (other)....

162/25} For Poe's half-dozen uses of this coinage for exaggeration see *PCW*, 28.

162/26-28} Hirst may have contributed to Poe's theory and knowledge of prosody, ripened in 1843 as the *PPA* rev. and *Pioneer* "Notes on ... Verse" show.

162/46} This is in *The Various Writings of Cornelius Mathews* (NY: Harper, 1843), pp. 91-115. Hirst's is on pp. 11-27.

162/52-62} The quotations are from 13, 16. Hirst wrote "teeth" not "tusks."

163/37-42} The quotations are from pp. 22, 25, 26, with "swept" for "slept" in line 23.
Poe coined the compound "Nat Leeism" as on 11/45 (where he uses a hyphen, q.v.). His praise of an allegory, although attenuated, is unusual. The poems discussed from lines 25-75 are found on pp. 31-39. Presumably Poe believes it to imitate Tennyson's "The Lady of Shalott" and treats its pedestrian awkwardness in kindly fashion.

164/5-89} These poems occur on pp. 48-52. The substantive variants are these: 11) swifts ... glide, 35) sung / sang.

164/90-91} This poem (pp. 53-56 in Hirst's vol.) was reprinted as "beautiful" in the 5/31 *BJ* (see 136a).

165/1-18} In the final line of the stanza from "Unseen River" (on p. 54) Poe apparently found exquisite the alliterative "r" at the very end; he seems to be exempting the poem from his condemnation of early and obvious allegory, as in his locus classicus of anti-allegory condemnation in the 11/47 *Godey's* rev. of Hawthorne's tales (see H 13.148-49), and also in Hirst's "Eros" (on pp. 60-63). In the Hawthorne rev. he had also exempted Bunyan's work, as well as Fouque's *Undine*, but omitted

Spenser's poem. In phrasing and idea lines 4-6 are a prelude to his ending for "Phil. of Comp." claiming that only at "the very last line" of "The Raven" "the intention of making him emblematical of *Mournful and Neverending Remembrance* is permitted distinctly to be seen" (para. 36).

165/19-46} These two poems are on pp. 64-69, 70-73. It may be Poe's occasional ref. to the general idea, as in "Israfel," that makes him "redeem" this quatrain. For the last phrase, see Pope's *Essay on Criticism* (2.162): "The sound must seem an echo to sense."

165/47-55} "Everard Grey" (pp. 74-75) first appeared in the 10/43 Snowden's *Ladies' Companion.* It could not be cited for a "dactylic line" in the "Notes on English Verse" of 3/43, so much earlier in the year, but in "The Rationale of Verse" of 1848 (para. 57, H 15.241), Poe illustrates the "caesura" (as he terms a truncated foot) by quoting a line (without author) which is obviously adapted from the second line of the *BJ* passage: "Pale as a lily was Emily Gray" (see TOM, *Poems*, 395). Is it of any significance that Poe had used, as his pseudonym "Edward S. T. Grey" in 1844, and repeatedly afterwards (*Discoveries in Poe*, 383-84) and that in 8/45 Frances Osgood published, in *Graham's*, a story called "rather indiscreet" by TOM (*Poems*, 383) because the beloved married man is very like Poe? (See the many Osgood items in the Index of the *BJ*.) We also note line 10 of "The Sleeper" (1841): "The lily lolls upon the wave," showing Poe's partiality for the flower and the situation.

165/56-60} The three poems are on pp. 76-79, 81, and 82-84. One might expect Hirst, proprietor for a time of a bird-seed store, to know the Latin name ("Fringilla") for a "chaffinch." The most noted poet, Bryant, would have approved of this sort of nature poem, probably inspired by one of his. Poe's adjective "equivocal" seems totally unwarranted, but strangely he does not mention the very limping meter of the lines. The second poem opens thus: "Hurrah for brown Autumn, hurrah! hurrah!"

166/1-23} The pages for these poems by Hirst are as follows: 85-87, 88-91, 92-94, 99, 100-103, 104-105, 106-107, and 108-110. Poe has changed nothing but accidentals and added the italics for pointed ref. or underscored approval. His point about "Eleanore" is simply that Tennyson's "Oriana" uses the title-name as a constant refrain (four times per stanza)--enabling him to avow his knowledge of Tennyson's works rather than to prove

Hirst's "source" of inspiration. "Eulalie Vere" is curiously linked to Poe himself in that Hirst published this as "Elenor Long" in *Snowden's Ladies' Companion* of 6/43. Since Poe's manuscript for his own "Eulalie" (1844), published in the 7/45 *American Review* and on 8/9/45 in the *BJ*, once belonged to Henry Hirst himself, we may assume some link between the two friends in Phila. concerning this curious name. (TOM, *Poems*, 348 also makes this point.) Moreover, the name from the French for "Eulalia" for "fair speech" after whom was named St. Eulalia, contributed to "Ulalume," especially as Poe pronounced that curious title (See *Poems*, 419-20). Even the second name "Vere" has a definite Poe connection, involving the important poem "Lenore" (q.v. in *Poems*, 334 n. to line 3, and Pollin, *Names*, 1974, 23.1-5). Last-- concerning the distich from "Ellena" it is strange that Poe ignores the obvious resemblance to Coleridge's mariner's report on the roars of the ice: "Like noises in a swound!" (I, st. 15).

166/24-76} The remaining poems in this column cover these pages: 111-112, 113-15, 116-17, 118-19, 120-21, 122-24, 125-26, 127-28. Only accidentals are changed (save for added italics/ and o'er / on on line 42). It is difficult to determine an error in line 26, whereas the plural verb "disturb" in line 32 should be singular. Barry Cornwall was the penname of Bryan Waller Procter (misspelled as "Proctor" by Poe) (1787-1874), writer of pretty songs, now forgotten, a tragedy, biographies, and a friend of the London literati (see 16, 126 above). Poe's appraisal is accurate. In line 62 Poe uses "nerve" to mean "force" or "strength" as often in his adjective "nervous."

Poe's arbitrary and idiosyncratic significance for the word "caesura" as here (line 75) is consistent with his definition of this "foot" in the disputed rev. of Griswold's *PPA* of 1/28/43, sometimes claimed as a joint product of Poe and Hirst (see above), q.v. in H 11.227-29. I doubt Hirst's ability to evolve this prosodic theory independently and persuade Poe into adopting it for his later essays. It has not convinced later theorists of poetry at all.

167/1-3} This vol. of 228 pages, priced at 50 cents, was no. 2 in the series "Library of American Books." The figure in the review looks like an "11"--showing perhaps Poe's indifference or distress over the vol. for its meagre and unbalanced selection (see below). The first in the series was *Journal of an African Cruiser*, ed. by Hawthorne (see pp. 147-48). Poe's vol. was announced as pub. in the *Daily Tribune* on 6/26/45 (see TOM, 1397-98 for a commendatory para. on the first three titles of the series in the

Weekly Mirror of 4/26/45). The pub. was certainly the result of the public acclaim over "The Raven" of January, but Poe privately and here in public took issue with the choices of Evert Duyckinck, the firm's literary adviser. For once Poe was promised a kind of European pub. in that Wiley and Putnam had a London office and used the American sheets with an English title page (apparently reaching the London reviewers by the end of July or early August).

167/1-23} The poems in these lines are located as follows: 127-28 (from preceding page), 129-31, 132-34, 135-36, 137-42, 143-45. No substantive changes are made save that for line 15, Hirst wrote "bard and glowing." In designating "one instance" as "hexameter catalectic" Poe seems to have erred, for the 4th line of the stanzas seems to read as heptameter. Below, Poe seems to be objecting to the irregularity (or variations of feet) in line 22, for he rigidly advocates strict, almost metronomic metrical patterns.

167/24-42} These sonnets are on pages 163, 162, and 168. No substantive changes are printed, but an accidental is highly significant, Poe's inserting parentheses around line 38. This involves two poems of Poe, thus: The last three lines of his second "To Helen," that is, to Helen Whitman, read: "While even in the meridian glare of day / I see them still--two sweetly scintillant / Venuses unextinguished by the sun!" (*Poems*, 447; TOM properly cites Hirst's "Astarte" and refers to the other poem). The earlier poem, "Eulalie," of 1844, includes, in its third and last stanza: "For her soul gives me sigh for sigh / And all day long / Shines bright and strong / Astartë within the sky" (p. 349; TOM indicates the name as that of the Phoenician for the planet Venus). One has the feeling that in the rambles along the Wissahickon Creek in Phila. Poe must have led the way in discussing such arcane, astronomical lore and that he was pleased to reprint Hirst's sonnet embodying his own hints, in the first poem, "Eulalie." Before taking leave of this rev., we must note an interesting MS., a verbal sketch of Hirst by Poe left to Griswold for posthumous publication, obviously dating from 1848, for after indicting Hirst for *hyperism*, as above, and imitativeness, he notes his *Saturday Courier* attack upon Poe for "stealing" concepts and language in "Ulalume" from Hirst's "Endymion" published in the 7/44 *SLM*. Poe refutes this and then shows that Hirst stole ideas from the early "Lenore" for his "Penance of Roland" in the 1/48 *Graham's*-- a passage moreover of atrocious grammar. Poe amusingly rebukes him. Hirst's obituary notice of Poe came out before this sketch (*Works*, 1850, vol. III, 209-213; H 13.209-213).

167/45-59} The twelve titles are given in the order of their printing with three errors, of a sort, proving, I think, that Poe merely handed the vol. to his typesetter for this part of the rev. He must have ignored the Table of Contents in favor of using the running heads of the tales, for the umlaut over "Maelström" and the circumflex over "Rogêt" (both erroneous and unnecessary) are omitted there alone (the umlaut is included in the Table of Contents and "chapter" title); likewise, the undifferentiated type might have led to the careless lower case form for "conversation" (line 48). This small matter, uncorrected, plus the brevity of the rev. typifies Poe's distress over the "arrangement" and lack of full scope. Poe repeated this criticism in public again via a para. in *The Aristidean* of 9/45 (p. 238), perhaps directly or else using the hand of English supplied with copy by Poe. (For vindication of Duyckinck's choices, see Jay B. Hubbell, Merrill Facsimile Text [1969], xxi.) Poe's letters discussed this theme often: on 1/8/46 he proposed for a second vol., another collection "far better than the first" (*Letters*, 309); on 8/9/46 he complained to P.P. Cooke that Duyckinck in stressing the "analytic stories" ignored his sense of "book-unity" respecting "the widest diversity of subject, thought, and ... tone and manner of handling" (328-29); similarly on 12/15/46, to Eveleth (332). Quinn explains his acceptance of the choice through the need for money, his royalty being eight of the fifty cents per copy (realizing, he said, about $120 for the successful sale of 1500 copies, pp. 464-66). Incidentally, much later in his "sequel to Mr. Lowell's memoir" of Poe, Philip Pendleton Cooke incorporated this information about the inadequate selection in the 1/1848 *SLM*.

Poe had fears about the narrowness of the selection as killing a varied critical and popular appeal, but the response was far flung and often favorable throughout America and abroad (see digests of the revs., *PS*, 1980, 13.24-26).

167/65} It has 327 p. and was announced on p. 157. Throughout, he praises Anthon as always (see Index entries). Poe may have owed his views on English prosody to the precursory vol. by Anthon. The incorrectly repeated "as" (line 70) shows Poe's haste in processing this rev.

168/1-5} The few specific points come from the Preface.

168/6-14} This book of 1-4 + 6-264 p., by the universally known "Christopher North" of *Blackwood's Mag.* is an Am. reprint of a much earlier British ed., with which Poe seems to be familiar in his 10/36 *SLM* rev. of another work (H 9.199). In general, he despises the criticism of Wilson, but respects his creative work, poetry and fiction. For details see SM 1 (plus notes) and SM 7, also Poe's rev. of his book on Burns in the 9/6 *BJ* below. The Preface, by R. Hamilton, tells of the book's popularity in England and Scotland and speaks of its "intense interest" and its "simple, natural and pathetic ... style."

168/15-21} This vol. is of 3-5 + 6-282 p. Its Pref. by the same person in ref. to (a) above speaks "of the same delicious pathos," lists the characters, discusses the background of the novel, and praises its religious and moral qualities.

168/22-28} Although this is a mere announcement, it suggests the ready availability to Poe of Macaulay's essays, which he frequently read and quoted. Judging from names mentioned in his work, he discarded (or sold) the other two vols. in the trio which appeared thus: I, 758 p., *Essays Critical and Miscellaneous*: T. Babington Macaulay, with portrait engraved by T. Sartain from a picture by Henry Inman. II, 1-6 + 390 p., *Critical and Miscellaneous Essays* of Archibald Alison (the correct spelling), with a portrait engraved by Sartain from a picture by J. Watson Gordon. III, 5 + 480 p., *The Works* of Rev. Sydney Smith, with a portrait engraved by Sartain.

168/29-41} This item reminds us of the rush to reprint British journals (as well as books) and the unfair competition that they offered to Am. magazines and their contributors. Pointedly Poe, ed. and magazinist, underscored their low prices. Yet today these Am. reprints have disappeared from almost every large library, and my page refs. must be to the British editions: the first, a rev. of *Old and New London*, ed. by the misc. author and publisher, Charles Knight, in 6 vols. (book of the same title), on pp. 259-318; the second, a rev. of the book by the same title, by the Hon. Caroline Norton, Sheridan's granddaughter, who had promoted Poe's friend Frances Osgood in London (see M 104 and note c [the rev. on pp. 460-72]).

168/43-46} Poe greatly respected this British publication, as his several allusions and short revs. indicate (see Index to *BJ*) and especially note his words: "No medical periodical equals The Lancet" (p. 92). His interest stems from the broad scope of the topics covered, such as "human magnetism," and the sober treatment.

168/48-54} For the numerous refs. to this journal see the *BJ* Index, and for its founder George H. Colton see M 191 (and Mott, pp. 750-54). Its importance in "first" publishing, after the *Mirror's* stolen march, Poe's "Raven" and other works in 1845 made Poe generally considerate in such summarizing revs. The first article is by Joel Tyler Headley, rarely called "clever" by Poe (see the abusive rev. in the 10/1850 *SLM*, H 13.202-209). Edwin P. Whipple (1819-86), broker, lecturer, lit. critic, was a fine reviewer and critic, even at this early stage, who evoked Poe's laudation (see his article of 1/1849, left in MS. in the Hirst papers at the Huntington Library, pub. in *Graham's* of 1/1850; H 13.193-202). The rev. of Griswold's book is on pp. 30-58, and the portion on Tennyson (45-48) would appear reprinted in the next issue of the *BJ*, 170-71 [facsimile text]. For numerous refs. to and articles on Tennyson in Poe's works, see Indices to *BJ* and *Br.* and, especially, M 44. Whipple's long rev. (pp. 30-58) was collected in the 1848, 2 vol. work *Essays and Reviews* (NY), 1.285-354, a slight proof of the popular appeal among thoughtful readers of his excellent searching essays. He starts with a discourse on poetry, discusses Wordsworth, Byron, Shelley, and Scott, and controverts Griswold's low ranking of Tennyson (see next issue's reprint).

168/54-61} William Ross Wallace (1819-81), Kentucky-born lawyer and poet of NYC, was friendly with the *Mirror* literati and always with Poe, whose extravagant praise, as here, 170, and 307, M 290, and even the Hirst-Poe 1843 rev. of Griswold's *PPA* (H 11.241) suggest a needed treatment of their relationship. A frequent magazine contributor, author of *Battle of Tippecanoe* (1837), he eventually won renown for his "And the hand that rocks the cradle" etc. in the 1851 *Meditations in America*. The cited poem (27-29) wins from ed. Colton the tribute of comparison with Elizabeth Barrett Barrett.

169/1-20} The ref. to Barrett and Schiller is easily explained in the headnote to her poem "The Dead Pan," which, with its slightly varied refrain for its 39 stanzas of "Pan, Pan, is dead" was another hint for the refrain-ingenuity of "The Raven." The first para. of the note is this: "Excited by Schiller's 'Götter Griechenlands,' and partly founded on a well-known tradition mentioned in a treatise of Plutarch ('De Oraculorum Defectu'), according to which, at the hour of the Saviour's agony, a cry of

'Great Pan is dead!' swept across the waves in the hearing of certain mariners,--and the oracles ceased." In her third para. she explains her inscription of the poem to her friend and fellow-poet, John Kenyon, whose "graceful and harmonious" paraphrase of Schiller's poem turned her thoughts to the topic. Since it was Schiller's poem of 1788 that awakened Goethe's respect for him, one may doubt that Poe had truly read it before his glib award of the palm to Wallace for the best treatment of the theme.

In collation this quotation shows a line omitted by Poe right after line 16: "And wed Creation to Divinity--". This stanza is full of the defect that Poe granted, Wallace's "excessive rhetoricianism," but thought him "richly eloquent" and "noble" as a man (see M 290a).

169/21-40} Late in 1835 Poe had conducted a "war" against the puffery of T.S. Fay's *Norman Leslie* in the *Knickerbocker*. His antagonism to this journal and its editor Lewis Gaylord Clark (whose name he probably deliberately misspelled) was so great that Briggs, one of the early contributors to it, took care of all notices for the journal in vol. 1 (see Mott, 606-611). Poe, annoyed at the scorn of his *Peter Snook* article, is overeager to mock Lewis G. Clark's ignorance, for his correction is partly incorrect in that Montaigne, in his *Essays* (Bk. 1, ch. 16) is here quoting an old French proverb for "Every man to his taste," in which the preposition "a" is needed. As for Clark's next "blunder"--it is true that this phrase from Horace's *Epistles* (I, 6.1.1) is usually taken to mean "wonder at nothing" but Creech translates: "To admire nothing, as most are wont to do" etc., while Pope, in his "Imitations of Horace" reads: "Not to admire, is all the art I know / To make men happy and to keep them so."

Concerning the derogation of his "wig"--see 315/37 [facsimile text] for the same remark, apparently stemming from the social significance of a well-kept, appropriate periwig in the 18th century--an item neglected only by a thorough reprobate (see "William Wilson," TOM, 428/34, 913/20, 1012/2, 1185/7, 1234/11).

169/41-47} Poe showed his awareness of the rich scientific contributions of Alexander von Humboldt (1769-1859) as early as "Hans Pfaall" (*Imaginary Voyages*, 403, footnote), but now the ensuing publication of *Kosmos* in parts (1, 2, 3, 1845-47) aroused his interest in a universally applicable theory of all scientific laws that eventually led to his writing of *Eureka*. To the world renowned German naturalist, traveler, savant in numerous fields of science, humanist, and humanitarian, Poe dedicated his cosmological "Poem" *Eureka* explaining that his plan was "synaeretical" (q.v. in *PCW*, 38), because "he discusses the universality of material relation" (H 16.187); at the end too he cites a passage from *Kosmos* on "Translatory Motion" with an English translation in his text (299), with the implication that it is his own. It certainly reads more idiomatically than the tr. that follows this one, obviously written by one more skilled in German than English. Needless to say, Poe was incapable of translating *Kosmos* or, according to Briggs, any German at all. His egregious errors in such words as "leiden" and "andere" support Briggs' scorn (see his letter to Lowell of 7/16/45 in Woodberry, 2.143). Note also that Mrs. Ellet, who knew Poe well, on 12/16/45, rescinded her request for a favor which contained a simple German phrase in part because "you would not decipher my German manuscript" (see Poe *Log* for 12/15 and 12/16).

The work "critick" for "critique" is a standard 18th century spelling, obsolescent for 1845, but not disallowed. It may represent the unchanged word used by the translator, like the "true" for which Poe would use "authentic" or "literal." The column (on p. 15) following this short note explains the provenance of vol. I of *Kosmos* which has just been published in Berlin, dedicated to the King of Prussia. It was developed from lectures of 1827-28 and seeks to "exhibit the worth and close connexion of all the laws of nature." It apparently comprised a letter sent to the ed. of the *Kölnische Zeitung* (i.e., of Cologne), the whole then reprinted in the New York *Deutsche Schnellpost* of 7/2/45 (page 2). This was a well established daily in German, with a long publishing history, whose name was equivalent to *Telegraph* (see *Discoveries in Poe*, 172 for Poe's use of the name in "Von Kempelen"). For other refs. in the *BJ* see 236 for the paper and for Humboldt, 234, 247, 281.

170/1-60} See 168/48-54 for Edwin P. Whipple's article in the 7/45 issue of *The American Review: A Whig Journal* from which Poe reprinted the section on Tennyson (pp. 45-48; 1.322-26 of the 1848 vol.), shorn only of the first three sentences of the para. concerning Griswold's "slip" in making the poet only of fourth rank. To Poe, Tennyson was supreme among living poets. It is Whipple's general view of poets also that causes this extraordinary praise of the critic. Surely, this sentence, second in para. 4, echoes or parallels sentiments voiced by Poe: "Poetry is that sublime discontent with the imperfection of actual life, arising from the vision of something better and nobler, of which actual life is still speculatively capable" (1.288 of the 1848 ed.). In sidelining most of this quoted passage for his own or Mrs. Whitman's attention, he seems to be stressing his view of lines 9-

10, oddly reminding us of Baudelaire's making a similar statement about Poe's expressing his own thoughts. The quotation is virtually perfect save for line 13: a keen / of keen. The quatrain in 41-44 is stanza 13 from "A Dream of Fair Women."

171/1-60} This too proves accurate upon collation with Whipple's original text, save that both texts misspell "Oenone" (with an "Ae" now corrected). Poe had independently misspelled that title in the 12/44 M 44. The ending quotation is from the first stanza of "The Lotus Eaters."

171/61-72} Even during his editorship of the *SLM* Poe had decried dependence in literary tastes and in shaping creative efforts upon the countries of Europe, particularly England; hence his satires of Disraeli and Bulwer Lytton and his stress upon originality. This indigenous development was a main objective in the establishment of the *Penn* magazine, then become the *Stylus*. Now he could join forces in 1845 with an increasingly vocal and well defined group, as shown through this speech, published as *Americanism: an address delivered before the Eucleian Society of the New York University / 30th June, 1845*, 34p. For Poe's role in voicing these fundamental views and associating himself with the group see Perry Miller, *The Raven and the Whale* (1956), p. 135, and Claude Richard, *Studies in Bibliography*, 1968, 21.25-58. Certainly, however, Poe's adherence was tentative and incomplete, as line 63 shows. Presumably he refers to the European "young" movements which had inspired the name and many of the platform principles, such as that of Italy, promoted by the exiled Mazzini, or that of Germany, which was eventually upheld by Heinrich Heine, or even of England, which was to be joined by Benjamin Disraeli (although very different in most of its aims). Poe's declaration of support here explains his favorable treatment of Mathews' nationalistic, allegorical *Big Abel and Little Manhattan* (see reviews on 257 f., 285 f.). In thus extensively excerpting the *Address* Poe is virtually publishing a manifesto for the *BJ*, although his commitment for the half year left of the journal would be tempered by his own individualistic tendencies and views, as always.

171/73-80} In the collations of the material (from pp. 19-32 of the pamphlet) I shall list not only substantive changes but several accidentals which aid the reading. These will cover the excerpts on 172-73, as the markings will indicate: 171/79 and

insist / and to insist; 172/4 proclaimed / declaimed; 13 in humor,
/ in humor, the copy of; 26-27 institutions; 29 sketchers; 45
Here,; 55 nature,; 66 whatever; 77 stranger might; 79 that single /
that; 83 in New / at New; 173/4 the engravers; 12 chanted; 14
pleasing and majestic; 21 and friend; 22 (3 pages deleted); 23 *A
National*; 30 of a national; 38 brother. Let him sustain his
interest against every other class.; 44 that he, one; 47 self-
justified and self-sustained etc.

173/52-62} There can be no doubt that this fairly long rev.
is by Poe, although carelessly presented. The content accords
well with his sentiments in other *BJ* revs. of and allusions to
Hazlitt works (see Index), and the style is typical of Poe's. A
reason for not signing it may be the obvious promotional aspects
of paras. 1-2, fully half Poe's content. Poe had to flatter Wiley
and Putnam, his own publisher for the tales and the soon to be
published poems. Moreover, he desperately needed their
advertising, and indeed elicited a sizable column on their new or
forthcoming or available books in most issues of the journal.
The firm was, apparently, taking the lead in issuing various
series that could provide a respectable library to the growing
middle classes with "improved taste"--a kind of Harvard Classics
plus Literary Guild concept. For example, it advertised in the
BJ of 9/27, different series: Books of Travels, Classic Fiction
(Fouqué, Peacock, Zschokke, Martin Tupper, et al.), "English
Literature" (Hazlitt, Hunt, Wilson), Biography, "Old English
Literature" (ed. by Basil Montagu and Lamb), its "American
Series" (Hawthorne, Poe, Headley, Mathews). Certainly these
were better than the "feuilleton" novels of the mammoth papers
or the newsprint pamphlets that sold for pennies, although
sometimes they were titles by Dickens or Bulwer in pirated
editions freshly set from the steamer-borne copy. We wonder
what Poe must have thought of his own *Tales*, very readable
indeed, but as drab and inelegant a volume in type and in
format as could be imagined. Soon he would be able to take
pride in the sale--he said--of 1500 copies (*Letters*, 301), proving
that the "juste milieu" had been attained; but Poe often enviously
commented on the sumptuous format of poems by Longfellow,
which subordinated text to design and pictures. Referring to the
"tact" of the selective editor was Poe's method of currying favor
with Evert Duyckinck, to whom Poe wrote a long series of letters
from 11/45 to 2/49 concerning books for loan, puffs of his work
to be placed, tales and poems to be inserted or recommended,
autographs to be supplied, etc. Despite all the favors conferred
(or perhaps because of them) Evert (and his brother George)

were far from flattering of Poe in their *Cyclopaedia of American Literature* article on Poe (1855, ref. ed. 1866).

173/60-76} In line 60 is a usage ("kind of books") that would have caused Poe to pounce on an author under rev. In line 71 he is using "quagmire" in a far less apt way than in M 276, where he says of "American Letters," "they are in a condition of absolute quagmire." As for a "happy medium" between "the ponderous and the ephemeral"--this is a third piece of evidence of the insincerity of the introduction of this rev.

174/1-12} The first five lines are so poorly written as to make one suspect that Poe had no or little hand in them; vide, "the ... sale of the Library was indispensible" (an allowed but old-fashioned variant) and "... of a gravity" etc., plus "well gotten up, but of a sufficiently standard character to warrant...." And this is followed by "whose" used for "of which" plus the words "implicitly following a good lead." But then we come to a favorite Poe phrase, "les moutons de Panurge" (Panurge's sheep), borrowed from *Pantagruel*, 4.8, as used in the 5/41 *Graham's* (H 10.122) and "Rationale of Verse" (para. 17) (H 14.217). And below we find a citation of Jeffrey and Gifford and of Wilson, typically full of prejudice, as Poe almost always claimed. Then the Poe origin becomes fixed.

174/13-19} This vol. by William Hazlitt (1778-1830), major essayist, especially on literature, philosophy, and art, was originally published with "Reign" for "Age" in 1821. When his *Literary Remains* were published by his son in 1836, Poe reviewed it for the 9/36 *SLM* (H 9.140-45) with unusual care. I suspect that the essays included in the vol. are the only ones by Hazlitt that he read, save for those conned for the *BJ* (see Index). Surely nobody would support his dictum in line 34.

This vol., vii-viii + 218 p., has a Preface by Hazlitt's son with a long complimentary excerpt from the *Edinburgh Review*, but the "quotation" is not found there; it sounds like Poe's invention. The phrase "vivida vis" is usually accompanied by "animi" to mean "the living force of the mind"--a rather unjustifiable truncation! What does he mean by "glowing fancy" in a critic, as a mark of comparison with the merits of Macaulay?

174/20-32} Poe is usually less favorable to Thomas Macaulay (1800-59) (q.v. via Indices for *Br.* and *BJ*). As seen, Poe had little respect for the poet and essayist Leigh Hunt, here alluding to his

Imagination and Fancy, No. 4 in W. and P.'s Library of Choice Reading (see rev. in 99-101 above).

For John Wilson, the great "Christopher North" of *Blackwood's*, who rarely drew a favorable word from Poe, see SM 1 and 7, and the *BJ* Index.

For Charles Lamb, whose ready wit and whimsy Poe seemed to like (lines 26-27 seem to allude to the second), see several *BJ* refs. and revs. and M 109 for a very good joke.

Francis Jeffrey (1773-1850), the founder and ed. of the *Edinburgh Review*, was often cited by Poe (see *PD*, 59; MM 61, 92, 181, 221). Every one knew about Wm. Gifford (1756-1826), first ed. of the *Quarterly Rev.*, Latin translator, assailant in print of Keats, ed. of the Elizabethans, but Poe probably read nothing by him (mere mention on p. 19 [facsimile text]). Certainly it was safe to see no point of "approximation" between them and the radical Hazlitt.

174/33-74} What can Poe mean by "an age of dishonesty"--an age that included Shelley, Keats, Byron, Godwin, Robert Owen, and their numerous friends? Having read and reviewed the *Literary Remains*, he knew of the frankness of *Liber Amoris*, his anti-Malthus stand and book on the subject, his vindication of Godwin in the face of the anti-Jacobin hysteria, and his attempt to deliver a balanced view of the great *mormio* Napoleon.

The excerpt comes from "Lecture VIII: On the Spirit of Ancient and Modern Literature--on the German Drama, contrasted with that of the Age of Elizabeth" (pp. 195-218). Collation shows the following changes: 53 five-and-twenty years; also the translation; 63 coffined / confined; opposition / oppression; 66 later / late; 71 that instant / at that instant.

175/17} By Poe's day everyone knew that this was by Thomas Hope (1770-1831), a wealthy dilettante and traveler, whose long picaresque novel had been published in 1819.

175/22-44} The vol. has 336 p. and a multiplicity of authors, of whom Murdoch (1811-93) would be best known (as a light comedian, as well as lecturer and teacher). Brief revs. of, or refs. to him or his work can be found on 105, 112, 247, 252, 296, 300. The section on metre is pp. 292-296, scarcely full enough to have given Poe any help with his theories. The age seemed to be obsessed with improving its standards of speech--probably as a means of social climbing. Note Anna Mowatt's and George Vandenhoff's public readings and the latter's book of model exercises (82, 90 [facsimile text]).

The word "orthophony" in the title is given by the *OED* without date as "the science of correct speech or enunciation" and with no ref. to its being obsolete, but the word is not given in two unabridged dictionaries consulted--of 1923 and 1945. The language of the last sentence is more colloquial than is Poe's wont.

175/45-68} Intro.: iii-xviii + 564 p. Alexander Reid (1802-60), professor and later headmaster of a Scottish school, had great success with this dictionary, now pirated in America, with an 18th ed. by 1864.

The four "improvements" laid down by the ed. are not those given by Poe who does derive his from the content of the preliminary matter. Poe's third point is not entirely tenable, although usually true. For Poe's reviews of other dictionary texts see the category of "dictionaries" in the Index and for his acute interest in language development and usage see preface to *PCW*.

176/1-6} This publication is by Henry Ustick Onderdonk (1789-1858), the middle initial being wrong for both author and publisher in the *BJ* text. The author was a physician and Episcopal clergyman who was suspended at his own request from office, for alcoholism. Far different was the suspension trial of his brother Bishop Benjamin T. Onderdonk (1791-1861), which was widely bruited in the press (see the humorous picture, "A Suspended Bishop" (*BJ* of 2/8, 1.89) with letter press not by Poe.

176/7-12} Anna Mowatt performed for two weeks at Niblo's to good reviews which were somewhat less spirited and laudatory than in her earlier runs (see 65-69, 76-78 [facsimile text]) as Odell indicates (5.156-57). Poe may have attended less regularly than the first run of *Fashion*, for he omits mention of her role in the comedy of *The Honeymoon* and in *The Pride of Lammermoor*, and also *Faint Heart* (Odell, 5.156-67).

176/14-38} Poe offers an interesting combination here of Anna Mowatt which perhaps stems from such factors as his increasing sympathy with the Young America's opposition to the domination of national taste by the British, the respect owed a talented, well to do socialite whose husband's reverses induced her to take up the pen and the buskin (see Odell, 5.99). Poe knew, as did all, that loyalty to her teacher in elocution and acting made her faithful to Mr. W.H. Crisp, regardless of the eminence of Edwin Forrest (1806-72), popular for his "animal vigor and sonorous voice" (*DAB*).

176/39-63} This para. with its proud avowal of his mother's profession has become a *locus classicus* concerning Poe's orientation to the theatre. Unquestionably, the low status of the actor, especially in Puritanical, moralistic America, had haunted Edgar ever since his entrance into the family of the prosperous, bourgeois, staid John Allan in 1811, after the miserable death (12/8/11) of Elizabeth Arnold Poe. Significantly, Poe omits mention of his inebriate actor-father David Poe, at times lampooned by the critics deriding his faltering presence and poor diction--all the circumstances of his death being entirely obscure. See Quinn for a thorough account of the life and career of Elizabeth Arnold (Hopkins) Poe (1787-1811) (*Poe*, ch. 1, "The Heritage," 1-50 and Appendix I, "The Theatrical Career of Poe's Parents," 697-724) and N. Bryllion Fagin, *The Histrionic Mr. Poe*, for the view of Poe's being peculiarly adapted to the life of the stage by nature, interests, physique, talents, associations and friendships (31-66). Certainly the final sentence has the defiant grandiloquence of a stage utterance.

177/1-31} The performance as Pauline was on 7/14/45 (see Odell, 5.156-57). Poe was sufficiently fond of the play by Bulwer and of this analysis to make it serve as M 177 in the 11/46 *Graham's*, which he starts with the following: "A hundred criticisms to the contrary notwithstanding, I must regard..." etc. For a full collation of his changes see M 177 note a; likewise, for further details about the play itself, including a summary of the plot. This is one of his then popular plays, others being *Richelieu* (1838) and *Money* (1840) (see 177b). Even Poe was captivated by the sentiments and "theatrical *flair*," vide his comparison to Shakespeare's "creation," and the intensity of his language in the last two sentences.

Poe's ref. to the heroine of Samuel Richardson is appropriate enough but shows no great knowledge of the book any more than other refs. to that novelist's works (H 8.54 and 10.218). We often have the impression that Poe's fictional reading was almost confined to the contemporary best sellers, a consequence of his career in reviewing.

Sentence 4 has a comparison derived from Jer. 4:19 and Sir Philip Sidney's *Defense of Poesy*, q.v. in M 177b.

177/32-66} Much of this section was lifted almost verbatim for the substance of part of Poe's "Lit." sketch of Mrs. Mowatt in 1846 (H 15.31-32). Poe confessed to seeing *Fashion* perhaps a half dozen times on 4/5 (see p. 76 and Odell, 5.98-99 for its 20 nights), so that he could have scrutinized her every feature and gesture for lasting memory. Certain predilections of Poe are prominent: his attraction to grace of movement (see his statements about Mrs. Osgood), to a strong, determined facial outline, e.g., what he terms a Roman or Hebrew nose, to a well-projected voice (American in accent!), in general to a "naturalness" rather than aristocratic reserve. We note that Poe italicizes the summarizing word "naturalness" at the foot of p. 177).

I must correct a blunder about this word as mistakenly printed by Harrison (H 12.188), namely "*naturalism*" from which I concluded in *PCW* that Poe preceded the "first usage of this meaning in the arts and in criticism" according to the *OED*'s "first" of 1850; reluctantly I withdraw the priority for Poe (*PCW*, 31).

In reordering his sentences for the "Lit." sketch, Poe did the following: lines 35-47 became para. 13 (on 15.32) and the last sentence, 47-48, cut down was merged above it. Lines 49-63 were the substance of para. 12, and the last two lines on 177 and 178/3 became the start of para. 12.

178/19-21} A new auditorium had just been opened at the Battery for Castle Garden, where light entertainment, such as varieties and dances, were regularly shown: on 6/18 a Hungarian *pas* by Desjardins (as one of several numbers--"dance and posings in scant attire" is reported by Odell, 5.160). Poe, who might have seen the great Fanny Ellsler in 1840-41, always evinced a keen interest in dance (see Pollin, *SAR 1980*, 169-82).

178/28} The Old Bowery had burned down on 9/22/36. Rebuilt by 1/2/37, this had lasted until a fire destroyed it on 4/25/45; it was to reopen on 8/4/45 as "the most beautiful ... in America," holding 4,000 persons (Odell, 5.161, 186).

179/1-12} Poe is unusually kind to this obscure poetaster (1806-78) for some reason, not known. He asked Duyckinck where he lived for his "Lit." sketch on 1/30/46 (*Letters*, 313), which remains a major source of information about him (H 15.37-38, although based chiefly on this *BJ* rev. [not in *DAB*]; Appleton's *Cyclopaedia* calls him a "very good man, and a rather good poet"). In the sketch Poe tells us that the work was never completed, and none of the essays or sketches were published. This part had 32 pages, of which 6 were front matter. Why indeed should Poe have devoted more than four pages to this mediocrity? Clearly, from the two publishers' names, we can assume Hoyt's involvement in a self-printing subsidy.

179/13-54} It was a medieval affectation of the age to insert a "u" in the spelling of words in "--ant" as Poe usually did in "Auncient Mariner." The two poems come from pp. 7-8. Poe is remarkably clement to this post-Augustan versification, full of cliches and second-hand sentiments and imagery. His italics for the selected "defects" certainly are warranted.

180/6-69} Poe's comparison justly suggests a similarity between the subjects in two different fields, both of which borrow from the pastoral tradition so popular in the narrative art of verse and genre pictures, typified by Goldsmith's "Deserted Village," known to all readers. Poe knew also that Asher Brown Durand (1796-1886) had recently shown his "new" picture, "An Old Man's Reminiscences" (its correct title), which is probably now in the Albany Institute and Historical and Art Society (see John Durand, *Life and Times of Asher B. Durand*, 1894, p. 173; see photographic copy in the Frick Museum, FARL 15718). The picture shows an old man with flowing locks, seated beneath a tree, retrospectively seeing children playing ball, riding on a hay cart, swinging, fishing, etc.--all normal activities exploited by both artist and poet. (See Briggs'review of the picture as exhibited, in the 5/3 *BJ*, 1.276.) We still esteem Durand for his illustrations and landscapes; his picture of Thomas Cole and Bryant overlooking the Hudson in the Catskills served as the cover for the 1982 telephone directory. Poe surely knew the article by Briggs on "The Art Union Pictures" in the 1/4 *BJ*, 12-13, which very warmly reviews the 12/20/44 exposition in New York City of works by the Hudson River School of artists: Durand, Cole, Weir, and Cropsey, starting with Durand's "large landscape," called "The Passing Shower."

In derogating the mechanical repetition of each first line at the end of the stanza Poe must be thinking of his own varied and integrated refrain in "The Raven." As for the italicized lines here and on 181-82, containing "pathos and imagination"-- we are struck by the conventionality and complacency of Poe's taste on this occasion. He even forgets to reprehend the frequent inversions (lines 24, 30, 42, 53). It is remarkable that for so long a transcription as this (180-82) only the accidentals were changed, save for one line that implies almost a rewriting by Poe: the morn shall no more bring / no more the morn shall bring (181/45).

182/25-30} Poe was very partial to the poems of Oliver

Wendell Holmes (1809-94), considered especially as a humorist and satirist; yet I doubt his knowing more than a few of his short poems, such as "Old Ironsides" and "The Last Leaf," the proper name of what he here terms "Old Man" (see also his ref. to the poem in the Hoyt "Lit." sketch and quotation of two stanzas in the 6/42 *Graham's* rev. [H 11.126]). His again insisting upon our being reminded "too forcibly" for one stanza out of twenty-four makes us aware that showing this kind of alertness in the "spotting" of likenesses with the implication of imitation or plagiarism is pretentious and basically misleading. Holmes' 7th stanza (the penultimate) reads thus: "I know it is a sin / For me to sit and grin / At him here; / But the old three-cornered hat, / And the breeches, and all that, / Are so queer!" (1st pub. in the 1/26/1831 *Amateur*). Mockery at his old-fashioned queerness is not basic to st. 2 of Hoyt's poem; it is the "pilgrim" whose feelings are primary and who reminisces upon his own past, melancholy over his own decline. As for Poe's pleasure in the "ninety-three" (181/23) it would be more pointed were we informed of the significance of a date that has no historical ref. (Washington's second inauguration?) and chanced to be two years away from Hoyt's birthdate. Presumably the year signifies simply the date of planting, fifty-three years ago. Is this truly "refined art" of "natural pathos"?

182/31-65} Concerning the "pencil" of the "white spire" (181/55)--if Longfellow had published this metaphor and moralistically developed the idea of a church steeple as tracing the man's life story, just imagine how harsh Poe's strictures would be. As for "New"--he continues to disapprove of the mechanical repetitiveness of the refrain device.

The title "Boemus" seemed to offer the typesetters much trouble, being so strange in appearance. Presumably it is Hoyt's creation, perhaps from the Greek root for "roar." By changing the "B" to "Pr" one produces a word that is somewhat familiar; moreover, Poe's capital "P" and "B" are not always clear; hence, the word in *Godey's* (for the "Lit." sketch) and in Griswold's and in Harrison's dependent ed. became "Proemus." It is the third stanza of Hoyt's poem. Poe is here invoking the well-known war-songs of Thomas Campbell (1777-1884), such as "Hohenlinden" and "Ye Mariners of England" (see H 8.306 for ref.). Poe makes frequent ref. to his numerous poems, reviewed his life of Petrarch, and respected his editing of the *New Monthly* (see *PD*, 17; *Br.*: Pin 4, 38, 78, MM 139A, 212).

182/66-68} Published by Wm. H. Colyer. See 145/20-22

[facsimile text]; also 213.

183/3-8}   *The Roman Pontiffs: or a sketch of the lives of the supreme heads of the Roman Catholic Church with a biography of one of the most distinguished of their number .... Translated from an original and very popular work, just published in France.* [1845] 40 pages
The biography is of Alexander VI, pp. 20-40.

183/9-14}   *Hammond's Letters on Southern Slavery: addressed to Thomas Clarkson, the English Abolitionist.* 32 p.
The letters, of 1/28/45 and 3/24/45, were written by Gov. James Henry Hammond (1807-64), apparently in retirement, since he states that he has "abundant leisure," in response to a Circular Letter written by Clarkson which was "addressed to professing Christians in our Northern States, having no concern with Slavery, and to others there." Hammond received the letter from the Rev. Willoughby M. Dickinson, who was then apparently residing in Ipswich, also Mr. Clarkson's residence. Hammond, a S.C. lawyer and planter, early advocate of secession, was governor of S.C. 1842-44. In 1858, in his reply to Seward, he called slaves and factory hands "mudsills of society" and declared "Cotton is King." Poe's "nervously" means "strongly" or "forcefully".
The brevity of this "rev." may result from Poe's knowing the anti-slavery views of his Northern readers. He discreetly merely hints his own views. Reared in upper-class Richmond circles, he could not be otherwise in his sentiments as Killis Campbell (*The Mind of Poe*) and others assume, but he was as rabid as the reviewer in the 4/1836 *SLM*, of Paulding's *Slavery in the U.S.* and Drayton's *South Vindicated*. Unfortunately Harrison included the rev. as Poe's (8.265-75), but Ostrom's *Letters* included one by Poe to Beverley Tucker, of 5/2/36 (190-91) conclusively showing Tucker's authorship of the rev. Even Quinn, assuming Harrison to be accurate, goes astray in this matter (248-49). Bernard Rosenthal's long article trying to restore the rev. to the Poe canon uses special pleading and casuistical reasoning which are still unconvincing (*PS*, 1974, 7.29-38).

183/15-55}   For details of these performances and casts at Niblo's see Odell (5.156-57). Poe still maintains his fervid admiration of Anna Mowatt's acting, appearance, etc., even roseately seeing her audience as "fashionable, and very intellectual" despite their objectionable love of "rhodomontade" below. On 7/14 she was Pauline in Bulwer's *Lady of Lyons*, and on 7/17, she was Juliana in John Tobin's (1770-1804) *The Honeymoon*. Poe's summary is sufficiently explicit about its absurd plot and poor characterizations--witness to the low average level of the theatre of the day. The 3 lines are in II, i of Tobin's play.

183/56-70} Poe's faithfulness in attending each of her varied vehicles is touching, especially since there are hints that his enthusiasm is waning. The distich comes from *Twelfth Night* (3.2.157) with "her lip" substituted for "his lip." Poe's remembrance of the music was of Donizetti, not of Bellini, who first produced the opera to a libretto by Salvatore Commarano. There are three other loci for Bellini in Poe's works, but none for Donizetti.

184/1-22} Poe is here developing more fervidly his praise of Mrs. Mowatt for her "naturalness" as stated in 177/66 [facsimile text]. He certainly wishes to foster a simple, inartificial style of delivery and stage presence such, we assume, as W.H. Crisp was disinclined to advocate (see lines 12 and 48 below). Poe insists upon her sense of "natural elocution" by contrast with the stylized gestures and deliberate phrasings enjoined by the "schools." In his tendency toward verbal flourishes here he produces a sentence far from clear in meaning: "Mrs. Mowatt, as she now stands ... to give lessons to her" (13-15). Obviously, the natural artist is said to be able to teach the trained disciple, but "routine" is scarcely the heart of her acting merit.

184/24-53} Poe was consistent in his devotion to Scott's novel, *The Bride of Lammermoor*, calling it, in the 12/35 *SLM* (H 8.64) "that most pure, perfect, and radiant gem" of fiction; and in the 2/36 issue "the purest and most enthralling" novel, "better than any by Bulwer" (8.33, 8.23). There is no doubt in Poe's mind that such a work could be transposed or adapted to the stage successfully, although here ineptly attempted, resulting in failure. In Poe's specifications of outstanding scenes involving Mrs. Mowatt, we clearly apprehend the marked variations from our present concepts of "naturalness" which then prevailed.
Poe's last sentence uses an adaptation of Byron's 1816 poem: "When we two parted / In silence and tears? Pale grew thy cheek and cold" (1-2).

185/1-9} Poe had left the employ of the *Mirror* during February when he became a member of the *BJ* staff (see the announcement to "Readers" in the 2/22 issue [1.127]). Willis and

Morris were then co-editors of the *Mirror*, but Willis, always afflicted by wanderlust and hoping to duplicate the success of his earlier reports from Europe, later collected into volumes (*Pencillings by the Way, Inklings of Adventure, Loiterings of Travel*), gave up his share of the journal (Hiram Fuller had bought a share) and had gone to England and Germany in 6/45. For Poe's generally favorable views on Willis, see his long "Lit." sketch (H 15.9-18) which incorporates much of his article in the *BJ* of 1/18 (see pp. 16-18 [facsimile text]). See also the numerous items on Willis in the Index.

185/10-24} From 1834 to the present, Willis had become the chief American reporter abroad, always moving about with light, bantering or descriptive pen in hand, and, especially in England, finding his way into socially distinguished or literary circles, fascinating to his readers back home. His letters about the salon of Lady Blessington, in 1836, had inspired the satirical "Lionizing" by Poe. The *Mirror* had first printed them; others were intended for Willis' new journal *The Corsair*, shared with T.O. Porter (1839-40), and always when collected into volumes they vividly provided Americans with the sense of sophisticated travel. This series was announced in the 7/5/45 *Weekly Mirror* (p. 198). The first letter of 7/12 (p. 216) spoke of Willis' illness (see above). Poe is quoting from his letter in the 7/26 issue, 251-52 (preceding week of the *Daily Mirror*).

185/25-47} The carriage described was named after Henry Brougham, Lord Chancellor of England. This whole article as reprinted from Willis' letter is, in a sense, a tacit apologia by Poe, whose article "Street-Paving" of 4/19 (94-96) had strongly advocated the very wooden blocks here discountenanced. No doubt Willis too is admitting his own error in the *Mirror* articles on the subject, q.v. in notes to 94/1 above, also showing the provenance in Poe's general interest in the topic.

186/6-8} Poe had long been interested in ballooning and devoted many tales to the subject, beginning with the 1835 "Hans Pfaall" and continuing through the "Balloon-Hoax" of 4/13/44, and "The Angel of the Odd" (10/44) to "Mellonta Tauta" of 2/49. A key figure in the history of the subject in England was Charles Green (1785-1870), an exhibition balloonist who made 526 ascents beween 1821 and 1852, first used carburetted hydrogen gas, went up from England to Germany in the "Great Nassau" balloon in 1836, and invented the guide-rope. For his background role in Poe's tales see *Imaginary Voyages.*, pp. 470-71,

475-76; *Tales*, 1063-66, 1306 n5; also, see *BGM*, 1840, 6.247 for 5 paras. on Green (Poe being ed. though not author). It is probable that this item comes from a newspaper of no very recent vintage, for Green made his 299th ascent by 7/30/44 and averaged almost one per month (q.v. in L.T.C. Rolt, *The Aeronauts*, 1966).

186/9-12} See *Punch* 8.256: "Bentley's Miscellany of this month contains a story of a husband being very nearly poisoned by the lover of his wife,--the poison having been sent to the cook to be mixed up with a dish of which the husband alone was passionately fond. This is afterwards explained away by the husband himself, as a trick he had resorted to in order to poison his wife's mind against the aforesaid lover. This story is very funnily told, and is called 'The Plum Pudding'; but unfortunately, the very same incidents were described in Hood's Magazine, two months back. The story was there entitled 'The Herring Pie.' We only mention this circumstance as a most extraordinary coincidence."
One doubts the French origin of this bit of fluff, and the accuracy of Poe's memory.

186/13-14} This little note to Richard Henry Stoddard was the start of a complicated and far-reaching relationship with Poe that produced two "memorial" poems on him and a continuation of the damaging "Executorship" by Griswold through the "editorship" of his works with newly derogatory "memoirs" (q.v. in Poe's follow-up on p. 198).

186/15-19} It was the obligation of Briggs to produce this Index, but he was no longer present. The statement of intention here indicates that a "rush" job would be performed--and so it turned out. The unpaged Index has been bound into the first vol. in the few bound copies that I have seen (see Canny and Heartmann's *Bibliography*, 1943, p. 168). It may bear traces of Poe's instructions to his staff if not of his personal selection and formulation of topics, but it is very far from representing everything of importance in the magazine or offering ready access to its materials. For a discussion of this Index, see my Intro.

187/1-2} The volume, by Thomas Holley Chivers (1807-58), is 32 pages in length (5 of them prefatory) in double columns. The preface is an apologue by Chivers concerning a stranger's choosing the best of a flock to comfort the father, who has lost his favorite child. Each poem is preceded by a poetic quotation, that before "To My First Born in Heaven" being from "Israfel," line 40: "Yes, Heaven is thine." These points may have influenced Poe's major emphasis in his brief review.

Chivers, as man and author, is intimately connected with Poe. Woodberry wrote a long account of this connection (App. V, *Life of Poe*, 2.376-90), a masterpiece of irony and abundant facts, explaining the difficult intertangle of influences whereby Chivers and some of his devotees contended that major poems and major strains in Poe's oeuvre are owed to this eccentric from Georgia, son of a rich planter whose medical degree from Transylvania Univ. was never used. For years he frequently lived in the North but his comfortable plantation life with his family at Oaky Grove and his numerous *offers* to help Poe with the *Stylus* roused Poe's interest; he knew Chivers' poems sent to periodicals, as early as 1835. The weirdest, most individualistic style of poetry certainly attracted Poe, as ed. and as recipient of numerous letters (Ostrom counts 36, 10 by Poe--only 8 extant). Poe's first is an apology for his cogently stated opinion of Chivers' poetry in the 12/41 *Graham's* "Autography" article (H 15.241-42). This needs partial quotation by contrast with the present 1845 article, issued just before Poe sent a private letter to Chivers urging his desperate need for funds to sustain and purchase a full share (one-third) of the magazine: He is "one of the best and one of the worst poets in America. His productions ... a wild dream--strange, incongruous, full of images of ... monstrosity, and snatches of sweet unsustained song .... Is there *any* meaning in his words--... His figures of speech are metaphor run mad, and his grammar is often none at all. Yet there are ... fine individual passages...." In his answer of 7/6/42 (*Letters*, 207-209; and 697), Poe spoke of some errors back in the early contributions to the *SLM*, of his own hastiness, and of the fine qualities of his poem about Shelley, q.v. in the present rev. Of course he asked for his help with subscribers to the projected *Penn. Mag.* The file of letters between them invariably concerns the same topics: Poe's grudging promise of individual poems by Chivers, his need for money for his mag., and his promise to give up drink. One variation is ironic, his inability after much effort to salvage some Florida bank bonds, via Wall Street, to save the wealthy Chivers $210 in losses. Another is his congratulations on the Southerner's invention of a silk-unwinding machine that was to bring him financial gain. But never did he keep any of his promises to aid the publishing venture (see pp. 214, 293, 296, 302, 325). Poe showed admirable self-control. For a covert ref. to "T.H.C." on 6/21, see 82/18 (end of note).

187/30} Poe's first para. obviously took its cue from Chivers' invoking his consolation over the death of his child, and he sounds the theme that became prominent in "Phil. of Comp."-- death of the beloved as apt for poetry. Poe's language is like that in a few of his poetic sketches (cf. "Shadow," sentence 1, on p. 188). The ref. to "Byronic affectation of melancholy" is rather inapposite, since the Corsair type of regret after conquest or the young-love-rejected theme of some of the short lyrics is not in Chivers' scope.

Poe's attempt to set up eras for the development of each nation's literature derives from the standard division into three levels: the epic, the classical, and (see M 181) the romantic. Surely strange is his representing the "critical era" through William Cowper (1731-1800), the pietistic, melancholy poet, but Poe knew and cited a few of his works (see *PD*, 23-34 for 10 loci).

Totally disproving Poe's insincere flattery in "an air of a rapt soliloquy" is a letter from Chivers to Poe, of 9/9/45, cited by Hull from a copy of the Huntington MSS.: "My poems have been spoken of in the very highest terms in this state, by all who have seen them. Several papers have republished your notice, with also remarks on their merits, of the most flattering nature, at the same time that *you* were spoken of in the highest terms." On the other hand, see Chivers' letter to a Georgia paper, the *Southern Courant*, defending Poe in this rev. against the Washington *Bee*'s charge that Poe was merely "puffing" Chivers' book (in Poe *Log* for September).

Poe's exempting Chivers in this small volume and in his many periodical poems from any "taint" of the major 19th century poets' works is hardly a tribute to Chivers' wide reading or sensitivity, according to what Poe has said about the lurking influences of the best models, but it does acknowledge the eccentric originality or mere oddity of his work, which in his odd coinages and compounds and riotous alliteration and stenographically truncated syntax appealed to the risibility of later Victorians, such as Swinburne and Bayard Taylor. It was the only kind of continuing appeal that Chivers could have (see Woodberry, 2.376, 388). Woodberry tartly notes that his next (4th) vol. of verse, in 1850, called *Eonchs of Ruby*, had a title "antiseptic against time" (2.377).

187/31-73} This poem on Shelley was entitled "The Wife's Lament for Her Husband Lost at Sea" (p. 14). Collations show two substantive changes that sound deliberate on Poe's part:

"Like lost Archytas from Venetia's Sea," (line 36) and "Like Orion on some dark Autumnal night" (188/3). In a now lost letter to the poet Poe had apparently argued *for* these changes, in terms of the accenting of the proper names. We have Poe's follow-up letter of 11/15/45: "You are wrong (as usual) about Archytas & Orion--both as I accent them / the first with a short y and the second with a long i/. Look in any phonographic Dictionary--say Bolles. Besides, wherever the words occur in ancient poetry, they are as I give them. What is the use of disputing an obvious point?" (302). Clearly, Poe's insistence upon improving the rhythm of the two lines and altering them in his *BJ* reprint entitles them to enter "Appendix III: Collaborations" in the Harvard ed. of *Poems* (491 ff.).

This poem, which is full of touches of "Adonais" despite Poe's "exemption," is an indication of Chivers' being "Shelley-mad" from 1837 on, a likely consequence of the publication in Phila. of the reprint of the large Galignani, Paris ed. of the three major Romantic poets' work (Woodberry, 381).

Concerning "a few extracts at random"--two more extracts aside from these testify to Poe's tactful promotion of Chivers, the earlier being a reprint of "To Isa Singing" at the start of this, the 8/2 number of the *BJ* (2.49). A curious correction made by Poe in 1842 warrants giving the five stanzas here: "Upon thy lips now lies / The music-dew of love; / And in thy deep blue eyes,-- / More mild than Heaven above-- / The meekness of the dove. [st.] More sweet than the perfume / Of snow-white jessamine, / When it is first in bloom, / Is that sweet breath of thine, / Which mingles now with mine. [st.] Like an Aeolian sound / Out of an ocean shell, / Which fills the air around / With music, such as fell / From the lips of ISRAFEL, [st.] Over thy lips now flow, / Out of thy heart, for me, / The songs, which none can know / But him who hopes to be / For evermore with thee. [st.] And like the snow-white Dove / Frightened from earth at even-- / On tempests borne above-- / My swift-winged soul is driven / Upon thy voice to heaven!"

In his letter of 7/6/42 to Chivers responding to the latter's protests over the "Autography" item, Poe wrote: "What I said of your grammatical errors arose from some imperfect recollections of one or two poems sent to the first vol. of the *SLM*" (*Letters*, 207) but not there printed, according to D.K. Jackson's checklist of the contributors to the *SLM*. Ostrom records an envelope notation, presumably by Chivers, that line 18 read "The song which none can know" through a copyist error, but that the original form should have been "Sweet songs"--now changed to "The songs." We may assume that its ref. to "Israfel" in line 15 caused its reprinting here. Another "extract" was reprinted by Poe in the 12/6 *BJ*, on 2.338; it was a sonnet "On Reading Miss Barrett's Poems," full of characteristic language: "god-enchanting," "Honey-tongued," "Crystal-shining," "sapphire-paven," "rapt the stars ... with wonder," "music-troubled ether-sea."

188/10-85} The first excerpt is from the title poem of the volume, pp. 5-12, specifically, p. 7. The second comprises the last three stanzas of "The Soul's Destiny" on pp. 16-17, and the last is "Sonnet.--to Isa Sleeping" on p. 20. There is an obvious misprint in line 38: "Upon thy mother's arm" is the obvious text.

188/88} Poe is being evasive in not specifying the "gross demerit" here and on the next page that lowers the rank of Chivers as poet, but he undercuts his own standards in claiming that mere conventionality determines the basis for criticism. The jumble of metaphors, the vagueness, the overworked themes which derive from third-rate sentimental poetasters--all these are regular targets for Poe's vituperation when he is not trying to please the writer.

189/5} See p. 296/20 [facsimile text] for an utterly noncommittal ref. to a magazine poem by Chivers.

189/12} Poe left it untreated in the *BJ* hereafter--a fuller justice.

189/16} *Childe Harold*, 2, st. 81.

189/33} Mrs. Mowatt, like Poe, was steeped in Byron's works; Poe also uses "Egeria" at the end of "Byron and Miss Chaworth" in the 12/44 mag. article (see SM 12 for full explication) deriving it from *Childe Harold* (4.115): "Egeria! sweet creation of some heart" for his pictured ideal of a youth.

190/57-64} This collection, pirated, of course, had vii-x + 189 p. This is only an announcement, with the proper rev. following in the next issue (see 198 ff.). The statement comes from p. vii.

190/65-73} The pagination is as follows: "Preface to Hood's Own" (1-6); "The Pugsley Papers" (7-20); "The Dream of Eugene Aram" (21-27), poem; "Black, White, and Brown" (28-33); "I Remember, I Remember" (34-45), poem; "The Portrait" (36-40); "Literary Reminiscences" (41-48, 51-100); "My Apology" (49-50);

"The Lost Heir" (101-105), poem; "An Undertaker" (106-108); "Miss Kilmansegg and her Precious Leg" (109-179), poem; "Fair Ines" (180-181), poem; "Ballad" (182), poem; "Ruth" (183), poem; "Autumn" (184), poem; "Song" (185), poem; "Ode to Melancholy" (186-189), poem.

191/1} This para. is from pp. ix-x of the Preface, and expresses very well Poe's views on the need for International Copyright laws.

191/12-19} The date is 1844. Each of the novels is in two columns, separately paged as follows: 3-136, 3-136, 3-139, 3-184, 3-138. See pp. 92, 150, 302.

191/20-22} This work appeared in parts at long intervals. It was finally published as one vol. (of 1104 p.) under the following title: *Pictorial History of the World, from the Earliest Ages to the Present Time.* New ed., with additions, corrections by the author. Ill. with 540 engravings from drawings by Croome, Devereux, and other distinguished artists. Richmond, Va.: Harrold & Murray, 1848. There were also Phila., 1851 and Hartford, 1855 eds.
For separate notices in the *BJ* see 215, 262, 281 [facsimile text].

191/24-28} This numbers 3-32 p., and is set in 1732.

191/29-34} Poe is correct about the pages (252 to be exact) and wrong about his placement of pointing before Author. She appears to be Maria Jane McIntosh, although not indicated on the book, which concerns one Frank Derwent, who seeks to answer the question, "For what shall I live?" and finds the answer, "God," on p. 252. It is didactic, like Thomas Day's classic, which contrasts the sons of the upper class and the yeomanry, but is far from "equal."

191/35-38} The cheap newsprint format of these novels in parts has guaranteed their extinction at present. For other notices of the continuing parts see 215, 259, 271, 295, 321, 333.

191/39-41} This 48 p. work is by Douglas Wm. Jerrold (1803-57), and has this title: *Mrs. Caudle's Curtain Lectures, delivered during thirty years by Mrs. Margaret Caudle, and suffered by Job, her Husband.* There are 29 lectures in all. For their inordinate popularity, through their many reprints from *Punch*, throughout

England and America, see p. 109 [facsimile text], which discusses their material and effect.

191/42-47}   Thomas De Quincey's "Suspiria de Profundis" is a continuation of "Confessions of an Opium Eater," correctly noted in Poe's rev. of the 4/45 *Blackwood's* (p. 111). This Am. ed. is paged differently: "Suspiria..." on 43-55, "Househunting in Wales" on 74-86, and not in the April British ed. In both instances Poe speaks well of this one of De Quincey's work.

191/48-53}   The author appears to be Harriet Maria (Gordon) Smythies (1838-83). The novel, pub. in London, then in NY, achieved a reprint in 1869, having 138 p. and leaving no copy in NYC. Poe avoids telling us what "class" of fiction it belongs to.

191/54-59}   This "select novel" is paged 5-72. No date is given on the title page but the translator's preface, signed W.H., is dated April 16, 1845. The translator further explains that, while all the previous translations were done by Mary Howitt, Mr. Howitt had to do *The Parsonage of Mara*. An "advertisement" by F. Bremer admits having "committed several minor offences against time and space ... knowingly and purposely."
   Frederika Bremer (1801-65), world-renowned Swedish novelist, wrote of middle class family relationships, with much melodrama and appeal for improving the status of women. She was on her way to America for a lecture tour, which finally had to be postponed. See 197, 238, 255 [facsimile text].

192/1-4}   The full title comprises 7 words detailing the content of the vol., ix-xiv + 1225 p., by Thomas Webster (from the 1845 L. ed.). The separate nos. no longer are available.

192/5-9}   This is one of the nos. of a series of "outlines" of the histories, "ancient and modern" of all nations by Samuel Maunder (1785-1849) with the U.S. history added (by John Inman). It is in 2 vols.: vi + 760; 638 p.

192/10-11}   See earlier reviews: 65-69, 76-78, 176-78.   Her "last" was 7/26.

192/15}   The theatrical "vaudeville" of Poe's day appears to have been a "piece, usually comic, the dialogue or pantomime of which is intermingled with light or satirical songs, sometimes set to familiar airs, and with dancing" (*Webster's New International Dictionary*, 1909, reprinted, 1923). *Johnson's Cyclopaedia* is cited for the word: "The early vaudeville, ... forerunner of the opera bouffe, was light, graceful, and piquant." It originated in the French satirical verses called vaudevilles, q.v. in Pin 154, explicated. Although prominent in the stage annals of Poe's day, it has received little attention in stage histories.

193/13} The last two are Poe's coined compounds.

193/31} While Poe here tries to temper his admiration, he generally belongs to the group of adulators, especially in the earlier reviews, reproved by the 7/26 *Spirit of the Times* (of NY) which said: "Mrs. Mowatt is decidedly a clever, pleasing, though not a versatile actress .... We conceive that ... her [friends] are doing her a signal injury, by the very fulsome flattery they are dealing out .... Every one, after reading the tremendous effusions of some critics, expected to find ... an angel ... they were naturally disappointed" (see Odell, 5.156-57).

193/32-37} At the Park appeared the French opera company from New Orleans, led by the singer Julie Calve, starting on 6/16, to 8/14, in a varied repertoire of operas and French "vaudevilles"; the former included the ambitious *La Juive* of Halévy, 6/16 (see Watson's long rev. on 2.58-59), Rossini's *William Tell*, Meyerbeer's *Robert le Diable*, and Donizetti's *La Favorite*. For the great acclaim see citations in Odell (5.103-106). Opera nights were Monday, Wednesday, and Friday.

193/39-41} On 7/21 Rosina Pico sang the "Brindisi" from *Lucrezia Borgia* and a cavatina from the *Prighionere di Edinburgh* and thereafter sang every night for awhile. On 8/5 appeared *The Veteran Returned*, arranged by John Cline and acted by him and others (Odell, 5.160). See Letter 4 (6/4/44) in *Doings of Gotham*, 47, for Poe's ref. to "Herr Kline's" "curvets upon a rope."

193/42-46} *The Female Horse Thief*, at the Chatham, presented Mrs. Jones playing Margaret Catchpole. Notice Poe's sneer at the tastes of the "Everyman" audience.

193/53-54} *Tait's Magazine* (London), pp. 373-74, reviewing *Poems on man in his various aspects under the American Republic* by Cornelius Mathews, NY. Here Poe is partial to the poet and novelist, friend of R.H. Horne and sponsor of "Young America" (see many refs. and articles in Index of *BJ*), but note the marked change in Poe's opinions in *Br.* (see Index).

194/1-68} Collation shows a few significant variations; all italics are Poe's. These lines are different as shown: (17) principle / social principle; (23) to a young person / to many a young writer; (37) believe the; (39) speaking even of; (48) associated / beyond the association suggested; (57) ragged / rugged; (60) and an American; (64) conclusions / convulsions; (66-67) at sight; (74) will yet be.

195/56-67} The selection and inclusion of this report on an important although now abandoned technological development evidences Poe's intense interest which made him a father of science fiction (cf. "Scheherazade," "Hans Pfaall," "Balloon Hoax," "Mellonta Tauta"). Several cols. in *BGM* and various items in *Doings of Gotham* also show this. The source of this excerpt is unverifiable. The "atmospheric railway," developed between 1840-45 by Joseph Samuda (1813-85) and his brother Jacob (d. 1844) and Samuel Clegg (1814-56), seemed to be a promising use of atmospheric pressure through air pumps for maintaining a partial vacuum for propelling trains. A two-mile installation in Dalkey, Ireland (1843) worked to 1855, but the London-Croydon stretch here described was not long lasting (see *En. Brit.*, 1929, 2.641-42).

195/68-72} Robert Taylor Conrad (1810-58), poet, dramatist, and jurist, issued *Conrad, King of Naples* in 1832, then *Aylmere* (1835), which, rewritten, as *Jack Cade, the captain of the commons*, entered Edwin Forrest's repertoire. For the sake of confusion-- this play was published in 1852 as *Aylmere, or the Bondman of Kent; and Other Poems*. The news of Poe's article seems abortive. Poe lauds Conrad in the 1841 "Autography" (H 15.232-33) and in the uncollected sketch in the 6/44 *Graham's* that he mentions at the end of Letter 2 of *Doings of Gotham*, p. 35 (see also 11.223-24). But there is no trace of this drama here mentioned. (Is it *Aylmere* again?)

196/1-9} The role of Frederick Wm. Thomas (1806-66) in Poe's life and work is considerable, for he was always a true friend who helped him with leads to posts, introductions, contributions for journals, and much sage advice through numerous letters (see 638, 662-- Indices in *Letters*). He was a magazine-poet, a novelist, a journalist and editor. Poe's "Autography" article, in the 12/41 *Graham's* (H 15.209-10), is based on a long autobiographical account that Thomas sent him as of 9/3/41 (H 17.95-100; H's date of 8/3 is one month off). Poe refers here to a life of Wirt on pp. 52-54, in this issue, and there will be one on "John Randolph, of Roanoke" in the 8/16 *BJ* (2.82-85) which contains a Shakespeare quotation that he will humorously use in *BJ* 2.339. Both these sketches derive from "two volumes of sketches of such persons as Wirt, John Randolph," etc. which dated from 1840-41, as mentioned in the autobiography of 9/3/41 (H 17.98). Clearly Poe was appealing to his friends for material for filling up the pages of the *BJ*. Hull prints an excerpt from a MS. letter from Thomas to Poe (9/29/45): "I see you have published two of my sketches (Randolph-Wirt)-- I observed them kindly noticed...."

The poem from the *British Critic* is reprinted on 2.52 of the current issue. In 28 lines, 7 stanzas, "Song" by E.H. Burrington is a slight allegory of the spirits of "Hope" and "Doubt."

196/10-59} This is from "Personal Recollections of Thomas Campbell, Esq. -- No. II," pp. 679-689 of the 1845 vol., specifically, 680. Poe's remark about literary Billingsgate is not a direct quotation, but rather is from a remark of Campbell's made anent an essay by Daniel Maginn entitled "De Arte Billingsgatoriâ" consisting of extracts from the writings of Swift. Collations show these variants: (18) would have sacrificed; (27) seduced by Hazlitt into; (41) henceforward. The book was *Conversations with James Northcote* (1830).

For Poe's views of Campbell see Index to *Br.* (and especially Pin 78, M 212) and Index to *BJ*; likewise for William Hazlitt (especially see 212 [facsimile text]). Obviously, "in" should be "into."

197/1-20} Poe here has taken up a question that shows great literary perceptiveness and a proper respect for authors' rights to a just voice in the publishers' arrangements. The proposed "literary agency" for German books, to my knowledge, never came about, but the idea was a tenable and valuable one. The "recent fair" must have been the renowned Easter book fair at Leipzig, an earlier holding of which had produced the celebrated translation of a book by Scott which never existed in the first place. The account of how this spurious Scott work, named *Walladmor*, was then translated "back" from the German by De Quincey is given in the *Br.*, SP 27. Poe also undertook the problem of proper translations from the French in M 176 (anent C.H. Town's hasty, careless translation of Sue's *Mysteries of Paris*). Poe was always much concerned with the exact shade of difference between an idea expressed in a foreign tongue and in English, even using the resultant misinterpretations as the basis for tales, such as "Why the Little Frenchman ...," and for many passages of criticism (e.g., H 10.138). Poe's deduction in the last sentence is entirely in keeping with his adherence to the "Young America" point of view.

197/21-37} This comes from the *Foreign Quarterly Review*, 7/45, p. 285 (NY ed.), 530 (L. ed.). All substantives are the same save for "fatigued" in line 32. There is meaning in Poe's choosing this derogation of Ludwig Tieck, whom he cites (I believe at second-hand) and to whom he imputes a joke that really comes from Bulwer (see M 78, and note b). Poe was now entering his complete disenchantment with German criticism and the solemnity of German scholarly and academic thought (q.v. under Schlegel in the *Br.*'s Index). Hence the appeal to him of this parody of hypocritical idolatry.

197/38-52} There are traces of a non-Poe hand in this short article, perhaps that of Henry C. Watson who did not share in Poe's nationalistic outrage over the derogation of American books by "Christopher North" (see SM 1) and Sydney Smith, notorious for his remark: "In the four quarters of the globe, who reads an American book?" (in the 1/1820 *Edinburgh Review*, which he helped to found, 1802; but see neutral refs. on 92, 168). Poe would not quote approvingly this way Carlyle, whom he always disparaged. On the other hand, Poe took the keenest interest in the dance, and especially in the legendary Maria Taglioni (see M 85, FS 27). His use of names and elements from the dance throughout his creative and critical work is manifold (see my "Poe and the Dance," in *SAR 1980*, 169-182). Hence the major topic and its decidedly pro-American culture orientation strongly suggest Poe's authorship. In the 6/28 no. (p. 638, 2nd col. top) in a rev. of *La Sylphide* is the opinion that she is past the age for the role but still graceful and charming. Another item in the 7/26 issue (p. 744) more broadly said that "she should *not* think of retirement," but this would have been too late to enter Poe's column.

197/53-57} Ida Marie Luise etc., the countess Hahn-Hahn of Germany (1805-80), a misc. popular writer (fiction, poems, and travel letters, many of them translated into English in the 1840s) wrote this "massacred" title, correctly *Zwei Frauen* (two women). Obviously the "z" and "e" have been read as "l", like the capital "H" in her name. Poe's script is usually too clear for this kind of misreading, but on the other hand he was interested in women authors (see 191[i] above) and particularly in George Sand (Mme. Dudevant; q.v. in SM 12 and *PD*, 81). The information comes from the same issue of the *Foreign Quarterly Review* as article (a) above. Poe is more likely to be responsible for the epigramatic last sentence than the stylistically dull and wordy Watson.

197/58-63} Early photography was a keen interest of Poe's, and this little note on the *Foreign Quarterly Review* article of 7/45 (pp. 534-35) would have fascinated Poe, even though this spelled the doom of his beloved anastatic printing (see 24, 83-86, 107, 135-36). Oddly, Poe did not here, as in 215 (g) [facsimile text], insist upon inserting the acute accent over the second "e" (daguerréotype, as in the original article), despite his words on the subject in *Alexander's Weekly Messenger* of 1/15/40 (reprinted by C.S. Brigham [Worcester, 1943], p. 20), nor did Poe use an acute accent in two articles in "A Chapter on Science and Art" in *BGM* of 1840, 6.193, 246, both printed under Poe's editorship, but not written by him (as is sometimes stated). Obviously, no one but editor Poe could have selected this topic for attention here in the *BJ*.

198/1-2} It would be difficult to determine the specific improvement mentioned among the numerous discoveries and theories of Dominique François Jean Arago (1786-53), the leading French physicist of his age. Poe derived a warped view of him from the disparaging, sensational treatment by Louis Loménie in the French original (which Poe did not directly know) of Robert M. Walsh's translated *Sketches of Conspicuous Living Characters of France*, reviewed in the 4/41 *Graham's* by Poe (see his refs. to Arago in H 10.134, 136, 138). Hence he introduced Arago into "Von Kempelen" (see ch. 10 on it in *Discoveries in Poe*; also TOM 1365, n. 1). This is a prelude of that interest.

198/3-14} In the first para. Poe scarcely conceals the ill-will he bore toward Briggs, the "former associate ed." and his doubt about being able to extract "Eudocia" from him. It did not appear in the rest of the vol.
    The "Correspondence" was printed, as he said, on pp. 23-26, anonymously. It is full of poetic quotations and refs. to classical and contemporary authors (such as Leigh Hunt) plus much flower lore. The ref. to the Boston agents (Redding and Co., according to the weekly advertisement) would indicate the provenance of the article. Clearly the writer has questioned Poe about his forthcoming *Raven and Other Poems*.

198/15-18} This is an insulting follow-up of the "loss" of the contribution mentioned on p. 186. It had very far-reaching consequences. The author, Richard Henry Stoddard (1825-1903), originally an iron moulder, persisted in self-education, reading and writing poetry, to become a critic and ed. in NYC in the center of literary circles, always second rate but enormously popular and influential. His experience with Poe, which included his calling on him and being evicted with menaces, his later leaving Poe in the rain, without an umbrella-- all this was repeatedly and unabashedly written up by Stoddard in magazine and newspaper articles and in the long *Recollections* (1903), pp. 145-60, as well as in his Preface to *Poems of Poe* (1875), 78-81, for Stoddard was to take over from his deceased friend Griswold the function of explicator, editor, and tacit assailant of Poe, especially in *Works of Poe* (NY, 1884, 6 vols.). He matched the Griswold "Ludwig" obituary with a depreciatory article, in 1853, ending with his own Poe poem, "Miserrimus," best epitomized by this line: "His faults were many, his virtues few." (For a full account, see ch. 11, "Poe as 'Miserrimus,'" *Discoveries in Poe*, 200-204.) Later Stoddard did acknowledge that it was "influenced by Keats but not copied from anyone," and later still he confessed that having read Major David Richardson's "Ode to a Grecian Flute" he "had to write a companion piece" which went to the *BJ*. Poe's insight was correct, undoubtedly, about the double plagiarism there admitted (*Lippincott's*, 1889, 43.107). It must be added that a year after Poe's death Stoddard came across an autograph poem of Poe's (for he inherited papers from many, including Rufus W. Griswold) and wrote a non-derisive, tributary sonnet on the reverse side, which he published, but since he cancelled the subject's name, it did not redress the balance at all. That odd story I hope soon to see in print.

198/19-24} This follows the previous week's announcement of the same book of 3 + 189 pages, but it does not quite accord with the initial para., which asserts that these are Hood's "More earnest writings," whereas we have had "heretofore his lighter effusions, his puns and quibbles...." The list of works on 190 shows several "punny" ones, such as "Miss Killmansegg" and "Pugsley Papers," confirmed by the first part of his discussion below.

198/25} The identity of the American editor has remained obscure; the Preface (see p. vii quoted on 191) differs from material in earlier or later American editions.

198/25-76} Poe seems to have thought so well of his material in this rev. that he incorporated it into the entire text of M 291, the last of the series published during his lifetime. I shall try to indicate how he adapted the substance, shorn of the illustrations from Hood and of the long excerpt (pp. 199-200, the major portion) from Poe's sketch of N.P. Willis, pp. 16-17 above. Para. 1 of M 291 uses 198/25-46; para. 2 uses 199/10-39; para. 3, the last, uses 199/42-45 plus 201/2-4 and 7-8 plus 202/6-7. For a collation of the material, see note a of M 291. Important is his dropping the "humor" at the end of the borrowed sentences in favor of stress on "imagination," which he thinks more justified after quoting his "essay" from the Willis sketch. Poe does not manage to clarify the distinction between "fancy" and "fantasy" nor does he manage to dispose of Hood's "humor" which he began by deprecating and ends by admiring in "Miss Kilmansegg" with its "brilliant points" (203/40), which he fails to explain. Basically Poe enjoyed humor, especially of the "punnage" variety (Poe's coinage), as we see in MM Intro., 87, 235, 253. His rather stilted rejection in this rev. misleads him about the appeal of Hood, while his partiality for the sentimentality of certain serious poems prevents him from seeing the same grotesquerie exhibited there.

Hood, in line 55, is quoting Burns' "John Anderson." In line 70, after "Sanitaire" is a missing line: "Above all, don't despond about it." In line 74 Meltonian is a ref. to hunting at Melton Mowbray, in Leicestershire, a traditional scene of skill for the sport.

198/26-27} This questionable statement is from p. viii of the Preface.

199/7-9} The excerpt from Hood is curiously reminiscent of one of Poe's most interesting tales, "The Imp of the Perverse," concerning our impulse to frustrate our own security and satisfied ambitions in a mad spirit of contradiction that brings us disaster. The date, language, and context (melancholy and mirth) suggest this: "Imp" came out in the 7/45 *Graham's*, just when he received the book for rev.; a key passage explains that "The most important crisis of our life calls, trumpet tongued, for immediate energy and action." "We struggle in vain .... The clock strikes, and is the knell of our welfare .... It is the chanticleer-note to the ghost that has so long overawed us" (TOM, 1222). Now it is true that *Hamlet* offers a closer and more apt source (see my treatment in *Etudes Anglaises*, 1976, 29.199-202), but multiple stimuli, all converging, explain the creative product, especially from so complex and associative a mind as Poe's.

199/21-39} Poe tries here to sharpen and individualize his language. Characteristic is "niaiseries" meaning nonsense, foolishness, or trifles (see M 291e); "grotesquerie" italicized as a sign of his new coinage. Indeed it is in this sense a word meaning "grotesque objects considered collectively." (See M 291e and *PCW*.) The word "ideal" sometimes meant little more than pertaining to the faculty for appreciating beauty. Poe was fond of "abandon" and "abandonment" often considered as French in significance-- freedom, unrestraint, lack of rules-- (see M 211 anent Shelley). His quotation from Horace, *Ars Poetica*, 1.385 means "Minerva being unwilling"; hence, without inspiration.

200/72} It is interesting that this entire reprint of almost the whole of the sketch of Willis was included as a footnote to the "Lit." sketch of Willis in the 5/46 *Godey's*, but this time numerous changes in the accidentals were introduced and about a half dozen variations in words were made (e.g., well-intentioned / benevolent). Obviously Poe thought well of his initial presentation on "Fancy" and "Fantasy."

201/1-10} These two poems appear in Part 1, pp. 21-27, and Part 2, pp. 202-205 of *Prose and Verse*, having been pub. respectively in the *Gem*, 1829, and *Hood's Mag.*, 5/44. In applying "imaginative" to these poems, Poe must be referring to constructing beauty out of deformities, as he has just explained, since "Eugene Aram" concerns the self-revelation of the notorious scholar-murderer (the subject also of Bulwer's novel) and the second concerns the suicide of the betrayed, pregnant, lower-class girl. The first, incidentally, draws on the language and emotions of "Ancient Mariner" and, in turn, lends a little to Poe's "Tell-Tale Heart" and much to Oscar Wilde's "Ballad of Reading Gaol." For Poe's fondness for the second poem see notes to text p. 229/13-17 below.

201/11-43} Hood having died on 5/3/45 in a melancholy state, Poe was naturally led to stress the link of "hypochodriasis" to his peculiar or grotesque "fancy" (as stated in M 291 f). Poe implies that this "malady" distorts the shapings of the "released" mind (cf. "abandon"), since, "in its pathological aspect" it was held "a disorder of the nervous system, generally accompanied by indigestion, but chiefly characterized by the patient's unfounded belief that he is suffering from some serious bodily disease" (*OED*). Roderick Usher is thrice called "hypochondriac" and also Julius Rodman; "hipped" (a colloquialism just coming into use for the idea) is used in "Never Bet the Devil."

These two stanzas as given by Hood, pp. 188-89, lack one intervening stanza, the penultimate one; also, the last line reads "But has its chord in Melancholy." It is possible that Poe retained a memory of lines 31-37, when he composed "Ulalume": "... Sadly this star I mistrust-- / / Ah, fly ... for we must. / ...letting sink her / Plumes till they trailed in the dust-- / Till they sorrowfully trailed in the dust" (lines 52-60, *Poems*, 417). The common elements are "sorrow," angelic wings trailed in vile dust, and three identical rhymes on "-ust."

201/47-50} Poe's Latin phrase comes from Cicero, who in *Pro Publio Sestio*, 45.48, wrote "cum dignitate otium" or "a peaceful life with honor." For Ramsbottom way, in line 50, his ref. is to Dickens' *Sketches by Boz*: "The tugs at Ramsbottom."

202/1-13} The poem in the *Gem of 1829* (separately published, 1831) exploited the well known story, as did Bulwer in his novel of 1832. Poe misprints line 10, which should start with "And," and which reminds us of "Four and twenty blackbirds" etc. despite the "serious subject," as Poe says. The last sentence of M 291 is a variation of part of this: "In a word, his peculiar genius was the result of vivid Fancy impelled by Hypochondriasis."

202/23-43} Whatever the novel that Poe meant in line 23, he seemed dissatisfied with the rest of the para., for he put a large X over it (inscribed here at the side in deference to legibility) in my facsimile text. Perhaps he felt that the "class *helter-skelter*" does not represent "the flattest ... prose," for in the Intro. to "Marginalia" (at note j) referring to his many random marginal notations, he speaks of "their helter-skelter-iness of commentary."
   In reprinting "Fair Ines" from the book (dating from the 1/23 *London Magazine*), Poe apparently overlooked the poem that most contributed to it: Burns' "Bonnie Lesley," which begins: "O saw ye bonnie Lesley / As she gaed o'er the border? / She's gane, like Alexander, / To spread her conquests farther. / To see her is to love her, / And love but her for ever?" In fact, Poe did not care much for Burns and could scarcely be expected to retain much of his poetry in memory. He might also have objected that "Oh, young Lochinvar is come out of the West," in the Intro. to *Marmion*, provides too close a model for one line.

203/17-45} It is true that "Miss Killmansegg," first pub. in the 9/40 *New Monthly Mag.*, is characteristic of Hood's genius, in that the humor has a strain of bitter criticism of a social order that worships gold and perverts all human and moral values to attain it. Of this objective Poe seems oblivious, even though it is not far from his own aim in "Von Kempelen." Poe does not specify the "brilliant points" (40-41) which are abounding, nor do his extracts clarify his term of "Fantasy." He has gone to some trouble to select them from various parts of the long poem, even interspersing some of them out of order, as my line indications below will show. In line 36 his French term means "swindler."

203/46-67 through 205/1-35} A collation of the text here and in Hood's original shows the following substantive changes: 203/47-- a very lively; 204/27-- washing his hands; 29-- besides / nothing but; 35-- cobwebs; 40-- or / and; 45-- is always / always is; 62-- tear her and / tear and; 205/55-- wretched that / wretched who; 56-- God himself / nature herself.

The lines of the excerpts below (and on 204-205) correspond to the lines of the poem as follows (only the first line of each separate excerpt is listed by number): 203/46-- line 22; 204/4-- line 87; 10-- line 114; 15-- line 303; 29-- line 350; 36-- line 499; 41-- line 546; 49-- line 596; 58-- line 673; 205/1-- 1734; 8-- line 1024; 15-- line 1322; 21-- line 1232; 31-- line 1303.

204/47-48} In the *Br.*, FS 15, Poe used these two lines for satire on a phase of women's clothing.

205/37-47} Massimo d'Azeglio (his correct name, not as Poe has it) was a marquis of great talent and ability, as painter, statesman, and writer, whose two historical novels (this and *Niccolò de' Lapi*) were strongly political in his effort to arouse nationalistic feeling. The serious undercurrent in this work, a widely reputed offspring of Manzoni's fiction, seems to have escaped Poe totally (see below). Later he took part in the government of the new monarchy of Italy as prime minister, repeatedly, and was influential directly and through Cavour in basic Italian policies. Charles Edwards Lester (1815-90), our consul (1842-47) at Genoa, was a former Presbyterian clergyman, a liberal journalist, and a misc. author, steeped in Italian culture as his books on art and this translation show (see my Index for numerous refs. to Lester). Poe may have disliked his authoring *Chains and Freedom* (1839), the sympathetic life of a run-away slave, followed by his exposé of exploited British labor (1841 and again, 1842). See 219 c) [facsimile text] concerning his error about the Medici Series' being devoted solely to Romances, probably corrected because of the arrival for rev. of nos. 2 and 3 of the series, Machiavelli's *Florentine Histories*, tr. by C. Edwards

Lester; see 232(b) [facsimile text]; see also 295 [facsimile text] for Poe's rev. of Lester's tr. of Alfieri's autobiography.

206/1-7} The phrase "autorial comment" needs mention both as a concept and also for its Poe coinage; he uses the first word in eight contexts, several of them similar in protesting against the lack of an author's involvement through remarks or commentary. In *PS.*, 1977, 10.15-18, I have discussed the fact that Poe was substituting for the awkward "authorial" this coinage, just before the more regular Latin-derived "auctorial" was separately created. The origin of this somewhat curious idea is Schlegel's discussion of the role of the chorus as an "ideal spectator" in his *Lectures on Dramatic Art and Literature*, and it was also from A.W. Schlegel that Poe drew some of his basic ideas on "intrigue" or complicated plot as being unmeritorious unless redeemed by a unifying plot arrangement and an inevitable drive toward a climax or dénouement. The 18th and early 19th century's frequent intervention of the author's voice seems to us so brash, so interruptive that we wonder at Poe's insistence here; clearly he wished to raise the narrative above the level of straight reportage, especially for a third-person method. It is the presence of the narrator (through the "autorial comment"), to which the modern reader takes exception.

In the five novelists listed by Poe there are certainly many differences in the use of this "comment," for Scott's novels are rich in forward-moving incidents, although a sense of planning is usually maintained by Sir Walter. Certainly, Poe was convinced about the total "shaping" by Godwin (about whom he learned, probably from Dickens) that the end of *Caleb Williams*, his major novel, had been planned *before* the first part-- see *Discoveries in Poe*, ch, 7 on Poe and Godwin). And likewise for Bulwer Lytton and Benjamin D'Israeli and Charles Brockden Brown-- there is often a plethora of author's comments (much of which we now find superfluous and distracting today). In an earlier examination of Poe's charge here against d'Azeglio's novel in Lester's translation I sought out every "commenting" passage in the 1845 NY ed., finding them to be on pp. 33-34, 76-77, 96, 197, and 273-74, the last being three paras. on the use of history by a novelist (*Discoveries in Poe*, 267). From Poe's whole critical outlook the objection made sense but not to a critic in the *Mirror*, whom he had to answer (see "Editorial Miscellany" on p. 224 [facsimile text]).

206/20-23} Pub. in 1845, this 28 p. work reached a 4th ed. in 1860, but NYC has no copy. For excerpt see *BJ* 2.331, of 12/6.

206/24-26} Joel Tyler Headley (1813-97), author of this work of v-vi + 224 p., managed to produce over 30 biographies, histories and travel books. "Prolific, superficial and popular" (*DAB*) characterize him well, and perhaps this explains Poe's distaste which flames into acerbic vituperation in the long posthumous rev. in the 10/1850 *SLM* (H 13.202-209) of *The Sacred Mountains*, in which he calls him "The Autocrat of ... Quacks" and "a *perfect* fool." He had been a Presbyterian clergyman (to 1842-44) and he became a prolific biographist, but Poe calls J.T. Headley "the Rev." and complains about his suppressed title. At this time Poe's antagonism had not grown so bitter, for he was willing to borrow for the 11/46 "Cask of Amontillado" from the *Letters from Italy* (the episode of "A Man Built in a Wall," first appearing in the *Columbian Mag.* of 8/44, reprinted in the *Mirror* of 7/5/44 and collected in *Letters from Italy* (see TOM, 1253-54). The *BJ* Index has several refs. to Headley; see especially 351 [facsimile text], a sardonic rev. of a travel book.

206/27-64} Poe so well states, initially, the essential nature (and charm) of Headley's writing that he unfairly tasks him later for the slackness that is almost intrinsic to such an approach-- likewise for his seeming serendipity. There did chance to be a young sculptor, Giovanni Dupré (1817-82), who worked in Siena, then in Florence and whose first exhibited work created a great stir. It was a model of "Dead Abel," which had first been refused by the jury as a mere copy and then was approved as artistic and different from "life," so that it was accepted and widely acclaimed. Later he scored great success with mythological and religious subjects and was commissioned for the statue of Cavour in Turin (1872).

In line 44 by Eustace and Forsyth Poe probably means John Chetwode Eustace (1762-1815) and Joseph Forsyth (1763-1815), authors of important guidebooks for Italy. The first published *A classical Tour through Italy* in 4 vols., which reached a 6th ed. by 1821 and a 7th in 1841. His *Letter from Paris* appeared in 1814. Forsyth published *Remarks on antiquities, arts, and letters, during an excursion in Italy, in the years 1802 and 1803*. There was a 2nd ed. in London in 1816, a 3rd in Geneva in 1824, and a London fourth in 1835.

207/6} Headley must describe well the effects of the avalanches, judging from Poe's witticism here, and from Poe's remark at the head of his two page reprint of the traversal of the Simplon Pass (see *BJ* of 12/6, 325 ff. [facsimile text].

207/52-62} Freeman Hunt (1804-1858) had been editing this highly successful journal for about 6 years with such success that Poe, with his perpetual ideal of the *Stylus*, feels vindicated in his goal. Obviously, on the verge of seizing sole control of the *BJ*, Poe confirms his boldness through Hunt's example of single proprietorship. For a fuller view of Poe's attitude and relationship with Hunt, see Pollin, *Texas Studies in Literature and Language*, 1974, 16.305-13. See also 89, 146, 242, 303-304 [facsimile text], especially the last which cites Willis' eulogy on Hunt.

207/64-66} The pages of these papers in order are 115-26, 127-38, 139-43, and 143-50.

208/1-26} The pages in the journal of these papers starting with the one on Peabody are: 150-62, 162-65, 165-70, 171-73. The para. about Mr. Peabody is taken almost verbatim from p. 157 (line 7: "... he built" and through line 16). The information about the *North American Review* and Carey and Hart is in a footnote of the article.

208/27-31} "Scene on the Schuylkill" was engraved by A.W. Graham from an original picture by J. Hamilton for *Godey's* American Views. "The Deliverance of St. Peter from Prison," painted by W. Hilton, R.A., was engraved by A.L. Dick.
The works referred to are: "Dudley Villiers" by Miss Leslie, a fiction about an army officer (39-45); "Error-- a Sonnet" by Mrs. E. Oakes Smith (37); Mrs. Hale's name is not listed, but various anonymous works might include hers. Poe's name is mentioned for the "Marginalia," 117-34.

209/1-15} See 282 and 288-90 [facsimile text] for a rev. of Hewitt's poems, and 328-32 for a rev. of Osgood's. For a considerate letter of 3/15 from Hewitt to Poe see Poe *Log* of that date; also H 17.272 for her kindness in 1846.

209/16-29} There is a good reason for the very full announcement of an annual due to appear three months from 8/9, namely, the inclusion of Poe's poem "The Lake," reprinted. Hence we find other announcements on pp. 247, 311, and 323, before a rev. on 344-45 [facsimile text], again telling us about the lovely format and Baxter's new color process.

209/30-34} Poe speaks well of Keese as ed. and also as anthologist of *Poets of America* (I, 1840; II, 1842: "a fine taste, a sound judgment, and ... a ... thorough acquaintance with our poetical literature" (H 11.150; see also H 12.228, 13.78, 15.254). See refs. in 221, 247 [facsimile text]. Poe had reason to mention the annual, *The Opal*, which had been edited by N.P. Willis and in which Poe himself had published "Morning on the Wissahiccon" (in the 1843 issue, that is *The Opal* of 1844). It had been illustrated by the well known artist John Gadsby Chapman, although somewhat inappositely (see Pollin, study of Poe and Chapman in *SAR 1984*).

209/35-38} Poe had no fondness for Arthur, the indefatigable ed. of dozens of journals in Baltimore, Phila., and NY over the years and prolific author of temperance tracts and moralistic stories (1809-85), mocked in FS 30 (q.v. for an account of Poe's views). Poe again announced the annual, characteristically entitled *The Snow-Flake and Gift for Innocence and Beauty* (220, 247, etc.).

209/39-43} The specimen sheets that Poe had seen were of his contribution, "The Imp of the Perverse," which TOM considered "one of Poe's great stories"-- supporting Poe's augury that this "souvenir" will be unequalled. Poe reviews a small game-book by Hamilton (243) in addition to the annual (247, 260 [facsimile text]).

210/1-2} Poe's faintly elegiac tone over the suspension of *The Gift: A Christmas and New Year's Present for ...*, published since the issue of 1836, stems from its hospitality to him for "MS ... in a Bottle," "William Wilson," "Eleonora," "Pit and Pendulum," and "Purloined Letter."

210/3-6} Edward Everett (1794-1865), eminent as educator, statesman, orator, and ed. of *North American Review*, was rarely praised or honored by Poe in half a dozen allusions and short notes (see loci in *PD*, 33). Everett wished to leave politics when he was ambassador to Great Britain (1841-45) and happily accepted the election (1845) to the Harvard post, which he left in 1849.

210/7-16} This "remarkable" story led to further submissions and a "lead-poem" in the 8/23 *BJ* signalized in 226 (h).

210/17-48} The editor and publisher mentioned are Briggs

and Bisco and finally Poe, who is, of course, being taxed with "severity" once again. The editor of the *Democratic Review* is John Louis O'Sullivan (35 [facsimile text]) and Henry G. Langley.

Poe's rejoinder seems to mix up two papers, the "Gazette" and the "Courier." In 255(e) he cites with tacit approval a notice for a new vol. of poems by Cist, stemming from the *Gazette*, and, 245/8-9, asks Cist to send him the *Gazette*. Poe cleverly evades the issue by speaking of Watson on the masthead, a name that had been and continued to be there, although it obviously was Briggs who was meant. He ignores the week of a lapsed issue (7/4) when the "flare-up" *was* being settled, for it was suitable to try to hush up the whole affair. See Quinn, 463; also, App. 9: three contracts for the *BJ*, of 2/21/45, 7/14/45, and 10/24/45 (751-53). The mild tone and attitude of judicious neutrality make it unlikely that the "Correspondent" could be the "unseated" Briggs, as does the ref. to the "flashy name," which was specifically chosen by Briggs and elaborately justified in para. 2 of his "Introductory" of 1/4/45, 1.1: "We have chosen it for the sake of individuality, and because it is indigenous, and ... is indicative of [our] ... spirit."

210/49-52} The plate of John Kearsley Mitchell is the frontispiece for "Our Contributors.-- no. XX: Dr. John K. Mitchell" by Joseph C. Neal, pp. 49-51. It was painted by Saunders, engraved by Welch and Walter. Joseph Clay Neal (1807-47) was a Phila. journalist and humorist whose satirical *Charcoal Sketches* (1838 and, second series, 1848) were popular here and in England. Poe seemed to know Mitchell personally, and included him in the second "Chapter of Autography" in the 12/41 *Graham's* (H 15.220-21) with a ref. to his "several pretty songs set to music" and his vol. of poems with one of "an old-fashioned polish and vigor." This is *Indecision, a Tale of the Far West and other poems* (Phila., 1838c.), containing "Come, come to me, my rover, / Let Araby boast. / Oh! fly to the prairies. / Oh, Home of my childhood. / The Prairie Lea."

210/54-56} "The Tower-Rock on the Mississippi" seems to be from a sketch of G. Bodmer, engraved by Smillie and Hinshelwood. The "Rock Mountain" northside view repeats the same large subject that was in the June *Graham's* (see 117/56 [facsimile text]). This is drawn by J. Smillie from a sketch by T. Addison Richards; engraved by Rawdon, Wright, Hatch, and Smillie.

210/56-58} "The Jugglers, a Story of New Orleans" is printed as "By a New Contributor" (pp. 61-71). Much more important is Poe's listing Mrs. Osgood's "Ida Grey," pp. 82-84, with the brief comment, "a tale of passion." This is another link in the long chain of exchanges in print between Frances and Edgar, a romance in the Della Cruscan style. She used the pages of the *BJ* and of *Graham's* chiefly, Poe the former. The names of "Kate Carol," "Violet Vane" and, in a sense, "Ida Grey" are some of the pseudonyms. The story is traced well by TOM in *Poems*, 379-84, 356-58. He indicates (383) that Poe's lately discovered poem, "The Divine Right of Kings," was probably a reply to a passage in "Ida Grey": "He bids me tell him that I love him, as proudly as if he had a right ... a divine right to demand my love." The hero of the tale is a married man much like Poe, who used "Edward S. T. Grey" as a pseudonym (see my account in *Ball State Univ. Forum*, 1973, 14.44-46). Surely Poe's phrase is significant here.

211/1} The poem of Mrs. R.S. Nichols of Cincinnati is "Farewell of the Soul to the Body" (p. 74). See p. 57 [facsimile text] for the reprint of 5 stanzas of her poetic "Address ..." and p. 69 for Poe's correction of his own error.

211/2-34} These are the final two stanzas of "Rain in Summer" (p. 71 in *Graham's*) and the "sick man" above is in the third stanza of the poem. In "To the Evening Wind" (st. 4) Bryant says "The faint old man shall lean his silver head / To feel thee;... / And they who stand about the sick man's bed, / Shall ... Softly part his curtains to allow / Thy visit, grateful to his burning brow." Longfellow writes: "The sick man from his chamber looks / At the twisted brooks; / His fevered brain / Grows calm again, / And he breathes a blessing on the rain." Poe's statement is a canard on Longfellow, obviously. All the italics in the excerpt are Poe's. There are changes in the accidentals, unlisted; the following need note: 12, which / that; 17, underground / under ground; 33, forever more / forevermore. The phrase "worthy the genius" is typical of Poe, often used.

211/35-50} The poem of James Russell Lowell appears on p. 52, with no variants in substantives from Poe's transcription. Wordsworth's lines in "Song at the feast of Brougham Castle" (last stanza) correctly read as follows: "Armour rusting in his halls / On the blood of Clifford calls;-- / 'Quell the Scot,' exclaims the Lance-- / Bear me to the heart of France, / Is the longing of the Shield-- / Tell thy name, thou trembling Field." Poe's half-remembered lines are almost a re-creation of those of

Wordsworth. Poe's challenging phrase "palpable plagiarism" naturally made Lowell-- always kind to the editor-- indignant, as seen in his letter to his good friend Briggs of 8/21/45: "In the last *BJ* he has accused me of plagiarism and *misquoted* Wordsworth to sustain his charge. 'Armour rustling on the walls, On the blood of Clifford calls,' he quotes, italicising [*sic*] *rustling* as the point of resemblance. The word is really 'rusting'-- ...My metaphor was drawn from some old Greek or Roman story which was in my mind & which Poe, who makes such a scholar of himself ought to have known .... There was no resemblance between the two passages" (letter cited by Hull from Harvard MSS.).

One minor aspect of Poe's comment is the indication of his bearing yet another poem by Wordsworth in his memory, although inaccurately. Poe's sharp attack on the English poet in the 1831 Prefatory "Letter to B_____" (*Poems*; H 7.xxxix-xliii) for "didacticism" is often taken as his basic and unaltered attitude, but all his later works show frequent refs. to his ideas and works (see *PD*, 99), markedly different. There is still no good, comprehensive study of Poe's views on and use of Wordsworth.

211/52-56} The magazine, pp. 133-53, prints a "Biographical Sketch of Harman Blennerhassett" (1765-1831), who aided and abetted Aaron Burr and went free with Burr. The article is based on documents from Burr's relative. Poe was very partial to Wallace, q.v. in 168, 251, and, especially, 307 [facsimile text].

211/57-65} A prefatory note explains the double number as stemming from H.G. Langley's ending his publishing control of the magazine, which continued to have John L. O'Sullivan, one of its founders; he had made it a leading literary and miscellaneous journal, with many contributions by Hawthorne, Poe and others (see Mott, 677-84).

Poe is surprisingly gracious to "Education" (40-50) by Henry Norman Hudson (1814-86), well-known lecturer on Shakespeare, about whom he has several unfriendly refs. (see 339 [facsimile text] and MM 146, 151, 165) although not in *BJ* 299/21 [facsimile text].

Poe is similarly surprisingly gracious about "Harry Franco's" tale-- tactfully showing the public their "good" relationships. However, Briggs continued to cherish animosity toward his former associate.

212/1-2} This is a long rev. article (263-78) on four books

concerning the Oregon Territory: by Duflot de Mofras (in French), by Robert Greenhow, by Thomas Falconer, and by John Dunn.

212/6} See 107 and 278 [facsimile text] for other Hazlitt revs.

212/3-25} This vol. has xxii + 229 p. Poe limits his discussion solely to *Hamlet* (70-76) and in his general remarks of para. 1 might be discussing any of the other works of Hazlitt, such as *Table Talk*. Numerous articles on Hazlitt (see *BJ* Index) can be consulted, but surely the rather generalized comparisons with Leigh Hunt and Macaulay are verbal filler; Poe is much kinder to the latter than is his custom.

212/26-60} The second para. is a restatement of Hazlitt's second para.: "Are not Hamlet's speeches 'real?' They are as real as our own thoughts. Their reality is in the reader's mind." Later he introduces the idea of identification, which Poe had already discussed for *Robinson Crusoe* in the 1836 *SLM* rev. (see Jacobs, 120-21, 384 n.14). Poe derived his emphasis on the idea from the preface to the ed. that he was reviewing (see Pollin, "Poe and Defoe," *Topic*, 1976, 30.3-22). Here is Hazlitt's hint: "The poet appears ... to be identified with each character .... Like ... the ventriloquist, he throws his imagination out of himself," etc. The original idea of Poe, however, is the concept that this leads to the inconsistencies of thought and action which are basic to the character of all men, including the author Shakespeare. Hazlitt says (p. 76) that the ideas and motives of the personae dramatis are like those of real men, and Poe adds-- "especially of the writer."

213/1-5} The Massachusetts proposal is on pp. 449-67. Mrs. Worthington's verses are "Love Sketches," 478-81. She was praised for the stanzas of "The Child's Grave" on p. 88 [facsimile text].

The "queer" inquiry on the cover must have emanated from Benjamin Blake Minor (1818-1905), the ed. of the *SLM* from 1843 to 1847. Mott reports a dispute between Minor and Poe over business matters anent the *BJ* (646), and this may motivate Poe's sarcasm.

213/9-26} John Stuart Skinner (1788-1851), lawyer, public official and agricultural publicist and editor, close friend of Francis Scott Key, founded the *American Farmer* in 1819, editing it to 1830, and founded and edited the *Farmers' Library* 1845-48. Poe's data comes from Skinner's article on pp. 25-26. The lectures of Petzholdt (Poe's spelling is an error) were probably those on agricultural chemistry by Alexander Petzholdt (1810-89).

213/27-34} This journal would end this year, after five years of publication. As an expression of the girl operatives it had attracted international attention in social history and even then among Boston literary groups. It was edited by Harriet Jane Hanson. The editorial (180-88) is part of the history of Miss Farley, one of the two publishers: her sad childhood, teaching, and work at the factory.

213/35} See Index for other announcements of this evanescent novel in parts.

213/37} This year saw the "battle of the illustrated bibles," each coming out in parts before issuance as a ponderous tome. R. Martin of NY used steel engravings for notes and "devotional reflections" by the Rev. Alexander Fletcher; hence, sometimes advertised as the *Devotional Family Bible* (see 243, 259 [facsimile text]). The Harpers had employed the well-known artist John Gadsby Chapman (1808-89) to do many hundreds of wood engravings for its *Illuminated ... Bible*, greatly preferred by Poe, who cherished wood engravings for his own dream magazine (see *BJ* Index for his revs. of this bible). Poe had long known Chapman's work, hanging his "Lake of the Dismal Swamp" on the model-salon wall in "Phil. of Furniture." Chapman also had illustrated Poe's tale (later termed "The Elk") in the *Opal* for 1844 (see Pollin, "Poe and Chapman" in *SAR 1983*, 245-274). Briggs, in his revs. of the earlier parts of the Harper bible, in *BJ*, vol. I, condemned the monotony of so many pictures by one illustrator; this probably stimulated Poe into a more laudatory rev. of the designs, title pages, etc. of the successive Harper part-issues.

214/7-45} There are several reasons to believe that this is not by Poe: 1. The style is atypical, as in "We know not who is the author" (10-11), "as well female as male" (38), the vague last phrase (44-45); 2. Poe would be unlikely to refer so flatteringly to Margaret Fuller (see 34 [facsimile text]); 3. Poe was not likely to espouse the cause of feminism so vehemently (see his views on "blue stockings" in 34 [facsimile text]) and would not derogate the South this way (lines 30-34 [facsimile text]). On the other hand, the length of the rev. makes it unlikely for him to assign any one else to it, and whom would he find for it? The books are of 1845, with 164 p. and no preface. Collation of the excerpt (pp. 33-34) aside from accidentals, such as the misspelled "million(s)" and the italics here and there, shows the following: 22 on to the stage; 25 nor in any; 28 power. In Ohio, more than one third of the children attend no school. In Indiana etc.; 32 read and write; 33 her hordes of ignorant....

214/46-58} John Abercrombie (1780-1844), a leading physician of Edinburgh, published papers and books on medical pathology. In 1830 he published *Inquiries concerning the Intellectual Powers* and in 1833 *Philosophy of the Moral Feelings*, works which were not particularly original but very popular. Poe's statement is taken from the prefatory "advertisement," although not verbatim.

214/59-65} The vol. had 192 p. Martin Farquhar Tupper (1810-89) had enormous popularity for his *Proverbial Philosophy*, four series of "truisms cast in irregular rhythmical language" (*Cassell's Enc.*), a "phenomenon in the history of taste" (Baugh, *Lit. History*). His novel came out in 1844. The theme stated by Poe (215/1-5) justifies the characterizing phrase "shot through with complacent Whiggery" (Baugh), although he himself was genial and humane in his political orientation and "did much to promote good relations with America" (*Enc. Brit.*, 11th ed., 27.411). Willis thought the first part of his *Proverbial Philosophy* to be a forgotten work of the 17th century. In the second part of this rev. (215/1-10), Poe seems to be impressed by the glibness and reputation of Tupper's works, but in a 3/46 *Godey's* rev. he drops a somewhat ambiguous remark about his standard "adages" (H 13.112), arising from the title of his major work. See 305-306 [facsimile text] for more on Tupper.

215/11-20} Sir Charles Lyell (knighted in 1848; 1797-1875), first a barrister, became the most eminent geologist of England. Poe alludes to him in the Intro. to the Marginalia (see *Br.*, p. 108, also TOM, 1117 n.10). In 1841-42 he traveled and lectured in North America; his studies of the alluvial matter in deltas led him to the "Great Dismal Swamp" of Virginia, well known to Poe (see "Poe and Chapman" in *SAR 1983*). Both vols. came out in 1845: I is v-vi + 251 p.; II, 197 p. Poe's remark implies his having heard Lyell in a lecture. He also alludes to the Pref. that gives a list of papers written by Lyell on more strictly scientific topics of geology, which are not for the "general reader." The book is written as a journal with dated entries.

215/21-24} For other notices of this novel in parts see 191/35-38 nn.

215/25-28} For another ref. to a rev. of this work by Caroline Norton, Sheridan's granddaughter, see 168/29-41 nn. Her *Child of the Islands* attacked the conditions of the laboring poor.

215/29-34} This consists of 140 p. of double columns. It is a series of travel sketches, probably unread by Poe. Poe uses his *High-Ways and By-Ways* for MM 114, 203, q.v. for details of the author who served as British consul in Boston, 1839-46. In the disputed rev. of the *PPA* in the 1/28/43 *Saturday Museum* (H 11.223) Poe objects to the ranking of T.C. Grattan before Willis and would put him last, but why is he even included among American authors?

215/20-22} For Poe's friend, Frost, see 72 [facsimile text] and for this book see 191/20-22 [facsimile text].

215/38-50} Poe's close association with Robert Sully, nephew to Thomas Sully (1783-1872), America's premier portrait artist after the deaths of Peale and Stuart (1827-28), makes this small item highly significant. See also 233 (f) [facsimile text], below. Robert Sully, a minor painter in Richmond, was the son of actor Matthew, who had acted on the stage with Poe's mother in 1803 (Hervey Allen, *Israfel*, 1834, 1-vol. ed., 683). They were boyhood friends in Richmond, also in Phila. in 1841, and again in 1849 when Poe visited his "home town" (Mary Phillips, *Poe*, 188-91, 1458; Allen, 81; Quinn, 85, 274). Susan Archer Talley Weiss relates Robert Sully's intimate views of Poe (*Scribner's Monthly*, 1878, 15.712, 715) and according to the Richmond *Whig* of 10/16/49 left an illustration of "Lenore" from Poe's poem (information kindly given by Michael Deas, author of the forthcoming *Portraits ... of ... Poe*). The picture of Jackson, in a red cloak, is famous. Poe's wonder at the term "original" can be explained, perhaps, in that Sully more than once made a "new" picture from one of his own works, an improved copy, so to speak, perhaps on commission-- or a slightly different version. There is a good reason for multiple versions and copies of the late General (and ex-President) Andrew Jackson (1767-June 8, 1845). His recent death must have led to a great demand by government agencies and historical associations for a portrait. We note in *The Life and Works of Thomas Sully* by Edward Biddle

(Phila., 1921) that in the List of Paintings, Nos. 875-888 are portraits of Jackson. Of these No. 880 is a "Bust, in uniform, high military coat, ... with red cape ... finished 8/6/29." The earliest portrait is that of No. 875, a drawing made 9/1817, but there is none listed for 1824. Yet No. 881 (finished 6/28/45) is inscribed on the back "From a study made in 1824 from Genl. Jackson. TS." No. 882 is described as "full length, standing in long military cloak ... finished 7/31/45." There might be an 1824 drawing or painting not in the current register of his works. Whatever the truth of the matter, and whatever the source of the *Sun*'s account, there is an easy explanation of the word "original" from which a new portrait could be made. Clearly Poe was in error also about the "younger Sully," his good friend Robert.

215/51-60} None of the available books on "Daguerreotypes" (see 197 [d] for a note on the acute accent) lists the name Martiner (is it an error for Martinez?) of Paris, and many in French are not available in this country. No doubt Poe is quoting from one of the local papers. His interest in photography and also in the theatrical panoramas and dioramas was always keen, q.v. in Pin 7 (*Br.*, pp. 14-15), and also 197 (d) above (in [facsimile text]). Richard Rudishill, *Mirror Image* (1971), pp. 54-55, 71, discusses Poe's interest and also his attempt to retain the French acute accent over the second "e."

216/1-6} Poe "last" spoke of the drama on 8/2 (p. 193 [facsimile text]). The Bowery theatre burnt down on 4/25 and reopened on 8/4/45. The opening bill was *The Sleeping Beauty* and J.H. Payne's comedy *Charles II*. The architect was J.M. Trimble (see Odell, 5.186 for details and for Jackson's statement). For additional information about the fire, see Mary C. Henderson, *The City and the Theater* (1973).

216/12} It seems obvious that Poe is describing the scene on the drop curtain-- the sort of monument-view that was being proposed for the ever a-building Washington Monument that intermittently concerned Poe himself; see my study, "Politics and History in Poe's 'Mellonta Tauta,'" *Studies in Short Fiction*, 1971, 8.627-31. The term "Pittite" was standard in England for one frequenting the theatre, especially sitting in the pit, but it did not have a capital letter. It is doubtful that Poe meant to pun on the other significance, one who espoused the policies of William Pitt, the British statesman.

216/16-26} Poe's advice here contrasts with his principles of private house decoration in "Phil. of Furniture," reprinted in the 5/3 *BJ*, opposing "glare" and "glitter" (TOM, 498-500).

217/8-10} *Les Huguenots* by Meyerbeer was performed on 8/11 with Calvé as Valentine.

217/11-13} Chippindale (properly spelled) and Sefton were in charge of the summer season at Niblo's, as well as acting. Wm. Burton, Poe's "boss" on the magazine in Philadelphia, first appeared on 7/11 in *Fright*. Henry Placide and Thomas Placide are mentioned, the former being the more prominent, and Miss Taylor is Mary. John Brougham appeared on 8/4 in *The Poor Gentleman*.

217/16-22} "Palmo's opened as a German theatre on 8/11, with a performance of *Roderich, der Sohn des Waldes, oder das Leben ein Traum*" (Odell, 136).

217/34} See the *Evening Gazette* of 8/8/45 (vol. 1, no. 135).

217/41-43} In view of the wordy and savage attacks by Poe in the "Longfellow War" articles and his long palliation below we must see exactly what the 8/45 *American Review* article on "The American Drama" said about Poe:
"Mr. Poe furnishes the next paper (in the 8/45 *American Review*), the first of a series upon the American Drama, The Tortesa of Willis, and the Spanish Student of Longfellow, are the subjects of his criticism, and the former is pronounced particularly successful, having received no stinted measure of commendations both on the stage and in the closet, while the latter is set down as totally devoid of any kind of merit, except as a mere poem. Tortesa, in the opinion of Mr. Poe, is superior to most of the Dramas of Sheridan Knowles, is full of fine passages and capital points, while Mr. Longfellow's play is condemned as unworthy of his genius, as utterly deficient in originality, in its plot and in the author's manner of handling it, and as exhibiting a radical want of the adapting or constructive power which the Drama so imperatively demands.
In Mr. Poe's own words, "as for the 'Spanish Student,' its thesis is unoriginal; its incidents are antique; its plot is no plot; its characters have no character; in short it is little better than a play upon words to style it 'A Play' at all. A somewhat sweeping condemnation, but Mr. Longfellow does not seem to please Mr. Poe in anything that he writes."

217/52} On 2/28 at the Society Library.

218/16-17} Poe regarded all the works of the distinguished critic H.T. Tuckerman of Boston (1813-71) with distaste (see "Lit." sketches, H 15.217, 227; *Tales*, 1101; *Poems*, 426 n.10). Perhaps Tuckerman's article on Petrarch in the 4/45 *American Review* led to this allusion to his book *Isabel*.

218/19-71 & 219/4-20} Poe had passed from disdain for William Gilmore Simms' carelessness of style and plotting in his numerous novels to considerable admiration and friendliness-- based on his wonderful variety and prolificity and the coincidence of their cultural and political views, as here (see *PD*, 84 for loci of numerous reviews and passages). See Index to *BJ* under "Simms" for numerous allusions showing this and see also "copyright" for a remarkable closeness of views (also MM 74, 113, 173). It is clear also that Simms' praise of the forthcoming Wiley and Putnam "Library" series of American books, including Poe's tales and his poems, motivates the reprint of this essay from Simms' *Southern and Western Monthly Magazine and Review*, which parallels the *BJ* in lasting from 1/45 through 12/45, before being merged with the *SLM*. It too was largely the product of Simms' pen and contained many of his tales and poems.

219/16-20} True to his promise, Simms reviewed Poe's *Tales* in a good-sized passage of the 12/45 issue, 2.426-27 praising Poe as a mystic and imaginative Prospero, despite his faults, the one specified being the liberties he takes with the Charleston area typography for "Gold-Bug," this being a natural criticism for the ed. of a Charleston magazine (and the only disparagement of Poe's "realistic detail"). He also complains of the slow diffusion from N.Y. of the American "Library" by contrast with the European series' distribution.

219/21-23} Samuel Colman was familiar to Poe for many publications, perhaps especially for the tr. of Fouqué's *Undine*, a Poe favorite, reviewed in the 9/39 *BGM* (H 10.30-39). Poe knew Kettell's *Specimens* well, mocking its status in a 2/42 *Graham's* rev. (H 11.17) and speaking of its currency in 11/42 (11.149).

Francis Lieber (1800-72), political scientist, reformer, educator, savant, won distinction after leaving Germany as ed. of the *Enc. Americana* (1829-33), prof. of History at South Carolina College, etc. Poe rev'd his book on Niebuhr (H 8.162-168) and charmingly includes him in "Autography" (15.170-71).

219/26-31} See 205 nn. for Lester's d'Azeglio tr. as only the first of the "series" and the Index under Lester for others.

219/40-46} Poe's information is only partially correct; Poe would review the Redfield ed. of Elizabeth Oakes Smith's *Poetical Writings* (221-22) and poems of Frances Osgood (328 ff.), but not of Alfred B. Smith or of Emerson. The former came out through Clark and Austin (more correctly) and the second came out in 1846 (England) and 1847 (Boston). Tuckerman never published such a volume.

219/48-60} Poe's opinion of mesmerism as a "science" and a therapy for illness had been changing considerably, and he was to use it effectively in several of his tales. In his rev. of Newnham's *Human Magnetism* he takes up Miss Martineau's advocacy citing the *Lancet* (more accurately, the March issue), q.v. on pp. 69-70 [facsimile text] (see also 254).

219/61-64} The ref. is to Henry Russell (1812-1900), vocalist and song-composer, who made a great reputation in England, Canada, and US with songs of a domestic character, some written expressly for him. This item comes from the Albany paper's issue of 8/4/45, vol. 16.

220/1-3} The "brief period" was May through August, for the April issue was to be followed by the September. Poe knew about this as a contributing "ed." and a friend at that time of Mr. English. In "Our Pigeon-Holes" (p. 242) of September, an editorial by English, is a long casuistical excuse for this four-months' interruption followed by a ref. to the editor's being "laid up" for over five weeks with arthritis. For Poe's future relations with the author of "Ben Bolt" see Moss, *Poe's Major Crisis* (1970).

220/4-5} Poe often wrote favorably about Lydia Sigourney (1791-1865), "the American Hemans" of Hartford, who wrote 67 books, mostly about death and its ravages. Gordon Haight's biography does not discuss this illness, nor does the short notice in the *NE Mag.* (5.15-30).

220/6-9} For Arthur and this annual see 209 [facsimile text]; also 247 [facsimile text].

220/10-19} This was originally part of the third installment of Marginalia articles, printed in *Godey's* of 8/45 (called "Marginal Notes") and accidentally attached to the preceding item (now numbered MM 122, 123 in *Br.*). Poe's explanation of the error springs perhaps from his concern over having antagonized Lowell through the charge of plagiarism in "To the Future" from a Wordsworth poem (see p. 211 [facsimile text]). In M 122 Poe is quoting from his own rev. of Lowell's *Conversations on some of the old Poets*, of 1844, a rev. originally printed in the *Evening Mirror* of 1/11/45. The passage rather tortuously criticizes Lowell for seeming to confuse an artist and a man of "some artistic ability" with respect to creating the same or a similar work (see text and note in *Br.*, p. 225-26). The following *Marginalia* item is a resounding slap at Griswold's "big book," the *Poets and Poetry of America* which Poe (and Henry Hirst) had lampooned in 11/42 (H 11.147-60). Jean Baptiste du Val de Grâce, Baron von Cloots (1755-94), was an eccentric nobleman of Dutch family, who titled himself "orator of the human race," assumed the name of "Anacharsis" from Barthélemy's romance, became a member of the Convention, and was finally guillotined by order of Robespierre.

220/20-25} The first name is possibly that of Thomas Warren Field (1821-81), an author, who edited several valuable historical works, and, much later, *An Essay Towards an Indian Bibliography* (1873).

The second item, "A New York Ghost," appeared in the 8/23 *BJ*, 2.101-102, by "Fidelius Bathos." It is conspicuously amateurish.

220/29-33} There is no doubt that "A Rare Opportunity" pertains to an investment in the *BJ*, so desperately short of funds. To clinch this assumption-- Poe is using his favorite pseudonym of E.S.T. Grey (q.v. re F. Osgood's "Ida Grey"-- the pseudonym treated by Pollin in *Ball State Univ. Forum*, 1973, 14.44-46).

220/34-55} Although Poe disapproved of Margaret Fuller, the blue-stocking, in many respects (see 34 [facsimile text]) he approved of her criticism of Longfellow, only a bit bolder than his own, as in the New York *Daily Tribune* of 12/10/45, which Poe partly reprinted in the 2/13 *BJ* (340-41). In this full page satire on Longfellow, he is pleased by the exposé of Longfellow's anti-feminism in the remarks of Victorian, the student, to Preciosa the Gypsy as expressed in *The Spanish Student*. Margaret Fuller uses a parodic or hoax approach to the question of "male superiority" as stated in the *American Whig Review*, 7/45, I, article by "Il Secretario," on "American Letters-- Their

Character and Advancement." The relevant pages are 577-78, 580. Pretending to state the man's opinion in the poem she uses five important excerpts from Act I of the play (Cambridge ed., Boston, 1882), p. 28. Poe's footnote comment shows him torn, but nonetheless firmly against Fuller's indignation over expecting women to be solely harem-companions. I see little reason to doubt Fuller's authorship here, since Poe himself docketed as hers a letter from "X", postmarked 8/9/45, which mentioned the anonymous article. "A Peep Behind the Curtain" (in the 5/24 *BJ*, 1.324-35) and offered this further "piece of pleasantry." Mary Phillips, *Poe*, 1166-67, first presented this item, and Ostrom in *AL*, 1974, 45.526-27, offers further evidence for its attribution to her. Joel Myerson, *Margaret Fuller* (1978), p. 147, however, points to the style and method of submission as uncharacteristic.

221/1-2} The vol. is paged 5-8 + 14-204. Many of the poems are repeated from an earlier vol., *The Sinless Child and Other Poems* (1842), to which Poe alludes below. Mrs. Seba Smith, wife and editorial helper of the prolific journalist, humorist "Jack Downing," first of Maine and then of NY, was renowned for her numerous mag. contributions, her fiction, essays, and poems-- usually strongly didactic or inspirational. Poe's partiality is so great as to indicate close association with the Smiths, and the "Autography" for Seba of 12/41, H 15.239, speaks of the signature as inscribed "in our own bodily presence," but other signs (e.g., a request to Duyckinck of 4/46, *Letters*, 316) imply a more casual acquaintance. There should be some explanation, aside from extraordinarily misguided taste, and the powerful literary position of the Smiths, for the lavish praise of this inept, sentimental rubbish. E.O. Smith (1806-93) continued her prolific, misc. writings well into the 1860s.

221/12} Poe appears to be cutting corners in this rev., filling it up with excerpts, as though short of time for thought and planning; yet while still on the *Mirror* staff, Poe announced in the 2/1/45 issue the pending publication of her work. In the 12/45 *Godey's*, 31.261 ff. he wrote a much longer "study" of the book, incorporating the same points but omitting the charge of Longfellow's borrowing "Rain in Summer" terms from "Water" (which is omitted as an excerpt). On the other hand, the *Godey's* rev. includes the final stanzas of "The Summons Answered," which served Poe as the germ of "Ulalume" (see TOM, *Poems*, 411). In the second rev. Poe gives information that certainly belonged in the first: 1. that R.W. Griswold edited the vol. and wrote the Preface; 2. that in her former collection of poems John

Keese, as ed., had included a biographical account written by her fellow Maine-citizen, John Neal of Portland. In a disparaging way, Poe then puts into service Griswold's "unnecessary" preface by quoting a full, long para., perhaps thereby revealing the sententious sentimentality of her poems: e.g., "the same beautiful vein of philosophy ... that truth and goodness of themselves impart a holy light to the mind which gives it a power far above mere intellectuality" (H 13.79). Oddly, Poe speaks merely of Keese's viewpoint, although this is expressed only in the 1842 vol.; it also leads us to think that the vol. of her poems for which he had thanked Keese in' May 1845 (see *Letters*, p. 289) was the first collection, requested in anticipation of the arrival of the 1845 vol.

221/33} The major excerpts, collated with Mrs. Smith's text, are paged thus: "Sinless Child" (15-90) with "The Stepmother" on 62-63; "Presages" (150); and "The Water" (141-43). Collations show these few changes: 221/39: new,; 222/35: When down it tumbles; 222/46: Released from out.

222/2} In the *Godey's* rev. Poe states the subject as "the progress of a plant from its germ to its maturity, with the uses and general vicissitudes to which it is subjected."

222/64} Poe's mention of the August number of the mag. is to show the priority of her poem. While both poems are based on imagistic clichés of the subject, it is true that Longfellow must have read her poem beforehand. Poe gives little credit to him for shaping it as a whole so much more artistically.

223/1-13} This vol. (part II) had no pref. and 212 p. in all. Poe initially alludes to his former rev. of part I (198-205 [facsimile text]). The articles listed are on these pages, in their respective order: 1-31, 32-56, 57, 73-122, 123-25, 126-37, 138-48, 149-52, 153-66, 167-82, 183-201, 202-205, 206-209, 210-212.

Of the serious poems three are works of social protest rather than simply poems of melancholy, dating from the final period of Hood's life: "Song of the Shirt" was first in *Punch*, Christmas No. of 1843; "Bridge of Sighs" in *Hood's Magazine* of 5/44; and "Lay of the Labourer" also in that journal, 11/44; the more purely Gothic poem of "The Haunted House" appearing in the 1/44 issue. Surely they spring not from Hood's "hereditary taint" but rather from his increasing awareness of the plight of the laboring, exploited poor and perhaps his own chronic illness, approaching its fatal conclusion-- rheumatic fever and other ailments. Poe, remarkably, seems to miss the social content of these works (even implicit in the last above) and regards the horror and somberness as the "theme" or "thesis."

223/21-29} This poem, based on a piteous police case of a widow's pawning her exploiting employer's "shirts," i.e., her "work," roused the public to the prevalence of starvation wages. Numerous lines hammer home the theme: "It is not linen you're wearing out, / But human creatures' lives!" and "But why do I talk of Death?.... / I hardly fear his terrible shape, / It seems so like my own" and "My labour never flags; / And what are its wages? A bed of straw, / A crust of bread-- and rags." From the viewpoint of carrying a clear "moral" the designation of "pure" poetry might be omitted, but Poe's view of the "*grotesquerie*" as explaining its popularity is a strange misconception. The term, incidentally, is one he first applied in this way in 1840-41 and continued to use for the whole decade (see *PCW*, 27).

223/30-35} Apparently Poe was enamored of the dimeter pattern of this poem, quoting it entire (*BJ* 2.153) and reciting it entire for his "Poetic Principle" lectures (see its pub. form, H 14.284-87). But his praise of it as "imaginative" (217 [facsimile text]), "of the loftiest order," and of "wild insanity" seems inappropriate. Rather hackneyed is the theme of the enceinte suicide, casting herself from Waterloo Bridge into the Thames (for that bridge won this title from such usage at the time). Its charm for Poe obviously lay in "singular versification," not pathos.

223/36-55} This is a collection of short stories many of which have surprise endings foreshadowing, as the *OCAL* avers, O. Henry's tales. Calling this vol. Part III of *Loiterings of Travel* (pub. in 1840, 3 vols.) is odd, since *Loiterings* were "Sketches of Travel," from the 1830s, chiefly in the British Isles, but also scenes of Washington life after Congress ended its session. For Nathaniel Parker Willis (1806-67), see 16-18 [facsimile text] and numerous other articles in the *BJ* Index.

The book is pages 110-220, with a Preface about its character (travel sketches and romantic fiction) and complaints about the unfair copyright laws that lead to mag. rather than book publication. Poe's statement is as evasive as can be, making one wonder whether he even scanned the contents, and his italics for "truest" and "pretence" remind us of the charges of affectation widely leveled against Willis. Yet he always proved a devoted friend to Poe, and perhaps this was truly meant.

223/56-63} This novel of 95 p. seems to have disappeared from all NYC libraries, existing only elsewhere whence it "does not travel" and for my part will not be traveled to. Poe appears to be in error about the first name, which is "James" and not "I." Moreover, he was mistaken about his existence, for the cataloguers tell us that he existed, 1818-47. Interested potential readers are referred to the Yale library.

224/1-5} See no. 35 of this bible (213 [facsimile text]) ed. by A. Fletcher, with all woodcuts by J.G. Chapman.

224/9} The series mentioned began only on 9/13, 2.153-54, being the composition of Henry C. Watson, essentially the music rather than art critic. He explains the formation of the National Gallery through a fund contributed to purchase the collection of "the late Lumon Reed." The Rotunda was a large brick building, built 1817-18 by John Vanderlyn, in City Hall Park as an art gallery, but it reverted to the city and was used for various other purposes until the NY Gallery of Fine Arts was allowed to occupy it. This lasted only until 1848 when it reverted to the city for public offices (and was demolished in 1870); information from Richard J. Koke, *Catalogue of the Collection* (NY Historical Society, 1982), p. 252, item 445. Subsequently Watson reviews the displayed pictures on 9/20, 2.169-70 and 10-11, 2.213-14. Thereafter Poe takes over the art criticism for several issues, and finally it disappears entirely from the journal (see Intro.).

224/10-40} Poe's ref. is to an item in the New York *Weekly Mirror*, of 8/23/45, pp. 318-19, obviously badly printed, since it has the wrong accent in "résumé" (the wrong word in any event), a misprint for "comment" (as "commaut") and for Macaulay's name. The article's allusion is to Poe's rev. of Lester's translation of d'Azeglio's *Ettore Fieramosca* (205-206 [facsimile text]); see the note for fuller explanation of Poe's meaning of the criticism. Poe clearly believes Lester responsible for the *Mirror* contribution; hence, his vituperative conclusion-- although in his many later revs. and statements about Lester he is far less harsh (see Index for loci). By this time his friend Willis had left the *Mirror* and Morris was preparing to leave, while Hiram Fuller was taking over full control. It was early in 1846 that Poe was going to sue Fuller for printing the libellous charge against him made by his former friend Thomas Dunn English (see Moss, *Poe's Major Crisis*).

225/3} This entire article offers proof positive that Poe did indeed visit Boston during July-- in fact, the first week, probably. It concerns a rather obscure episode involving Frances Osgood about whom Hervey Allen writes that during the summer of 1845 she went to Albany to live, with Poe following after her. "She later went to Boston, it is said, to avoid him" (*Israfel*, 527), but Allen is mistaken in thinking this the occasion of his Lyceum reading, which was in October. (My thanks are owed for the date to Dwight Thomas, author of the forthcoming *Poe Log*, with D.K. Jackson.)

225/28} The two Boston ed. vols. of Hawthorne's 1842 *Twice-Told Tales* numbered 331 and 356 p. Poe had reviewed them very favorably in the 4/42 and 5/42 *Graham's* and would again mention their being "scarcely recognized by the press or the public" in the Intro. to the "Lit." sketches (H 15.3) as well as in his collective rev. of this work and *Mosses...* in the 11/47 *Godey's* (H 13.142): "a poor man" and "publicly-unappreciated man of genius." Poe's noble solicitude ties in with his Young American bias, his anti-New England prejudices, and perhaps the initially encouraging sales of his *Tales*, issued two months earlier by Wiley and Putnam. The poor grammar of "profit ... are" is doubtless a typesetter's oversight.

225/31-45} Jean Paul Richter, *Flower, Fruit and Thorn Pieces*, tr. by Edward Henry Noel, in 2 vols.: I, xiv + 348 p.; II, 398, 1845. William and Anna Russell, *The young ladies' elocutionary reader*, 1845 (rep. ed., 1851). Joseph Buckingham, *Devotional Exercises*, 1842 and 1845. Poe had offered "Epimanes" to Buckingham on 5/4/33 for the *New-England Magazine*, without success (*Letters*, 53).
William D. Ticknor (1810-64) of Boston published the works of his friends, Longfellow, Holmes, Lowell, Emerson, et al. but not these two books to my knowledge. Wiley and Putnam published Lamb's *Specimens of English Dramatic poets* in 1845. Poe would review *Festus*, by Philip James Bailey, of 412 p., more accurately pub. by B.B. Mussey of Boston (240-41 [facsimile text]).

225/47-48} This cinerary urn of transparent blue glass, coated with opaque white glass cut in cameo fashion, found in an antique Roman tomb, had been acquired by Sir Wm. Hamilton for 1,000 guineas and then by the Duke of Portland who exhibited it in the British Museum. In a fit of delirium one Wm. Lloyd smashed it utterly, and, by a legal quirk, could be fined only 3 pounds, the value of the case. The restoration made the damages imperceptible.

225/49-53} The original bill was introduced in 1841 after David Salomons was barred from his position as elected alderman of London, but it was lost in the House of Lords; it carried in both houses in 1845 under Sir Robert Peel's government. Poe, friend of Major Noah and depictor of several characters as Hebrew in appearance, might easily choose this "pregnant item," brought by fast steamship.

225/53-226/4} This item reflects two of Poe's major interests: classical studies and scientific history and biography. For his interest in the extraordinary genius G.W. Leibnitz see MM 38, 67, 161B. For his contacts with Peter the Great see *Dictionary of Scientific Biography* (1973) 8.150.

226/5-7} This comes, verbatim, from the New York *Sun* of 8/12/45. It is inaccurate, for Guizot, the Prime Minister, had tried to have the order suppressed and succeeded only in having some of the houses dissolved and scattered. Popular literature, e.g., by Eugene Sue, influenced this move.

226/8-13} There is an ambiguity about this stemming, perhaps, from someone's failure to recognize that the standard French word for "race-course" then was "hippodrome," in use as early as 1651. Paris had only a rudimentary race-course at the Champ de Mars until 1857, when the French Jockey Club had one built in the Longchamps meadows on land leased from the government.

226/14-17} The source is only partly correct. The actress apparently covertly left for London and then contracted for a St. Petersburg engagement after marrying Auguste Arnould, a minor playwright, of no flaring republican views (see the Paris rev. *L'Art*, 1876, vol. IV, 157-59).

226/18-19} This comes verbatim from the *Sun* of 8/12/45. For many years lighthouses had been erected on this danger point off the south coast of England, but each one was battered down or collapsed. One had just been rebuilt in 1/45. Sir Samuel Brown's proposal this year led to a more permanent plan (see G.B. Gattie, *Memorials of the Goodwin Sands*, 1890). Poe's interest in lighthouses grew into his unfinished tale, "The Light-House" (see TOM, 1388-92, and *Discoveries in Poe*, 71, 150-51).

226/23-27} Abbott Lawrence (1792-1855; N.B. his first name corrected), prominent Mass. manufacturer and philanthropist, founder of Lawrence.

226/28-37} Perhaps this is the first item after the Boston visit account to be all or partly from Poe's pen. Poe must have enjoyed much of Shea's company (he was a resident civilian at West Point) while Poe was at the Academy, 1830-32. Born 1802 in Cork, he migrated here in 1827, dying on 8/15 (not 8/17) after newspaper work and verse publication. TOM notes the echoes of "To Helen" in Shea's "The Ocean," which started out in the Boston *Ariel* of 5/1/30 (cf. lines 37-38: "The glory of Athens, / The splendor of Rome)," and was reprinted by Shea in vols. of 1831, 1836, and 1843 and newspaper columns (TOM, *Poems*, 170). Poe's last ref. is to the dimeter of both poems.

226/38-41} The poem is on *BJ*, 2.96. Poe refers to an ed. comment (210 [facsimile text]).

226/42-48} Poe had exchanged letters with Lewis Jacob Cist (1818-85) concerning Cist's poem, submitted to Poe for the abortive *Penn* and being printed by Peterson in the *Saturday Evening Post* (*Letters*, 150-82). In the 12/41 "Autography" Poe speaks of his popular poems as "disfigured by false metaphor" and "straining after effect." See 255 [facsimile text] for a follow-up.

226/50-59 + 226/1-6} James McHenry (1785-7/21/1845) was known to Poe in Phila. as contributor to the mags. and as victim of the *Knickerbocker* "cabal" as Poe says in the flattering "Autography" note (H 15.258). *The Antediluvians*, was the only "tolerable American epic" (pub. in London, 1839; Phila., 1840). This blank verse chronicle of the flood was savagely attacked by "Christopher North" in the 7/39 *Blackwood's*, as Poe said.

227/7-8} The Sears Observatory on Summer House Hill was finished on 6/23/47 (see Elias Loomis, *Recent Progress of Astronomy*, 1851, pp. 185-89).

227/9-12} This mammoth paper, like the *New World, Brother Jonathan* and *Boston Notion*, in size, lasted from 6/45 to 2/47, achieving five volumes.

227/13-22} Ever since excavations began in 1748, new

discoveries continued to be made at the incinerated and buried city of Pompeii at the foot of Mount Vesuvius, only half of which is still revealed. There is, indeed, a cemetery on the outskirts that has been uncovered, but this particular detail, and its source have not been readily discovered. The "duumvir" (more correctly "duovir") had various functions, depending on the period of use of the term: "Men for building or dedicating a temple," a Roman board or court of two, officers in the "municipia and colonies, who had charge of the streets of the suburbs of Rome" (Liddell and Scott) and "officers in Pompeii corresponding to the Roman consul" (*Library of Entertaining Knowledge*). Poe always showed much interest in classical antiquities and especially in the destroyed city (see M 49), often in connection with Bulwer's *Last Days of Pompeii* (see *PD*, 139 for over a half dozen passages).

227/25} See article (a) above on 227 [facsimile text] for this observatory. Poe's interest in astronomy was demonstrated as early as in "Hans Pfaall" (1835).

227/30-38} Poe's interest in Egyptian hieroglyphics was always keen, a sideline of his cryptographical involvement and also part of the current Egyptological fad. For his references to hieroglyphics see "Mummy," "Mellonta Tauta," and *Eureka* (TOM, 1129/29, 1298/6, H 16.196). As an ed. and calligrapher himself Poe would naturally find Dubois' achievement fascinating.

227/39-46} The Eisteddfod of 1845 was a major event in the revival of this old convening of Welsh "bards and musicians" (now much more varied with chorus, and other arts, such as drama and literature). The modern revival of the ancient tradition dates from 1792. Henry Brinley Richards (1819-85), pianist and composer, eventually was to compose the Welsh national anthem (1862).

227/47-49} Poe's inordinate interest in Thomas Campbell (1777-1844), poet, biographer, editor, anthologist, would cause him to favor selecting this item (see *PD*, 17 for 14 loci, and many *Br.* items, q.v. in Index). Campbell's nephew did not enter the *DNB*.

227/50-53} Poe's interest in ballooning, as in "Hans Pfaall," "Balloon-Hoax," and "Mellonta Tauta" would justify reprinting this item which, clearly, refers to a gliding mechanism.

227/54 + 228/1-7} While this is mere advertising copy, it is very possible that Poe wrote it for the firm of Bagley because of his use of old and new pens for his successively planned *Penn* and *Stylus*, the cover picture of the latter (see *Discoveries in Poe* 223-29), his play on the words for old and new types of pens in M 256, his buried ref. to Byron's "grey-goose quill" (*English Bards*, line 1), and the editorial tone of the "sales talk" here.

228/11} See 223 [facsimile text].

229/1-4} The essay "Copyright and Copywrong" is on pp. 73-122, "Bridge of Sighs," on 202-205, and "Haunted House" on 126-37. Concerning the first-- Poe is, of course, firmly supported by Hood and the other pirated English authors in his basic premises.

229/5-9} For Poe's strange reasons for his high praise of this poem see note to 223/21-29 [facsimile text]. Poe was happy to oblige a friend and fill up a page with the quoted poem-- *BJ*, 2.153, on 9/13. His ranking it below the Gothic sensationalistic verses of "The Haunted House" is odd.

229/10-65} Poe plucks out stanzas from the 88 of the text without warning. The excerpts come from the following: "O'er all" (127); "The coot was swimming" (128); "Howbeit, the door" (130-31); p. 230 [facsimile text]-- "The very stains" (132); "Those dreary stairs" (133); "Yet no portentous shape" (134); "Rich hangings" (135); "The death-watch ticked" (136). A collation of Poe and Hood shows no variations in substantives save for 229/45: reedy / weedy.

Here at last Poe gives us the meaning of "phantastic" (line 30): discordant, ill assorted, etc. The quoted stanza, used as a sort of refrain, occurs seven times at various points in the three parts of the poem of 352 lines.

230/1-42} Poe chooses as excerpts stanzas that remind us of some of his own tales in minor details, "Usher" and "Oval Portrait" and (in the ticking death-watch beetle) "Tell-Tale Heart"; yet, this dates from the 1/44 issue of *Hood's Magazine*. Clearly there was an underlying similitude of mind in some aspects.

230/43-60} This consists of various papers from magazines, *The Indicator* (1819-21) and *Companion* (1828) of James Henry Leigh Hunt (1784-1859). Poe always seems unsettled in his opinions of his essays and his poems, which range over a wide field and long period of time (see *PD*, 47 for many loci). In M 179 Poe coins the word "rigmarolic" for his essay discussing "What is Poetry?" (from the vol. that Poe reviews, 99-101 [facsimile text]), but adapts his answer in part in the Preface to *ROP*. Poe ignores his early recognition of such poets as Keats, Shelley, and even Tennyson and his political courage. In exalting the satire *The Feast of the Poets* (1811, with frequent later revisions) over *The Story of Rimini* or a few charming lyrics, Poe is very partial, but in his stress upon Hunt's mere "taste" and, in the conclusion of the present article, on the "entertainment" value of his essays over original ideas and depth, Poe fairly well epitomizes our present evaluation of Hunt's essays.

231/1-17} The "absurd eulogies" are in the essay, "Of Dreams" (93-103), and the next essay is on 52-57. Poe, in his critical bent, anent the preposition "upon," did not notice Hunt's error in the name of Pietro Andrea de' Bassi or da Basso, author of "Canzone della donna cruda." Poe does not explain why the "*ennuyé*" is dissatisfied with "entertainment."

231/18-43} The vol. numbers 5-11 + 25-423 p. Thomas Arnold (1795-1842), Headmaster of Rugby, which he reformed in spirit and curriculum, and Regius Prof. of history at Oxford (1841-42), especially renowned now as the father of the poet Matthew, was hymned in Henry Reed's Pref. which is largely the source for Poe's few comments. This book was announced in 92/5 [facsimile text], the n. to which has data on Henry Reed. By Apostle of Liberty does Poe refer to his advocacy of church reform or reorganization of schooling? Arthur P. Stanley (1815-81), a former Rugby student, absorbed the spirit of Arnold, and exerted a liberal influence through his long and influential career, finally becoming dean of Westminster (1864-81). Both works (final para.) came out in 1845.

231/44-54} Catherine Esther Beecher (1800-78) was daughter of the celebrated preacher Lyman Beecher and sister of Harriet. She too was a reformer and educator. The pages are 5-9, 25-356. Poe's para. is based on the Pref., p. 6.

231/ 55-63} The mag. is *Southern and Western Monthly Mag. and Rev.*, q.v. in 218/19-71 nn. Despite his adverse criticism of Simms in the *SLM* Poe and Simms had developed considerable admiration for each others' positions on the literati of America and the neglect of Southerners by NE writers and editors. See the *BJ* Index for Poe's numerous refs. to Simms. The articles mentioned are seriatim on 87-94, 95-105, 73-85, and 107-118 (by Prof. J.H. Gueneboult).

232/1-4} As we have seen (nn. to 121-27 [facsimile text]), this is a far from accurate account of the numerous revs., some very enthusiastic, of Lord's poems. It is strange to see Poe's French treatment of now Englished words like "mediocre."

232/5-28} This comes from p. 134 in the mag. Collation shows a few changes, of some significance: 14-- temple / haunting; 17-- "Poe" is inserted between the other two poets by Simms; 18-- at the end of this sentence are five sentences, dropped from Poe's transcription. These start with this: "Now, it so happens, that all of these poets are exquisite artists." It is curious that having omitted his own name (out of editorial modesty?) he finds it impossible to record the praise by Simms of the others-- especially of Longfellow.

232/29-35} Poe's response to good illustrations is always enthusiastic. The Harpers advertised nos. 61-62, which began *The Tempest*, as having "exquisite designs after Kenny Meadows, Weir, and others ... it combines the best features of the two best London editions, by Charles Knight and Tyas" (2.111, 8/23 *BJ*).

232/36-53} The typical view of Niccolò Machiavelli (1469-1527), derived from the advocacy of immoral expediency in *The Prince*, was usually that of Poe (see *PD*, 59, for 8 loci and several in Index of *Tales*). Here Poe is much more sophisticated and just toward the brilliant, versatile author of the *Historie fiorentine*, thanks to prefatory material. This is one of the several translations by Lester that Poe apologized for ignoring (219 [facsimile text]).

233/1} See 268 [facsimile text] for a second fuller rev. of the book by Brooks, Poe's friend. The title correctly lacks "an" before *Accurate*.

233/15} This 1845 vol., also by Nathan Covington Brooks (1809-98), had vi + 234 p.

233/25} See 334-35 [facsimile text].

233/26-31} In the British edition these are respectively: "MacFlecnoe and the Dunciad" (229-56) and pp. 173-84.

233/32-44} For Poe's friendship with Robert Sully, implied here, see nn. to 215 (f). The picture is a frontispiece for "The Rose and the Lily." Annan's tale is on 86-91, "Sense and Sensibility" by "F.E.F." on 92-96, and Simms' "Mesmerides in a Stage-Coach; or, Passes en Passant" on 111-119, but there is nothing signed by Mrs. Hale. Poe must have been privately informed. Simms' story has nothing in common with those in the genre by Poe save that he tells it from the first person viewpoint of the mesmerist, who puts a young fellow-traveler, over-loquacious, into a spell, causing him to miss his stop and mistake strangers for his relatives. We note the gratuitous flattery of Godey at the end.

233/45-59} The three revs. are on 1-85, 238-65 (collective rev. of 10 books) and 86-92. For Chambers' *Vestiges* see nn. to 88, 234.

234/8-14} See 192 (a), also 259 (a).

234/15-23} See n. to 169/41.

234/24-37} The plate is for "The Western Captive," by James Smillie and Hinshelwood (see also 117, 210). "Paris Fashions" is "from La Follet." The rest are as follows: "Blanche Neville" by Mrs. Ann S. Stephens (103-106); "The Cherokee Braves of 1760" by Mrs. Caroline H. Butler (107-113); "Born to Wear a Coronet" by Fanny Forrester (114-118); "The New Neighborhood" by Mrs. A.M.F. Annan (125-131); "Foreign Literary News" from Brussels (138-142). The music is "The Appeal," poetry by Mrs. Ann S. Stephens (136-137); the poetry is "Lines to a Fat-cinating Young Lady" by P[ark] B[enjamin] (113); and "Afternoon in February" by Longfellow (118).

234/42-49} See earlier Poe refs. to Mowatt's *Fashion* (65-69, 76-78, 234-35).

235/9-13} See also 78/41-45 [facsimile text].

235/29-32} For James E. Murdoch see 235 (c) and other refs. in Index.

235/33-34} See his agency below (e).

235/46-47} "Mazeppa" starred C. La Forest.

236/1-4} Poe could thoroughly agree for once with Griswold, but the book never came out.

236/5-9} James Montgomery (1771-1854), *Poetical Works of James Montgomery*, "With a memoir of the author," by Rufus Griswold (Phila.: Louis and Ball, 1845-52), 2 vols.: I, 7-18 + 392; II, 468. For Poe's adverse views of this popular poetaster see the several articles in *Br.* (Index).

236/10-13} John Pendleton Kennedy (1795-1870), *Memoirs of the life of William Wirt* (Phila.: Lea and Blanchard, 1849), 2 vols.: 417 and 450 pp.

236/14-15} *Poems* by Henry Wadsworth Longfellow, illustrated by Daniel Huntington (Phila.: Carey and Hart, 1845), 387 p.; and William Cullen Bryant, *Poems*, illustrated by E. Leutze, engraved by American artists (Phila.: Carey and Hart, 1847), 378 p.

236/16} Elaborated in Poe's rev. (256).

236/23-26} William Greenough Thayer (1820-94) was graduated from the University of Vermont in 1839 (he entered at fifteen). He was professor of English literature there from 1845-52. It is possible that as a result of this little notice by Poe, he was "elected Poet for their ensuing Anniversary in August" (1846, q.v. in his letters of 4/28/46 and 6/16/46, showing Poe's efforts to place this news in the press, *Letters*, 316, 321).

236/27-30} For other refs. to this *German Telegraph* see 169 [facsimile text] and "Von Kempelen" of 1849 where it is a name given to a Presburg paper (TOM, 1360). It is highly unlikely that either here or in 169/47 Poe could manage to read much less translate the newspaper columns for his "editorial miscellany" (q.v. in 169/41-47 n., end of para. 1).

236/31-34} Frederick Wm. Thomas (1806-66), most noted now for his friendship with Poe, was then a prolific, popular novelist, a poet, editor, especially in Ohio and S. Carolina, as Poe favorably reports in his "Autography" (H 15.209-10; see other loci in *PD*, 90-91 and *Letters* Index, 662, the last of which is that of 2/14/49). He contributed to Poe's *BJ* long sketches of Wm. Wirt and John Randolph of Roanoke (2.52-54, 8/2, and 2.81-85, 8/16). Alexander B. Meek (1814-65) was a lawyer, legislator, author, and later public school sponsor. Poe had easily solved his cryptograph sent him by Tomlin in 8/43 (see *Letters*, 235-36).

236/35} Amos Kendall (1789-1869). His *Life of Andrew Jackson, private, military and civil* (NY: Harper and Bros., 1843-44) was to have been completed in fifteen parts, but only seven were published.

236/36} This paper, of a Phila. suburb, lasted from 1830 to 1930, and must have been familiar to Poe from his *Graham's* period.

236/38-43} The masthead on no. 17 (4/26) shows 153 Broadway as the office address, changed in the next issue, of 5/3, to 135 Nassau Street, but changed in the 11/29 issue (2.21) to 304 Broadway, fulfilling Poe's prediction. The centrality of Broadway to the city and the nation-- typographically, financially, and culturally-- can be seen in the non-Poe article of "Broadway" (1.259-60) by "I. M." and in the illustrated article "Glimpses of Broadway. No. 1. From Union Square looking down Broadway: The National Academy" (5/10, no. 19).

237/3-4} Poe must have had in mind a specific person for Mr. T-----. Perhaps it was John Tomlin, who was involved in his contretemps with Wilmer (see 82/18). As for the root of "sycophant"-- the reason that "fig shower" (the second element being roughly like "discoverer" in an old-fashioned sense) in the Greek usage of the word has come to mean parasite or flatterer today is unknown.

237/5-7} See *BJ*, 1.35, 5/31. For Robert M. Bird (1806-54), physician, novelist, playwright, whom Poe admired see H 8.63-73, 15.203-204.

237/8-17} It is in the *Weekly Mirror* of 8/30/45, 2.323. Collation shows the following changes: to the school; and imparts light. Poe was very partial to Catharine Sedgwick, the novelist (see 26/7 n. and *PD* for 9 loci). In the 9/20 *BJ* (2.174) the Advertisements begin with a five-line entry on the 9/10 "reopening" of the school.

237/18-22} The sentence quoted is in "Foreign Literary News" in a piece in the September *Graham's* (p. 141), excerpted from "On the Organization of the Trades and Handicrafts in Germany, during the Middle Ages" by Archivarius (C.L. Stock,

Magdeburg, 1845). The para. concerns salutations of the masons, and it may have given Poe the idea of a "grotesque movement" for the greetings or intercourse of masons as interwoven into "Cask of Amontillado," written the very next year.

237/23-48} Poe indicates the importance to him of para. 2 by the sidelining. He repeated the Paris *Charivari* in his 12/30/46 letter to Duyckinck (*Letters*, 336), but in fact that journal was not then being published, as C. Cambiaire has shown in *Influence of ... Poe in France* (1927). It was in *Bentley's Miscellany* of 8/40 and the *Notion* of 9/5/40; for details, see Pollin, "Poe and the ... *Notion*, in *English Language Notes of 9/1970*. Both the "abuse" and "laudation" are exaggerated here.

237/50-64} Owen, the son of the prominent British social reformer and mill owner, was himself prominent since settling in America (1801-77) and founding New Harmony in Indiana (also publishing and editing the radical "Free Enquirer"). His efforts in politics made self-exoneration vital. The charge appeared in the 8/5 issue (p. 3) and the rebuttal in the 8/26 issue. Owen continues by expressing his revulsion at literary plagiarism and adds an original song.

238/1-11} Poe always praises the Southern gentleman Legaré (1797-1843), for "talent and scholarship" ("Autography," H 15.215; also, 9.172). The date on the two vols. (1846) must be proleptic; the frontispiece portrait is signed "T. Doney, sc." The vols. are lxxii + 558; 5-598 p. All of Poe's information is from the subtitle. There is no record of the publication of the Simms' "Selection."

238/12-14} For F. Bremer, see 191/51-59 n.

238/15-17} See the rev. on 257-58.

238/18-20} TOM (*Poems*, 509) indicates that this poem, which begins, "O, where shall our waking be?" was tentatively assigned to E.A. Stansbury by Killis Campbell in his *Mind of Poe*, p. 192.

238/21-23} For *America and the American People* see 255, 311, and the rev. on 317-19.

238/24-29} John Britton (1771-1857), of humble origin, became eminent for his *Beauties* of Wiltshire, England and Wales, et al. Poe's ref. is to the 7/7/45 dinner which set up the Britton Club, for collecting 1,000 pounds for publishing his autobiography (1850).

238/30-38} Poe's information, correct as to the plans, proved partly wrong in the facts of the occurrences on 9/2 and on 9/3, Commencement Day, according to issues of the *Providence Journal*. The oration by Dr. Lambert sponsored by one of the two debating societies, The United Brothers, was not given, nor did Andros, editor of the New Bedford *Register*, appear for the poem, scheduled for Manning Hall, the chapel. However, Dr. Williams delivered the "oration" on Blaise Pascal in a feeble voice audible only to those near the speaker (data kindly supplied by Martha Mitchell, Brown University Archivist).

238/39-44} Poe is referring to an item of 8/9 on p. 210 [facsimile text]. He seems to have settled for the title "Gazette," which was there somewhat confused.

238/45-46} See 210/3-6 note.

239/1-3} In the 10/11 *BJ* is a long description of the organ by Dr. Edward Hodges who is supervising the construction of the instrument. He refers to the contractor Henry Erben and furnishes an unpaged steel engraving of the large organ (the article headed "Musical Department" is on 2.214-15). He furnishes many technicalities, but does not confirm the 30-men figure of Erben.

239/4-5} Nathaniel Jocelyn (1796-1881), portrait painter and engraver, received the "gold palette award" in 1844 for the best portrait exhibited in Connecticut-- this being of Gov. Roger Sherman Baldwin.

239/12-15} Poe refers to his treatise "Notes Upon English Verse" in the third and last issue of Lowell's *Pioneer* of 3/43, in which he says, as in the work based on it, "Rationale of Verse," "We are without a treatise on our own verse" (H 15.211). The correspondent "A. M. J. of Attleboro'" must be Abijah M. Ide, Jr., of South Attleboro (see items in Checklist of *Letters*), four of whose poems were published in the *BJ* and were ascribed to Poe by Ingram. See TOM, *Poems*, 509 concerning this young ed. of the Taunton *Gazette* and writer also for the *Columbian Magazine*. The *BJ* poems were dated 9/13, 9/27, 10/25, 12/6. See also 264 (g). It is amusing that Ide's rather obvious imitation of Poe's style (as in "To Isadore" on 2.243) should have caused the modern attribution of his poems to Poe.

239/20} The book had 222 p. with no preface.

239/21-27} This para. plus the remainder on p. 240 became SM 7 in *Br.* with no changes save for the idiosyncratic spelling of "Preeminent" and "pre-eminence" (240/19), both of which receive the dieresis over the first "e" in the copy that Poe left for the "new" Marginalia (q.v. in *Br.*'s Intro. xxxvi-lx). Either Poe thought it a detraction from the sketch of Christopher North to include the second para. or thought that he had derogated Burns a bit too much. In SM 7a, I indicate why I would deny to Poe the 1/42 *Graham's* rev. of the earlier reprint of the same book.

For Poe's attempt to differentiate between moral and physical courage see also MM 185, 234.

240/1-12} For the quiet loveliness of the *Isle of Palms* (1812) see SM 7b. Poe's insistence on ranking the subjects of his criticism shows a kind of formalistic, neoclassical tendency.

As often, he uses the French "niaiserie" or "foolishness" as a term of contempt, but here without specifying the nature of Wilson's offenses.

240/13-40} Aristarchus, editor and harsh critic of Homer (see Pin 144, LST 1) was a favorite term of Poe's, but it was also applied by editors of other journals to him in the days of the *SLM* editorship. Wilson's great authority made his abuse of Americans, such as Lowell, particularly offensive to Poe, the "Young American" (see SM 1). The view of posterity has supported Poe in his complaint about the shallowness of Wilson as critic. In line 35, the Latin comes from Horace, *Epistles*, XXX, 1.1.14.

The clever turn of language at the end of the para., is used elsewhere by Poe as in his "Literati" sketch of L.G. Clarke (H 15.115).

240/41-55} This is the most reserved of any of Poe's refs. to Burns, who certainly occurs infrequently in his critical works: a praise of his "pure ideality" in "Tam O'Shanter" (H 8.299) and a mere repetition of Mrs. Hemans' dictum about his "wretched stuff" in one poem (H 9.203). Yet, the ballad-quality of some of Poe's lyrics makes one suspect his partiality (see TOM, *Poems*, 80, 203). We must note Poe's saying that Burns' profligacy and tipsiness are to be disregarded in judging his literary merits.

240/56-64} The ed., proleptically dated 1846, has a short Preface (pp. 3-4 + 7-413), of which the first line reads: "We here present to the American public a book which has produced no little sensation in England." This best seller by Bailey (1816-1902), of 1839, enlarged in subsequent editions (see 225/46) to 40,000 lines, had a succession of 52 semidramatic scenes, sometimes noble in style but usually "inflated and absurd," with "a theme of universal salvation" (Baugh, 1406 n5).

241/1-17} Poe probably never managed to read its 40,000 lines and he carried out this promise by quoting a full two-para. condemnation on 12/6 (p. 327 [facsimile text]) from the New York *Evangelist* (q.v.). Probably these laudations were from the publisher in the book or in advertisements. Poe seems trying, against his better judgment, to take the work seriously, especially in citing Horne, whose *Orion* he had glowingly reviewed (see H 11.249-75). Mrs. Hall must have been Anna Maria, i.e. Mrs. Samuel Carter Hall (1800-91), author of nine novels and two plays.

241/18-39} "L'Envoi" shows well the "affected" and poetastical quality of the verse. As often happens, Poe's statement of a "theme" is often far off the mark, as here. Certainly there are far worse faults in these "jottings" than the final "defective rhyme." Collation (p. 413) shows only one substantive change, which scarcely improves the thought: line 25--was of the soul-rack.

241/43-68} This thoroughly didactic novel of 9-332 p. by Elizabeth Missing Sewell has no Preface to indicate its origin, probably England, to follow Poe's lead (p. 242) and the fact that it was edited by the Rev. W. Sewell, probably Rev. Wm. Sewell (1804-74), with a long series of clerical posts, author of miscellaneous works, and finally an emigré to escape his creditors (see the *DNB*). Is Poe being mildly ironic about "more decorous ... of the British journals" for so exemplary and didactic a work?

242/17-23} This is by A. Henningsen and has a one page Preface which Poe equably chooses to ignore, for the author intends to "popularize some knowledge of the condition of the Russian Serf among a people who sacrificed twenty millions sterling to the enfranchisement of its own colonial blacks."

242/25} See 213/37 n. for the full account of this bible.

242/28-45} See 89 (a) notes for Poe's high regard for Hunt and his magazine (also Index items). The pages of the articles, in the order given by Poe, are these: 211-21, 252-55, 256-59, 227-32, 250-52, 222-27. Poe's jesting designation shows his conviction about the inadequacy of the term "American," q.v. in 55-56, 80 nn.

242/46-56} This work, published in 1844, has xii + 13-428 p.

242/57-62} This is the third ed. of a book published the same year (1845), with Preface (pp. 9-12 + 15-160) that deals with the nature and proper treatment of children. One suspects that Poe did not scan more than the Preface of this collection of poetry and stories for the young. For Elizabeth Oakes Smith see 221-22.

243/4-10} This book of 128 p. is by the ed. of the annual *The May-Flower* with Poe material. For brief refs. see 209, 247, 260 [facsimile text].

243/11-22} The whole of this installment-bible is in 2 vols., 1622 p., giving good competition, as Poe indicates, to the Harpers' work (see Index).

243/23-45} This is truly conciliatory to the magazine, whose ed., L.G. Clark, Poe detested. The pages of the items, seriatim, are: "To My Wife" (202-203), 203-212, 245-52 (signed M. S. P.), 252. For Pike (1809-91), "Autography," H 15.257-58.

For Mary E. Hewitt see the rev. of her book, 288-89 [facsimile text]. His quoting this bit of didactic fustian is surprising.

243/57} Clearly this is by the music ed. Watson, who would not stay for the rest of vol. 2 of the *BJ*. For Poe's comment on this play see M 221.

The equivalent of three full columns on pp. 139-140 is devoted to views by Murdoch about his life as actor and elocutionist and the state of the theater in America early in his career and in the 1840s in London, ending with two paras. on the present performances at The Bowery and The Chatham (perhaps by Watson). All this is prefaced by a statement which may be by Poe (cf. 247/16-17): "We gladly avail ourselves of the author's permission to occupy, this week, some portion of our usual space under the head of 'The Drama,' with an extract from a forthcoming work--'The Stage or Sketches of Dramatic Art' By Jas. D. Murdoch." (See 247/16-17.)

244/1-6} It was rather a hope than a fact that the advertising matter was usurping review space, for that of 8/30 was longer by four inches than the advertising of the present issue. It is true that the critical columns were shorter, but Poe filled up space with two of his own tales ("The Little Frenchman" and "Silence" plus "The Valley of Unrest") as well as Act I of a tedious play by "the author of 'The Vision of Rubeta'" (i.e. Laughton Osborn) with II and III on 2.149-51 and 164-66, the work being called "The Magnetizer." Poe's proposed "eight additional pages" never came about, nor did the "new type."

244/7-24} For Poe's initial response to the dictionary of Bolles, see 144, 148-49 [facsimile text]. He was highly favorable to the "completeness" of the contents (85,000 words), but apparently further exploration of its pages showed its flaws and its biases-- its origins being New England (see notes on the above and *PCW*). Poe's sense of logic required the language to coin derived adverbs, adjectives, etc. from all the basic words. Yet he finally accepts Bolles' work and probably consults it frequently. But it never won out against the ubiquitous Webster's lexicons, and disappeared from almost every great American library.

244/25-64} Poe used this article for Marginalia 219, shorn of its first paragraph and newspaper column title and of its last two sentences, but with another para. added giving his opinion of *Saul*, finally read some time before the *SLM* of 5/49 published the reprint. Poe was obviously flattered by "Green" of the *Emporium* (no copies of the Hartford *Columbian* or of relevant issues of the weekly *Saturday Emporium* of New York are available). Moreover, the implied play on words in line 1 of para. 2 seems to derive from a pun by Poe himself in *Alexander's Weekly Messenger* and used again in the *Weekly Mirror* in the Outis series (see 31/23-26 [facsimile text] and nn. Sidney Lanier's citation of the first three lines of this squib on *Saul* as model humorous verse, in *Science of English Verse* [1880], pp. 229-30), may have come from either the *BJ* or the Marginalia article rather than from the Hartford newspaper.

For collations of the two texts of 1845 and 1849 see M 219 n. in *Br*. In general, Poe changes only the accidentals and the editorial "we" of the *BJ* into "I." His added para. puns on the "Mystery" of Coxe's pretentious "drama." Rev. Arthur Cleveland

Coxe (1818-96) was an Episcopalian churchman at Hartford and Baltimore who eventually became bishop of western New York. Before *Saul* he published *Advent, a Mystery* and *Christian Ballads* (1840), the latter popular among conservative readers. Earlier, in the 5/10 *BJ* (1.296-97) Briggs had reviewed *Saul* as the longest American dramatic work yet written, deliberately delayed in publication since 1842 and remarkable for the author's refusing to read Sotheby's epic on the same theme. Briggs mocks the subtitle "A Mystery" as did Poe in his 1849 addendum to his 1845 article, but otherwise he shows no awareness of the earlier review in an issue full of his own material.

The phrase with "tory" (line 48) must come from the Gaelic original meaning for pursuer, then outlaw, marauder, brigand, moss-trooper (cf. "swear like a trooper") prior to its 1689 shift in meaning to one of the political factions (*OED*).

The complete dog ref. (line 58) is "Give a dog an ill name and hang him," cited by Scott in *Guy Mannering*, ch. 23, with the added explication, "and if you give a man, or a race of men an ill name they are very likely to do something that deserves hanging. The *Oxford Dictionary of English Proverbs* (3rd ed. 1970), p. 400, gives a 1721 citation, and Bergen Evans (177/11) cites John Ray's different form for 1670.

245/1-7} The other New York publishers had hastened to compete with various series, such as the Harpers' "Complete Library of the Best Literature of the Age" which announced: "Original productions from American writers will also occasionally be introduced" (see the advertisements in the *BJ*, e.g., 2.185). Poe knew of the "success" through his *Tales* for which he claimed 1500 copies sold at 8 cents' royalty per copy in a letter of 11/13/45 to Duyckinck (*Letters* 301). Poe was to print his long rev. of Simms' novel in the 10/4 *BJ* and also in the 1/46 *Godey's*, q.v. in H. 13.93-97). The "Astronomy" is William Augustus Norton's *An Elementary Treatise on Astronomy*, xvi + 367 p., + 112 p. of illustrations, tables, and diagrams.

245/7-11} "L. I. C." is clearly Lewis J. Cist of Cincinnati, the New York correspondent for the *Gazette* (see 210 [c] and note), whom Poe regarded as a friend (see *Letters*) and whose *Trifles in Verse* he reviewed in the *BJ* (342-43; see also 255), using it for the *BJ* reprint of "Blanche" on 2.149, next issue. "The Village Street," on 2.145--the opening article--is the first of four poems by Abijah M. Ide that Poe published in the *BJ* (see TOM, *Poems* 509, 70-73). See also his reprint of a poem from the *Aristidean* (322 [facsimile text]).

245/12-27} This was in two parts, apparently published both in two vols., as here, and also in one, although separately paged (193 and 169), q.v. in 251 (b).

Poe, who likes the quirky humor of Lamb, elsewhere too speaks of both Jerrold (1803-57), miscellaneous author and humorist, and Webbe, author of *The Man about Town* and other garrulous works, as being of Lamb's school of "extravaganzists," in his coinage (q.v. in M 67). See *BJ* Index for other refs. to Lamb. For Jerrold, see 109/50-68 and 302 nn. and for Jones (1817-1900), even then a well-known critic and also author of "American Prose Writers. No. 3: R. H. Dana." in the 2/1 *BJ* (1.69-71) under the sway of Briggs, see 250-251, 263 nn.

Poe's ref. to "entozoa" in "Scheherazade" of the 2/45 *Godey's* and the 10/25 *BJ* explains his ref.: "Intestinal worms ... repeatedly ... observed in the muscles, and in the cerebral substance of men" (Wyatt's *Physiology*, p. 143), q.v. in TOM 1165 ftnote.

245/29-60} Collations (of the passages here given) show the following changes: 29 there yet stands; 37 what a beating; godfather (plus two more accidentals).

246/1-8} This book, of 230 p., was by Eliza Thayer Clapp. Poe had coined the last two nouns in M 109 in a discussion of Coleridge's *Table Talk* of 1844. It bears quotation for its wit and its being the prototype of this epitomization: "Its character can be fully conveyed only in 'Post-Prandian Sub-Sermons' or 'Three-Bottle Sermonoids.'"

246/9-18} The author of this 168 p. vol. is given as Elbridge Gray Paige, by the cataloguers of the New York Public Library. It is difficult to see how Poe could have ascribed it to his very good friend Jesse E. Dow of Philadelphia and Washington, often mentioned in the Poe-Thomas correspondence (see 11 items in the Index of *Letters* of Poe) and so much a journalist there that essays in the New York *Mercury* could scarcely be thus overlooked by Poe. This must be a Poe *blague* (see Quinn, *Poe*, p. 381, for Dow's attempt to secure a post for Poe in Washington).

246/19-28} This 268 p. book has a subtitle which obviously parodies Willis's *Dashes at Life with a Free Pencil*, although Poe chooses to ignore that (see 233 [facsimile text] nn.). The ref. to *Chronicles* is to William Tappan Thompson's *Chronicles of Pineville, embracing sketches of Georgia scenes, incidents and characters* (1845), in turn, perhaps the offshoot of A. B. Longstreet's *Georgia Scenes* (1835), which Poe had favorably reviewed in the *SLM* (H. 257-65). In the last sentence Poe is consistent with his strong feeling that American books must not seek preferential treatment apart from their intrinsic quality.

246/29-31} For Poe's enchantment with this poem, which he often read from the lecture platform, see 201, 223, 226 nn. and many entries under "Thomas Hood."

247/1-15} This is a mere announcement of "La Sortie du Bain" by Jean Baptiste de Cuyper (1807-52), again announced on 282 and reviewed on 297 [facsimile text]. In every instance Poe shows a certain defensiveness because of the Puritanical outcry against this nude statue and also "The Greek "Slave" of Hiram Powers, as in his list of merits, especially "intellectuality." This attribute is stressed for "The Ivory Christ" (see 282/36) and probably borrowed from a passage in *The Artist* etc. of C. E. Lester, the importer of that sculpture (see 282/21 n).

247/16-17} For Poe's friend James E. Murdoch, actor and elocutionist, see 105, 112, 175 [facsimile text] and other items in the Index. The "extracts" have as their theme the need for and possibility of developing plays of every type based on American themes and settings for the American stage--in short, the Young America movement now espoused by Mathews and Poe. The extracts follow from those of 9/6, *BJ*, 2.139-40 (see 243/57 n).

247/18-30} For *Cosmos* see 169/41 n and 234 (b); for the Dante text see 290-91 (b); and for the Gift Books see 209 (c).

247/31-40} Clearly this was one of the exchange papers received in the *BJ* office (this from Virginia), now enabling us to add this unauthorized version to the Poe reprints (noted in TOM *Poems* 333). By omitting the accent over the altered word, Poe indulges his irreverent humor.

247/41-44} The soirée took place on 10/23/45. Sir Thomas, according to the *DNB*, made his most celebrated speech, printed in the 1848 ed. of his *Critical and Miscellaneous Writings*. It is a tribute to and a history of the Manchester Athenaeum.

248/1-16} The book comprises xxii + 437 p. Para. 1 is adapted from p. 1 of the Prefaces and the Appendix is on 389-437. The engravings of sheep are signed "E. Bookhout." There are other illustrations, mostly technical and architectural, which are not signed and are probably by different, less skilled artists. The sheep engravings are based on paintings "by the celebrated animal painter, Harvey, of London." William Harvey (1796-1866), wood engraver and designer, was Thomas Bewick's pupil.

248/22-25} *The Bosom Friend* by Elizabeth Caroline Grey numbers 134 p.

248/26-36} On 8/9 there appeared a three sentence notice of the first number of this book (p. 206/9). This is not a full notice, and there is no mention of a second number in the *BJ*. Hull suggests an error in Poe's memory, and the possibility of his confusing this work with *An Encyclopedia of Domestic Economy*, noticed 8/30 (p. 234/8).

248/37-49} The novel numbers 151 p. Poe was probably responsible for notices of *Nan Darrell* and *The Frigate*, the two by her, in *BGM* (11/39, 5.286, and 2/40, 6.106) and both with the same critical view. *Santo Sebastiano*, by Catherine Cuthbertson, was published in 5 vols. (London, 1806). See 281 (b) for another Pickering work.

249/1-27} The book by Daniel Denton, published first in London in 1670 had a 57 p. text. This reprint ed. included "advertisement" (p. 7), Intro. (9-17) and "To the Reader" (19). Poe's first para. is taken almost verbatim from the "advertisement" and his second is based on the first para. of the Intro. The third para. is based on the second page of the Intro. His devotion of so much space to this recherché item must be owed to the very cordial relations of Poe with William Gowans (1803-70), bibliophile, bookseller and publisher, who came to be called the "Antiquarian of Nassau Street," specializing in Americana, although migrating from Scotland only in 1821. For eight months of 1837-38 Gowans boarded at the Poe's quarters, maintained friendly relations thereafter, and defended warmly the pleasant atmosphere of Poe's home years later (see Quinn 267; H. Allen, *Israfel*, 1934 ed., pp. 330-35).

249/28-37} Charles Lyell's *Travels in North America*-- see 215 (a) [facsimile text]-- is reviewed (199-202). The title for "The Feud" is "La Vendetta" (173-82). Mrs. Ellet's story is on 185-89. Tuckerman is reviewing Headley's *Letters from Italy* (203-12). Benjamin's poem is said to be words for music (202), and Mrs. Osgood's "Labor" is on 220.

250/11-30} The article on "American Humor" by William Jones of Boston, on pp. 212-19, is discussed again by Poe on 263 [facsimile text]. He had deprecated him on 245/19 (see n.) as here, for his New England prestige as well as more problematic causes (see below the opinion of Briggs). Poe, as the former ed. of *Graham*'s, would have known this type of office gossip. The statement by Jones (p. 218) is this: "With the aid of one of the most ingenious critics, and a prose poet of much force, imagination, invention and versatility, Mr. Poe, this weekly cannot fail to become in its way a classic, like the 'London Journal' or the 'Athenaeum.'"

250/31-56} Poe frequently tried to foster a more exact and logical type of criticism with opinions supported by a chain of arguments and objective data. By this time Poe, who had frequently assailed the slipshod, melodramatic, loosely constructed novels of Simms, was his firm ally in resisting the denigration of the New England "coterie" as he would call it. The first quotation should be: "however slightingly we may regard the ..." (p. 212) and the second (line 47) has "this" for "his." Poe's ref. is to Augustus B. Longstreet's *Georgia Scenes* which Poe had lauded in the *SLM* (H 8.257-65).

250/60-66} Briggs gives this interpretation of Poe's insults to himself (Harry Franco) and to William A. Jones (1817-1900) (continued on p. 263 [facsimile text]) in a letter to Lowell of 10/13 (Woodberry, 2.146-47): that Poe hates him for his knowledge of Poe's despicable character and that Jones omits Poe as humorist and ranks Briggs high. Surely Briggs had grounds for taking umbrage at this contumely, knowing that Poe had worked closely with him earlier in the year on material demanding a knowledge of art, other tongues, and literary judgment. The first quotation comes from p. 215, the second from p. 218: "Paulding in his novels, and ...."

251/7-15} The magazine pages are as follows: Ingersoll's on "National Institute" (235-55), "The Bhagvat Geeta, and the Doctrine of Immortality" (267-73), "Helicon ..." (310-25), Browne's paper (230-34) and "Statuary" (287-91). Poe's typesetter misspelled the then acceptable title of the Hindu "Song of the Blessed" which is in Book 6 of the "Mahabharata." His deprecation of Lord's poem is consistent with his other refs. to Lord (see Index and, especially, 121-27r). John Ross Browne (1821-75), brought early from Ireland to Kentucky but widely traveled, first as a sailor on a whaler, may have influenced *Moby-Dick* through *Etchings of a Whaling Cruise* (1846). Poe shared with editor Colton of the journal great respect for Wallace's poetry (see 168/54-61 n.); also 211 and 307 [facsimile text]. The collation of the poem shows only these changes of importance-- 1.39: whispered and 1.66: we/ye.

251/69-70} For Poe's previous rev. see 245 (c) n. and for his invariably favorable ref. to Charles Lamb see Index and *PD* 53 for other loci.

252/1-2} See the Poe *Log* for 2/8/45 for the account by the office boy, Alexander T. Crane, of Murdock's private recital of the "Raven." For the prior extracts see 247, and for other favorable refs. see numerous Index items.

252/3-24} The date is given by Poe (on 264) as 6/19/41. While Poe is most particular about the date, he is wonderfully vague about the source of "Bulwer's text." Surely the charge against Whittier is serious enough to justify our knowing by whom the source passage is attributed to the English author. Moreover, Poe regards his expansion of the general topic as fit for his repeating the next para. on plagiarism in general in the posthumous SM 11 (q.v.). The follow-up letter to the *BJ* by "A Friend who knows," in 275 below scarcely clarifies the matter, nor even specifies whether Whittier or Prentice had previously been copartners in the same sort of accusation.

253/5-26} The real anomaly (see 1.25) is the tissue of disclaimers, innuendoes, and accepted although denied conclusions in this para. Since Poe could expect a real friend of the Abolitionist poet and widely known newspaper editor and writer to deny totally the *Courier* tale as Whittier's if falsely attributed, it could only have been this poet's passage. It was among his less memorable works, indicated by T. F. Currier, *A Bibliography of ... Whittier* (1937), p. 396, as first in the 1839 *Ladies' Garland* of Philadelphia, III, no.6, pp. 143-44, and reprinted in *The Villager* of Amesbury, Mass., for 5/1/51 and in the *Boston Museum* (*Dodge's Literary Museum*) of 6/7/51. He omits the *Saturday Courier* reprint. Like much of Whittier's ephemeral prose, it was never collected in the prose volumes of the Riverside ed. or of others based on it. The six paras. tell about the decline and death of a young girl whose fiancé has died. The appallingly sentimental excerpt, from the last para., is in the style of the rest of it and needs no source in a putative

Bulwer.

Collation of the *Ladies' Garland* text for errors of transcription shows a virtual identity of the two passages: 252/8: cast off / cast up; 17: And why / And, finally, why; 18: are present / are presented; 19: affection / affections; 22: like islands / like the islands. Surely Poe did not devise the Bulwer-passage charge to discredit the "somebody" who obviously was Whittier. Poe had never favored Whittier, whom he called a "fine versifier" whose themes "are *never* to" his liking (H 15.245, and 1841 "Autography"). It is the didacticism of his verse plus his hostility to slavery that earned him Poe's condemnation.

For this para. Poe coins two words: "pick-pocketism" and "soul-uplifting," the latter matching his coinages of "soul-elevating" and "soul-exalting" (see *PCW* 64-65). Poe's exaltation of the "thirst for fame," prominent in his own nature, may derive from Milton's "Lycidas" (line 70; see SM 11, n. b).

253/34-56} Neither poem has been collected or anthologized, and Poe's sources are unknown. Bushnell's poem "A Touch of Nature" appears in the third ed. of Granger's *Index*. The parallel between the two formally occasional poems rests on a cliché scarcely individual or original.

254/19-23} Poe tends to deprecate the title of "Professor" as though disgruntled over his own degreeless state, often using it for Longfellow almost mockingly (see H. 15.73, for example).

254/21-63} Poe's tale, "Mesmeric Revelation," had appeared in the 8/44 *Columbia Magazine* and the 1845 *Tales* with many reprints in the occult or fringe-religious magazines here and in England. Poe is citing a letter from John S. Clackner of Rochester, N.Y., to the *Regenerator* of Fruit Hills, Ohio, of 7/18/45 (see TOM *Tales* 1024-29 for data). The two offending sentences to which Poe refers are at the bottom of 1033 and 1034 with only 4 paras. between (the second is actually near the end of the third--a very long one). What Poe intentionally wrote for his "it" subject was this: "Destroy the idea of the atomic constitution and we should no longer be able to regard the ether as an entity, or at least as matter .... Term it spirit .... It" (etc.). Poe is correct technically, but he has somehow contrived to shift attention to "spirit" by means that are as illogical and incoherent as those imputed by Clackner. Poe was disinclined to think seriously about the whole matter, for he had lost all credence in the occult science of Mesmerism save for its medical uses through plain hypnotism. For his numerous comments and gradual shift of view, as well as modern critics on that shift, see 69-70, 355-56 (for "Valdemar") and *Brevities*: MM 130, 180, 200, CS 3.

254/64-67} Poe refers to the 9/45 *Southern and Western Monthly Magazine and Review*, q.v. in 231/55-63 n. The correspondent is unknown, but signs himself "C. M." in a subjoined, quoted "epistle to a friend." It is the major portion of the "Editorial Bureau" (pp. 205-207), and gives "Literary Statistics of New-York" including the editors of the various monthlies, weeklies, and dailies. Poe and Watson are listed, along with the two discussed by Poe (p. 255). At the end a long list of "general retainers of the Press" of the Metropolis omits Poe--this fact being the probable source of his animus here.

255/1-12} Poe often mentioned Lydia Child and reviewed her novel *Philothea* in one of the longest *BJ* articles (128-36) (see Index), so that he is being ironic about the incorrect "s" given to her last name. As for Thomas Holley Chivers, there were so many "extracts" quoted in Poe's rev. of *The Lost Pleiad* in the 8/2 *BJ* (187-89 [facsimile text]) that the correspondent might easily have become confused. Poe's laudation ("do honor" and "might be proud") is a stroke of diplomacy for conciliating the powerful and the alienated, in part. He had accused Lowell of plagiarism and grossly insulted his friend Briggs. He had mocked Laughton Osborne's *Vision of Rubeta* in an article which he falsely denied writing (see 36-37 nn and Ostrom, letter of 8/15/45 with note, 293-95). He had attached a satirical para. to a caricature (34) of Margaret Fuller. Miss Mary L. Lawson's eight-stanza, sixty-four line poem "Estelle" in the 4/12/45 *BJ* (1.235) had been side-lined by Poe in the Whitman-gift copy of the magazine for lines strongly pointed toward "Annabel Lee." Earlier (1/28/43) Poe had praised her "faultlessly correct" ear (see Pollin, *American Notes and Queries*, 1981, 19.7-8). The other persons mentioned can be traced via the Index for Poe's respect or earnest consideration.

255/15-19} This comes, almost verbatim, from the *Mirror* of Saturday, 9/6/45, p. 341. It is interesting that Poe still rephrases such items, not for rhetorical improvement but apparently to avoid the onus of direct copying. For other Bremer entries see 191, 197, 238.

255/19-20} Frederick T. Tiffany, rector of the Episcopal Church of Cooperstown, on 5/12/45 resigned his post and Judge

Samuel Nelson and J. F. Cooper were elected delegates to the Diocesan Convention (see G. P. Keese, *Historical Records of Christ Church, Cooperstown*). Later Tiffany became a chaplain in Congress.

255/27-36} For other refs. to Von Raumer in the *BJ*, far less adverse, see the Index. Poe as editor had good relations with the New Orleans *Picayune* which defended him the next year in the "Literati" contretemps (S. Moss, *Poe's Major Crisis*, 65-66). Poe's relations with Elizabeth Ellet (1818-77) were critically uneven, and despite his praise of her translating ability here (see other refs. in Index), he gradually came to detest her officious tendencies and interference in the Osgood letter case (see Quinn, *Poe* 497-99; also *Discoveries in Poe* 59-62).

255/37-44} This book was announced on 226 and would be reviewed on 342-43 (q.v.). As correspondent he seems to have been closely associated with Poe at the time.

256/1-10} Poe announced this in 236 (e), unusual in being free from aspersions on Griswold (but see p. 257). These two vols. number iii-xi + 548 and 5-550 p. The tribute paid to Milton, the republican, comes from Griswold's Intro.

256/11-33} The "Areopagitica" is on 1.166-92 where Poe could have read it for this panegyric. Clearly he is affected by the wonderful organ tones of Milton's style and describes a new genre of writing for which he created the word "prose-poem," that he used first in the 1842 "Exordium" (H 11.6) and as the subtitle of *Eureka: A Prose Poem* of 1848 (see *PCW* 61).

257/1-52} Poe is a bit confused here about details. The manuscript of the *De doctrina christiana* was that of Milton's last amanuensis Daniel Skinner, from whom it was taken after Milton's death. In 1823 in a parcel of Milton's papers it was discovered and was published in 1825 by C. R. Sumner, keeper of the Royal Library; the same year he published his English translation which Poe calls "feeble." Poe refers (32) to the passages that Sumner cites in his "Preliminary Observations" in the American ed. (Boston, 1825, 1.xliv), for the treatise. Poe had long known this 1825 print, for he cites Sumner's notes in "Al Aaraaf" (*Poems* 103, n 11 and p. 118); likewise, in his 2/42 *Graham's Magazine* rev. of Brainard's poems. Poe's considerable interest in Milton is attested by the many refs. in the *PD* 63-64 and *Brevities*, Index). Poe's penultimate para. is less a deprecation of Milton than of Griswold.

257/53-67} The volume numbers 93 p. and has no Intro. The main points of this are to be repeated in Poe's 11/45 *Godey's* rev. of the work. Poe is still most congenial toward Cornelius Mathews, especially as primary spokesman for Young America, as numerous refs. in the *BJ* (q.v.) show. Later he objurgates the writer for some obscure reasons (see 9 passages or articles in the *Br.*). Since he regards the rather callow book as an allegory (see 258/25) he finds it necessary to explicate and yet accept the idea of an "under current" for the "true theme" (see Poe's reservations in Pollin, *Studies in Romanticism*, 1975, 14.59-74).

258/31} Poe's fulfillment of his last two words of promise is on 285-86 [facsimile text], which instance "the author's very peculiar style and tone," also called "idiosyncratic." Clearly his esteem was falling.

258/32-52} There are two prefaces: vii + ix + 13-527, which provide Poe with his information. The first concerns the history of the Puritans. Whatever Poe meant by his adjective "nervous" (first line), it could scarcely be the same as for Mathews' "style" (l. 28).

258/53-66} The volume, dedicated to John Quincy Adams, is paged: v-xii + 21-190. It is another proof of Poe's error about the "Medici Series" in 205/53, which he had corrected in 219 (c). Poe's ideas here are derived from x-xi of the Preface, but are not verbatim. His last sentence (on 259) corresponds to the translator's "full of years and ripe in experience."

259/10-21} Clearly Poe was delighted by a long, descriptive title which enabled him to fill the space and avoid even glancing into the work for an evaluative statement. For his fuller comment see 243 (b); also Index under *Martin's Illustrated Bible*.

259/22-68} This vol. numbers vii-viii + 16-487 p. As with the preceding work, Poe limits his comments to reprinting the title and borrowing from the preface; his quotation (which corrects the author's "won and lost") in para. 2 comes from p. vii, but at least Green's "reflections" comes from pp. 382-435, while the excerpts on these two pages come from 323-26. The only other change in text is "labour" for "labours" (260/6).

260/54-70} Poe's word about "next week's review" was

fulfilled only in the 12/20 number (see p. 345); earlier refs. are on 209 and 247. His graciousness toward Hamilton appears also in 243. Note the ideal "annual" qualities given comment here: beautiful or showy covers, pictures showing well dressed women, sentimental poems, and prominent names. Ironically, the LC lists only one copy--at the Antiquarian Society. The vol. numbers 354 pages.

261/1-37} This work was mentioned by Poe at the end of 231 (a), the rev. of a companion vol. Most of this is a pastiche of ideas and phrases from the vol. or paraphrases. The Pref. covers iii-vi and the text 519, which is, coincidentally, the same as the London text, despite the recasting of the whole. Poe's knowledge of the "omissions" and "redundancies" comes from iii and the fourth sentence is a paraphrase of iv. para 1. The designated additions are on pp. 2 and 5, and the rest derives from v-vi.

261/38-54} This "socially conscious" fiction has a Pref. of v-viii and text (9-162). Poe's word "persecutions" is not quite the right interpretation of Burdett's Pref.: The author attests to the truth of facts in the story that testify to "the sufferings of female operatives of this city" and are an incentive to social change.

261/55-67} The pages number vii-viii + 288. Poe had previously treated of Russell in 175, 225, 242 (q.v.).

262/1-3} See 226 (g) and n for Poe's obit. of James Augustus Shea, also mentioning his "Ocean" and its resemblance to Hood's "Bridge of Sighs." In Shea's *Poems* (N.Y., 1846), pp. 118-20, it is called "To the Ocean."

262/4-50} William Whewell (1794-1866), master of Trinity College, Cambridge, displayed a wide range of knowledge and original thought in moral philosophy and various scientific subjects in numerous publications. Poe had paid brief tribute to his Bridgewater Treatise in 1836 (H 8.210). The three-vol. work on the "inductive sciences" in the title came out in 1837. The present vol. had been pirated by the Harpers immediately after its London (1845) publication. Poe chiefly follows the table of contents for the substance of his notice: I, Preface, vii-x + xi-xxvi + 27-401; II, iii-xxi + 25-424. It was dedicated to Wm. Wordsworth. It would appear that the Harpers aimed to compete with the "Libraries" being published by Wiley and Putnam, more belle-lettristic in content.

262/51-54} See 191/20-22 n for data on this book by a man whom he knew and respected (see "Autography" in H 15.242-43).

262/55-63} See 268 (a) and (b) for slightly fuller notices of these two works.

263/1-56} For Poe's animus against Jones, see 245/18-21 and n, plus 250-51. The "warm personal friend" was, most likely, Evert Duyckinck (see Poe *Log* for the date), whose opinion he was bound to respect and acknowledge (see 29-31). The article on Dana (line 41) was in the 2/1 *BJ* (1.69-71), the insertion of Briggs, of course. Poe's animus clearly derives from Jones' origin and position in Boston (53).

263/57-58} See 210 and 238 for other comments on Everett.

264/1-4} Joseph M. Field (London, 1810-St. Louis, 1856) maintained a warm friendship with Poe, chiefly by mail and by supportive statements in the *Daily Reveille*, of which he was ed. after a career as itinerant actor and playwright, and also writer of sketches of humor (see Intro. to reprint of *The Drama in Pokerville*, 1843, 1847, 1969). Poe used his influence over the New Orleans *Picayune* for favorable notices, especially during the libel suit of the next year. See Sydney Moss, *Poe's Major Crisis* for Poe's sending notices for Field's adaptation (20-24; see other refs. via the Index). Moss lists these dates of 1845 for *Reveille* notices of the *BJ*: 9/24, 10/10, 29, 11/9, 12/4 and 4/12/46. Possibly Field's libel suit, here mentioned, gave Poe a notion for his own suit against Hiram Fuller of the *Mirror* the next year. See Poe's refs. to Field in H 11.224, 13.6 and 12.

264/8-23} Most of these can be traced in the *BJ* through the Index. For Miss Lawson, see 255/11 n. Laughton Osborn was author of *The Vision of Rubeta*, this being another tactical stroke by Poe. We must enjoy the joke of his listing himself twice as both Poe and "Littleton Barry," his pseudonym for five tales reprinted in the *BJ*--a name probably derived from Thackeray's *Barry Lyndon* (see TOM *Tales*, 77 n41). The correspondent's statement was noted in 254 (b) above.

264/31-44} Although this is an advertisement, the copy was surely written by Poe--somewhat ingeniously. Poe here is giving Mr. Oliver B. Goldsmith good value for his purchase of space on

p. 185--probably in surplus supply. The notice is of the reopening of the "writing academy" and of his "gems of penmanship" for sale there.

264/45-47} Henry C. Watson was still the music editor of the *BJ*, the 10/18 issue being the last masthead bearing his name.

264/50 and 55} We recognize Poe's "friends": Abijah M. Ide, Jr. [see Index and *Poems*, 509 for 70-73 and see 239 (d) above; for Philip Pendleton Cooke and Thomas Holley Chivers see the Index].

265/1-3} The vol. consists of two "series," separately paged, 233 plus 238 p. and a single page "Advertisement" by Simms, preceding the first "Contents" page. Series I has seven "tales" and II has six. The first (1.1-36) consists of "Grayling; or, Murder will Out" (excerpted below), itself divided into 5 "chapters." Poe used the following (first) three sentences of the "Advertisement" for his first para. and successive sentences for the top of 265, there verbatim: "The Tales which follow have been the accumulation of several years. They were mostly written for the annuals--an expensive form of publication which kept them from the great body of readers. However, they met with favour, and it is thought that their merits are such as will justify their collection in a compact volume."

265/4-11} Poe's relations with William Gilmore Simms, during the year of the *BJ*'s publication, steadily improved, in part because of the firm and regular support lent Poe through Simms' journal columns, especially during the Lyceum episode. This is reflected in this rev., numerous other passages in the *BJ* (see Index), and the decided muting of criticism of his style, which he calls "verbose, involute, and ... ungrammatical" in a parallel rev. of this very book in the 1/46 *Godey's* (H 13.93-97); it is one-third longer in its criticism, shorn of the long excerpt attached to the *BJ* rev., but similarly touches upon the numerous fictions of Simms and highlights the distinctively Southern and American qualities which *should* entitle it to more praise, especially abroad.

Poe's use here of "generic" is odd, since it either means the opposite of specific (thereby rendering general redundant) or "pertaining to a class" which certainly has no relevance to the title, unless he intends American dwellings and frontier life to be so characterized.

265/12-58} For the first sentence of this para. see the Poe *Log* of 10/6 for Hiram Fuller's derision of this in the *Mirror*. In line 17 Poe misspells the name of Lope de Vega, which he had probably derived from references in A. W. Schlegel's *Lectures on Dramatic Art* (see under Schlegel in Index to *Br.*). The title of Frederick M. Reynold's notorious novel *Miserrimus* plays a large and ironic role in Poe's criticism, life, and posthumous reputation (see Ch. 11, pp. 190-205, "Poe as Miserrimus," in *Discoveries in Poe*). This is the third instance of Poe's associating the work with *Martin Faber*, the first two dating from 1844; and another would follow (*Discoveries in Poe* 195-97), in the 1/46 *Godey's* rev. of Simms' work.

The dates of Simms' works given here are not without significance: *Martin Faber* (1828 as a tale; 1832 as a novel); *Partisan* (1835); *Beauchampe* (1842); *Richard Hurdis* (1838); *Castle Dismal* (1845); *Helen Halsey* (1845). Poe's 1835 verse drama "Politian," part of which was in the 12/35 *SLM*, early exploited the story of the "Kentucky Tragedy" which figures also as the basis for *Beauchampe*; this renders significant his remark about "historical *truth*" (see *Poems* 242-45). While this is Poe's only ref. to Walpole's Gothic novel, Poe showed a nodding acquaintance with many of Walpole's writings (see *PD* 96 and *Br.* MM 109, 209, 259). His ref. to Charles Brockden Brown (1771-1810) in connection with Simms parallels that in M74 and recalls the influence of Brown on Poe so often attributed (see M74, note c; also loci in *PD* 13).

266/15-17} For Poe's studied animosity toward Jones of Boston see text and notes of 150-51, 263, 276-77.

267/57-71} This is Poe's second notice of this book, the first having been in the 4/36 *SLM*—longer and specific about his charming whimsy, like Lamb's and Irving's (H 8.319-20). Even there Poe too literally believed in the age of the "old man," for Sir Frances Bond Head (1793-1875) was vigorously serving as lieutenant-governor of Upper Canada (1835-37), causing him to be knighted in 1836. He had previously published an account of his travels in South America and contributed to eminent journals.

268/15-25} This article and the subsequent one were announced the preceding week (p. 262). This book, of viii + 276 p., was by Tayler (1797-1875), a clergyman who wrote religious manuals and homiletic fiction for the young, as here. There is a trace of tongue-in-cheek attitude in Poe's few sentences.

268/26-43} Henry Melvill (1798-1871), after a long, varied, distinguished career in education and church posts (ending as Canon of St. Paul's Cathedral), published numerous sermons that were less "peculiar" than these.

268/44-68} The vol., of vi + 211 p., is dated 1844 and again 1845, with reprints in 1848, 1857, and 1864. Poe announced this book on 8/30, 233 [facsimile text]. Nathan Covington Brooks (1819-98) was a good friend to Poe in the 1830s in Baltimore and later, to the very end of his life (see Quinn, 269, 292, 637). He first published "Ligeia" and "The Haunted Palace" in his short-lived *American Museum*. Poe mildly praised his magazine papers and poems in the "Autography" (H 15.222, 225; see also *Letters*, 111-13). Poe briefly reviewed his *First Lessons*, based on Ross's *Latin Grammar* (233 [facsimile text]), as he notes on 269/29-32. The present relatively long rev. presumably is based on the Introductory material of the book itself. Poe acknowledges this himself on 269/13.

269/1-33} Then as now, textbooks were far more remunerative than original or scholarly works, as Brooks seemed to know. The *First Lessons in Grammar* by James Ross (1744-1827), on which Brooks based his text, first came out in America in Chambersburg, Pennsylvania, in 1798 and reached a tenth ed. in 1842. The letter from Frietog must have been part of the publisher's advertisement, despite its recent date. In thus featuring it, Poe willingly promoted the work and filled up his space.

269/33-39} The items in *Blackwood's* seriatim are these: The first is a rev. of C. R. Leslie's *Life of Constable* (257-65); the second surveys the state and writers of historical fiction at present (341-56); the third concerns Goethe's Bettina Brentano (357-65); the fourth is about A. Dumas' book with excerpts (312-27); and the last (366-88) in several sections treats of Dryden, Pope (with Lowell's criticism thereon and disparagement thereof) and Charles Churchill.

269/40-48} All the parts were collected for a one-vol. publication in 1846, of iii + 576 p.

269/49-51} See Poe's irritation over the promotion of this work on 334-35 (d) and earlier announcements (192, 233). The twelve parts had been "borrowed" from the one-vol. British publication (Longman, Brown, 1844) of xviii + 864p, which comprised "a general introductory outline of universal history," etc.

269/56-65} The material in the magazine of Poe's friend Simms ran thus: "The Epochs ..." (145-54); "A Foreigner's First Glimpse" (166-79); "Marion Family" (200-204); "Maiden's First Dream" (165-66) and "Elodie" (179-80), both the poems being by Simms (see his *Poems* of 1853, 210-11). The first essay is relevant to Poe's interests, for J. G. Gadsby, the artist and illustrator, somewhat connected with Poe, was famed for his Capitol Rotunda mural of "The Baptism of Pocahontas," executed between 1837-40 (see Pollin, "Poe and Chapman," *SAR 1983*, 245-74, specifically 252; for Poe anent Chapman's 1400 engravings for the *Harpers' Illuminated Bible*, see 270-71).

270/1-10} While there are changes in accidentals, including all the italics, the stanza is correctly cited. Here is a sample of the lauded "Elodie," which has about it touches of "The Raven" (such as a single-word refrain from a bird's beak, a pining lover, a lugubrious nightly atmosphere): "A bird that had no song by day, / But crouch'd in sadness in the shade, / As soon as came the evening's ray, / Took wing and soar'd aloft, / And, with a music soft, / Sweet melodies for all the forest made. / Elodie! Elodie! / Thus evermore the plaintive ditty rose-- / Elodie! Elodie!" (beginning). The poem explains the sad fate of the "denied" lover who sought oblivion in the forest, and died, giving rise to the bird of the sad song.

270/11-33} The two plates are at the beginning; J. P. Frankenstein's painting is engraved by J. W. Steel. The other is engraved by W. H. Ellis. Poe is being very conciliatory of editor Sarah Josepha Hale here. Mrs. Ellet's piece is fiction (151-58). The rest follow: Mrs. Caroline Lee Hentz's poem (133); Miss Rand's poem (134), Miss Leslie's fiction (135-42); Lois Adams' poem (142); Mrs. Hale's poem (144); Tuckerman's poem (144); Mary Lee's fictions (145-50 and 160-68) and T. S. Sullivan's song (176-77). Poe may have known which of the anonymous poems was Frost's. Poe had nothing in this issue of the magazine which issued two installments of the Marginalia in 8/ and 9/45.

270/34-51} Poe favored Robert Morris (see 78 and 79 [facsimile text]), here subject of a sketch by Charles J. Peterson, with long excerpts (183-85). The Warrior precedes the title page of the magazine. Grund's is on 145-50; Street's "Callikoon" (*his* spelling) is on 155-59; and Osgood's fiction on 151-54.

270/52-63} Thomas Dunn English's *Aristidean* includes a long series of short reviews by Poe himself, delicately mentioned (p. 271). The contents run thus: "Sir Albert" (168-70), "Travels in Texas" (170-86), "Popular Governments" (187-92), Hirst's poems reviewed (cf. 162-67 [facsimile text]), "Leaves" (227-32), "Alas" on 270 (225) and "Our Book-Shelves" (234-42).

271/1-19} The verses bear all the earmarks of Thomas Dunn English's humorous verse (see his "Ode to the Muses" on 323 [facsimile text]). Poe's good will to the author here (also on 272-73 [facsimile text]) is great, but his prediction was erroneous for the short-lived magazine, which died, along with the *BJ*, from inadequate financing.

271/20-30} The vol. of 128 p., 5 in the Intro., is "By an Adept in the Science" who remains unknown. The Intro. maintains that astrology, a "serious" science, is worthy of being studied, both in its "natural" (or astronomical) and "judicial" (star-influencing) forms. Sir Francis Bacon, whose essays Poe admired and often quoted, within limits, wished for a reformed alchemy and astrology, but his older views of the latter lacked the light of Kepler and Galileo's presentation of Copernicus through the chances of time and place (see *Enc. Brit.*, 2.885).
      In line 26 Poe must be referring to an oft reprinted book of xxxiv + 32 p., by Herman Kirchenhoffer, *The book of fate: formerly in the possession of Napoleon ... now first rendered into English from a German translation of an ancient Egyptian manuscript, found in the year 1801, by M. Sonnini, in one of the royal tombs, near Mount Libycus, in Upper Egypt* (9th ed. London, C. S. Arnold, 1825).

271/31-38} For fuller treatment see 279 (b) + n.

271/39-41} Poe usually spoke disparagingly of H. W. Herbert, son of the Dean of Manchester and writer on field sports as "Frank Forester" as well as novels, misc. articles, et al. before his suicide (1807-58); e.g., see MM 116, 253. For other refs. to other editions of Sue's *Wandering Jew* see the Index. This vol., of iii-v + 668 p. was pub. by Richards of N.Y. but "entered by E. Winchester."

272/1-7} Poe's kind words toward English (1819-1902) contrast sharply with his derision in the "Literati" sketch of 1846 (H. 15.64-68) and the even more scornful sketch written later (H

15.266-70). This ballad, published anonymously in the 1843 *Mirror*, speedily became popular, inducing English (called later "Brown" by Poe) to acknowledge it and even compose his own music for it (it received 26 settings and was revived in Du Maurier's *Trilby*). Poe's noting that publishers were promoting this bathetic "song" (see line 50) accords with his own interest in song-writing (see Pollin, *Prairie Schooner*, 1973, 46.229-35).

273/46-56} This para. reiterates Poe's outrage against an undetected case of plagiarism two weeks earlier (253/5-26 [facsimile text]) in a passage used as SM 11; see the Index to *Br.* for numerous other passages on the immorality of plagiarism. See 291 (e) for the exoneration of Webster by his friend, which Poe graciously printed.

273/57-66} This entire article (also on 274-75) was used verbatim as SM 1, in *Br.*, in which full notes are supplied. Several will briefly be repeated hereafter.

274/1} Although marked "P" by Poe in the Whitman copy, this article was omitted by Harrison. Poe's interest in American "nationality" in letters was shown earlier in the "Exordium" (not his title) to the "Review of New Books" in the 1/42 *Graham's* which has similar ideas and language (H 11.2). The Latin for "player" can be traced to Petronius, Fragment 10. For Poe's coined "autorial" used nine times see Pollin, *PS*, 1977, 10.15-18 and *PCW* 84.

274/2-36} Poe's ref. to a "cockney critic" balances Wilson's insult to Lowell as a "Yankee-cockney" below. Poe's three American writers were, in fact, highly respected and popular in America: Irving, Bryant, and W. H. Prescott (1796-1859), the nearly blind, detailed historian of the Hispanic world. The sub-sub-editor coinage was to be used again in the 1/46 *Godey's* rev. of Simms' *Wigwam and the Cabin* (H 13.96-97). Poe's ref. is, obviously, to Sydney Smith's remark in the 1/1820 *Edinburgh Review*: "In the four quarters of the globe, who reads an American book?"

274/37-38} Poe had expressed early interest in Hassan-ben-Sabah of Lebanon, founder of the anti-Crusader sect of the Assassins in Pin 24, but he seems to confuse him with the "Old Man of the Sea" in Sinbad's tale in the "Arabian Nights," q.v. in "Scheherazade." Poe's word "rhapsodist" for "a person who uses extravagantly enthusiastic or impassioned language" (not an "epic singer") must refer to John Wilson's unrestrained style in harangue. For Poe's generally unfavorable views of "Christopher North" (1785-1854) of *Blackwood's* see Index to *BJ* and SM 7.

274/42} Poe was ambiguous about T. B. Macaulay, to whom he often alluded and from whom he borrowed (see Index to *BJ*, *PD* 59, and TOM, Index on 1433).

274/46-53} Poe's "running ... read" came first from Habbakuk 2.2, but probably through many later adapters. Wilson could scarcely be termed "ignorant," especially in his seven Homer essays springing from the new translation of Wm. Sotheby (see SM 1 note i). Wilson's adverse rev. of E. B. Barrett's *Drama of Exile* in the 11/44 *Blackwood's* was answered (as to poor constructions) in the 1/3/ *BJ* rev. (1.7).

274/54-66} Wilson's article appeared in the 9/45 issue (368-70) for the Lowell criticism. Lowell's book, *Conversations on Some of the Old Poets* (1844; actual date, 1845) is a youthful but sincere discussion or "dialogue" between "Philip" and "John" (hence Wilson's error in naming the author). Poe's scornful name "Sawney" is a variant of "Sandy" (short for Alexander), used to denigrate a Scot. The *OED* credits Wilson with the 1818 coinage of "squabash" from "squash" and "bash." "Faugh" is merely an expression of disgust. The Poe *Log* for 10/11 notes that editor Lawrence Labree of the N. Y. *Illustrated Magazine* notes and approves this defense of Lowell.

275/1-11} The Coventry expression means to mark with disgrace by universally ignoring the culprit. The Latin is quoted in reverse order from Cicero's first oration against Catiline: "Quo usque tandem abutere, Catalina, patientia nostra? quam diu etiam furor iste tuus nos eludet?" (How long will you continually abuse our patience, Catiline? And now how long will that madness of yours mock us?) The final ref. is to the history of Rome by Livy, Book 28, for 205 B. C., in which Livy vividly reconstructs the speeches by and about Scipio Africanus Major who "kept saying that he could not finish the war unless he should himself transport his army to Africa" (Loeb Classical Library, 1949, 8.161).

275/12-23} The article on the "parallel" was on 252-53 [facsimile text]. The "friend" did not have his data quite right. Wm. D. Gallagher (1808-94), associated with the Cincinnati *Gazette* (q.v.) and author of the popular poetry collection *Erato*

(H 9.73-75), was founding ed. of the Columbus journal, *The Hesperian*, during its three-vol. life (1838-39). In the 6/39 issue (3.41) he included "Lines to a Lady" by "Rigel" which began thus: "Upon the verge of womanhood / Thou tremblingly dost stand,/ Before thee all that's bright and good / In youth's sweet fairy land!" There is no trace of the opening quoted in the para. The legal maxim at the end means: "The law is not concerned with trifles." See 358/9 below for a veiled ref. by Poe to Gallagher.

275/24-66} For Poe's utter loathing of Wm. W. Lord's poems and the puffery used in publicizing his book *Poems*, published by D. Appleton, see 121-27 [facsimile text] (and other loci in the Index). George Washington Doane (1799-1859) was Episcopal bishop of New Jersey. The poem "A Hymn to Niagara" mentioned at the end of this article (see 276/1) is thoroughly derided on 124 [facsimile text]. The first Latin phrase comes from the *Epodes* of Horace, 1.7.27, referring to the half-brother of Ajax, Teucer: "under the protection of Teucer." The second comes from Horace's *Ars Poetica*, line 155, referring to the applause demanded of the crowd by a player or singer.

276/3-9} For Poe's general attitude toward the Wilkes' Expedition and also Reynolds' lack of participation in it, see 116-17 (b).

276/10-15} For Tucker's Southern novel as "on the whole" the "best and noblest" American work unjustly suppressed by Northern chicanery, see M 206 and SM 25. For "the author of the Vision of Rubeta" (lines 25-26), that is, Laughton Osborn, and for Poe's conciliatory gestures, including this article and also (c) below, see 255/1-12 n.

276/16-24} Poe alludes to 264 (b), the list of which is partly repeated in the present one. Several date from the days of Briggs as editor. He has his joke again with his own pseudonym of "Littleton Barry" (see notes to the earlier para.). For various of the individuals named see the Index.

276/29-38} Poe alludes to Margaret Fuller's rev. of his *Tales* in the Wiley and Putnam ed., in the New York *Tribune* of 7/11/45 (1/col. 2) which objects to Poe's "inaccuracies in the use of words. As a formalist in diction (see his reviews of Bolles' *Dictionary*), he knew the basis for her criticism. See 34 and 220 (and nn) for Poe's view of Miss Fuller.

276/39-54} This comes from *The Builder* (London) of 7/19/45, pp. 344-45, "On Mosaic Floors and Tessellated Pavements" (34-45), taken over verbatim, save for 1.45: "was one which / is that which" and save for some accidentals ("Giacomo"). In the 9/44 tale "The Oblong Box," much is made of a supposed "copy of Leonardo's 'Last Supper'" which misleads the narrator (TOM 925); see also 355/1n (below) which concerns a new engraving of this work.

276/55-60} Poe mentioned this figure of 1500 copies sold in his 11/13/45 letter to Evert Duyckinck (at eight cents a copy, for a total of $120), q.v. in *Letters*, 301. His joke about the speech of each country is repeated in his "Literati" sketch of Margaret Fuller in 1846, when he complains (H 15.78) of her "murders committed on the American of President Polk"-- perhaps a lingering trace of his resentment of her criticism of his own diction in the rev. which he had cited in article (d) directly above this.

276/61-63 + 277/1-3} Poe had spoken of the relations of Graham and Jones in the 9/20 issue on 250/27-30. He manages to include a barb against Jones even at the end of the apology, however.

277/4-10} It is possible that "M.O." refers to Maria Brooks, given the name by Southey of "Maria del Occidente" (the "del" often being dropped), for Poe spoke very highly of her in the *BJ* and elsewhere (see *PD* p. 13 for loci). See 328, 340, and 357 [facsimile text], in the last of which is a long notice of her life and death in Cuba on 11/11/45. The "W. G." may refer to W. Gilmore Simms, for his two-stanza poem in the 10/18 issue (2.219), called simply "Stanzas" (presumably by Poe himself). The last title is, as printed, "To Constance" by "W." on 2.208.

277/11-55} The volume has 324 p. and appears to be funded by the author herself (although Poe assumes a forthcoming second ed. on p. 278). The pages of the three poems mentioned are 187-90, 244-46, and 264. Poe objects to the Latin as meaning "To him to whom [my] songs apply," although this was not the meaning of the verb in classical Latin. The poem "The Moon" is correct in transcription save for numerous changes in accidentals.

278/14} In his 1832 tale, "A Decided Loss," Poe had shown his familiarity with Peter Schlemihl (editorially corrected), hero of Adelbert von Chamisso's romance, involving a bargaining away of his shadow to the Devil (TOM, *Tales* 54-- with the same misspelling.)

278/14-32} The vol. has a Preface (vii-xii), a Catalogue of authors quoted (xii-xvi) plus 17-242 pages of text. The inclusion of Mrs. Osgood's work perhaps explains even this much space as being devoted to the work. Allston (1779-1843), a pupil of Benjamin West and a friend later of Coleridge and Irving, had a somewhat abortive career as painter and also as poet.

278/33-67} For the first part, see Poe's rev. on 107 (b), and for his rather varying opinion of Hazlitt see other items in the Index. Poe's interest in the subject was intense (q.v. in the *Br.*, Index, three rubrics for "genius").

279/1-36} The reason for reprinting in the facsimile text the end of the material that Poe quoted from Hazlitt is to indicate his emphasis through the sidelinings, the basis (in small measure) for his final comment, and the persistency of his error about the name of Lope de Vega (see 265/17, where it is uncorrected).

279/37-57} This large book, of 642 p., has a short pref. that provides Poe with the material for his brief rev. The elaborateness of its apparatus, including good maps, leads to his comments.

279/58-70} The book numbers 508 p. plus Index.

280/1-51} The first quotation, on p. 61, concerns Timothy Pickering (1745-1829), soldier, administrator, and senator. The passage is correctly transcribed, except for a dozen changes in accidentals and, for line 6, the phrase "firm in the convictions"; likewise excerpt two, which freely changes the accidentals.

280/52-66} Unfortunately, a copy of this work has not been available to enable me to see how much of the material is taken from the Preface and the text itself. The manner is certainly that of Poe, causing both Hull and TOM (in his notes) to ascribe it to him, but the authority with which the reviewer speaks belies a man capable of such blunders in German as Poe's (see "André" on p. 33). See the second para. (p. 281) for Poe's typical language and details, however. The further rev. promised at the end never materialized.

281/10-24} Despite Poe's middle initial for the publisher

(and author), this is by Benjamin Moore Norman (1809-60), numbering vi + 206 p. Poe's "design" in reprinting the full title is probably the filling of space. The engravings were executed by Messers Shields and Hammond after drawings by M. Cowell.

281/31-41} Poe's sketch of Epes Sargent (1813-80) in the "Literati" papers (H 15.91-93) shows some intimacy and partiality as here (see also 321 [facsimile text]). Poe suggests that Mrs. Mowatt's *Fashion* owed something to Sargent's 1839 play *Velasco* or at least to his advice. *Ion*, on a classical theme, was the popular play of 1836 by Thomas Noon Talford; *Fazio* was the 1816 Italianate-Elizabethan drama by Henry Hart Milman. Bulwer authored the 1838 *Lady of Lyons* and the 1839 *Richelieu*. For another rev. of this series see 321.

281/47-50} Poe's tolerant praise of the October *Knickerbocker* is so unusual as to make one doubt the authorship, but it is scarcely possible that this was assigned to any one else. See 307A nn. He is referring to the article "By Our 'Salt-Fish Dinner Correspondent'" signed at the end "J. K., Junior," 26.331-41. It maintains that Negro slaves are the only truly national poets, especially coming from Virginia, with a native love of songs which infuses the widely popular music.

281/51-56} For Poe's keen interest in *Kosmos* see 169, 234, 247 nn. D'Israeli had just published *Sybil*, addressed to the social problems of industrial England with its "Two Nations."

281/57-59} See numerous items (in Index) expressing his detestations of Lord's poems.

281/60-62} Cave Johnson (1793-1866) was a lawyer and Tennessee Congressman, and under President Polk Postmaster General, who would introduce the use of stamps in America. For Elizabeth Frieze Ellet, now a friend but markedly hostile in 1846, see the numerous Index items.

282/21} The forthcoming vol. by Charles Edwards Lester, U.S. Consul at Genoa (1815-90), caught Poe's interest and contributed greatly to the material and even language of this article through the autobiographical material by the American sculptor, living abroad, Hiram Powers, whose nude female Greek slave statue was a *cause célèbre*. The book, in two vols., each separately published, was *The Artist, The Merchant and The Statesman, of the Age of the Medici, and of our own Times*, noticed as follows: Excerpts, I, *BJ* 10/28, 2.228-29; Table of Contents printed as a summary (by Poe), *BJ* 11/8, 2.274 (p. 301 below); review of I with many excerpts (not by Poe), *BJ* 11/15, 2.286-87; rev. of II (by Poe) in *BJ* 12/13, 2.355 (see p. 333 below). The following para. of 10/18, 2.229, is Poe's basic source:

"But a step further. I have seen either the originals or good casts of nearly all the celebrated representations of our Saviour; and, with a few exceptions, they portray the humility, meekness and benevolence that are supposed to have been peculiar to him; but in none of these, if I except the Ivory Christ of yours--cut by an uneducated monk at Genoa, have I ever seen that expression of mind, of divine gracefulness which must have been just as peculiar to his wonderful character. It would be enough for us to know that that [*sic*] he were the Prince of Peace to know the one, and it is enough for us to know that he is the Son of God to convince us of the second. When we read the New Testament we are guided to a conclusion in which we cannot be mistaken; and I have always felt that Milton was the only Christian of modern writers who has drawn the person and the character of the Son of God with just conceptions of his intellect, his majesty and his grandeur, as we find it drawn by the simple but inspired pens of the apostles."

It is likely also that Poe derived a few ideas and words (see "agony" and "anatomical truth" below) from the para. devoted to this figure in a column "Works of Art" in the 7/5/45 *Weekly Mirror* (p. 200):

The other gem of art we referred to is a modern work executed by a monk belonging to a convent in Genoa. It is a crucifix scene. Our Saviour is represented on the cross in all the agony of his painful death. The body is wrought of one solid piece of ivory, the largest we have ever seen, and which is of itself a curiosity. The anatomical truth of every part of the form--the perfect representation of nature in every detail, astonishes the anatomist, while the character of the face--nay the expression of agony in every muscle, and in the whole attitude fills the artist with admiration. Even Mr. Powers looked on it with wonder. The intellectual and majestic brow is knit in the extremest agony, while around the glorious mouth, plays the smile of resignation. The brow is the bitter prayer in the garden, while the mouth is the embodied exclamation, "Thy will be done." We have never seen any thing equal to this of its kind. Even the distended veins are seen coursing under the skin and the exquisite finish of every part is equalled only by the perfect harmony and wonderful expression of the whole. It is a gem of art, and what renders it stronger still, it is the only work the artist has ever executed.

282/30} The *BJ*, 11/15, 2,283, starts with the following, "Sonnet. On Seeing the Ivory Statue of Christ," by his literary and social friend, Anne C. Lynch (see 15/20-29), evidence of the stir it evoked: "The enthusiast brooding in his cell apart / O'er the sad image of the Crucified, / The drooping head, closed lips and piercéd side, / A holy vision fills his raptured heart; / With heavenly power inspired, his unskilled arm / Shapes the rude block to this transcendant form. / Oh Son of God! thus, ever thus, would I / Dwell on the loveliness enshrined in Thee, / The lofty faith, the sweet humility, / The boundless love, the love that could not die. / And as the sculptor with thy glory warm / Gives to this chiselled ivory thy fair form, / So would my spirit in thy Thought divine / Grow to a semblance, fair as this of Thine."

283/1-6} In type font sizes brevier, in 8 point, is smaller than bourgeois, of 9 point size. Willis went to Europe in midyear. As usual, Poe is punning on the star-system of theatres and the asterisk, for the anonymous writer, but often, as here, the editor himself--this being Hiram Fuller in the *Mirror*.

283/7-63} By coincidence, Poe had attacked "Mr. Asterisk" of the *Mirror* in 12/35 for lauding *Norman Leslie* by Theodore Fay, one of its own editors. The uproar in literary circles consequent upon Poe's campaign against this "bepuffed" and second-rate but enormously "successful novel" plunged him and the *SLM* into a deleterious battle that affected his status even in 1845 (see Moss, *Poe's Literary Battles*, 38-45). Even his praise of Simms reflects the sectionalism that underlay the Knickerbockers' support of Fay against the Southern critic, and their closer orientation then to British standards and works. Poe had written of a forthcoming edition of his works in England, where "bug" was reserved for "louse" and not used respectably. The pun in the first word of the quoted article would have pleased Poe, who liked that on "Poe + t = poet" (see 31/24 [facsimile text]).

284/1-37} Poe rightly objects to the crude pragmatism of the editor's idea of artistic merit, just as his predecessors had done ten years earlier. Poe had stated, 265/57-58, that Simms showed more skill than anyone since C. B. Brown. Poe derided Dr. Richard Emmons, author of the bathetic "epic" *The Fredoniad* (1827), before this instance (see H 11.160, 235, and especially,

TOM *Tales*, n. 1 on 1146, to the 12/1844 "Thingum Bob").
Poe's ref. to a "republication" of the *Tales* is somewhat misleading, since the American ed. came out late in June, and the London Wiley and Putnam ed. was simply the American sheets with an English title page; the date of 1846 on some of the English copies may be a clue to its lateness (see TOM *Tales*. 1398). Poe's attack upon his friend and supporter Willis, as the author of Mr. Star's remarks, is surprising since he certainly knew that Willis was abroad and in process of separating himself completely from the *Mirror*. Poe was to continue his humorous remarks at the end of this article when he discussed La Place's "Nebular Cosmogony" in *Eureka* (1848), q.v. in H 16.260-69.

285/1-4} For Poe's reading of a poem before the Boston Lyceum on 10/16 see 297-99 and the notes.

285/5-53} See 257-58 nn. for Poe's first (and only) rev. of Mathews' native American book extolling New York. Poe, still adhering to Mathews' cause of Young America, was perhaps cooling off toward his "allegory" and poetry, but the reason for his merely excerpting the novel instead of properly reviewing it is plausibly stated by Hull. He probably left New York for Boston on Tuesday and had no time to prepare copy for going to press by Wednesday for the Saturday issue of the journal. The two "articles" of magazines on 287 required little time and the gross typographical errors in the second indicate no proofreading. His promise to attend to "new works" (aside from the excerpt) was fulfilled in the 11/15 issue (see 307A, 307B [facsimile text]). It must have been right after his return from Boston that Poe addressed himself to the task, for the 11/34 *Godey's* carried a sizable rev. by Poe of Mathews' "original" and "emblematical romance of homely life" (H 13.73-78), close in some ways to that in the *BJ* of 11/15.

287/1-12} Eliakim Little in Boston followed his successful formula for a journal reprinting articles mostly from the British magazines, which he had developed through the Philadelphia *Museum of Foreign Literature and Science* (1882-42, with slight change of title). His journal was to last to the end of the century and, when merged, well into the twentieth. Allibone and Mott (748-49) pay tribute to the scope and wise selections of Littell, Mott saying: "Nearly all the comment of British periodicals on American affairs appeared in the *Living Age*," contrary to Poe's indictment.
In this issue (Vol. 7, no. 73, the magazine reprints a notice

from the *Spectator* (on p. 18) which objects to Prescott's *Biographical and Critical Miscellanies* on the grounds that they are rather brief notices of books than essays of criticism like those of Sydney Smith; the New Yorker Joel T. Headley, author of *Letters from Italy* is mildly criticised by the *Examiner* (pp. 20-21) for his strange interpretations of Italian phrases and customs and breezy style and observations. Both somewhat belie Poe's comments.

287/35} Poe published the rev. in the 11/1 issue (p. 294).

287/36-50} Now that Poe was taking over the duties of art critic, he obviously exploited sources that would lend him material, Lester's two vol., work being pressed into service for "The Ivory Christ" and rev. material (see 301, 308-10, 333). Poe's inclusion of this excerpt by Hiram Powers, on his celebrated, even notorious statue, "The Greek Slave," argues an implicit defiance of the widespread Victorian condemnation of the representation of a beautiful victim intended for a seraglio, despite Powers' evasive language. In his treatment of the statue "La Sortie du Bain" (247, 282, 297), Poe shows the courage and tact needed for such art matters.

288/1-15} Mary Elizabeth Moore Hewitt (1807-94) lived her life in New England, but wrote chiefly for the New York journals, such as *Arcturus* and *Knickerbocker*. This vol. of 156 p. is dedicated to her brother Josiah Moore. Poe had more time to evaluate her work critically for a more pointed rev. in the 2/46 *Godey's* and for a "Literati" sketch (H 15.123-26). In both he praises her metrical skill but not her use of inversions and her lapses from smoothly concorded consonants. The "sketch" shows clearly that he has "become acquainted with the woman." He still admires the format of the vol., so much more sumptuous than his own vols.

288/16-63} The poem about the mariner, pp. 32-34, is quoted accurately here and in *Godey's* (first pub. in the 9/43 *Boston Miscellany*, 2.103). Likewise, "Alone" (of 10/43), with its motto from Victor Hugo's *Les Voix intérieures* is quoted. By the next year Poe had decided to reprehend her for the first stanza's inversion (line 4) and he adapted his two para. "lecture" to the text of M 218 (*SLM*, 5/49). However, she still remains among the top dozen of nearly 100 of Griswold's *Female Poets* (1849 ed., pp. 157-63), Poe notes. For Poe-letters exchanged and soirées co-frequented, see M 218 note a. For Poe's partiality for the title

"Alone," much before this time, see TOM *Poems* 146-47.

289/21-70} The three sonnets (each with a mythological name), on pp. 35-37, appeared first in *Arcturus* of 4/42, 3.376. They are transcribed correctly save for 1.35: "All vainly struggling." Since we know that Poe admired *Arcturus*, edited by Duyckinck, and read it faithfully (see *PD* 107 for seven citations), traces in "The Raven" of Sonnet III may be significant: 62--"with fiery eye" / 75: "To the fowl whose fiery eyes now burned into my bosom's core"; and 65--"With whetted beak deep in the quivering heart" / 101: "Take thy beak from out my heart."

290/13-14} See the Poe *Log* for 11/10 for Hewitt's letter of thanks to Poe for the rev. and the enclosure of "a little song" for possible publication in the *BJ*, soon to be printed on 2.290 in the 11/15 *BJ* (3 stanzas) as "Song." See also H 17.272-73, for Hewitt's letter of 12/20/46 to Mrs. Osgood, on her efforts to relieve the misery of the Poe family in Fordham.

290/15-52} According to the LC *List of Geographical Atlases*, the *Cerographical Atlas of the U.S.* of Sidney E. Morse and Samuel Brease was published 1842-45, with the title page bearing the final date. Poe's nine items are almost verbatim from various portions of the work. Poe may have derived information also from a prospectus carelessly looked at for the tenth number, since that, rather than no. 1, "embraces" the Indian Territory, nor are the maps colored as originally promised.

290/54-68} & 291/1-7} The vol. has 570 p. plus the index. As always, the physical format of a book is of primary importance to Poe and worthy of mention. Poe's information about the frontispiece came from the caption under the engraving, which is labeled "Giotto" and "Phillibrown," but Poe miscopied the word "lost" as "last" and "castle" instead of "chapel." Poe praises John Flaxman also in H 9.201 and 11.84. For his refs. to Dante see *PD* 25 and, in *Br.*, Pin 14, 33, MM 7, 139A.

291/25-32} This "unusually good" issue of *Graham's* starts with Poe's "System of ... Tarr and ... Fether" on pp. 194-200. The "Correspondent's" article has a Brussels dateline (pp. 231-33). For Mrs. Hale's *Alice Ray* see p. 292.

291/37-40} For Poe's reading at the Boston Lyceum on 10/16 see 297-299 [facsimile text]. Even in this ref. he shows the belligerence over his own "hoax" that was to make this a major crisis in his life.

291/41-64} For the occasion which required this explanation see 273 above.

292/1-6} The same "business" in Boston that occasioned 291 (d) caused this: the Lyceum affair, q.v. in 297-99.

292/7-17} Samuel Lover of Ireland (1797-1868) was a song-writer, novelist, painter of miniatures, magazinist (helped found *Bentley's* with Dickens), Irish entertainer, lyrist, and parodist. Poe's judgment is sound here.

292/18-41} Poe praises this small book of 37 p. out of proportion to its quality for the most obvious of reasons. Sarah Josepha Buell Hale (1788-1879), author and editor, was a formidable power in the realm of opulent annuals and ladies' magazines, especially when she became Godey's literary coworker. Of her 36 published volumes and smaller works, "Mary's Lamb" (1830) is chiefly remembered. Even in the 12/37 *SLM* he handled her *Traits of American Life* with rare delicacy and his letter of 10/30/36 (*Letters* 105-106) is a model of tact in answering one of her objections, offering a contribution to her in the future, and suggesting his acquaintance with her son at West Point (see other letters in Ostrom's Index). On 10/26/45 Poe addressed a letter to her, apologizing for not responding to her sending him this volume for rev. and also a poem for the *BJ* called "The American Pioneer" of 36 lines, printed in the 11/15 issue (2.284). In earlier letters he advised her about minor aspects of her publications, upon her request, as he does in this, about a publisher. Neither in this poem about the "warrior, in panoply arrayed ... " who "drives Despair before him, while Ruin stalks behind," nor in "Alice Ray," do the "pitiable conceits" seem to trouble Poe. Marvelous that after reading her for over a dozen years, he was "prepared for nothing so good." Yet Poe does manage to find a minor merit in the rhyme scheme, without commenting on the cliché-ridden rhymes employed.

294/11-33} This, the first vol. in the new "Foreign Library" series, has ix-xv + 254 p. while the second vol., about to be issued, q.v. on p. 303 (b), has x + 256. The advertisement, that Poe mentions in para. 2, printed on *BJ* 2.266, includes the Walpole quotation also on the title page that ends Poe's first para. Poe supplements this "scant" rev. with a long one quoted from the *Evening Post* in the 11/15 *BJ* (see 310 below). Poe's ideas are taken from the Preface to vol. 1, which speaks of his unstable character, but not of his "madness" (see the *Enc. Brit.*, 1940 ed., 5.99, for the "splendidly gifted and barbarically untameable" genius of 1500-71).

294/34-54} The notice of the masterpiece (1827; rev. ed. 1842) of Manzoni (1785-1873), universally known and praised, is especially significant as being Poe's sole ref. to a work that may have influenced "Masque of the Red Death" through its graphic plague scenes. The long rev. included by Harrison (8.12-19) is not by Poe but by Beverly Tucker. In para. 1 Poe seems to object to the didactic aim of Manzoni in this historical novel--to advocate resignation to the apparent evils of life and reliance on sincerely held religion. The last para. on the use of English (or "American" as Poe humorously termed it) is often controverted by Poe himself with his "niaiseries" and "bizarreries" and "lorgnon" and "fierté" (295/13) et al.

294/55-66 + 295/1-8} Anne McVicar Grant (1755-1838), of Scotland, lived as a girl near Albany, where her father, a British captain, was stationed. This record of her early life, published anonymously in 1808, was popular; Poe reviewed a reprint in the 6/36 *SLM* (H 9.70-71). Grant Thorburn (1773-1863), writer of the Preface, was a migrant from Scotland who became a successful merchant and author in New York.

295/9-23} This is the fifth of the "Medici Series of Italian Prose," being advanced by the translator C. Charles Edwards, q.v. in 205 (a) nn., (and my Index) and by the publisher Paine and Burgess (see advertisement on 2.280). Poe's previous refs. to Vittorio Alfieri (1749-1803), the outstanding romantic poet and tragedian of Tuscany, are purely peripheral (H 8.138, 9.204). Passion and boldness are poor points of comparison with Cellini. Lester acknowledges that he has merely "edited" an anonymous translation of the *Memoirs* pub. in 2 vols. (London, 1810). Poe's cliché terms--"vivid" and "intensely interesting"--seem to reflect a most rapid skimming.

295/24-33} This vol., of 7-9 + 13-311 p., is a collection of short stories by "Christopher North" whom Poe detested (q.v. under John Wilson, in the Index).

295/34-41} The text is preceded by prefatory material of 36 p. Poe's ready acceptance of the evils of tobacco assumes more rationality than America has since demonstrated concerning the addiction. Poe's smoking habits have not been thoroughly investigated or depicted; the reminiscences of Gabriel Harrison, then a tobacconist, are revealing (see Hervey Allen, *Israfel*, 1934 ed. 499-501).

295/57-61} Poe did not return to this textbook, by Marcius Wilson (1813-1905).

296/9-15} Wm. Gilmore Simms had been in New York during October, as Poe certainly knew. The first article (pp. 249-54) is about the danger of cannon accidents and how to avoid them; the second concerns the Partisan leader of South Carolina, Francis Marion, who greatly hampered the Tories and the British troops (265-76). Poe was now "courting" Thomas Holley Chivers, Georgian planter, whose book he had favorably reviewed (187-89 [facsimile text]), perhaps because he had hopes for financial support which Chivers often pledged but never paid. Certainly this "Elegy" is more rational and composed than Chivers' usual extravanganzas. Each of its eight quatrains starts with "Thou art gone to the grave!"--an initial repetend, pleasing to the author of "The Raven" and also of "The Conqueror Worm" (cf. Chivers' stanza 4: "Yes, the earth-worms are creeping / Where beauty since laid on thy cold breast her head!"). In the 12/6 *BJ* (2.338) Poe would print Chivers' sonnet to E. B. Barrett to whom Poe had dedicated his recently published *Raven and Other Poems*.

296/16-23} The engravings in *Graham's* are of "Leonora" by Sir Thomas Lawrence, Bodmer's "Indians Hunting the Bison" and Hinshelwood's drawing, from T. Addison Richards, of "Medical College of Georgia"--variety enough. Poe's contribution is "The System ...", Chivers' is "The Cottage Girl" (p. 226). Poe adroitly demolishes the merit of Longfellow's didactic poem with his phrase "rhetorically considered."

296/24-29} Darley had painted the "Indian Captive" (engraved by Cushman) and J. Burnet painted a second plate, of "The Dancing Dolls." Poe's contribution was the rev. of Mathews' "Big Abel ..." (218-19), q.v. in 257 nn.

296/30-35} This is John Gadsby Chapman (1808-89), prominent Virginian and New York painter, who had illustrated Poe's "The Elk" (for his relations with Poe and refs. in the *BJ*, see Pollin, *SAR 1983*. 245-73, especially *ad finem*). The other plate is called "The Black Mask." The proposals for improvements had been included in the October issue at the end:

"Looking Ahead."

296/36-47} T. Doney's plate, "Moses Commanding the Water Out of the Rock," is extremely dark; the other is "The White Mouse" by T. Kelley. The "strong list" includes two alleged rivals for Poe's favorable attention: "Lady Jane--a song" by Frances S. Osgood (196) and "The Maiden's Leap," Elizabeth Fries Lummis Ellet's fiction (205-208). For the tangled affair, climaxing in 1846, see S. Morse *PLB*, 208-220, 240-43, who notes Poe's printing, in the 12/13 *BJ*, veiled Della-Cruscan-style tributes to himself from both the ladies: "Coquette's Song" (Ellet's on 2.349) and Osgood's "A Shipwreck" (352).

296/51-58} This small item seems to augur drama criticism from Poe for the duration of the journal, but the internal evidence of style and content argues against the realization. A few commentators have toyed with ascribing a column or two to Poe, according to his pledge in the last sentence. It is worth a small space to explain my omissions from the canon of this material, save for that on 354 [facsimile text]. In the 11/8 *BJ* on 2.276-77 is a rev. of Murdoch's performances not at all in Poe's style. It concludes with a curtain call speech that he gave on a benefit night, introduced by two sentences which may have been inserted by Poe as editor: "At the end of the performances he was summoned before the curtain and delivered the following speech, which was rapturously welcomed, and which we place on record for future reference. We have many reflections springing from this success of Mr. Murdoch's, and the new light it casts upon our present Drama, to lay before our readers hereafter." Even for these sentences the phrasing is too awkward to lay them at Poe's door. On 11/15 the *BJ* published another accolade to Murdoch, including long notices from two Philadelphia journals. Neither the style nor the blandness of the refs. to such persons as Epes Sargent and Wm. Burton, his former proprietor and co-editor of the *Gentleman's Magazine*, seems of Poe origin, although Hull thinks that "one sentence points to Poe"--concerning Mowatt's *Fashion*, whereas it leads to the opposite view, in my opinion. TOM, in some private notes on the text, also ascribed it, probably on the grounds of the unfulfilled pledge of the first article (on 296). The 11/22 *BJ* (2.208-209) has a rev. of music and dramatic events, largely devoting its space to another benefit curtain call speech by Murdoch, but the style is not that of Poe. The 11/29 *BJ* (325) has a brief survey of events in various American cities and in London. On 12/13 a column of drama news was probably written by Poe (p,. 356), with one mention of Murdoch. Likewise, the 12/27 issue (354 [facsimile text]) savors of Poe, but the last col. on "The Drama" in the 1/3 *BJ* is a mere listing of events which Poe could obviously not then have witnessed, in a cliché-ridden style, probably that of Murdoch himself (2.406).

297/1-40} Poe initialed this article in the Whitman copy, enabling Harrison to list it on H 16.375, but it was not reprinted by Harrison or any other editor of Poe. Poe had twice preannounced his critique of this sculpture: on 9/13 (p. 247 [facsimile text]) when he mentioned its unsurpassable qualities and purchase by an American visitor to Belgium; and on 10/11 (p. 282) when he mentioned "those who decry it"--obviously for its nudity, mentioned again at the start of this article.

The circumstances of its showing do not yield to investigation, thanks to the poor indexing of art events at that time. Jean-Baptiste de Cuyper (1807-52), member of a family of artists, was a pupil of Ivan der Neer and Matthew van Brée of Antwerp. His most famous work is a marble statue of King Leopold I at Antwerp. There is little information available on the "Bathing Girl" which seems to have disappeared. An article in the *Bijdragen tot de Gesehiedenis* (Contributions to History) of Antwerp, 10/15/1924, 16.307-24, on him, says that he showed in New York "a Venus at the water's edge." This seems to refer to a marble composition that he spoke of in two letters of 7 and 8/1843, which he describes as "a young girl seated at the edge of the water and amusing herself with a tortoise" (p. 317). Clearly, the beauty of the figure derives from that of Venus herself, although the "girlish innocence" that Poe insists on noting is a new interpretation of the goddess. It is interesting that on 247 Poe mentioned attributes of the figure omitted from this article: "intellectuality, gentleness, and modesty" not to be "excelled" and these correspond to adjectives that he applied to "The Ivory Christ" (p. 282): "dignified, meek, ... eminently intellectual." Understandably the last is dropped from the detailed description of the "Venus." The idea of "truth" occurs in both: for the Christ, "the absolute *truth* of the entire design" and for this, that of "the attitude." For both, Poe tries to analyze the anatomical fidelity of the representation. Amusingly, Poe objects to the discordance of the "girl's" tempting a vegetarian reptile with live bait. One suspects that Poe was much more apt and certainly knowing in commenting on the graphic, two-dimensional arts than the field of sculpture.

297/41-59} This begins Poe's public accounts of the

unfortunate "hoax" that he played on the literary and journalistic "establishment" of Boston, initially cordial and financially supportive despite the "Longfellow War" that he had foolishly waged early in 1845. The best account of this "reading" of a so-called "original" poem (in reality, "Al Aaraaf" renamed the Messenger Star" of Tycho Brahe," but 298/66n) is given by TOM (*Poems* 559) and Sidney Moss in *PLB*, 190-207, including choice excerpts from the press of Boston and the rest of the nation, proving the notoriety and discredit that it was bringing to Poe just when he took over control of his magazine (see also Quinn, *Poe*, 485-89, treating Poe's unwise savagery and levity too mildly). Briefly, Lowell, early in 1844, offered to arrange for Poe's appearance before the prestigious Boston Lyceum for a reading of poetry, necessarily original. The stipend (probably $50, q.v., in TOM, *Poems* 559) and the distinction of opening the series (together with Cushing) were enough to cause Poe to accept (for 10/16/45) but he had no new, long poem and no time, as a busy editor, to write one. After the long speech of the statesman Caleb Cushing, recently returned from a commission to China, Poe read his obscure early poem and concluded with "The Raven." Later in the evening, Poe privately confessed his "hoax" to four men, including the Shakespeare critic and lecturer Henry Norman Hudson who had been treated rather off-handedly in the *BJ* (by Briggs) after his New York lecture. The editor of the Boston *Transcript*, Cornelia Wells Walter, friend of Longfellow and Hudson, first published a blunt statement about Poe's failure in the lecture (10/17) and then about the hoax (10/18). Soon the publication of Poe's poems in *ROP* would emblazon the deception about "Al Aaraaf" as an unpublished juvenile poem everywhere in the nation. The subsequent charges and countercharges by Poe, Cornelia Walter, Hudson, and others can be followed, in part, through Poe's *BJ* columns below (and in Moss's fine survey).

For Poe's friendly relations with Mordecai Noah, see 151/1-11 n.

298/6} A friend and admirer of Longfellow, Cornelia Walter was so termed by Poe at the end of the 4th "episode" of the Longfellow War (66/37 [facsimile text]), where Poe assumes that Longfellow had advised her "to pierce me to death with the needles of innumerable epigrams."

298/8} The expression "stand and deliver" was then the standard imperative of a footpad, meaning "Halt and hand over your valuables." Below (1.28) Poe puns on its meaning "to turn over goods as ordered, at the door."

298/13} Caleb Cushing's speech lasted 2 1/2 hours, and Poe's 15 minutes, as he says. The former is often described as 3 hours. In any event, Poe could scarcely expect an eager and receptive audience, but he is gracious in this part of his account.

298/15-16} Poe was distinctive, even unique at that time, in decrying moralistic poetry. His reasoned antipathy is stated in the 4/42 rev. of Longfellow's *Ballads* (H 11.58-85); for his stand see Robert Jacobs, *Poe: Journalist and Critic* (1969), 298-301. S. Moss (196) quotes the full Boston *Daily Courier* 10/18 editorial on the Lyceum talk as an exception to the "baiting" of the rest of the press: The prefatory "prose, showing that there existed no such thing as didactic poetry ... The poem containing the essence of *true* poetry ... (with) a graceful delivery."

298/17} The word "indefinitiveness" was coined by Poe for its special use in his esthetic, especially for poetry and music. See the ten instances in *PCW* 29, 90.

298/61} The 1845 version of "Al Aaraaf" consists of Part I, 155 lines, and Part II, 264, or a total of 419. Poe is probably correct that "Miss Walter" invented the title (but it must have been after his oral hints). Her editorial states: "We believe ... it was a prose introductory to a poem on the 'Star discovered by Tycho Brahe,' considered figuratively as the 'Messenger of the Deity,' out of which idea ... Poe had constructed a sentimental and imaginative poem." Soon the other papers must have been terming it "The Messenger Star," as did "Miss Walter" herself.

299/1-8} According with this "confession" by Poe is a curious bibliographical fact presented by TOM in the preface to the Facsimile Text Society ed. of *Al Aaraaf* (Columbia UP, 1933), TOM ed., with no allusion to the *BJ* passage. The edition bore the date 1829 (making Poe 20 at the time), but one copy, included in the 1924 sale of the "Wakeman Collection," had "on the title page the date 1820, usually described as a misprint. But that copy belonged to Elizabeth Herring, a cousin of Poe's, and was used by Poe in preparing copy for his 1845 volume *The Raven and Other Poems*.... The suggestion that the date may have been altered, either idly or hoaxingly, by the poet himself, seems to me quite credible" [3-4]. The altered date falls within Poe's tenth year, as stated here.

299/10-14} In addition to Moss's transcription of the

Transcript and *Courier* reviews, see the Poe *Log* for the *Traveller* and TOM (*Poems* 559 n 12) for the much later reminiscence (perhaps by T. W. Higginson in the Boston *Museum*).

299/19-22} Poe's loquacity, due probably to the wine, gave Miss Walter's friend Hudson (see 211/52 n) the information that he anonymously put to use in the 10/18 *Transcript's* subsidiary column of abuse of Poe. His avowal of this in a letter to Duyckinck of 11/24 was soon conveyed to Poe, motivating his shift in feelings and his scurrilous *BJ* article of 12/13 (see p. 339 [facsimile text]; see Moss, 195-96, n. 8).

299/23-24} "The soft impeachment" is from Sheridan's *The Rivals*, 5.3. The Latin is from Vergil's *Aeneid*, 1.11, and also from Terence, *Andria*, 1.1.99, quoted by Horace, *Epistolae*, 1.19.41: "And hence this anger?" (used also in "Marie Rogêt", TOM 767).

299/25-35} There seems little doubt that the editor had seen the "Outis" letter and the replies, which included a pun on "Poe, the Poet" (see 60/1-2 above). No trace of this paper is given in W. Gregory's *American Newspapers*.

The word "lick" has many colloquial meanings, several of which are here possible, such as "a spring" (ironically referring to the great falls) or as "a slap or a quick stroke"; or "a burst of speed." Similarly, the word "fits" means not only "violent attacks" or "moods" or "spells or periods" but also "adjustments." Poe puns on two meanings of "fits" in *Br.*, M 160. Here he also puns on the temperance "resolution" advocated for his drinking problem, which he "took" in 1849 from the Richmond Sons of Temperance.

299/36-44} By 1844 Poe had become disillusioned in his hopes that Dickens would help him to have his work published in London; he assumed to be Dickens' the allusion to Poe as an imitator of Tennyson, in a rev. of Griswold's *Poetry and Poets of America* in the *Foreign Quarterly Review*. He first affirmed this in letters of 3/30/44 and 5/8/44 addressed to Lowell, who correctly ascribed it to John Forster (see Lowell's letter of 6/27/44 in H 17.180-82). This article shows Poe's persistence in error, especially since Sir John Bell was a military and diplomatic-corps person, without literary or journalistic tendencies. Poe had previously published a denunciation of this journal's abuse of American authors in his rev. of C. F. Hoffman's *Poems* in the 12/10/44 *Evening Mirror* (1/2).

299/45-55} *The Travels of Marco Polo greatly amended and enlarged* ... by Baldelli Boni, had copious notes by Hugh Murray (N.Y.: Harper and Bros, 1845). *The Memoirs of Father Ripa* was a recent Wiley and Putnam vol.

299/56-64 & 300/1-5} The *Critic* of London, 9/6/45, 2.378-379 carried the rev. (5 brief paras.) plus a long excerpt from "Mesmeric Revelation"; in the issue of 9/20, pp. 420-22, it printed a long excerpt from "The Maelström," to show the "thrilling" description which gives the reader a "frightful and giddy interest." The *Mirror* of New York reprinted the first of these (daily: 11/25; weekly: 12/6). Poe is stretching several points in his "sufficiently complimentary," for the rev. speaks of the disappointment in finding the "poet of considerable power" issuing tales so strange, so merely ingenious (especially to the police), so replete with horrors and cruelties, so passé. "Mesmeric Revelation" is cited as of "masterly treatment." It is curious that the *Critic* writer has sniffed out the trail of *Zadig* by Voltaire as one of the general sources for Poe's use of circumstantial clues in his detective fiction (see Tom, *Tales* 521-22).

300/6-19} It may be suspected that the motto of the anonymous essay (2.241-43, by "Schrev."--Schrevelius?) consisting of three Greek words might have been "jumbled up" through Poe's poor Greek, not his "hurry."

The "exquisite poem" with the incorrectly spelled title *here* but not on 2.240 where it is printed out reads as follows (lines 1-4): "Not of earth's common mould was she, / On whose young soul Futurity-- / The veil from those dark features raises-- / With sad and solemn aspect gazed!" Poe favored Gibson, printing "Stanzas" (p. 206, 10/11), "The Unattainable" (p. 223, 10/18), and "To Helen" (pp. 258-59, 11/1).

Despite the correction of this oversight (on p. 243) John H. Ingram preferred to consider "Ide" a pseudonym for Poe (see Tom *Poems* 509, items 70-73). Poe scrupulously wrote Ide's name in the Whitman copy (see Index for other Ide entries). There likewise Poe inscribes W. G. Simms next to the "Sonnet" on p. 235, which leads off the number.

300/20-22} Mrs. Hale's N.Y. publisher in the 30s and 40s was Edward Dunigan of 137 Fulton Street and the Harpers (see 73 [facsimile text]).

300/23-28} *The Book of Christmas* by Thomas Kibble Hervey, contributor to annuals, numbered ii + 220 p. Frederick de la

Motte Fouqué's two romances (the second being *Aslauga's Knight*) came out in December (see the issue of 12/6 for announcement), too late for a rev. prepared for the *BJ*. Poe's article was used as M 181 in the 12/46 *Graham's* (q.v. in *Br.*). The poems of Mrs. Southey are probably *Solitary Hours* (159 p.) together with *The Birthday and Other Poems* (179 p.), which bears the proleptic date of 1846.

300/29-32} Robert Hasell Newell (1778-1852) wished to correct the errors in zoology made by English poets (London: Longmans, 1845). We note Poe's insistence upon putting the dieresis over the first of the two syllables rather than the second--the common custom (cf. *Br.*, xxxviii-xi).

300/33-41} Poe was conciliating Wm. Gilmore Simms (1806-70) in every way possible, knowing his ready pen and wide influence in the South.

300/45-47} This "romance" of Edward Maturin (1812-81) came out in two vols.: ii + 270 and 287 p. (N.Y.: Paine and Burgess, 1845).

300/48-51} For the rev. of her *Western Clearings* see 316-17.

300/61} "The Autumnal Leaf" by G. H. Mildeberger appeared in the 11/15 *BJ* on 2.285-86.

301/1-22} The vol. has viii + 237p., devoted largely to Hiram Powers (1805-73), America's first internationally celebrated sculptor (see 308-309 [facsimile text]). The sections are respectively pp. 1-18, 19-24, 25-147, 148-153, 155-237. Campbell (1806-81) was a jurist, historian and congressman. Note Poe's use of the "fine portrait" on 308 [facsimile text].

301/24-40} The vol. had viii + 143 p. No copy of this book has been available to me to verify the error mentioned at the end. Presumably Casserly's Chrestomathic Institutions (one of several?) taught foreign tongues through a selection of passages with notes--a kind of reader.

301/41-50} This vol., of 222 p., from the third London ed., was titled *Lectures on the English Comic Writers*. The pagination is this: 2-13, 32-54, 55-79, 80-105, "On the Periodical Essayists," 106-123, 124-156, 157-177, 178-222.

301/51-57} This vol., of vii-xvi + 175 p., has numerous footnotes and a section at the start of "Criticisms" consisting of comments on the book by Scott, Irving, Goethe, and Mrs. Barbauld.

301/58-64} This vol., of 288 p., was published in 1826 as *Sabbath recreations.*

302/7-17} This vol. of 235 p. is one of numerous texts reshaped by Wm. Ruschenberger (1807-95) once pervading the schools of America and now almost nonexistent; one copy in "Rare Books" at Harvard was unavailable for examination. See 73 (a) for another title.

302/18-22} Mrs. Thomas C. Hofland (Barbara Wreaks Hoole) (1770-1844) has 62 titles in the British Museum Catalogue. Poe was correct about reprints: 1809, 1814, 1830, 1834, 1839. Her *Young Crusoe* may have influenced *Pym* (see *Imaginary Voyages,* p. 6).

302/23-30} Mary Botham Howitt (1799-1888) (who often collaborated with William, q.v.) wrote children's books and did translations, of great popularity. This has 71 double-column pages, the first sentence being used almost verbatim for this notice.

302/31-35} For the English humorist see 245/17.

302/36-47} See 92, 150, 191 for earlier comments. Poe's desire to see reading more widespread transcended his love of fine editions, as here.

302/48-57} Adolphe Thiers (1797-1877) was a noteworthy figure in historical writing, whose books would induce this kind of "fresh off the boat" piracy. For the interesting sportsman, son of the literary dean of Manchester and well known as "Frank Forester," see 102 [facsimile text].

303/3-9} Robert A. West was well known to Poe for his being coeditor, with John Inman, of the *Columbian Lady's Magazine* from 1845 to 1848, while it published works of Poe. See 105/19-22 for his own poem and song reviewed by Poe.

303/10-14} This numbers x + 256 p. See 294 (a) for the notice of No. 1 and 310 for a further token of Poe's respect.

303/15-68} For Poe's admiration of Freeman Hunt and his magazine see 207/52-62 and other items in the Index as well as *Texas Studies in Literature and Language*, 1974, 16.305-13. The articles seriatim are on pp. 403-412, 412-417, 417-426, 426-434, 434-449, 450-459, and 459-468. The article by Willis appeared in the *Evening Mirror* of 11/13/44 while Poe worked there.

304/1-22} Unquestionably Poe speaks of Hunt, the successful and sole proprietor of the magazine, in terms wishfully parallel to himself on the *BJ*, far from the goal of success of course.

304/23-30} The articles in this issue of the *Aristidean* of Thomas Dunn English are as follows, seriatim: 254-59; 260-66; "Petrus"--267-72; "The Cobbler"--273-76; 296-303; 304-14; and 287-92. This time Poe's promise of further comments was fulfilled in the 11/29 issue, 322/23.

304/31-44} The articles are paginated thus: 437-51, 498-503, "Adventures ..." by Charles Winterfield--504-18, 532-36. The 9-stanza poem "Elfland" is on 457-58 and the 20 stanzas of "True Death" on 494-97. Poe was most partial to Wallace's banal poems, q.v. in the items of the Index, and see 307-49, which discussed the poem "True Death" defensively. The "Critical Notices" are on 543-46.

304/45-52} The chief conductor was Lewis Gaylord Clark, relentlessly hostile to Poe since the *SLM* attacks on Theodore Fay. See 307A.

304/53-63} Poe had reviewed this at length on 116 (a), but enthusiastically and without this reservation. It is impossible to discover from the scant art records of the day which exhibition is here intended.
For Lester on Powers, see 287, 301, 308-309.

305/22-52} For the popular, highly overrated poet and moral philosopher Tupper, see 214-15 n. His *Proverbial Philosophy*, "truisms" in "rhythmical language," first came out in 1838, the novel in 1844. Poe's rev. above is favorable. Herman Hooker's ed. of the *Philosophy* (1843) is from the 5th London ed. with a 3rd American ed. following in 1846, all proof of the value of the rights. For Poe's very definite views on the issue of international copyright see Index under "copyright"; also, *Br.*, M 139C. For Willis' misconception see 214 n. above.

The quotation from Poe's favorite, *Essay on Criticism* is slightly inaccurate (Part 2, 11.220-221): "But let a lord" and "How the wit brightens! How the style refines!"

306/1-40} The Oxford man was George Smith Green, a watchmaker of the town, who published a "paraphrased *Paradise Lost*" (1756), a curiosity recorded by Poe in the *Br.*, SP 20. This is proof enough of Poe's authorship of the whole, apart from the main theme, his previous rev. of Tupper's work, and the lively style. Only his mildness concerning the generally objurgated Carlyle (line 35) is uncharacteristic.

307/1-49} For Wallace, see 168-69 (f) above and M 290. For a link of Dow, Wallace and Poe see *Letters*, 8/27/42. See also the Poe *Log* of 1/29/45, for an amusing anecdote anent "The Raven." See 251 [facsimile text] for a long excerpt from "The Statuary" (1.34). Concerning the word "Tennysonism," see Poe's coinage of the term in the 8/1843 rev. of Channing's *Poems* (H 11.181), according to *OED*. Poe himself had been so accused, and significant is his own footnote to the Preface to the section, "Poems Written in Youth," in the *ROP* just now being issued; it has a sly ref. to plagiarism and Tennyson (see Quinn, *Poe* 482).

307/55} Poe here misspells the name of Richard Monckton Milnes, friend at Cambridge of Tennyson, promoter of the Copyright Act, and active in various reform movements.

307/62} Like the *BJ*, Simms' *Southern and Western Monthly Magazine and Review of Charleston*, having become a one man affair, had grown "irksome, and ... compensative neither in money or other reward" (11/45, 2.344). Hence it was to be merged with the *SLM* in 1846, under the title *The Southern and Western Literary Messenger and Review*, Benjamin Blake Minor, editor.

307/63-70} This is a mere puff for the one-para. advertisement by H. Johnson on p. 280, col. 1, of the *BJ*, but apparently written by Poe. In one of his tales he uses "recherché" with this meaning of "sought after" (TOM 175/3, 180/26).

307A/1} This article has obviously caused some uncertainty in the sifting processes anterior to the layout of the pages of vol. 1 and the final preparation of the notes of vol. 2. It was first included for its internal evidence: adverse criticism of the

Knickerbocker and its chief editor, general respect for Coleridge, John Neal, and Simms, the stenographic style as used in certain tales, the personal ref. to lecturing soon after the Lyceum affair, a generally clever development, et al. (see below). On the other hand, some things were uncharacteristic, particularly the flattery of Hudson, so very different from Poe's abusive comments on 339 [facsimile text], 12/13. But Poe's great shift in attitude there was explained later by a letter of 11/23 from Hudson to Duyckinck (see 339 n). This removed my last reason for doubting this article, which had to be inserted on two pages labeled 307A and 307B, to preserve the folio odd-even pagination. This required subjecting the readers to a worse than *Knickerbocker* tininess of print, for which my apologies are here due. Poe shows adroitness in using long quotations from a book that must have caused him some distress, despite his loyalty to Mathews and especially to his friend Duyckinck as well as the Young America movement.

In the 11/8 *BJ* (304 [facsimile text]) Poe had curtly referred to the November *Knickerbocker* attack on Mathews' book as "beneath notice and beneath contempt." Duyckinck had dispersed his support of Mathews and denunciation of L. G. Clark (under the pseudonym of "S.T."-- Samuel Taylor [Coleridge]?) to "the city press" which promptly published it. The 12/45 *Knickerbocker* response of Clark was likewise sent to the press, for publication (see the *Weekly Mirror* of 12/13, pp. 148-49), the entire sequence being given by Sidney Moss in the *American Book Collector*, 1967, 18.8-18, specifically, 10).

307A/2-11} On 169/21-24 Poe had censured the abominably small type of the *Knickerbocker Magazine's* "Editor's Table." Usually he reprobated the journal for Clark's comments or orientation (see 304), but sometimes seemed to be making conciliatory remarks, as did Clark in the 10/45, 26.378, when agreeing with Poe's scorn for Wm. Jones on "humor in America." Likewise, Poe had liked an article "Who are our National Poets?" (q.v., p. 281 [facsimile text]).

307A/11-13} Poe's pun on "table" involves a once common expression involving the tomb of Sir John Beauchamp (d. 1358) in Old St. Paul's, known erroneously as that of Duke Humphrey of Gloucester. "To dine with Duke Humphrey" was to starve among the debtors and beggars frequenting his "Walk" in the Cathedral (*En. Brit.*, 12.848, n. 1).

307A/19} More than once Poe advanced his narrative

through the semi-dramatic device of a "Memorandum" (or "Mem") read aloud to the reader, as in "Blackwood Article" (*Tales,* 337/1, 2), "Business Man" (487/6 and 13) and "Balloon Hoax" (1080/10). Equally important is the stenographic, inner-speech-revealed method throughout the para., as in the "Day-Book" section of "The Business Man" (p. 487), which is the tale with one of the "Mems."

307A/29-34} For Poe's long, tangled "relationship" with Coleridge, still the best treatment is in Floyd Stovall's *Edgar Poe* (1969), pp. 126-74. See also the *Br.* items, MM 109 (on Coleridge as a boring preacher or talker), 133, 213, SM 19, and Poe's coinage of "sermonoid" (see *PCW*).

307A/35-41} For Poe's cordial relations with John Neal, who always defended him, even after his death, see the Index entries, MM 197, 216, and Benjamin Lease on the two authors in *PS*, 7.38-41. The 2-vol. Revolutionary romance *Seventy-Six* (1823) is often considered his best work.

307A/41-51} There is no need to underscore the growing closeness of Poe and Wm. Gilmore Simms in their present views and support of each other (see Index items). There is an implied intimacy here that might easily follow a personal meeting of the two the preceding month in New York. A brief but nasty remark against Simms is in the 10/45 *Knickerbocker,* 26.378.

307A/51-62} Certainly Poe should have been "tired ... with lectures of all sorts" after his own in Boston of 10/16. It was there that he had drunk with Hudson and admitted the hoax. Poe publicly confessed to never having heard Hudson before, q.v. in 339 (b). Poe's angel ref. is to John 5:4--"For an angel went down at a certain season into the pool, and troubled the water: whosoever the first ... stepped in was made whole of whatsoever disease he had."

307A/70-93} These two excerpts are taken from *Big Abel,* pp. 53, 64-65.

307B/37} This excerpt comes from *Big Abel,* pp. 40-41.

307B/72} It may have significance that above and here, the reader of all the objectionable material and the examples as well is "John," while in "X-ing a Paragrab" it is John Smith, the aggrieved victim of Mr. Bullet-head, who insulted him and deformed the text read aloud (*Tales* 1368-1375).

307B/73-81} This para. is a composite of passages from two pages of the *Knickerbocker* of 11/45 (the top of 452 and also of 453). The "thimble" ref., quoted from Clark's text, was cleverly used by Poe in 307A/35 for a contrast of Clark and Coleridge.

307B/82-83} Poe refers here to Dogberry's foolish wish: "O that he were here to write me down an ass!" (*Much Ado*, 4.2.80). The omitted word is one of Poe's favorite terms of disdain.

308/1-13} For data on contents see 301 (a), and 333 (a) for vol. 2. Poe is here giving a phrenological description of Powers, whose "fine portrait" embellishes the vol. (304/21). The great success of the Greek slave (a woman) was owed, in large part, to the popularity of the cause of the Greeks versus their Turkish rulers. It is instructive to compare Poe's remarks here and elsewhere on "La Sortie du Bain" (q.v. in the Index) with the review in the London *Athenaeum*, reprinted by Briggs in "British Criticisms on American Art" in the 6/28 *BJ*, 1.403, which lauds Hiram Powers whose "genius [in Florence] fed on the Greek inspiration, and outlived ... the chastening apprehension of the prudes at home."

308/28-38} For more details tied to Robert Kerr's monument-proposal see M 15 c and the 2/8 *BJ*, 1.92-93 (an article by Briggs). See also Poe's "Mellonta Tauta" (TOM 1303-04 and "Mummy" (*Tales* 1200 n 34) for Poe's objection to the Washington Monument and the enormous, tasteless Bowling Green Fountain (see also my study in *Studies in Short Fiction*, 1971, 8.627-31).

309/18} Poe's view of Jackson, whose policies were unfortunate in 1837-38 for his journalistic hopes in New York, can be traced through the Index entries in TOM, *Tales*, and H. Allen's *Israfel*.

309/40} Thomas Crawford (1813-57), having studied in Rome, won fame with his "Orpheus" (in the Boston Athenaeum). He imitated classical forms, presumably a basis for Poe's remark.

310/10-47} This is presumably Poe's although the evidence is not direct. George Barrell Cheever (1807-90) was a Congregational clergyman and reformer, whose book was announced on 282; another of his is to be reviewed on 359. Reasons for assigning it to Poe follow: Poe would justifiably be indignant at the crudity of the humor described, especially with reference to books--that deserve serious treatment--and the term "Penny-a-liners" is not uncommon in Poe's work. The long string of Church worthies' names is typical of Poe--overshooting the mark to display his knowledge. Richard Corbet was mentioned by him as a poet (H 9.91, 98-100, *BJ* 114, as well as Bishop of Oxford and Norwich here--a not very likely choice for this instance. Finally Poe often cites the white Parian marble statue, mentioned by Lucian (see FS 21, "Man of the Crown," TOM 510 at n 7, et al. loci). The dramatic form of the imaginary episode of the "dirty fellow" is also in Poe's style.

311/1-20} This para. is obviously editorial and explains a new policy for cheaply and entertainingly filling up space. The kind of lurid "news" items mentioned were common in the press and, perused by Poe, to judge from the thematic motive of "Berenice" (TOM 207) and the start of "Angel of the Odd" (1101). An almost full page devoted to four of these "Items"--clearly copied verbatim--gave his readers "a new work by Ariosto," "News of Tycho Brahe," a fabulous gold and diamond "strike" in Brazil, and two anecdotes about books. The brief continuing life of the *BJ* enabled Poe to insert only two more sets of this sort: the issues of 11/29 (326) and of 12/6 (341).

311/22} This item at the very end of the 11/15 number is preceded by a box which reads as follows: To the Public.-- *Edgar A. Poe, Esq.* having purchased my interest in "The Broadway Journal," is now sole proprietor of the same. All persons indebted to the paper will please make settlement with him.

John Bisco.

New York, October 24, 1845.

For the general significance, please see my Intro.

311/39-53} Poe modestly omits mentioning that *The Missionary Manual* includes his poem "The Lake" on pp. 324-35, once again reprinted. The "hustle" was occasioned by a move from 135 Nassau Street to 304 Broadway, corner of Duane (at the head of 11/29 issue).

312/1-3} Poe's statement is rather disingenuous since "The Spectacles," occupying pp. 299-307 of the current issue, had been published first in the *Dollar Newspaper* of 3/27/44. He had then copied over the entire tale to be sent to Elizabeth Barrett's friend, Richard Hengist Horne, author of *Orion* which Poe had reviewed (see letter of 3/15/44 to Cornelius Mathews and Ostrom's note; also, my study of "The Spectacles" in *American Literature*, 1965, 37.185-190. More recently, in *SAR 1977* J. J. Moldenhauer has supplied details; see TOM 883-86). Almost the whole issue, then, was devoted to a tale which TOM and Woodberry thought a "weak piece of humor" and which was derived closely from the plot and ambiance of a tale in the 7/1836 London *Belle Assemblée* (see my study, given above). Four columns also were spent on the Lyceum affair.

312/11} This long article by Wm. Gilmore Simms appeared in the 11/10/45 issue of the Charleston *Southern Patriot* (vol. 54, no. 8201, p. 2/2). Obviously it was sent immediately by Simms to Poe personally.

312/53-65} This section was used by Poe himself for his parody of *Evangeline*, dating probably from 1849, first printed (by TOM) in *Poems* 395-95. See also my study of the hexameters in *Mi Q*, 1984, 37.475-82. TOM correctly points out the dependence upon this passage of Simms' article in key ideas and wording: "Do tell when shall we make common sense men out of the pundits ... who lost in a fog-bank / Strut about all along shore there somewhere close by the Down East / Frog Pond munching of pea nuts and pumkins and buried in big-wigs...." As for Longfellow's "comeliness" -- see Poe's clothing metaphors attacking the well-dressed Professor on 38/46-56.

313/15-27} This was from the Boston *Courier* of 10/18, a sentence from which was quoted in the *Sunday Times* 10/26 issue that was excerpted by Poe in his 11/1 "Editorial" (see 297, art. b). It is likely that Poe had collected all the critical comments in the press and sent the whole *Courier* column to Simms for his present write-up--a strong suggestion that he had arranged for this *Southern Patriot* column. In short, Poe was promoting a nationwide journalistic campaign or "war."

313/70} Invariably Poe meant the *North American Review* by this sarcastic colloquial term for New England, which suggests a crude or homespun approach.

314/1-14} Poe apparently had met Joseph M. Field (1810-56), actor, playwright and journalist who edited the St. Louis *Reveille* (a paper of 1844-1850), for in a very "newsy" letter of 6/15/46, mentioning his warm friendship, Poe speaks of their meeting (Ostrom 318-20). The whole context makes it clear that Field had been solicited for favorable comments on Poe's conduct of the Lyceum affair. Poe later was to insult Thomas Dunn English with the wording "Done Brown." Curiously, Poe is half punning on the similar sound in "dona ferentes," completing the *Aeneid* line (2.49), "I fear the Greeks even when they bear gifts." The article cited here by Poe is from the 11/9 issue of the *Reveille* (see Moss, *PLB* 202 and the Poe *Log*.

314/26-31} Poe uses "had" as meaning tricked or hoaxed here. His god "Momus" is in charge of carping criticism or ridicule. The rhyme in "blustered and flustered" is typical of the "comic rhymes" that TOM listed from 24 of his prose passage in *Poems* 485-90; from these it is omitted, perhaps because it has a traditional tone.

314/69} It is clever of Poe to give a sales talk here for his new volume *ROP*, just published on 11/19, but he is not entirely accurate, for this edition is properly the third of "Al Aaraaf," which first appeared in 1829, next revised in 1831, and now substantially in the text of 1829 again. The Boston paper, *The Star*, could not have "copied our *third* edition of the poem" before the new book came out. For the publishing history see TOM *Poems* 97-99, and observe, in the collations, that Poe read "The Messenger star" for "The wandering star" (line 15) according to a special set of manuscript changes. This influenced Miss Walter and other editors in designating the poem read at the Boston Odeon for the Lyceum series.

315/1-44} Numerous commentators have deplored the intemperance, ill-will, and petulance of the whole editorial and, especially, this portion, which reeks of insobriety in the writer. We note the changing and deliberately confused names (the two proper adjectives for "Teetotaler") as he had done in the first "Autography" for the "Joseph ____ Miller who elicited the letters (TOM 259-64). Also obvious is Poe's disapproval of bluestockings, especially common among the Transcendentalists of *The Dial*, the literary circle, and even the newspaper staffs.

315/45} Poe's "thanks to W. W." are to Walter Whitman for his article "Art-Singing and Heart-Singing," indicated directly below. This may be Whitman's only *BJ* contribution, or it may be the second, for in the 5/31/45 *BJ* (1.347) is a harbor description, "Delightful Sights," which I have ascribed to him (see *WW Review*, 1969, 15.180-87), with the approval of the eds. of the supplementary vols. of the critical ed. of his works. This small editorial note and the footnote below represents the only direct tie of the living Poe to Whitman (see the study for the full links).

315/47-53} Whitman's thesis in this six-para. article concerns the songs of Europe, full of art and aristocratic artificiality, by contrast with the wholesome, homespun naturalness of the American folksongs sung by such groups as the Hutchinsons and the Cheneys, who have been touring the country and concertising. Poe's agreement savors of his review of G. P. Morris' *National Melodies of America* (H 10.41-45), repeated in M 202 (q.v. for the notes).

316/1-36} The book, of viii + 238 p., was by Mrs. Carolina M. Kirkland née Stansbury (1801-64), actually a Michigan frontier resident 1831-43. She used the pseudonym of "Mrs. Mary Clavers" for *A New Home--Who'll Follow? or Glimpses of Western Life* (1839; 1840). Poe incorporated most of this rev. into the "Literati" sketch of C. M. Kirkland (H 15.84-88). Changes from this text are mainly verbal and positional, but not substantive. It is clear that the depiction of the frontier keenly touched an interest of Poe. See also my Intro. to "Julius Rodman" (*Imaginary Voyages*, p. 508; also, E. S. Fussell, *Frontier*, "Poe," pp. 132-74). The *Macbeth* tag (1.7.19) occurs also in *Poems*, 293, and "Imp of Perverse" (TOM 1223 at n 3).

316/66} *Forest Life* in two vols. came out in 1842. The pages, given after a rubric are these: "Fever," 1-14; "Huddle," 15-26; "Changes," 94-117; "Love," 35-56; "Bee-Tree," 66-86; "Ambuscades," 118-43; "Half-Lengths," 168-93. Several of these sketches had been published in the *Gift of 1842* and *Gift of 1844*, where Poe had read them. The collection contains fourteen sketches in all.

317/1-41} The sketches cited are "Progress," 153-67; "Embroidered Fact," 194-204; and "Bitter Fruits," 205-38. The *OCAL* observes that only her first book, *A New Home*, was humorous, the others being "self-conscious and sentimental."

317/42-68} This vol., viii + 512 p., has Prefaces by translator and author, F. von Raumer (1781-1873), q.v. also for 238, 255, and 311 [facsimile text]. The letters "G. H." for the publisher are transposed inaccurately. The passage, from p. 111, is correct save for line 54: "wholesome, and not with."

318/1-68} Lines 16-39 contain quotations from p. 307, which also praises the copyright of 28 years. The para. with the "Down-East Review" (*sic* for *North American*) exudes a bit of the animus displayed in refs. to the Lyceum affair (see 297-99 above). The para. on the lyric and R. W. Griswold is from p. 314, with Poe's italics added. As often, the size, as well as the influence and frequent reprintings and revisions of the anthology, infuriates Poe.

319/1-25} The first ten lines are as contemptuous toward Griswold as any others by Poe; yet Poe still expected support for the needy *BJ* from Griswold.

The quotation of Paulding's poem is on 319; it was first published in the 8/36 *SLM* (2.538). Bishop Doane's poem (on p. 316) was "What is that, Mother?" Mr. William Kirkland (1800-46), husband of Caroline (see above) learned French and German through living in Europe. Poe mentions the aid for this translation in the "Literati" sketch (H 15.23). For further praise and data concerning Mrs. Ellet see 296/45-47 n. and the Index. It is to be assumed that when Poe gave the journal to Mrs. Whitman in 1848, with his markings, he "X'd" this passage in his disaffection with Mrs. Ellet.

319/26-45} Dendy (1794-1871) was a surgeon who published medical and also speculative works such as *Zone* (1841) and others later. This work, of 7-442 p., has no preface to state its purpose clearly. Poe implies that it is the "useful" rather than the merely "pleasing," but surely Sir David Brewster's *Letters on Natural Magic* (1832) combines these two eminently. Brewster's scientific and editorial achievements and contributions can scarcely be listed. Poe owed a debt to this work for much of "Maelzel's Chess-Man" (and for the "sail-illusion" in "MS. in a Bottle," q.v. in *PS*, 1982, 15.40); see *PD* 13 for 12 passages anent Brewster.

319/46-61} This numbers 291 p. with a one-page publisher's advertisement which furnishes Poe with ideas for the beginning of para. 2. There is no hint of who did the "best" British translation. Does Poe imply in the second sentence that he knows of a Preface in the French ed.? It is not easy to reconcile Poe's last two sentences, especially since Poe had thoroughly studied and absorbed Hugo's major novel (q.v. in *Discoveries in Poe*, 1-37).

320/5-38} The book has 281 p. "Fanny Forester" (more

correctly) was the pseudonym of Emily Chubbuck (1817-54), who married the prominent Baptist missionary-scholar Adoniram Judson in 1846. She was prolific in verse and prose, especially favored for the pages of the *Mirror* from 1844-46; hence, Poe's ref. to the "kindly" notices of Willis. See the *BJ* Index for frequent refs. to her pieces. We must note that the "Mrs." on line 38 is purely honorific at this date. This item is deplorably wanting in any evidence of proof-reading. I have left most (but not all) the typographical errors, being content to list them here: 14: taunt/tint; 19-20: produced plan/*delete*; 25: boddice/bodice; 28: and/*repeated*; 31: father/farther; 36: more/*upside-down letter*.

320/39-43} This vol. of xi-xiv, 15-126 p., bears the half title "Morris's Melodies," perhaps reminiscent of its popular prototypes, Moore's *Irish Melodies* and Byron's *Hebrew Melodies*, similarly printed usually without music. Poe respected immensely the lyrist (and *Mirror*-editor) George Pope Morris (1802-64), as 79/45-50 and his rev. of an earlier book show (see *Br.*, M 202 nn.). The "songs" (that is the *paroles*) were both popular and far more lucrative than magazine poetry.

320/44-67} Poe's agitated life now and his heedlessness anent the *BJ* perhaps are evinced in the errors uncorrected here too (*Mouths / Months* and *Prorpietor / Proprietor*). It is difficult to avoid concluding that he needed far less room than this to express his contempt for the "sales pitch" of the publisher. With the disappearance from all libraries of this contemptible work, as Poe presents it, we cannot even verify whose typographical error is that in 321/3: "moughn n't."

321/6-12} This is an American pirated ed. of *Poems in Two Volumes* (London, 1842), each vol. having 231 p. The lapse of years, so rare at the time, shows our slow appreciation of the poet who was "*the greatest....* " In M 44 of 12/1833, Poe expressed the same conviction about Tennyson, and in numerous refs. to the poet (see *PD* 90) he never deviated from this adulatory worship, although it could scarcely be considered "heretical" by this time.

321/13-17} For Milnes, Baron Houghton (1809-85), see 307 [facsimile text]. The vol. of 275 p. was dedicated to the Conversazione Society of Cambridge.

321/18-23} For long extracts by Poe from this address on "Young America" and the need for promoting American genius and literature, see 171-73 [facsimile text]; also, 324/41-47. Has Poe forgotten his already printed extracts? The pamphlet consisted of 34 p. plus letters exchanged by the Eucleian Club committee and Mathews.

321/24-37} This narrative by John Charles Fremont (1813-90) was reprinted from the official version in iii-iv + 186 double column pages. The Preface emphasizes its accuracy and then traces the history of exploration in the West of the USA. Poe's "Julius Rodman" of 1840 shows his intense interest in this field. Poe invariably praises *Robinson Crusoe* for its verisimilitude (see my full study in *Topic: 30*, 1976, 30.3-22).

321/38-42} The illustrations, by Chapman, are discussed in 296/30-35 n.

321/43-46} For more on Sargent and this series, see 281/31-31 note.

321/54-64} The plates are these: First, drawn by T. Allom, engraved by A. L. Dick; second, painted by Overback, engraved by H. S. Sadd. The separate articles follow: "Remembrance," p. 241; fiction by F. Forrester, 242-50; essay by Child, 251-53; "Lake Michigan," 254 (the beginning: "Calmly each crested wave / Sank to its crystal grave / On the blue waters"); fiction by Brougham, 255-59; poetry by Benjamin, 268; essay by Kirkland, 273-79, poetry by C. S., 250.

322/3-63} See this issue as discussed briefly in 322 (a). For Ide's many contributions to the *BJ* see the Index. This starts with the fourth stanza and comes from pp. 314-15. The italics are added by Poe. "The Hope of the Broken-Hearted" is an 18-stanza poem (pp. 292-95) by "Captain" Thomas Mayne Reid (1818-83), a colorful friend of Poe's in Philadelphia, originally from Ireland, who was novelist, journalist, and adventurer in various fields. He left reminiscences of the Poes, whom he cherished (see the *DAB*; see H. Allen, *Israfel*, 354, 391, 452). His poem starts thus: "God of heaven! has she perished? / All on earth I ever cherished-- / Can a hope not yet be nourished? / Say not, every hope is fled." English's poem, on p. 259, "The Parting," shows his aptness in rhyming which enabled him to shine in humorous verse, as in "The American Poets," 289-92, and in the many contributions later in the magazine *The John Donkey* of 1848. The letter and poem, "The Mammoth Squash," by "Poe" (that is, English) are on p. 290. For the poem see H 7.236. The letter reads as follows: "New York City, Sept. 28th, 1845. My dear Sir: (para.) For old acquaintance sake, I comply with your request; but your attempt will be a failure. Reasoning a priori, I could demonstrate that it cannot succeed. But I will not waste my logic on an obstinate man. Your obedient servant, Edgar A. Poe."

323/6-42} The Rev. John Pierpont, Unitarian minister of Boston (1785-1866), author of *Airs of Palestine* (1816, 1840) and other popular works, was highly praised by Poe (see H 15.191-193, 15.239). It is a curious coincidence that Poe wrote a short article on "The Swiss Bell-Ringers," known as the Campanologians, for the 10/10/44 *Mirror* (TOM 1118-1120). They had appeared at the Tabernacle on 10/7 (also the 11th and 16th), so that Poe indirectly or directly, through advice and perhaps direct intervention, may have contributed to this good-natured squib by T. D. English. A significant lead to this conclusion is the strong animus Poe felt against both Wm. W. Lord and Coxe's *Saul* (see *BJ* Index), and also his reprinting it here in its entirety. For another sample of English's humorous verse see 271 [facsimile text].

323/43-54} Poe did not quite fulfill his intention about the reviews the next week, for the annuals had to wait until 12/20 (pp. 344-45), but the books, mentioned below, did appear on 12/6, while he contented himself with excerpting from Simms' editorial farewell on p. 326. The "Illustrated" was the New York *Illustrated Magazine*, lasting from 9/45 to 3/47 and continuing *The Rover*.

324/1-3} Poe's serenity was temporary, for he soon learned that Miss Walter and her cohorts were not "dried up" -- witness her 12/1 editorial on "Al Aaraaf" as it appeared in the *ROP*, q.v. in 325 (d). Moreover, the organ of the Brook-Farm group, the *Harbinger* would join the fray on 12/6 with abuse of the book. Poe devoted much space to the attack and his counterattack (see 336-38 [facsimile text]); see Moss, *PLB*, 204-206, for coverage of this stage of the quarrel).

324/4-55} See 171-73 and 321 (c) for this address by Mathews. The open and declared reprinting of British magazine articles had long been a method for constructing a popular type of journal in America, called museums, repositories, etc. Poe's indignation is entirely warranted. But he too was to become disaffected with Mathews as the spokesman for the broad Young

America movement, aiming to promote native genius and letters. The *Mirror's* animus is not that of Morris and Willis, however, but rather of the rising star (or asterisk), Hiram Fuller, who would show himself to be Poe's implacable enemy in 1846. The "saying" of Dr. Johnson is probably this from Boswell's *Life*: "I have found you an argument; but I am not obliged to find you an understanding." This, in turn, is much like that of Goldsmith's dialogue in the *Vicar of Wakefield*, ch. 7: "You want me to furnish you with argument and intellects too" (both given by Burton Stevenson, p. 98). For Poe's defense of Mathews' manner in *Big Abel* see 307 A, B.

324/56-62} Here Poe is alluding to a set of mawkish "Lines. To Her Who Can Understand them," being a setting for the "*Air*-- To Ladies' eyes a round--boy." This composition by Fitz-Greene Halleck starts: "The song that o'er me hovered / In summer's hour--in summer's hour / To day with joy has covered / My winter bower--my winter bower." It creeps its way, through regular repetitions for six stanzas, each of twelve lines, along two columns on p. 319, *BJ* of 11/29. Poe's printing the tedious trifle, despite artless "refrain," perhaps springs from Halleck's having lent (i.e., given) him $100 for refinancing the *BJ* (Quinn, *Poe*, 491-92).

325/1-8} This introduces a reprint of a full chapter, which occupies 4 full cols. (pp. 331-32). It contains much about storms and an avalanche, q.v. on 207/6. The book, by Joel Tyler Headley, of vii + 138 p., is proleptically dated 1846.

325/19-28} S. Moss, *PLB*, 206-207, records a few of the bits of doggerel, scorn, and exchange items of derogation (e.g., from the *Knickerbocker*) that Miss Walter continued to publish well into 1846, to indicate her continuing sense of outrage over Poe's behavior and remarks. She was able to excerpt the Lyceum censure of Poe as an "unprincipled" man "defiled" by his own "venom," in its 18th annual report.

325/29-69} The start of this has an odd connection with an earlier article in this vol. of the *BJ*: In the 8/16 issue, is the long sketch of "John Randolph, of Roanoke," by Poe's friend F. W. Thomas (2.81-85), and in one anecdote Randolph quotes from King Lear: "The little dogs and all, / Tray, Bianch (*sic* for Blanche), and all, / See--they bark at me" (13.6.65-67). The *Nassau Monthly* exemplified a trend of the period whereby the major colleges were founding general journals--chiefly literary, this being that of Princeton which, soon changed to the *Nassau Literary Magazine*, would last into the twentieth century. The commentator may have read "The Imp of the Perverse" "among the mass" of journals or annuals on his table, for it came out in the 7/45 *Graham's* (27.1-3) and also in the newly issued *Mayflower* of 1846 (that is published at the end of 1845), pp. 11-22. The suggested source here is from Byron's *Don Juan*, 14.5, pointed out by no student of Poe. In *Etudes Anglaises*, 1976, 29.199-202, I traced the passage to Shakespeare, without comment on this source. Poe usually cites earlier works of Byron, but the suggestion sounds reasonable.

326/6-7} For the unplumbed relationship between Poe and Anne C. Lynch see 151 (c) nn above. There are touches of Poe in this tribute to Ole Bull's music that enable us to read between the lines: the "vulture of Unrest, / That whets its beak upon my heart, / Lies, charmed, within my breast" (ll. 14-16). Surely this comes from the turmoil of "The Raven," just as the "wild melodies" (37) might come from "Israfel."

326/19-21} The second sentence is Poe's self-quotation from his rev. of *Twice-Told Tales* of Hawthorne, of 5/42 (H 11.107) which he was to repeat in the Hawthorne sketch of 11/47 (H 13.151) and develop in the "Philosophy of Composition." Poe's understanding of "fugitive" is uncommon, for it usually means "temporary" or "ephemeral," while the dictionary adds, "occasional" in its theme. Poe implies "brief" as in almost all lyric poetry. But it is true that Simms gives him the lead for this idea. Please note that the footnote for line 48 is on the next page (327).

327/43} For "Scheherazade" (TOM 1165 ftnote.) Poe had used a similar fact derived from his friend Wyatt's *Physiology*, the basis of his *Conchologist's First Book* (1839). His asseveration of the leech-like behavior of publishers matches his own article of the *BJ* of 2/15 (1.103-104), reprinted by TOM, 1206-1210: "Some Secrets of the Magazine Prison-House."

327/44-48} See notes to 88, 234 [facsimile text] for other attributions and views. See rev. in *New World* of 1/15/45, p. 108, which pins the book on Sir Richard Vivian (*sic*) and gives a summary which is very close to Poe's thesis in *Eureka*.

327/49-53} This journal seems not to have been launched, despite its hopeful name. Hoffman (1806-84), prominent as editor on many major journals, author of the Kentucky Tragedy novel *Greyslaer* (1840), many poetry collections and accounts of the West, left the literary scene through insanity in 1849. Poe's interest in the nascent magazine savors of his hopes for his own *Stylus.*

328/1-60} This is the first of four long articles on Mrs. Frances Sargent Locke Osgood (1811-50), "prolific author of rather thin poetry" (*Concise DAB*), who was perhaps the most meaningful object of Poe's ardent but Platonic attention at the time of Virginia's final decline and during the year following. The next article was in the 3/46 *Godey's* (promised at the very end of this article), followed by the "Literati" sketch of 9/46 and finally that in the 8/49 *SLM*. Each piece was reworked from the previous ones, with the last combining all three. The third (H 15.94-104) was one of the longest of the sketches. See *PD* 69 for ten loci of Poe comment on her. Poe is correct about the pages of the volume; the London *Wreath* (1838) had 364 p. The Preface is correctly cited from p. 5.

In lines 30 and 45 Poe touches as always on her "grace" as an indefinable quality--a notion that he acquired from Horace Walpole (see M 209), and which is the burthen of his "sketch" of her. Unfortunately, Poe does not explain *his* meaning for "emblematical" (in 53), usually defined as symbolical. The three poets with whom she is compared were all reviewed and discussed by Poe; see M 104, notes a-d, for the links among them in his mind; also the *BJ* Index and *PD* 13 for "Brooks," 39 for "Gould," and 97 for "Welby." See also 54/55 and 210/56-58 above.

329/} This poem, from pp. 13-16, is transcribed faithfully save for a few accidentals and save for line 61 which read "dreams" for "beams." Was it Osgood--through Poe--or Poe himself who "improved" the line? Is Poe reprinting the whole poem as a covert tribute to himself, object of her love, despite the "smokescreen" of stanza 2, ambiguously referring to her "dreaming childhood"? It is a strange coincidence that two tributary poems, "The Ideal" and "The Ideal Found," by Anne Lynch, in the 6/21/45 *BJ* (see 151 (c) above), with Poe's headnote, set the tone and the verbal orientation of this one. But both are characteristic of the sentimental, Della Cruscan genre.

330/9-60} From the first, on pp. 105-106, Poe omits the subtitle, "A Song." Collation reveals no substantive changes; similarly in "Aspirations," pp. 131-33. Here too one can easily find a parallel to the situation facing Fannie Osgood, unhappily married and in love with "Israfel," the selecting editor.

331/14-42} Poe's choice of "Lenore" (from p. 136) can not be without significance; first, it bears Poe's title for a poem about unhappy love, and it is set in Venice with a glass which breaks when touched with poison, just as in the Venetian tale of "The Assignation," the covertly administered poison produces "a cracked and blackened goblet" in the revelation of the last sentence (TOM 166). In the "Literati" sketch (H 15.101) Poe similarly comments on this poem, but calls the verses "false dactyls"--a correction made in the 12/20 *BJ* on 347 (f) below.

331/43-61 & 332/1-27} There were five poems in all with the same title, this being on pp. 223-24. Two changes of text make one wonder whether F. Osgood determined them: 332/1: shrink / drink; 332/8: sigh / smile. In his "Annals" TOM, *Poems*, 556, notes this as a plea by the wife to her errant husband Samuel Stillman Osgood, who left us one of the few portraits of Poe. This poem came out first in the *Evening Mirror* of 12/10/44.

332/28-66 & 333/1-4} This volume is by Clinton G. Gilroy. Surely Poe is being slyly humorous about the indispensability of the book to scholars in the first three paras., the ideas of which come from the Preface (p. vi). In fact, Poe is really mocking the style and approach of Gilroy, exemplified in the excerpt. The Chinese Loom picture faces the title page and the other one faces p. 93.

333/5-25} This volume, by Charles Edwards Lester, has 239 p. To the title as given, should be added *of the age of the Medici, and of our own times.* Poe's first para. shows the effect upon him of the Young America movement. His sections on the men listed are these: Michael Angelo--26-72; Galileo--73-99; "The Quaker Painter, Benjamin West"--220-29 and Bishop Berkeley--212-19. As always Poe notices and mentions the physical appearance of the make-up and the pictures.

333/26-34} It has Introductory remarks on 2 pp. plus 419 of text.

333/35-40} This vol. of iv + 357 p. was by Charles Bindley (1796-1859), a writer on sporting subjects who regularly used this pseudonym. His revised and corrected ed. of Delabere Blaine's *Encyclopaedia of Rural Sports* came out in 1852. *Harry Lorrequer*

(1837) was one of Charles Lever's (1806-72) accounts of the fox-hunting Irish society of the period (mentioned in H 10.197, 11.10-11; see also *Charles O'Malley* by C. Lever in H 11.85-98).

333/41-48} This reprint of xxvii + 19-134 p. was published by Lea and Blanchard of Philadelphia. Poe infuses his characteristic humor into it and possibly his curious notion that the medical specialty comes from "pes, pedis" in Latin and not the Greek root "pod-" with two errors in the title and the last word of the rev. Or should we lay the blame at the door of the typesetter? Both the London and Philadelphia editions spell "chiropodist" correctly.

333/49-54} The poem, dedicated to General Zachary Taylor, numbers 5-7 p. of Preface, plus 8-69 plus 73-88 (Notes). From the poem, about the Florida war, I quote two lines to illustrate Poe's dictum: "Still from the watchful sentinel / Was heard the cheering sound, 'All's well'" (I, 11.7-8).

333/55-57} This novel, published in London, 1845, was by Thornton Leigh Hunt (1810-73), son of the essayist and poet. The Harper's ed., of 148 p., was reissued in 1864 and 1871. He became a journalist-associate of G. H. Lewes, poet, editor of his father's memoirs, and essayist.

333/58-61} The separate parts were collected in two volumes in 1846 in "a new and elegant translation profusely illustrated by the most eminent artists of Paris," of 680 p. Part 5 covers pp. 192-236.

334/1-9} Poe here evades the slightest gesture toward a proper rev. of the worthy Thomas Arnold's sermons. For earlier revs. see 231 and 261.

334/10-22} Poe often mentioned the beautiful socialite, Carolyn Norton, Sheridan's grand-daughter, who had befriended Frances Osgood in London (see M 104 note c). Surely he enjoyed the seeming paradox that "passion" destroys the effectiveness of a poem. Poe did not again take up or explicate this thesis in the *BJ*, but elsewhere he did (see R. D. Jacobs, *Poe*, pp. 346, 390-91). Two of the 23 stanzas of "The Dying Hour" (pp. 116-20) may be illustrative: (Stanza III)-- "Stoop down, and kiss my brow! / The shadows round me closing / Warn me that dark and low / I soon shall be reposing. (Stanza IV)-- "But while those pitying eyes / Are bending thus above me, / In vain the death-dews rise,-- /

Thou dost regret and love me!"

334/23-41} This is one of the few refs. by Poe to Mozart, the others being two allusions made by other writers of 1835 and 1836 (H 8.52, 9.200) and a bon mot by Mozart in M 271; Poe's preferences in music were invariably for a more florid and romantic style. The ref. in the excerpt is to a brief life of Mozart (1814) by Stendhal, pseud. of Marie-Henri Beyle, the great novelist.

334/42-59 & 335/1-5} See 269 (c) note, for this history in parts. Poe's protest in being circularized with propaganda accords with his opposition to puffing and all efforts to deprecate critical judgment.

335/7-45} Poe must have derived this news of his favorite, Anna Mowatt, from the daily press.

James E. Murdoch was a good friend of Poe and a probable assistant for dramatic material in the *BJ*, but Poe's evaluation is biased, for the press complained that Murdoch, especially in Shakespeare roles, was a good elocutionist, not a spontaneous actor (see Odell, 5.169, 181).

Mrs. Charles Kean had achieved tremendous success as Ellen Tree. They were at the Park Theatre in October, and opened in Thomas Noon Talfourd's stilted but then successful *Ion* in November; it had been played by Ellen Tree in 1837 (Odell, 168, 171). Poe's judgment here has been amply vindicated. After performing *Twelfth Night*, they left the city in mid-December.

The amateurs gave the play for charity, but very poorly (see Odell, 225).

The German opera was one of a series of attempts to bring foreign operas authentically to NY, and it failed like the others, after an elaborate *Der Freischütz* (of Weber) as part of a series of 24 performances, which were cut short in 1/46 (Odell, 224-25).

336/1-24} The "Brook Farm Institute of Agriculture and Education" was a cooperative community (1841-47) nine miles from Boston, which included, during the years of its organization and growth, Dana, G. W. Curtis, Orestes Brownson, Alcott, W. H. Channing, Margaret Fuller, and, briefly, Hawthorne. In 1843 it came under the influence of Albert Brisbane, fresh from his studies under Charles Fourier in Paris and became the "Phalanx" as Poe derisively states. From 1845 its official organ was *The Harbinger*, a serious, reflective, and prevailingly Transcendentalist although varied and independent journal. After the demise of the Roxbury organization, following a fire, the magazine was continued at a New York "association" until 2/10/49. Its abolitionism and philosophical viewpoint naturally alienated Poe, who coined "Crazyites" for its supporters.

337/1-68 & 338/1-18} It was probably written by the editor George Ripley (1802-80), who graduated from Harvard into the Boston Unitarian ministry, and a keenly active life of writing and editing philosophical and reform literature, often translated from the German. He founded the *Dial* and helped organize Brook Farm; here he shows a broad and serious acquaintance with Poe's works and major ideas--perhaps the reason that Poe reprints it verbatim, despite its hostility. Poe might have even been flattered by the allusion to Wordsworth's "Peter Bell" (337/16-17) and the excerpt from Tennyson's "Palace of Art" at the end. He certainly enjoyed the grounds for his own abuse given him in "insanity" and "singed."

338/19-} Prince Hal is from *1 Henry IV*, 2.4.312, with "thou lovest me." Poe's "Dutch uncle" traditionally reproves sharply but not unkindly (1.23). "King Log" in the "Fable of the Frogs" was the spiritless king of wood, followed by the esurient King Stork.

Concerning the imputed "motive of the publication," Poe's reply seems confirmed indirectly according to Ostrom's Check List of the letters, ascribing two letters to the Lyceum Committee in 9-10/45 (see p. 608, nos. 570-71) but on indirect evidence only. Concerning the article in the *Foreign Quarterly Review* see 299 (b) note for the proof of its being by John Forster (see also TOM, *Poems* 581), but since Forster, in 1/44, was finding a debt in "The Haunted Palace" (1839) to Tennyson's "Deserted House," Poe's rejoinder ignores chronology seriously.

"Reform it altogether" is from *Hamlet* (3.2). In the last para. Poe quotes his favorite, Alexander Pope: "Worth makes the man, and want of it the fellow; / The rest is all but leather or prunella" (*Essay on Man*, 4.203-204).

339/1-42} This account and excerpt seem to come from a contemporary journal, probably British, but it might have been adapted by Poe, whose word-awareness might have dictated his singling out "saudade" (nostalgia) for comment. João Baptista da Silva Leitão. Visconde de Almeida Garrett, as of 1852 (1799-1854), was the leading Portuguese poet, novelist, and playwright, active in liberal politics which drove him to live in England and

Paris in the 20s and 30s.

339/43-62} The explanation for Poe's savage attack on H. Norman Hudson lies in the information given in the notes to 299/1-22 above--basically Poe's recent discovery of Hudson's role in the Boston *Transcript*'s abuse of him for the Lyceum reading. Poe always reprehended the excessive use of antithesis, q.v. in *Discoveries in Poe*, 12, concerning Victor Hugo. Line 47 indicates that previous refs. to Norman in the *BJ* are the work of Briggs, Watson, et al.

340/1-18} Clearly Poe enjoyed the misconceptions and notoriety arising from his "repulsive masterpiece" (TOM 1228) and used it all for magazine copy here and below [342 (a) and 355-56]. Colton's *American Review* of 12/45, 2.561-65, carried "The Facts in the Case of M. Valdemar" (its correct title). The *Tribune* reporter (just possibly Margaret Fuller) obviously knows Poe's works well, the second one being a reference to *The Narrative of Arthur Gordon Pym* of 1838. The "bump" of faith comes from phrenology. In the word "transcendentalist" is a hint that Poe thought that it might be Fuller, author of the "just review" of Longfellow quoted in article (e) below. This *Tribune* article dates from 12/10 (pages 2/col.2). For fuller treatment of this whole affair see TOM 1228-32.

340/19-28} This para., taken verbatim from the 12/10 *Tribune* (to the word "Professorship"), alludes to a complicated academic situation owing its presence here to a request to Poe from Mrs. Ellet for an editorial on Dr. Henry's fitness but lack of "popularity" (see Poe *Log* of 12/15), followed by her withdrawal of the request on 12/16. Wm. C. Preston (1794-1860) served as college president from 1846-1851. Robert Henry (1792-1856) had a long career at the college (from 1818) teaching various branches of philosophy and literature, but sensitive and troubled in his presidency, declared terminated on 11/24/45. Mrs. Ellet's change of mind and the termination of the *BJ* revoked Poe's final intention.

340/30-42} For a full account and Poe's longer consideration of Maria Brooks ("Occidente") see 357-58 [facsimile text], with a tempering of the comparison with Miss Barrett (see also *PD* for both names of "Brooks"). By this time, Poe had no link of friendship with the *Mirror*'s editor--now Hiram Fuller.

340/50-60} This comes from Margaret Fuller's *Tribune* rev.

(12.10, 1/2-3) of Longfellow's *Poems*. While often at variance with the "bluestocking" he is delighted to air her marked reservations about Longfellow as person and writer.

341/1-42} It is clear that M. Fuller has been reading Poe's disparaging criticisms of Longfellow in the *BJ* and earlier journals, since so many strains are the same. Concerning the "dandy" charge, see notes to 38/46-51 and 312/65 above. The stanza is quoted from "Hymn to the Night" of 1839 with "cisterns" in the plural both in the *Tribune* and in Longfellow's page. Similarly, there should be a dash after the third line.

341/43-47} Poe here refers to the poem by R. S. Rowley, in the 12/6 *BJ*, 2.337-38, which has four eight-line stanzas. The third has only seven lines, lacking between lines 2 and 3: "They are fading, they are fading-- / And, as one by one they set, / I do struggle to forget!" "They" are "Dim dreamings of the future" in this very faint offshoot of Wordsworth's "Intimations" ode. R. S. Rowley was also the author of "A College Reminiscence" in the 1/3/46 *BJ*, 2.401-403.

341/51-59} A few of the names in initials are obvious. "P. P. C." is Philip Pendleton Cooke (q.v. in Index), his longstanding Virginia friend and correspondent. See his five-part poem "The Mountains" in the 12/20 *BJ*, 2.368-69, printed without editorial comment. "F. W. T." must be Frederick W. Thomas, Poe's very close Washington friend (q.v. on 196 and 236 nn.). "A. M. I." is probably Abijah M. Ide, Jr., contributor to several issues (see 239/10, 245, 265, 322 [facsimile text]).

342/1-9} Poe is delighted to reprint his "Valdemar" and continue the banter over its veracity, begun in 340 (a) and proceeding into the next issue of the *BJ* (355-56). For the international aspects of the "case"-- of especial delight to Poe-- see the next phase and TOM's fine summarizing account (1228-32).

342/10-41} Prescott (1796-1859), the eminent, socially distinguished, handicapped historian of the Hispanic world, was too universally admired to be attacked. Poe borrows the information from para. 2 of the Preface, but deprecates the *North American*, as always, if not Prescott himself. When he speaks of the volume again, in 350 (a), it will be solely to introduce four paras. from the article on C. B. Brown, the first and last one mentioned here. Poe's interest in this precursor in narration was always keen.

342/42-53 & 343/12-62} The book has numbers ix-x + 13-184 p. See the Index for several passages on Cist and the notes, indicating a closer relationship than biographers have indicated. Poe's comment on the portrait duplicates that on T. C. Grattan (M 203). Poe had faithfully copied the first poem in the collection (pp. 13-15). He is apparently too cursory in reading even to notice the inversions in lines 45, 60. Perhaps Poe was rounding up his journalist friends throughout the country, since he sensed his growing need of allies.

344/1-33} This annual of 96 p., which features its *"Ten Engravings"* in the title, epitomizes the one-sided development of these gift books that started out with an emphasis on reading material with subsidiary illustrations. John Sartain (1808-97), the leading mezzotint engraver (and a good friend of Poe, his editor on *Graham's*), deplored the increase in number and the decline in their literary quality in the forties in the 2/49 *Union Magazine* (1.154; quoted in Mott, 421), but he grants an improvement in the art work. Poe clearly pays tribute to the latter in the full treatment of each of the engravings, and acutely singles out the best "article" in the volume, even though it was by Emerson, his customary butt of attack. Certainly Wm. Henry Furness (1802-96), Unitarian pastor, student of German literature, and abolitionist, was an undistinguished editor. Sartain was probably totally responsible for the art work choice and execution. Henry Inman (1801-46), immensely popular portrait and landscape painter, was to be mentioned by Poe in his "Literati" sketch of Halleck (H 15.56); his brother John (1801-46) had become a powerful influence in journalistic and publishing circles of the city. Emanuel Leutze (1816-68), famous for his large historical pictures, left America to study and work in Germany (1841-59). Sarah Setchel-- the correct spelling-- (1803-94) was a well-known British water-colorist. Sir Edwin Henry Landseer (1802-73) has left us a rich and now deprecated legacy of groups of animals and their masters. Poe's comment is perceptive. Frank Stone (1800-59) was a friend of Dickens. Joshua Cristall (1767-1847) was a successful water colorist and china painter. Paul Falconer Poole (1807-79) was a self-taught historical painter of some temporary fame then.

344/34-57} Poe was ferociously adverse to Emerson, for his "mystical" transcendentalism, his "aping" of Carlyle, and perhaps for his success as a lecturer and place as the Concord seer; see the ten refs. in *PD* 31, of which only one is neutral (also M 188). But he acknowledged that some of his poems showed beauty "by flashes" (1841 "Autography" in H 15.260); hence his quoting the entire text of "A Fable" (from p. 38 of the annual). Poe inserts the stanzaic pattern but otherwise is accurate save for a few accidentals in his transcription. This was the first appearance of Emerson's poem, which would be collected in his 1847 volume.

344/58-62 & 345/1-9} Poe's rev. of this vol. is noteworthy for his reticence since "the best of Poe's early poems," that is, "The Lake" (see TOM *Poems* 82-84) is contained in it. Two or three reprints of the vol. under different titles came out later. It uses G. Baxter's new color process for the frontispiece. The names mentioned by Poe, many of them his friends, have compositions, both prose and poetry, on the following pages: Sigourney, 13-15, 142-45, 371-37; Whittier, 31-36; Lowell, 47-51; Hoyt, 100-103; Tuckerman, 104, 337-39; Gould, 122-23, 264-65, 325; Simms, 199-219; Mowatt, 220; Mancur, 266-79; Sargent, 302-303; "others" (Poe), 324.

345/10-18} The frontispiece is an engraving entitled "The Cottage Children," with no artist given, serving as illustration for the first poem, of that title. The title page shows a child holding a banner, without the artist's name.

345/19-31} Robert Hamilton, the editor of this 354 p. annual, has four previous loci in the *BJ* (see the Index). The Hermann Winterhalter painting is called "Innocence." "Cup Tossing" by Mrs. S. C. Hall, wife of the editor of the *Book of Gems* (see 112-15 [facsimile text]). The "noted pens" can be headed by E. A. Poe, for "Imp of the Perverse" (11-22). Others are Robert Hamilton, Elizabeth Oakes Smith, F. de la Motte Fouqué.

345/32-58} Perhaps it was the mystery of authorship or the "editing" by J. F. Cooper or the interest of the narrative-- or all, which contributed to the relative success of this work, published in a 3-vol. ed. in London (1845), reprinted in Phila. in 1846. P. K. Foley, *American Authors, 1795-1875*, asserts that Cooper was certainly the author, but F. R. Lounsberry, in *J. F. Cooper* (1883), p. 299, denies it to him. R. E. Spiller, *A Descriptive Bibliography of ... Cooper* (1934), p. 209, attributes it to his daughter Susan Cooper. To use Poe's coinage-- her grammar and dialogue were expectedly "Cooperish." Perhaps Cooper père helped to choose her pseudonym from the character in Scott's *St. Ronan's Well*, namely, Lady Penelope Penfeather, a patroness at the Spa; his novel *The Pilot* (1823) had been a deliberate analogue for Scott's *The Pirate* (1822).

346/7-28} The first is by the renowned innovative educator, Eliphalet Nott (1773-1866), and has 129 p. The second was by John McVicar (1787-1868), renowned clergyman and economist, who held the subject to be a branch of moral philosophy. The third, of 94 p., exploits the renown of Sir Humphry (correctly spelled) Davy (1778-1829), the renowned scientist, whose writings Poe may have used for a tale (see *Br.*, Pin 135). How gratuitous and characteristic is the way Poe uses the atrocious writing for an insult against the detested Thomas Carlyle (see other refs. in Index)!

346/29-36} John Kitto (1804-54) worked his way up from workhouse poverty, although deaf, to writing for periodicals, narratives of his travels abroad, illustrative lives of the handicapped and illustrated works connected with the bible. This vol. is the renamed *Pictorial History of Palestine* (1840).

346/37-40} Horatio ("Horace") Smith (1779-1849), banker and literatus of London, wrote satirical verses and a string of popular novels, which Poe used and discussed in various ways (see 144/52-58 for an article on the subject). This vol. of 168 p. contains two short novels, issued earlier this year in London.

346/45-48} All the parts, numbering well over 100, were collected into a 3-vol. set in 1847, entitled *The Illustrated Shakespeare*, ed. G. C. Verplanck. The hundreds of woodcuts were executed by H. W. Hewet, after designs by Kenny Meadows, Harvey, and others.

346/49-55} for the *Lancet* and John Frost's *Pictorial History* see the Index for previous issues.

347/1-9} Poe never managed more than this brief announcement for this "true poetry," but see the Index for other refs. to C. F. Hoffmann. See 349 (a) for a rev. of Foster's ed. of Shelley's poetry and 350 (b) for Street's poetry.

347/14-28} Concerning article (d), Poe's statement here proves his assurance about managing to finance and promote the journal, now so close to the end of its tether.
    Article (f) is a correction for 331/35, q.v.

Article (g) which extends onto p. 348 lengthily concludes this Editorial Miscellany, and bears Poe's "P" at the end. Yet his footnote "Mem." clearly indicates that the long article, commenting on Leigh Hunt, as criticized in the *SLM* of 12/45 is not by Poe but by "L." for that journal (pp. 737-42). The method and language of the excerpts are strikingly like Poe's. We must, however, attribute it to Henry Charles Lea (1825-1909), of Philadelphia, grandson of Matthew Carey, who was to be an historian, publisher, and reformer, and author of important scholarly studies. The identification is made by D. K. Jackson, *Contributors ... to the SLM* (1936), p. 75, based on E. S. Bradley's biography of Lea (1931), p. 367. Amazingly, he was only twenty at this time. Collation of the long excerpt (p. 742) shows no substantive changes, with only the spelling of "Shakespeare" (line 41) worth mentioning. The Latin, in line 28, should be "tetigit" as Poe says, in his note.

349/1-19} George G. Foster, enterprising editor of the first American "complete" ed. of Shelley, was more important in Poe's literary life than biographers and students have granted. See, e.g., Poe's praise of his periodical verse, his articles and his varied journalism in Alabama, St. Louis, and New York ("Autography" in H 15.237, and *Letters*, 117 n, 212, 212n). He was highly perceptive in his Preface here, a keen wit, as in his *John-Donkey* magazine of 1848, and a singularly unfortunate man, retrieved from prison by Rufus W. Griswold. Despite his wide scope and circle of associates, he is ignored by the *DAB* (1810 or 11-1856), but not completely by Mott (p. 780). For a fine résumé, see Dwight Thomas, "Poe in Philadelphia" (diss., 1978), pp. 765-66. The text was obviously pirated from the Moxon ed. of Shelley's works, edited by Mrs. Shelley, but the Preface is highly original, and perhaps offensive to Poe in linking the poet's thought to that of Fourier, but a curious footnote links Poe and Shelley (p. 12). Foster cites "Lines to an Indian Air" (now called "Indian Serenade"): "I arise from dreams of thee, / And a spirit in my feet / Has led me-- who knows how?* / To thy chamber-window sweet!" His footnote reads: "Mr. Poe tells me that this was originally written 'God knows how?' But I have not felt at liberty to change the text sanctioned by Mrs. Shelley." The text of 750 p. is truly well-printed for the period. Poe's objection to the "Fragments" of his beloved Shelley is strange. In the 1852 expanded ed. Foster indicates that the first was exhausted in less than 18 months, and he is "now" printing the full notes of "Queen Mab" (784 p. in all).

349/20-36} This was the fifth year for this well-known annual (of 304 p.) with the many illustrations by the famous John Gadsby Chapman, who had illustrated Poe's "The Elk" in the *Opal* published in 1843 (see 209 [facsimile text]). Poe is rather petty about refusing it a full rev., even though he obviously has a copy in hand, used for his reprint of the poem. The pages of the contributions are these: Osgood, 252-53; Lynch, 120-22; Mowatt, 98-99; Smith, 11-35 (prose), also, 125-32, also 135 (poem); Embury, 101-19 (prose) and 242 (poem); Gould, 195-96; Tuckerman, 38-52 (prose), 123-24; Hoffman, 91-97 (prose); Paulding, 136-37; Schoolcraft, 179-80, 197-201 (prose); Whittier, 202-208, 209-12 (poems). The Chapman illustrations are these: frontispiece, title page, facing pp. 53, 91, 125, 181, 209, 242, 245. At the end of the article, as if to strike out again at the ed. and his art "director" Poe concludes thus: "The engraving and general getting-up of 'The Opal' are discreditable in the last degree. A more wretched set of mezzotints we certainly never beheld." For Poe's friendliness toward Lynch see 151, 326-27 n. above.

350/1-5} On 342 [facsimile text] Poe had promised another "discussion" of Prescott's book, now called by its subtitle, *Miscellanies*, but he too has great interest in Brown and probably approves Prescott's sensible analysis of Brown's weak use of ingenious machinery or such phenomena as ventriloquism in *Wieland* to explain the "supernaturalities" of his fiction. The quoted column and a half comes from the first essay, pp. 1-56, on Brown.

350/6-30} In more than one passage Poe deprecated the poems of Street (1811-81), poet, journalist, lawyer and NY State Librarian at Albany, for mere descriptiveness following Bryant's style. See M 167 and FS, "Autography" (H 15.254) and "Rationale of Verse" (14.255-56). It is noteworthy that Poe exempts Emerson's "Fable" (p. 344 [facsimile text]) from this sweeping denunciation of "Frogpondium."

350/31-36 & 351/1-13} Poe had reviewed the first, 1839 ed. of *Hyperion* in 10/39 *BGM* (H 10.39-40), as a "farrago," with much "rich thought" but little "labor" or "trouble," shapeless and formless. He changes this contention here but continues to charge superficiality and an imitation of Germanic models. It has indeed been said to reflect Paul Richter and is, manifestly, a travel account through Germany, with German legends, works, and themes incorporated. Clearly, Poe is unsympathetic with the genre, and the author as well.

351/14-42} See 206-207 [facsimile text] for Poe's rev. of Headley's *Letters from Europe*, which contributed much to "Cask of Amontillado." His criticism is similar in admiring his vivacity and pace and deploring his slack diction and grammar. Poe thoroughly reprehends him in a posthumous (1850) rev. of Headley's *Sacred Mountains* (H 13.202-209). Poe's scorn leads him to coin "Irishy" and "neck-or-nothingness" in para. 2. See Index for other passages.

351/43-57} This is the American reprint of George Gilfillan's *First Gallery of Literary Portraits* (1813-78), a reflection of Gilfillan's wide acquaintance with the British literati. There is a kind of poetic justice in Gilfillan's commenting on Godwin as having founded a small but distinguished school of writers in England and America, for Poe was among them in many ways. There are seventeen passages on Godwin or his works in Poe's writings, as I first noted in preparing my book *Godwin Criticism* (Toronto, 1967). This led to my study, "Godwin and Poe," (Ch. 7, *Discoveries in Poe*, 107-27). Poe admired Godwin as a novelist whose prefaces adumbrated his own theories of fiction, not as the advanced social thinker of *Political Justice*. Emphasizing his opinion is the sidelining next to para. 2 in the Whitman *BJ*.

352/10-21} Edward Maturin (1812-81) migrated from Ireland to become professor of Greek in the College of South Carolina. Poe, having read the Gothic *Melmoth* (1820) as his refs. in "Letter to B_____" and a 1/42 rev. (H 11.13) show, flatters the son via the father, Charles Robert Maturin (1782-1824). Both the proper names are Poe coinages, the second after the 1816 play *Bertram*, which Kean produced at Drury Lane.

352/22-30} Charles Burdett was the author of the *Wrongs of American Women (Trials of New York Seamstresses)*, reviewed on 261 [facsimile text]. In *Chrysal or the Adventures of a Guinea* (1760-65) by Charles Johnstone, a guinea is made to describe its various owners.

352/31-38} Perhaps the publication of this was motivated by the success of *Plato Contra Atheos*, by Tayler Lewis (q.v. on 153-55). Is the last sentence Poe's honest conviction or simply pious tact?

352/41-61} Perhaps Poe is referring to the large "1846" on

the title-page surrounded by Victorian curlicues. The Sartain mezzotint is of a painting by W. Salter, and Smillie's of a battlefield painting by R. Hinshelwood. The unsigned fashion plate recalls Poe's usual objection to the "namby-pamby" plates, as he called them. The contributors are these: N. C. Books, 1-3; Ann S. Stephens (the correct spelling), 4-12; Caroline Butler, 13-19; A. B. Street, 20; T. H. Chivers, 20; Fanny Forrester, 33-39; Lowell, "To the Past," 39; E. J. Eames, 44.

353/9-16} The author of *The Froissart Ballads* was Philip Pendleton Cooke, long a valued correspondent of Poe, whom he praised highly in the "Autography" of 12/41 (H 15.234) and mentioned often in the *BJ* (see Index). In his long, chatty letter of 8/9/46 he promised to review this collection of Cooke's poems (issued 1847), but never did. The "Pröem" (notice Poe's dieresis) was the subtitle for "Emily" on pp. 30-32 of *Graham's*. Poe is quoting from Richard Lovelace's "To Althea: From Prison": "The gods that wanton in the air / Know no such liberty" (st. 1)--scarcely a very close parallel.

353/17-31} As usual, Poe lavishes high praise on Hunt's magazine (see the Index). The contents, given seriatim, by pages are these: 499-506 (John Spare); 507-12; 512-25; 526-34; 534-46; 546-50; 550-53; 553-55; 555-57; and editorial section, 557-92.

353/32-43} The Sadd mezzotint for "A Scene from the Pioneers" is opposite p. 43; the other, of "Mary Queen of Scots," is opposite p. 41. These are the contributions: Osgood, 7; John Neal, 8-12; Sedgwick, 13-17; Sigourney, 18; Tuckerman, 19-22; E. F. Ellett (*sic*), 26-28; Gould, 28; Embury, 29-34; Paulding, 35-40; Maria Child, 43; Inman's is probably "Vogue la Galère" by J. I. (i.e., John Inman, brother of Henry Inman). For Miss Blackwell, an Englishwoman, see Poe's *Letters*, p. 370, 394, 397n.

354/1-9} The production of *Richard III* (in Cibber's version) on 1/7/46 was considered a great event of the year. The total cost for scenery, costumes, machines, etc. was $10,000 borne largely by Charles Kean (Odell 5.173-74). It set an example for lavish and realistic theatrical display that crossed the Atlantic during the next decade in London.

354/10-22} This criticism is in line with Poe's extensive campaign while editor of the *SLM* and also his anti-puffery comments in the *BJ*; see 334-35 (d).

354/23-28} Poe must be referring to 335/13--not a very effusive statement. The excerpts are extremely favorable to Murdoch, being taken from the Boston *Post*, *Daily Times*, and *Evening Transcript*. His italics under "this" indirectly allude to his quarrel with the press over the Lyceum affair.

355/1} At the top of the column in the *BJ* is a three line item which may be by Poe. In style it differs from the full column to the left, "The Fine Arts," and it oddly concerns a subject which entered into "The Oblong Box," in the 9/44 *Godey's*, namely, a copy of Leonardo da Vinci's "Last Supper," said to be "done by Rubini the younger, at Florence" (TOM 925). Here, we find the following:
"The Last Supper, from Leonardo da Vinci, has been engraved by A. L. Dick, in the most superb style of the art. It is a close copy of Raffaelle Morghen's engraving."
Raphael Morghen (1758-1833) was a well known Italian engraver, a pupil of Volpato, celebrated for his burin engravings of excellent technique, among them being the "Last Supper" of da Vinci. The copy here discussed is by the staff engraver, apparently, of *Godey's* (q.v. on 80 [facsimile text]), where Poe may have seen this.

355/12-40 & 356/1-7} For this bantering article and letter see 340 (a) and the note. The whole account is given in detail by TOM 1228-32, who also follows in detail the parallel case of "Mesmeric Revelation" (1024-28), which gave Poe an article on 9/20 (see 254 [facsimile text]). Poe is inconsistent in the spelling of the name of the "eminent Mesmerist"--left uncorrected. Dr. John Elliotson of London (1791-1868), a prominent physician and founder of the Phrenological Society, lost his medical post through his mesmerism prominence (1838), after which he started a "mesmeric hospital" and founded the *Zoist* for the cause. I have searched the magazine for news of this affair--fruitlessly. See TOM for other responses to the weird tale in the London press; also for P. P. Cooke's 8/4/46 interest and that of George W. Eveleth in 1848. The "universally copied" statement of the letter (sentence 1) has not led to the discovery of Boston reprints, as TOM indicates.

356/8-16} Philip Pendleton Cooke's "The Mountains," a five part set of tercets, appeared in the 12/20 *BJ*, 2.368-69. Parts III and IV are largely devoted to a retelling of the legends of the heroes William Tell and Arnold Winkelreid; hence, Poe is reminded of Macaulay's *Lays of Ancient Rome* (1842), in which

"Horatius at the Bridge" tells a like heroic tale. For Poe and Cooke, see pp. 42 and 353 [facsimile text], and note the possible effect on "Annabel Lee," appearing first in the 3/35 *SLM*, opposite Poe's "Berenice" (TOM, *Poems*, 480 n on title).

356/17-20} "The Modern Poetical Literature of Germany" was on pp. 369-373 of the *BJ*. Poe seems somewhat confused here about the authorship, since there were three brothers: the poet Adolphus, Theodore L. and Johann Ludwig Tellkampf (1808-76), who came to the U.S. in 1838, became Professor of German language and literature in Columbia College, returning to Germany in 1847 to participate in the politics of his country. The author was probably this J. L. T. Poe knew about the "celebrated German poet" from the account itself (p. 371), which mentions his "poems ... scattered through a great variety of periodical and fugitive publications."

356/49} For John Neal of Portland, see the five entries in the Index. Neal (1793-1876), a most prolific author and editor of many publications and journals, early encouraging to Poe and his eulogist after death, wrote on "American Writers" for *Blackwood's* (1824-25), while living in England. This perhaps started this false rumor.

356/50-64 & 357/1-16} The memoirs of Henry Wikoff (1813-84) do not mention any such commission, but his travels and service in various diplomatic capacities gave him ample opportunity to be thus engaged.

The "charming book" was *A Treatise on the Theory and Practice of Landscape Gardening* (1841) by Andrew Jackson Downing, whose further works on landscaping and domestic architecture, service on the *Horticulturist*, and designs for great estates helped him to make over "the face of rural America" (*DAB*) (see Briggs' long review-summary of the second edition of Downing's book in the 4/5 *BJ*, 1.213-15). Poe's interest in the *Treatise* is evinced in "The Landscape Garden" of 10/42 (see TOM 700-702), which was expanded into "The Domain of Arnheim." Poe's awareness of the control of environment as a basis for mankind's esthetic and spiritual growth has been increasingly studied (e.g., see Kent Ljungquist, *The Grand and the Fair*, 1984, pp. 129-37). We note also Poe's hostility to honors conferred by monarchs of no intrinsic superior qualifications.

357/62-67 & 358/1-11} Maria Gowen Brooks (1794-1845) was given the flattering name "Maria del Occidente" (Maria of the

West) by Southey, who saw her long narrative poem *Zóphiel, or The Bride of Seven* through the press (1833). Poe thought it surpassed even E. O. Smith's *Sinless Child* (H 13.97) and praised her "abandon" and "*sustained* ideality" (13.156, 192). It is true that he never assigned the very highest rank to her (as in M 105). Poe's deprecation of Lamb's taste is based on an arguable premise-- concerning the feminine nature of poetry, made even more untenable in his conclusion about the nonexistence of the "greatest poems" as yet; thus Poe obliterates Homer, Vergil, Dante, Shakespeare, and Milton!

358/9} For Wm. D. Gallagher, see 275/12-23 n. Poe early considered his poems critically, as in the 7/36 *SLM* (H 9.73-75) and the 1841 "Autography" (H 15.223), mixing high praise with sharp cautions, but there seemed to be a real friendship.

358/12-29 & 359/1-15} The two vols. number 560 and 412 p., with the first 3-80 comprising Carlyle's Introductory chapters. Poe uses a double plural in "Anakims." Poe's dislike of Carlyle (see loci in Index of *Br.*) is tempered in this rev. by the need for tact about two Wiley and Putnam volumes.

359/16-24} The vol. has vii-x + 214 p. For notes on Cheever and Poe see 282 and 310. A fair amount of the book consists of excerpts from poets such as Dante, Wordsworth, and Dana, one of Poe's least favorite writers. Poe was correct about his coining the word "Cheeverish"--in his typical style.

359/25-34} Katharine Thomson, née Byerley, (1797-1862) wrote books of anecdotal biography and historical fiction. It is very doubtful that she is the author of the book that Poe ascribes to her, but it helps to establish the catholicity of Poe's reading.

359/35-45} The pages run, seriatim, thus: 649-72, 673-87, 688-703, 704-10, 711-12, 713-34, 735-51, four poems (signed "J. D."): 752, do., 753, do., 754-68, and 769-84.

359/51-59 & 360/1-9} It was almost natural that there should be a survey-rev. of two issues of the *Aristidean* in the last pages of the *BJ*, since Thomas Dunn English was helping to put it out, including whatever material Poe had prepared, plus some of his own (excluded of course from the facsimile text). These were also the final numbers of the dying *Aristidean*, which had some Poe material. The "Ferrando" story is on pp. 354-61. The

"Dearborn Poems" are on 335-37. The long article, "American Poetry," pp. 373-82, is a recasting of previous essay material by Poe. Most of the so-called "Exordium," beginning the 5/1/42 *Graham's Magazine* (H 11.1-8) has been adapted for this essay, and likewise a great deal of Poe's rev. of the third ed. of Griswold's *Poets and Poetry of America*, which Poe inserted into the *Boston Miscellany* of 11/42 (H 11.147-56). Poe deals with the lack of true critical principles in American criticism and the narrow, venal bases for selections in poetry anthologies. The essay on "Death" is on pp. 390-93, and Herman S. Saroni's fantasy about a "self-performance" of a symphony by the instruments, still warm from the actual concert, is on pp. 362-65 (see 2.405).

360/17-24} Poe is making the best of things in this farewell statement. It was lack of funds and of subscribers that caused the termination of the magazine, instead of permitting the start of a new volume, announced on 355/6, the preceding week. Surely, Poe had had a small role in the "objects" (objectives) for which the journal "was established" and, with proper funding and sufficient departments, the *BJ* could have become equivalent to his long-projected "Stylus." Ironically, the next year he was to issue a legal challenge to those very "foes," such as Hiram Fuller of the *Mirror*. See Moss, *PLB*, p. 206 for Walter's doggerel in the Boston *Transcript* on the demise of Poe's *BJ*.

This "valedictory" is a good place with which to conclude Poe's writings in the journal, but it is possible that he was at least responsible for two more half columns of "filler" on pp. 407-408, below the "Valedictory." On the other hand the items might equally well have come from the scissors plus editorial pen of English. The first is a long account of "Herr Faber's ... speaking automaton," now being shown in Philadelphia. It is presented with the same delight in human ingenuity that Poe voiced in "Maelzel's Chess-Player" (H 14.6-37), and the last para. begins with Poeian sardonicism: "There remains only one achievement-- a machine to think. We should say, perhaps, there *has* remained; for certain books lately printed induce us to believe that some people think by a machine." The next item is about "N. C. Brooks, A. M., of Baltimore, well known as a terse and vigorous writer, as well as a poet of much absolute power and refined taste ... [now] preparing a series of works for the use of schools and colleges." The next article concerns the retirement of Willis and Morris from the *Mirror*, but its praise of Fuller as the continuing editor makes me ascribe it to English, rather than to Poe. The last item discusses the purchase of one of Leutze's pictures by the art patron, Mr. Towne of Philadelphia-- a bland clipping of no definite provenance.

INDEX

The following index items refer solely to the text, by Poe, in the First Part of this section of his *Collected Writings*, that is, volume 3, and not to any of the material in the Annotations (volume 4). The following letter-symbols are attached to the page-numbers to indicate the nature and scope of the material being indexed, as follows:

a: an article, no matter how short, on the subject
c: a comment, usually one sentence or shorter
m: a mere mention by Poe of the subject indexed
p: a passage, often of a few sentences, on the subject
r: a review, often very brief, of the book
q: a quoted remark or article on the subject
s: a magazine survey by Poe, in a *BJ* column, usually summarizing the articles in an issue of a given magazine

Combinations are possible, such as "47q+c" or a quotation from an author plus a comment by Poe on him; "344pq" or a quoted passage on p. 344; "268rp" or a review of passage-length. Occasionally the line pertaining to an entry is added after a slash, to aid quick finding, as "Ide: 341/58c." Authors are given in parentheses after the book title and also alphabetically. Occasionally, Poe's error in a name is corrected via a cross reference (see Pinckney).

Rimini (Hunt): 99c
Ripa, Father: 299m
"(The) Rivulet's Dream" (Kate Carol [Osgood]):
    75q+c
road-making: see street-paving
Robinson Crusoe (Defoe): 19m, 321m
Rocchietti, Joseph: 21-22r
Rogers, Professor: 41m
Roman Pontiff: 183rm
Roman: street-paving, 94-95a
Rose, or Affection's Gift: 345rc
Ross, James: 233rc(2x), 268-69r
Rotunda--National Gallery: 224c
Rowley, R. S. "Epicedium": 341c
Royal Corporation of the Literary Fund: 109p
Royale, Anne: 1m
Ruschenberger, W. S. W.: *Elements of
    Entomology*, 73rc, 302rc
Russell, H.: 219c
Russell, Wm. (elocutionist): 175rp, 225m,
    242rc, 261-62rc

Sadd (engraver): 104c, 353m
(The) Sale of a Distillery (Bourne): 128rc
Samuda, Joseph: 195cq
Sand, George (Mme. Dudevant): 197c
sarcasm or wit: 17c
Sargent, Epes: 281rc, 321c
Saroni, Herman W.: 105c, 360m
Sartain, John (artist): 344c, 352c
satire: 36-37a
"Satirical Poems" ("Infatuation"): 36-37a
Saul (Coxe): 92m, 244c, 323m
Saunders *(Missionary Memorial)*: 209c, 247m,
    344rc
Scenes from "Politian" (Poe): 63-64q
Schiller: 169m, 174p, 287m, 307m, 311m
Schlegel, Augustus W.: 89m
Schnell Post (of N.Y.; a newspaper pub. as
    Deutsche Schnellpost): 169m, 236c
Schoolcraft, Henry: 80m
Scott, J. M. (impresario and actor): 235c+m
Scott, Sir Walter: 19m, 92m, 150m, 191m,
    206m, 224m, 302c, 324m
sculpture: 77m, 80c, 90c
Sears, David: 227c
"Sea-Weed" (Longfellow): 58-59p
Sedgwick, Catherine: 26c, 237c
Sedgwick, Misses: their boarding house, 237c
Self (Gore): 150r
Senefelder, Alois: 84m
Sewell, Elizabeth M. *(Gertrude)*: 241-42r
Seymour, Agnes: 198m
Shakespeare, William ("Shakspeare" to Poe):
    23q, 61m, 78m, 102m, 120q, 122q, 125q,
    149m, 177m, 192-93p, 197c, 212p, 232m,
    232r, 243c, 268q, 296c, 348pq, 354c
Shakespeare *(Harper's Illustrated* ed.): 296m
Sharpe, John: 65m
"She Loves Him Yet" (Osgood): 330q+c
Shea, J. Augustus: 226p, 262c
Shedd, Wm.: 236c

Shelley, Percy Bysshe: 14-15p, 100-101q,
    126m, 170m, 187m, 348c, 349rp+q, 351c
Shelley's Grave (Tomlin): 82rc+q
Sheridan, Thomas B.: 148p
Short Patent Sermons (Dow Jr. = E. G. Paige):
    246rc
Siborne, W.: 279rp
(The) Sibyl's Book of Fate: 146m
(The) Sibyl's Wreath: 320-21r
Sidney, Philip: 64q+c
Sigourney, Lydia H.: 78m, 220c
Simms, Wm. Gilmore: 26c, 137m, 149c, 218-
    19aq, 231-32r, 237m, 238c, 245m, 250c,
    254-55m, 265-67r, 269-70s+q, 277c (see
    note; also see Gibson), 283aq, 284c, 296c,
    300p, 307c, 312aq, 326q
Simm's Magazine: 231s, 255-56p, 296s, 307rp
Simpson, Mr.: 78m, 354m
"Sir Oracle": 87-88p+q
Skerrett: in *Fashion*, 68-69c
Sketches of Modern Literature (Gilfillan): 351r
Skinner, John S.: *Farmer's ... Journal*: 213s
slander of *BJ* by "R. C.": 93c
Smillie, James (artist): 117m, 210m, 234m,
    352m
Smith, Elizabeth Oakes: 221-22rc, 242-43rc
Smith, Horace (Horatio): 144/56m, 346rc
Smith, Seba: 78m, 80m, 104m, 118m, 219m,
    221-22r; see also Elizabeth Oakes Smith
Smith, Sydney: 92m, 168m, 197q
Smith, Wm. (ed.): 81m
Smith's Weekly Volume: 144s
Smollett: 19m
Snapp (see Stapp): 106-107r
(The) Snow-Flake (Arthur): 220c, 247m
Socrates: 153m
"Some Words with a Mummy" (Poe): 87m
"Song of the Shirt" (Hood): 223p

(The) Songs and Ballads (Morris): 320rc
(The) Songs of our Land (Hewitt): 282c, 288-
    90r
Sophocles: 3m, 7mq, 89-91r, 96-97c
"(La) Sortie du Bain" (sculpture): 247a, 282c,
    297a
South American: 96m
Southern Literary Messenger: 54a, 59m, 60m,
    63m, 88s, 116-17s, 212-13s, 219c, 221m,
    281c, 307m, 347c
Southern Monthly Magazine: 307m
Southern Quarterly Review: 105rc, 300c
Southey, Mrs.: 300m
Southey, Robert *(The Doctor)*: 150/27m
(The) Spanish Student (Longfellow): 62-63q+c
Sparhawk, E. V. *(SLM)*: 54m
Specimens of American Poetry (Kettell):
    219/23+41m
Spenser: 13m
"Spirit of Poetry" (Osgood): 329-30q+c
"Spirit of the Age" for *New Spirit of the Age*
    (Horne): 105c
Spitzner: 110c